D0813528

The Democracy Reader

The Democracy Reader

From Classical to Contemporary Philosophy

Edited by
Steven M. Cahn
City University of New York Graduate Center

Andrew T. Forcehimes
Nanyang Technological University

Robert B. Talisse
Vanderbilt University

ROWMAN & LITTLEFIELD
Lanham • Boulder • New York • London

Credits and acknowledgments for material borrowed from other sources, and reproduced with permission, appear on the appropriate pages within the text.

Published by Rowman & Littlefield
An imprint of The Rowman & Littlefield Publishing Group, Inc.
4501 Forbes Boulevard, Suite 200, Lanham, Maryland 20706
www.rowman.com

86-90 Paul Street, London EC2A 4NE, United Kingdom

Copyright © 2021 by The Rowman & Littlefield Publishing Group, Inc.

British Library Cataloguing in Publication Information Available

Library of Congress Cataloging-in-Publication Data Is Available

ISBN: 978-1-5381-5755-8 (pbk. : alk. paper)
ISBN: 978-1-5381-5756-5 (electronic)

♾™ The paper used in this publication meets the minimum requirements of American National Standard for Information Sciences—Permanence of Paper for Printed Library Materials, ANSI/NISO Z39.48-1992.

Contents

PART II: CONTEMPORARY ISSUES

A. JUSTIFICATION

B. DELIBERATION

C. VOTING

D. CHALLENGES

Preface

Democracy places political power in the hands of the people. But why should they have a say in the operations of government? Are democratic states preferable to non-democratic ones? If so, is democracy intrinsically good or only instrumentally so? How can the voices of the ignorant be prevented from drowning out the insights of the wise? Such questions are explored in the following readings, chosen for their importance and, where appropriate, edited to enhance their accessibility.

We wish to express gratitude to our editor Natalie Mandziuk for her unwavering support and insightful guidance. We also thank He Fan for his conscientious assistance in preparing the manuscript as well as the staff of Rowman & Littlefield for valuable help throughout production.

A final note. Many of the selections were written when the custom was to use the noun "man" and the pronoun "he" to refer to all persons regardless of gender, and we have retained the authors' original wording. With this proviso, we begin our study of democracy.

Introduction

Robert B. Talisse

Democracy is commonly regarded as a crucial social good and an indispensable ingredient of a decent society. Along with freedom and justice, democracy is frequently cited as something to fight for, both at home and abroad. Accordingly, in describing a country as non-democratic, we thereby criticize it; similarly, in characterizing a country as democratic, we thereby attribute to it a significant degree of political legitimacy. It is not surprising that many of the most brutal dictatorships of the past century claimed to be democracies.

The term "democracy" has come to enjoy this positive valence only recently. For most of the history of Western thought, the term was associated with unconstrained and direct rule of the many, conceived as a fickle and foolish mass. Democracy thus was widely regarded with suspicion—popular with the common people and politically ambitious rhetoricians, but socially degenerative. Indeed, in documents surrounding the founding of the United States, democracy is contrasted with the *republican* form of government, an arrangement whereby citizens are ruled by their laws and the public institutions that enact them, rather than by the "many." In contemporary discussions, however, this hard distinction between democratic and republican forms of government—between the rule of the many and the rule of law—has been eased. Today, we nearly always mean by "democracy" a constitutional and representational form of government; according to modern usage, in a democracy, the citizens rule themselves by means of elected representatives who function within the legal constraints established by a public constitution that affords to each citizen significant legal protections—most often articulated as civil rights—against the majority and the government. These legal protections ensure that democracy respects the citizens' fundamental political equality; our rights establish that there are certain political outcomes that not even a vast democratic majority can rightfully enact. In this way, none of us is ever reduced to being merely a political *subject*; even when we find ourselves at odds with the political opinion of the majority of our fellow citizens, we retain our social standing as full and equal citizens. This more recent understanding of democracy differs importantly from the simple majoritarianism that is described, and in many cases criticized, in this volume's earliest historical selections. We might go so far as to say that, far from being rivals, contemporary democracy is a republican form of government.

That modern democracy has embraced the traditionally republican mechanisms of representation and constitutionalism renders it less vulnerable to one line of criticism that looms large in the history of political thought (and is consequently well-represented in this volume). Taken as rule by the many, democracy is objectionable simply because it affords equal political power to those who are not equal in knowledge, wisdom, public-spiritedness, or good will. As the objection is commonly presented, this commitment to the political equality of those who are unequal with respect to politically relevant dispositions and capacities ensures that democracy will enact unwise, ineffective, and unjust policies. Indeed, in the version of the objection found in Plato, the wise and public-spirited citizen *suffers* under democratic arrangements: he is forced to live under laws that he knows are unjust and thus lives at the whim of a haphazard citizenry. Famously, Plato inferred from this that the best political arrangement is the rule of the wise—what David Estlund has characterized as "epistocracy."

The introduction of constitutional constraints designed to protect electoral minorities and individuals from the will of the majority goes a long way toward evading this classical objection to democracy. However, related challenges remain. Consider that, even in the presence of robust constitutional protections, democracy nonetheless requires you to live according to political decisions that you oppose, simply because a relevant number of your fellow citizens favor them. This is true even when the decisions in question are demonstrably unwise and imprudent. And it is nonetheless true even when your fellow citizens prove to be ill-informed, irrational, or positively deluded about facts pertaining to the decision set before them. Even when one can *demonstrate* that one's fellow citizens are largely ignorant of the things they would need to know in order to make a responsible political choice, provided that the decision they favor does not violate a constitutional protection, one is required to abide by the majority's decision. Thus, even in the presence of robust constitutional protections, democracy exposes individuals to the tyranny of the majority.

It is not obvious how such an arrangement could be justified. To fully feel the pinch of the problem, recall that democracy is committed to a kind of *equality* among citizens. And yet democracy inevitably imposes on some citizens the requirement to live according to political decisions that they have voted against. Thus, democratic citizens who find themselves in an electoral minority are forced to live according to the majority's political will, not their own. Such citizens are, in effect, required to subordinate their individual judgment to the judgment of the majority. How could such an arrangement be consistent with the equality of all citizens?

Unlike Plato's challenge, which contends that democracy fails to satisfy a requirement external to itself (namely, that of producing wise outcomes), this challenge holds that democracy is *internally* conflicted in that it embraces a kind of equality that it must nonetheless violate. Accordingly, much of modern and contemporary democratic theory is devoted to addressing this fundamental conflict between collective self-government and citizens' political equality. Beginning most explicitly with John Locke's social contractarian defense of democratic government, one finds in this volume a broad range of responses to this challenge.

Consider first an intuitive response that captures the sense of democracy that children learn in the schoolyard: when a group has to make a decision, take a vote and the majority rules. This "schoolyard" view treats equality as procedural fairness. It says we retain our equality even when we are required to go along with decisions we oppose, simply by virtue of the fact that everyone in the group had an equal say in the decision-making process: a single vote. When it is scaled-up into a conception of democracy, the result is a view variously known as the "procedural" or "aggregative" theory of democracy. According to this view, democracy has little to do with equality in any lofty sense of that word. Instead, democracy is presented as an instrument for producing political decisions in a way that suppresses revolt and other forms of civic unrest. In establishing a fair procedure according to which each citizen gets an equal say and the majority rules, democracy tends to produce results that satisfy most of the citizens. Those who find themselves on the losing side of a vote must look to the next election.

This procedural view has an intuitive appeal; however, as several authors in this volume argue, it is too simplistic. As emphasized by W. E. B. Du Bois and John Dewey, the idea of democratic government as simply a mechanism for collective decision-making overlooks the need for political policy to be responsive to the concerns of all citizens, not only those who form a majority. Picking up on this idea, many of the contemporary authors challenge the assumptions underlying the procedural view. In particular, David Estlund argues that procedural fairness is not sufficient to capture the democratic commitment to political equality; meanwhile, Seyla Benhabib notes that the procedural view presupposes that citizens bring to political decision-making a set of fixed and ordered preferences, but it does not investigate the social and political processes by which such preferences are formed. In general, although the procedural view still has advocates, it is widely rejected as providing too thin an account of democracy. According to most theorists, our understanding of democracy needs to incorporate the idea that it is not only a form of government, but a *kind of society*, or, as John Dewey and Elizabeth Anderson express it, a *way of life*.

What does it mean to say that democracy is a kind of society? Among the historical authors, the conflicting responses of Jean-Jacques Rousseau and John Stuart Mill provide a sense of the philosophical spectrum.

Taking the challenge to be that of finding "a form of association" where each individual unites with all, but nonetheless "obeys only himself" and thus "remains as free as before," Rousseau argues that, when properly enacted, democracy requires no one to subordinate their judgment; in a true democracy, elections reveal the *general will*, which is the will we each must embrace in our role as citizens. Hence, on Rousseau's view, in finding themselves on the losing side of a democratic election, those in the minority discover simply that they had voted in error; consequently, they must revise their judgement so that it accords with the general will. In a democracy, then, we obey only ourselves because we each are required to tailor our wills in conformity with the general will. To be sure, many find Rousseau's proposal unacceptable, and many theorists question whether it is psychologically possible.

Taking a different approach, Mill begins with a significant concession to Plato that the purpose of politics is to produce good outcomes; he then argues that democracy—what he calls "representative government"—performs better overall than the available alternatives. However, Mill then makes a further concession to Plato that may seem objectionable. Given his initial concession to Plato, Mill embraces the idea of *plural voting*. That is, Mill winds up endorsing the view that although all citizens are to be afforded at least one vote at the polls, certain citizens—namely, those who have greater knowledge of political affairs—are entitled to additional votes. Hence Mill embraces the Platonic view that political power ought to be apportioned according to political wisdom. Mill adds that the collective endorsement of processes that empower political wisdom is no deviation from democratic equality, but rather is its essence. As explained by Richard Arneson (who on this point follows Mill), this view holds that political equality is satisfied when the entire political system tends to produce the best results as compared with the available alternative systems. Many object that the idea of plural voting involves a gross violation of political equality and an overt departure from democracy (though note the debate between Jason Brennan and Julia Maskivker over voting).

Most of the contemporary authors included here promote views of democracy that fall within the spectrum set by Rousseau and Mill. All tend to agree that although government by means of elections wherein each citizen has an equal vote is *necessary* for democracy, it is nonetheless *not* sufficient. This is because circumstances in which each citizen has equal voting power are consistent with there being broader social conditions under which citizens are marginalized, excluded, silenced, and effectively barred from exercising their power. Hence it has occurred to many philosophers that the democratic ideal requires not merely that each citizen has an equal *voice* or vote, but that each has the opportunity to get an equal *hearing* as a citizen. The thought is that in order to manifest the democratic ideal, the mechanisms of government must operate in concert with a vibrant culture of democratic participation. And, according to what is presently the predominant conception of these matters, democratic participation must take the form of public *deliberation*.

Broadly, "deliberative democracy" is the view that, if collective political decisions are to be legitimate and hence binding on all citizens, they must be the products of decision-making processes that include occasions where citizens have the opportunity to *reason together* about the political questions they face. In this way, the deliberative democrat understands democracy neither simply as the rule of the many, nor as the rule of law, but instead, as John Rawls would have it, the rule of *public reasoning*. The contention is that, even though they are required to accede to political outcomes that they reject, electoral minorities retain their status as equal citizens because the decision-making process was responsive to their attempts to *rationally persuade* their fellow citizens. The democratic way of life, then, involves something more than collective decision by means of elections in which each citizen's vote is *counted*; according to the deliberative democrat, the legitimacy of collective political decisions rests rather with the fact that the democratic process involves *weighing* the reasons that citizens offer in support of their political judgments. As emphasized by Seyla Benhabib and Elizabeth Anderson, democratic citizens thus are expected to vote on the basis of their *reasons*, rather than, say, their brute *preferences*.

Deliberative democracy is currently the predominant conception among democratic theorists. This, of course, is not to say that the deliberative democratic program is unchallenged in the contemporary literature. Note that many of the authors included in this volume explore their own reservations concerning the view (see, for example, the contributions by Robert B. Talisse and Iris Marion Young). To be sure, these reservations tend to focus on the feasibility of deliberative democracy, and many authors propose strategies for overcoming the most obvious practical challenges facing the project of implementing a system of widespread public deliberation. Still, challenges of a different kind lurk: in calling for the "rule of public reasoning," what, *exactly*, are the deliberative democrats expecting of democratic citizens? Under deliberative democracy, how much time and attention are citizens required to expend on politics? One worries that on the deliberative view, the democratic way of life will be unacceptably *demanding*, leaving precious little time in citizens' lives for things other than political discussion.

This consideration raises a different concern about the demandingness of deliberative democracy. Given that, as Rawls emphasizes, the deliberative democrat proposes that citizens should vote on the basis of their *reasons* (rather than their brute preferences), one wonders about the degree of political *expertise* that is expected of the democratic citizen. After all, reasons undeniably have an *epistemic* component in that they can be justified or not, weighty or not, sufficient or not, and so on. More generally (and glossing over a host of philosophical complexities), reasons are signals of truth. In attending to reasons while formulating our political judgments, we manifest the aim of satisfying an *epistemic* goal—judging correctly, coming to hold the truth, being justified in holding our political opinions, and so on. Now, according to deliberative democrats, citizens are expected to exercise their political power on the basis of their assessment of the reasons that figure into the decision at hand. And, as David Estlund stresses, it is difficult to make good sense of that expectation without introducing the idea that the legitimacy of a political order depends on its capacity to produce outcomes that are wise.

Perhaps, then, one may conclude that democratic theory has come full circle. Back in Ancient Greece, Plato objected to democracy on the ground that it is necessarily unwise, and thus incapable of securing justice. Today's deliberative democrats contend that properly conducted public deliberation is capable of achieving collective wisdom. Thus democracy's most formidable historical critic and its most prominent contemporary defenders share a common conception of what it would take to vindicate democracy. Taken together, the selections contained in this volume provide a historically informed but nonetheless state-of-the-art snapshot of this persistent philosophical dispute.

I

CLASSIC SOURCES

Chapter 1

Funeral Oration

Pericles

Pericles (495–429 B.C.E) was an Athenian statesman. In the speech below, delivered at a public funeral during the Peloponnesian War between Athens and Sparta, he describes the virtues of Athenian democracy. He lauds the distinction between a private sphere where citizens are free to live their own lives and a public sphere in which all are subject to the law. This equality was also exemplified in Athens's open border, which provided free access to all who wished to come and learn. Pericles maintains that such freedom and equality are the source of the society's strength.

Thucydides, *Thucydides: On Justice, Power, and Human Nature*: Selections from *The History of the Peloponnesian War*, trans. Paul Woodruff (Indianapolis: Hackett Publishing Company, 1993).

We have a form of government that does not try to imitate the laws of our neighboring states. We are more an example to others, than they to us. In name, it is called a democracy, because it is managed not for a few people, but for the majority. Still, although we have equality at law for everyone here in private disputes, we do not let our system of rotating public offices undermine our judgment of a candidate's virtue; and no one is held back by poverty or because his reputation is not well-known, as long as he can do good service to the city. We are free and generous not only in our public activities as citizens, but also in our daily lives: there is no suspicion in our dealings with one another, and we are not offended by our neighbor for following his own pleasure. We do not cast on anyone the censorious looks that—though they are no punishment—are nevertheless painful. We live together without taking offense on private matters; and as for public affairs, we respect the law greatly and fear to violate it, since we are obedient to those in office at any time, and also to the laws—especially to those laws that were made to help people who have suffered an injustice, and to the unwritten laws that bring shame on their transgressors by the agreement of all.

Moreover, we have provided many ways to give our minds recreation from labor: we have instituted regular contests and sacrifices throughout the year, while the attractive furnishings of our private homes give us daily delight and expel sadness. The greatness of our city has caused all things from all parts of the earth to be imported here, so that we enjoy the products of other nations with no less familiarity than we do our own.

Then, too, we differ from our enemies in preparing for war: we leave our city open to all; and we have never expelled strangers in order to prevent them from learning or seeing things that, if they were not hidden, might give an advantage to the enemy. We do not rely on secret preparation and deceit so much as on our own courage in action. And as for education, our enemies train to be men from early youth by rigorous exercise, while we live a more relaxed life and still take on dangers as great as they do.

The evidence for this is that the Lacedaemonians do not invade our country by themselves, but with the aid of all their allies; when we invade our neighbors, however, we usually overcome them by ourselves without difficulty, even though we are fighting on hostile ground against people who are defending their own homes. Besides, no enemy has yet faced our whole force at once, because at the same time we are busy with our navy and sending men by land to many different places. But when our enemies run into part of our forces and get the better of them, they boast that they have beaten our whole force; and when they are defeated, they claim they were beaten by all of us. We are willing to go into danger with easy minds and natural courage rather than through rigorous training and laws, and that gives us an advantage: we'll never weaken ourselves in advance by preparing for future troubles, but we'll turn out to be no less daring in action than those who are always training hard. In this, as in other things, our city is worthy of admiration.

We are lovers of nobility with restraint, and lovers of wisdom without any softening of character. We use wealth as an opportunity for action, rather than for boastful speeches. And as for poverty, we think there is no shame in confessing it; what is shameful is doing nothing to escape it. Moreover, the very men who take care of public affairs look after their own at the same time; and even those who are devoted to their own businesses know enough about the city's affairs. For we alone think that a man who does not take part in public affairs is good for nothing, while others only say he is "minding his own business." We are the ones who develop policy, or at least decide what is to be done; for we believe that what spoils action is not speeches, but going into action without first being instructed through speeches. In this too we excel over others: ours is the bravery of people who think through what they will take in hand, and discuss it thoroughly; with other men, ignorance makes them brave and thinking makes them cowards. But the people who most deserve to be judged tough-minded are those who know exactly what terrors or pleasures lie ahead, and are not turned away from danger by that knowledge. Again we are opposite to most men in matters of virtue: we win our friends by doing them favors, rather than by accepting favors from them. A person who does a good turn is a more faithful friend: his goodwill towards the recipient preserves his feeling that he should do more; but the friendship of a person who has to return a good deed is dull and flat, because he knows he will be merely paying a debt—rather than doing a favor—when he shows his virtue in return. So that we alone do good to others not after calculating the profit, but fearlessly and in the confidence of our freedom.

In sum, I say that our city as a whole is a lesson for Greece, and that each of us presents himself as a self-sufficient individual, disposed to the widest possible diversity of actions, with every grace and great versatility. This is not merely a boast in words for the occasion, but the truth in fact, as the power of this city, which we have obtained by having this character, makes evident.

For Athens is the only power now that is greater than her fame when it comes to the test. Only in the case of Athens can enemies never be upset over the quality of those who defeat them when they invade; only in our empire can subject states never complain that their rulers are unworthy. We are proving our power with strong evidence, and we are not without witnesses: we shall be the admiration of people now and in the future. We do not need Homer, or anyone else, to praise our power with words that bring delight for a moment, when the truth will refute his assumptions about what was done. For we have compelled all seas and all lands to be open to us by our daring; and we have set up eternal monuments on all sides, of our setbacks as well as of our accomplishments.

Such is the city for which these men fought valiantly and died, in the firm belief that it should never be destroyed, and for which every man of you who is left should be willing to endure distress.

That is why I have spoken at such length concerning the city in general, to show you that the stakes are not the same, between us and the enemy—for their city is not like ours in any way—and, at the same time, to bring evidence to back up the eulogy of these men for whom I speak. The greatest part of their praise has already been delivered, for it was their virtues, and the virtues of men like them, that made what I praised in the city so beautiful. Not many Greeks have done deeds that are obviously equal to their own reputations, but these men have. The present end these men have met is, I think, either the first indication, or the final confirmation, of a life of virtue. And even those who were inferior in other ways deserve to have their faults overshadowed by their courageous deaths in war for the sake of their country. Their good actions have wiped out the memory of any wrong they have done, and they have produced more public good than private harm. None of them became a coward because he set a higher value on enjoying the wealth that he had; none of them put off the terrible day of his death in hopes that he might overcome his poverty and attain riches. Their longing to punish their enemies was stronger than this; and because they believed this to be the most honorable sort of danger, they chose to punish their enemies at this risk, and to let everything else go. The uncertainty of success they entrusted to hope; but for that which was before their eyes they decided to rely on themselves in action. They believed that this choice entailed resistance and suffering, rather than surrender and safety; they ran away from the word of shame, and stood up in action at risk of their lives. And so, in the one brief moment allotted them, at the peak of their fame and not in fear, they departed.

Such were these men, worthy of their country. And you who remain may pray for a safer fortune, but you must resolve to be no less daring in your intentions against the enemy. Do not weigh the good they have done on the basis of one speech. Any long-winded orator could tell you how much good lies in resisting our enemies; but you already know this. Look instead at the power our city shows in action every day, and so become lovers of Athens. When the power of the city seems great to you, consider then that this was purchased by valiant men who knew their duty and kept their honor in battle, by men who were resolved to contribute the most noble gift to their city: even if they should fail in their attempt, at least they would leave their fine character to the city. For in giving their lives for the common good, each man won praise for himself that will never grow old; and the monument that awaits them is the most splendid—not where they are buried, but where their glory is laid up to be remembered forever, whenever the time comes for speech or action. For to famous men, all the earth is a monument, and their virtues are attested not only by inscriptions on stone at home; but an unwritten record of the mind lives on for each of them, even in foreign lands, better than any gravestone.

Try to be like these men, therefore: realize that happiness lies in liberty, and liberty in valor, and do not hold back from the dangers of war. Miserable men, who have no hope of prosperity, do not have a just reason to be generous with their lives; no, it is rather those who face the danger of a complete reversal of fortune for whom defeat would make the biggest difference: they are the ones who should risk their lives. Any man of intelligence will hold that death, when it comes unperceived to a man at full strength and with hope for his country, is not so bitter as miserable defeat for a man grown soft.

Chapter 2

Crito

Plato

Plato (c. 428–347 B.C.E.), the famed Athenian philosopher, wrote a series of dialogues, most of which feature his teacher Socrates (469–399 B.C.E.), who himself wrote nothing, but in conversation was able to befuddle the most powerful minds of his day. In the *Crito*, Socrates offers an early articulation of social contract theory, according to which a contract or agreement serves as the basis of morality. If parties to a contract agree on certain rules and then act in ways forbidden by the agreed-upon rules, they act wrongly. Socrates explains that because he failed to leave Athens, he tacitly agreed to its laws, and hence he would act unjustly if he now disobeyed.

Plato, *Dialogues of Plato: Euthyphro, Apology, Crito, Meno, Gorgias, Menexenus*, trans R. E. Allen (New Haven: Yale University Press, 1984).

———

SOCRATES: Why have you come at this hour, Crito? Isn't it still early?

CRITO: Very early,

SOCRATES: What time, exactly?

CRITO: Depth of dawn, before first light.

SOCRATES: I'm surprised the guard was willing to admit you.

CRITO: He's used to me by now, Socrates, because I come here so often. Besides, I've done him a kindness.

SOCRATES: Did you come just now, or a while ago?

CRITO: Quite a while ago.

SOCRATES: Then why didn't you wake me right away, instead of sitting there in silence?

CRITO: No, Socrates. I might wish I weren't in such wakeful pain myself, and I've been marveling for some time at how sweetly you sleep. I didn't wake you on purpose, so that you could spend the time as pleasantly as possible. Often before, through the whole of our lives, I've thought you happy in your ways, but never more than now in the present misfortune—so cheerfully and lightly do you bear it.

SOCRATES: But surely, Crito, it would scarcely be appropriate in a man of my age to be distressed that he now has to die.

CRITO: Other men as old have been taken in similar misfortune, Socrates, and age did not relieve their distress at what faced them.

SOCRATES: True. But why are you here so early?

CRITO: I bring grievous news, Socrates. Not grievous to you, it appears, but grievous to me and to all your companions, and heaviest to bear, I think, for me.

SOCRATES: What is it? Has the ship come from Delos, on whose arrival I'm to die?

CRITO: Not yet. But I think it will come today, to judge from the report of some people who've arrived from Sunium and left it there. From what they say, it will clearly come today, and then tomorrow, Socrates, your life must end.

SOCRATES: Well, Crito, let it be for the best. If so it pleases the Gods, let it be so. Still, I do not think it will come today.

CRITO: From what do you infer that?

SOCRATES: I tell you. I am to die, I think, the day after the ship arrives.

CRITO: Yes—so the authorities say, at any rate.

SOCRATES: Then I think it will come tomorrow, not today. I infer that from a dream I saw a little while ago tonight. Perhaps you chose a good time not to wake me.

CRITO: What was the dream?

SOCRATES: A woman appeared to me. She came, fair and beautiful of form, clothed in white, and she called to me and said, "Socrates, on the third day shalt thou go to fertile Phthia."

CRITO: A strange dream, Socrates.

SOCRATES: But Crito, I think a clear one.

CRITO: Yes, too clear, it seems. But, please, Socrates, my beloved friend, please let me persuade you even at this point. Save yourself. As for me, if you should die it will be a multiple misfortune. Quite apart from the loss of such friendship as I shall not find again, people who don't really know us will think I didn't care, because I could have saved you if only I'd been willing to spend the money. Yet what could seem more shameful than the appearance of putting money before friends? People won't believe that you refused to escape even though we were eager to help.

SOCRATES: But Crito, why should we be so concerned about what people will think? Reasonable men, who are the ones worth considering, will believe that things happened as they did.

CRITO: Surely at this point, Socrates, you see how necessary it really is to care about what people think. The very things now happening show that they can accomplish, not the least of evils, but very nearly the greatest, if a man has been slandered among them.

SOCRATES: If only they could work the greatest evils, Crito, so that they might also work the greatest goods, it would truly be well. But as it is, they can do neither; they cannot make a man wise or foolish. They only act at random.

CRITO: Very well, let that be so. But tell me this, Socrates. Are you worried about me and the rest of your friends? Are you afraid that, if you escape, the sycophants will make trouble for us for helping you, so that we may be compelled to forfeit our estates or a great deal of money, or suffer more besides? If you're afraid of something of that sort, dismiss it. It is right for us to run that risk to save you, and still greater risk if need be. Please, let me persuade you to do as I say.

SOCRATES: Of course I'm worried about those things, Crito, and many other things too.

CRITO: Then don't be afraid. In fact, it's not a large sum which certain people are willing to take to manage your escape, and as for the sycophants, you see how cheaply they can be bought; it wouldn't take much money for them. You have mine at your disposal, and it is, I think, enough, but if you're at all worried about me and think you shouldn't spend mine, your friends from abroad are ready. One of them, Simmias of Thebes, has brought enough money, just for this purpose, and Cebes and quite a few others are ready, too. So as I say, you mustn't hesitate because of that. Nor should you be troubled about what you said in court, how if you went into exile you wouldn't know what to do with yourself. There are many places for you to go where they'd welcome you warmly, but if you want to go to Thessaly, I have friends there who will honor and protect you, so that no one will cause you distress.

Furthermore, Socrates, I think the thing you're doing is wrong. You betray yourself when you could be saved. You hasten a thing for yourself of a kind your very enemies might hasten for you—and have hastened, wishing you destroyed. In addition, I think you're betraying your sons. You desert them when you could raise and educate them; so far as you're concerned, they're to take what comes, and what is likely to come is just what usually comes to orphans in the poverty of their orphanhood. No. Either a man shouldn't have children, or he should accept the burden of raising and educating them; the choice you're making is one of the most heedless indifference. Your choice should be that of a good and courageous man—especially since you say you've had a lifelong concern for virtue. I'm ashamed, Socrates, ashamed both for you and for your friends, because it's going to seem that the whole business was done through a kind of cowardice in us. The case was brought to court when it needn't have been. Then there was the conduct of the trial. And now, as the final absurdity of the whole affair, it will look as if we let slip this final opportunity because of our own badness and cowardice, whereas we could have saved you or you could have saved yourself if we were worth anything at all. These things are bad, and shameful both to you and to us. Decide. Or rather, at this hour, it isn't time to decide but to have decided. This is the last chance, because everything must be done this coming night, and if we wait it will not be possible any longer. Please, Socrates, be persuaded by me and do as I ask.

SOCRATES: My dear Crito, your eagerness is worth much, if rightly directed. But if not, then the greater it is, the worse. We must consider carefully whether this thing is to be done, for I am now and always have been the sort of man who is persuaded only by the argument which on reflection proves best to me, and I cannot throw over arguments I formerly accepted merely because of what has come; they still seem much the same to me, and I honor them as I did before. If we can't find better ones, be assured that I will not give way to you, not even if the power of the multitude were far greater than it now is to frighten us like children with its threats of confiscation, bonds, and death.

Now, how might we most fairly consider the matter? Perhaps we should first take up this argument of yours about beliefs. We often used to say that some beliefs are worth paying attention to and others not. Was that wrong? Or was it right before I had to die, whereas it is now obviously idle nonsense put for the sake of arguing? I'd like to join with you in common inquiry, Crito. Does that appear in any way changed now that I'm here? Let us dismiss it or be persuaded by it. We often used to say, I think—and we used to think it made sense—that among the beliefs men entertain, some are to be regarded as important and others are not. Before the Gods, Crito, were we wrong? At least insofar as it lies in human agency, you aren't about to die tomorrow, and the present situation won't distort your judgment. So consider the matter. Don't you think it's satisfactory to say that one shouldn't value the beliefs of every man, but rather of some men and not others, and that one shouldn't value every belief of men, but some beliefs and not others? Isn't that right?

CRITO: It is.

SOCRATES: Now, it's useful beliefs which should be valued, not harmful or bad ones?

CRITO: Yes.

SOCRATES: Useful ones being those of the wise, bad ones those of the foolish?

CRITO: Of course.

SOCRATES: To continue, what did we use to say about things like this? Suppose a man goes in for athletics. Does he pay attention to the opinions, the praise and blame, of everybody, or only the one man who is his physician or trainer?

CRITO: Only the one.

SOCRATES: Then he ought to welcome the praise and fear the blame of that one man, not of the multitude.

CRITO: Clearly.

SOCRATES: So he is to train and exercise, eat and drink, in a way that seems good to a supervisor who knows and understands, rather than anyone else.

CRITO: True.

SOCRATES: Very well. But if he disobeys that supervisor, scorns his judgment and praises, values those of the multitude who are without understanding, won't he suffer an evil?

CRITO: Of course.

SOCRATES: What is that evil? Whither does it tend, and into what possession of the man who disobeys?

CRITO: Into the body, clearly, for it ruins that.

SOCRATES: Right. And isn't this also true in other matters, Crito? We don't need to run through them all, but isn't it especially true of what is just and unjust, honorable and shameful, good and evil—just the things our decision is now concerned with? Are we to fear and follow the multitude in such matters? Or is it rather the opinion of one man, if he but have knowledge, which we must reverence and fear beyond all the rest? Since, if we do not follow it, we will permanently damage and corrupt something that we used to say becomes better by justice and is harmed by injustice. Or is there no such thing?

CRITO: I certainly think there is, Socrates.

SOCRATES: Very well then, suppose that, by disobeying the opinion of those who understand, we were to ruin what becomes better by health and is damaged by disease. Would life be worth living for us once it has been damaged? That is the body, of course?

CRITO: Yes.

SOCRATES: Well, would life be worth living with a wretched, damaged body?

CRITO: Surely not.

SOCRATES: Then is it worth living when there is damage to what the just benefits and the unjust corrupts? Or do we think that this—whatever it is of ours to which justice and injustice pertain—is of less worth than the body?

CRITO: Surely not.

SOCRATES: Of more worth?

CRITO: Far more.

SOCRATES: Then perhaps we shouldn't give much thought to what the multitude tells us, my friend. Perhaps we should rather think of what he will say who understands things just and unjust—he being but one man, and the very Truth itself. So your first claim, that we ought to pay attention to what the multitude thinks about what is just and honorable and good, is mistaken. "But then," someone might say, "the multitude can kill us."

CRITO: Yes, Socrates, it is very clear someone might say that.

SOCRATES: And yet, my friend, the conclusion we've reached still seems much as it did before. Then too, consider whether this agreement also still abides: that it is not living which is of most importance, but living well.

CRITO: It does.

SOCRATES: But "well" is the same as honorably and justly—does that abide too?

CRITO: Yes.

SOCRATES: Then in light of these arguments, we must consider whether or not it would be right for me to try to escape without permission of the Athenians. If it proves right, let us try; if not, let us dismiss the matter. But as for these other considerations you raise about loss of money and raising children and what people think—Crito, those are really fit topics for people who lightly kill and would raise to life again without a thought if they could—the multitude. As for us, the argument has chosen; there is nothing to be considered but the things we've already mentioned—whether it is right to give money with our thanks to those who are going to manage my escape, whether in actual fact we shall do injustice by doing any of these things. If it proves to be unjust, then perhaps we should give thought neither to death nor to anything else except the doing of injustice.

CRITO: You are right, Socrates. Look to what we should do.

SOCRATES: Let's examine the matter together, my friend, and if you can somehow refute what I'm going to say, do so, and I'll be persuaded. But if not, then please, my dear friend, please stop returning over and over again to the same argument about how I ought to escape from here without permission from the Athenians. For I count it important that I act with your agreement, not against your will. So look to the starting point of the inquiry. See whether it is satisfactorily stated, and try to answer what I ask as you think proper.

CRITO: I'll certainly try.

SOCRATES: Do we say that there are any circumstances in which injustice ought willingly or wittingly be done? Or is injustice to be done in some circumstances but not others? Is the doing of injustice in no way honorable or good, as we often in the past agreed, or have those former agreements been cast aside these last few days? Has it long escaped our notice, Crito, that as old men in serious discussion with each other we were really no better than children, or is it rather precisely as we used to claim: that whether the multitude agrees or not, whether we must suffer things still worse than this or things more easy to bear, still, the doing of injustice is in every circumstance shameful and evil for him who does it. Do we affirm that, or not?

CRITO: We do.

SOCRATES: Then one must never do injustice.

CRITO: Of course not.

SOCRATES: Nor, as most people think, return injustice for injustice, since one must never do injustice.

CRITO: That follows.

SOCRATES: Then does this? Ought one work injury, Crito?

CRITO: No, surely not, Socrates.

SOCRATES: Then is it just to work injury in return for having suffered it, as the multitude affirms?

CRITO: Not at all.

SOCRATES: No, for surely there is no difference between doing ill to men and doing injustice.

CRITO: True.

SOCRATES: Then one ought not return injustice for injustice or do ill to any man, no matter what one may suffer at their hands. Look to this, Crito. Do not agree against your real opinion, for I know that few men think or will ever think it true. Between those who accept it and those who do not, there is no common basis for decision; when they view each others' counsels, they must necessarily hold each other in contempt. So consider very carefully whether you unite with me in agreeing that it can never be right to do injustice or return it, or to ward off the suffering of evil by doing it in return, or whether you recoil from this starting point. I have long thought it true and do still. If you think otherwise, speak and instruct me. But if you abide by our former agreements, hear what follows.

CRITO: I do abide. Please go on.

SOCRATES: I say next, or rather, I ask, whether one is to do things he agreed with someone to do, given that they are just, or is one to deceive?

CRITO: One is to do them.

SOCRATES: Then observe what follows. If I escape from here without persuading the City, am I not injuring someone, and someone I least ought? And am I not failing to abide by agreements that are just?

CRITO: Socrates, I can't answer what you ask, for I don't understand.

SOCRATES: Look at it this way. Suppose I was about to run off from here, or whatever the thing should be called. And suppose the Laws, the common constitution of the City, came and stood before me and said, "Tell us, Socrates, what you intend to do. Do you mean by this to destroy us? To destroy, as far as in you lies, the Laws and the City as a whole? Or do you think that a city can continue to exist and not be overturned, in which legal judgments once rendered are without force, but may be rendered unauthoritative by private citizens and so corrupted?"

How are we to answer that, Crito, and questions like it? A good deal might be said, especially by an orator, in behalf of that law, now to be broken, which requires that judgments judicially rendered be authoritative. Or are we to reply that the City did us an injustice and didn't decide the case correctly. Is that what we're to say?

CRITO: Most emphatically, Socrates.

SOCRATES: Then what if the Laws were to reply, "Socrates, was that really our agreement? Or was it rather to abide by such judgments as the City might render?" And if I were surprised at the question, they might go on, "There's no reason for surprise, Socrates. Answer the question, especially since you're so used to questions and answers. Come then, what charge do you lay against us and the City, that you should undertake to destroy us? We gave you birth. It was through us that your father took your mother to wife and begot you. Tell us, then, those of us who are the Laws of Marriage, do you find some fault in us for being incorrect?"

"No fault," I would say.

"Then what about the Laws governing the rearing of children once born, and their education—the Laws under which you your self were educated. Did we who are the Laws established for that purpose prescribe incorrectly when we directed your father to educate you in music and gymnastic?"

"Correctly," I'd say.

"Very well, then. We bore you, reared you, educated you. Can you then say, first of all, that you are not our offspring and our slave—you, and your fathers before you? And if that's true, do you think that justice is on a level between you and us—that it is right for you to do in return what we may undertake to do to you? Was there such an equality relative to your father, or your master if you had one, so that you might return whatever was done to you—strike back when struck, speak ill when spoken ill to, things like that? Does such a possibility then exist toward your Country and its Laws, so that if we should undertake to destroy you, believing it just, you in return will undertake so far as you are able to destroy us, your Country and its Laws? Will you claim that this is right—you, who are so profoundly concerned about virtue? Or are you so wise that you have let it escape your notice that Country is to be honored beyond mother and father or any forebears; that it is more holy, more to be revered, of greater apportionment among both gods and men of understanding; that an angered Country must be reverenced and obeyed and given way to even more than an angered father; that you must either persuade it to the contrary or do what it bids and suffer quietly what it prescribes, whether blows or bonds, whether you are led to war for wounds or death, still, these things are to be done. The just lies here: never to give way, never to desert, never to leave your post, but in war or court of law or any other place to do what City and Country command—that, or to persuade it of what is by nature just. It is not holy to use force against a mother or father; and it is far more unholy to use force against your Country."

What are we to say to that, Crito? Do the Laws speak the truth?

CRITO: Yes, I think they do.

SOCRATES: "Then consider this, Socrates," the Laws might say. "If we speak the truth, aren't you attempting to wrong us in what you now undertake? We gave you birth. We nurtured you. We educated you. We gave to you and to every other citizen a share of every good thing we could. Nonetheless, we continue to proclaim, by giving leave to any Athenian who wishes, that when he had been admitted to the rights of manhood and sees things in the City and its Laws which do not please him, he may take what is his and go either to one of our colonies or a foreign land. No law among us stands in the way or forbids it. You may take what is yours and go where you like, if we and the City do not please you. But whoever among you stays, recognizing the way we render judgment and govern the other affairs of the City, to him at that point we say that by his action he has entered agreement with us to do as we bid. And if he does not obey, we say that he commits injustice in three ways: because he disobeys us, and we gave him birth; because he disobeys us, and we nurtured him; because he agreed to obey us and neither obeys nor persuades us that we are doing something incorrect—even though we did not rudely command him to do as we bid, but rather set before him the alternatives of doing it or persuading us to the contrary. Those are the charges, Socrates, which we say will be imputable to you if you do what you're planning. To you, and to you not least, but more than any other Athenian."

And if I were to ask, "Why is that?" they might justly assail me with the claim that, as it happened, I more than most Athenians had ratified this agreement. They might say, "Socrates, we have ample indication that we and the City pleased you. You would not have stayed home in it to a degree surpassing all other Athenians, unless it pleased you in surpassing degree. You never left to go on a festival, except once to the Isthmian Games. You never went anywhere else except on military service. You never journeyed abroad as other men do, nor had you any desire to gain knowledge of other cities and their laws—we and this our City sufficed for you. So eagerly did you choose us, so eagerly did you agree to live as a citizen under us, that you even founded a family here. So much did the City please you. Even at your very trial, you could have proposed exile as a penalty, and done with the City's knowledge and permission what you're now attempting to do against her will. But at the time, you made a fine pretense of not being distressed at having to die. You'd choose death before exile—so you said. But now you feel no shame at those words, nor any concern for us, who are the Laws. You attempt to destroy us by trying to run off like the meanest of slaves, contrary to the compacts and agreements you entered with us to live as a citizen. First of all, then, tell us this: do we or do we not speak the truth when we say that by your actions, if not by your words, you have agreed to live as a citizen under us?"

What am I to say to that, Crito? Must I not agree?

CRITO: Necessarily, Socrates.

SOCRATES: "Very well then," they might say. "Aren't you trespassing against your compacts and agreements with us? You didn't agree under constraint, you weren't misled or deceived, nor were you forced to decide in too little time. You had seventy years, during which time you could have gone abroad if we did not please you, or if your agreement came to seem to you unjust. But you preferred neither Sparta nor Crete, which you often used to say were well governed, or any other city, Greek or barbarian. Quite the contrary; you traveled abroad less often than the halt, the lame, and the blind. So the City pleased you, to a degree surpassing all other Athenians. Therefore, we pleased you, too, for to whom would a city be pleasing without laws? Are you, then, now not to abide by your agreements? If you are persuaded by us, Socrates, you will. You will not make yourself a butt of mockery by escaping.

"Consider too what good you will accomplish for yourself or your friends if you transgress or offend in this way. That your friends risk prosecution themselves, with deprivation of city and confiscation of estate, could hardly be more clear. But you first. If you were to go to any of the cities nearest Athens—Thebes, say, or Megara, for both are well governed—you would go as an enemy to their polity. Those concerned for their own cities would eye you with suspicion, believing you to be a corrupter of laws. Again, you would confirm the opinion of your judges and lead them to think they rendered judgment justly, for a corrupter of laws may surely also be thought, and emphatically, a corrupter of young and ignorant men. Will you then shun well-governed cities, and men of the more estimable sort? Or will you associate with them and without sense of shame discuss—What will you discuss, Socrates? What arguments? The ones you used to offer here, about how virtue and justice are of highest worth for men, along with prescriptive custom and the Laws? 'The affair of Socrates'—don't you think it will look indecent? Surely you must. Then will you keep clear of such places and go to Thessaly among Crito's friends? There is plenty of license and unchastened disorder in Thessaly, and no doubt they'd delight in hearing you tell your absurd story about how you ran off from prison dressed up in disguise—a peasant's leather coat, perhaps? Disguised like a runaway slave, just to change your looks! That you are an old man with probably only a little time to live, and yet you cling boldly to life with such greedy desire that you will transgress the highest laws—will there be no one to say it? Perhaps not, if you give no offense. But otherwise, Socrates, you will hear many a contemptuous thing said of you. Will you then live like a slave, fawning on every man you meet? And what will you do in Thessaly when you get there, besides eat, as if you'd exiled yourself for a banquet. But as for those arguments of yours about justice and the other virtues—what will they mean to us then?

"Still, you want to live for your children's sake, so you can raise and educate them. Really? Will you take them to Thessaly and raise and educate them there, and make foreigners out of them so they can enjoy that advantage too? If you don't, will they be better reared for your being alive but not with them? Your friends will look after them. Will they look after them if you go to Thessaly, but not if you go to the Place of the Dead? If those who call themselves your friends are really worth anything, you cannot believe that.

"Socrates, be persuaded by us, for we nurtured you. Put not life nor children nor anything else ahead of what is just, so that when you come to the Place of the Dead you may have all this to say in your defense to those who rule there. It will not appear better here, more virtuous, more just, or more holy, for you or any of those around you to do this kind of thing here. And it will not be better for you on your arrival there. You now depart, if you depart, the victim of injustice at the hands of men, not at the hands of us who are the Laws. But if you escape, if you thus shamefully return injustice for injustice and injury for injury, if you trespass against your compacts and agreements with us, and work evil on those you least ought—yourself, your friends, your Country and its Laws—we shall be angered at you while you live, and those our brothers who are the Laws in the Place of the Dead will not receive you kindly, knowing that you undertook so far as in you lay to destroy us. Do not be persuaded to do what Crito bids. Be persuaded by us."

Crito, my dear and faithful friend, I think I hear these things as the Corybants think they hear the pipes, and the droning murmur of the words sounds within me and makes me incapable of hearing aught else. Be assured that if you speak against the things I now think true, you will speak in vain. Still, if you suppose you can accomplish anything, please speak.

CRITO: Socrates, I cannot speak.

SOCRATES: Very well, Crito. Let us so act, since so the God leads.

Chapter 3

The Republic

Plato

In the *Republic*, Plato's central concern is the relationship between justice and happiness. He maintains that a just life is superior to an unjust life, both intrinsically and instrumentally. To arrive at this conclusion Plato draws an analogy between individual persons and states and levels forceful criticisms against democracy. He compares democratic arrangements to a ship on which all the sailors have some say in decision-making. Those that have learned the art of navigation have equal clout as those who lack this crucial skill. Plato's message is clear: just as there are better and worse sailing decisions, there are better and worse political decisions. Just as it would be foolish to allow the incompetent to have an equal say in running a ship, it would be foolish to allow the incompetent to have an equal say in running the state. Properly organized states, according to Plato, are those ruled by a small group. Whether men or women, these elites are chosen on the basis of their natural aptitudes and specially educated for their role as rulers. The remaining roles of the state are assigned similarly. Those apt for the military form the army, while those apt for various trades form the commercial sector. Justice is done, on Plato's view, when all are in the roles for which they are fit. Since democracy treats unequals as equals, it is unjust.

Plato, *The Republic*, trans. John Llewelyn Davies and David James Vaughan, revised by Andera Tschemplik (Lanham, MD: Rowman & Littlefield Publishers, 2005).

＝◢◣◢◣＝

If . . . we were to trace in speech the gradual formation of a city, should we also see the growth of its justice or of its injustice?

Perhaps we should. . . .

Well then, I proceeded, the formation of a city is due, as I imagine, to this fact, that we are not individually self-sufficient, but have many wants. Or would you assign any other principle for the founding of cities?

No I agree with you, he replied.

Thus it is, then, that owing to our many wants, and because each seeks the aid of others to supply his various requirements, we gather many associates and helpers into one dwelling-place, and give to this joint dwelling the name of city. Is it so?

Undoubtedly.

And every one who gives or takes in exchange, whatever it be that he exchanges, does so from a belief that it is better of himself.

Certainly.

Now then, let us construe our city in speech from the beginning. It will owe its construction, it appears, to our needs.

Unquestionably.

Well, but the first and most pressing of all wants is that of sustenance to enable us to exist as living creatures.

Most decidedly.

Our second want would be that of a house, and our third that of clothing and the like.

True.

Then let us know what will render our city adequate to the supply of so many things. Must we not begin with a farmer for one, and a house-builder, and besides these a weaver? Will these suffice, or shall we add to them a shoemaker, and perhaps some other person who ministers to our bodily wants?

By all means.

Then the smallest possible city will consist of four or five men.

So it seems.

To proceed then, ought each of these to place his own work at the disposal of the community, so that the single farmer, for example, shall provide food for four, spending four times the amount of time and labor upon the preparation of food, and sharing it with others; or must he neglect of them, and produce for his own consumption alone the fourth part of this quantity of food, in a fourth part of the time, spending the other three parts, one in making his house, another in procuring himself clothes, and the third in providing himself with shoes, saving himself the trouble of sharing with others, and doing his own business by himself, and for himself?

To this Adeimantus replied, Well, Socrates, perhaps the former plan is the easier of the two.

Really, I said, by Zeus, it is not improbable: for I recollect myself, after your answer, that, in the first place, no two persons are born exactly alike, but each differs in his nature, one being suited for one occupation, and another for another. Do you not think so?

I do.

Well, when is a man likely to succeed best? When he divides his exertions among many skills, or when he devotes himself exclusively to one?

When he devotes himself to one.

Again, it is also clear, I imagine, that if a person lets the right moment for any work go by, it never returns.

It is quite clear.

For the thing to be done does not choose, I imagine, to await the leisure of the doer, but the doer must be at the call of the thing to be done, and not treat it as a secondary affair.

He must.

From these considerations it follows that all things will be produced in superior quantity and quality, and with greater ease, when each man, being freed from other tasks, works at a single occupation, in accordance with his nature and at the right moment.

Unquestionably.

More than four citizens, then, Adeimantus, are needed to provide the requisites which we named. For the farmer, it appears, will not make his own plough, if it is to be a good one, nor his hoe, nor any of the other tools employed in agriculture. No more will the builder make the numerous tools which he also requires; and so of the weaver and the shoemaker.

True.

Then we shall have carpenters and smiths, and many other artisans of the kind, who will become members of our little city, and create a population.

Certainly.

Still it will not yet be very large, supposing we add to them cowherds and shepherds, and the rest of that class, in order that the farmers may have oxen for plowing, and the housebuilders, as well as the farmers, beasts of burden for hauling, and the weavers and shoe-makers wool and leather.

It will not be a small city, either, if it contains all these.

Moreover, it is scarcely possible to plant the actual city in a place where it will have no need of imports.

No, it is impossible.

Then it will further require a new class of persons to bring from other cities all that it requires.

It will.

Well, but if the agent goes empty-handed, carrying with him none of the products in demand among those people from whom our city is to procure what it requires, he will also come empty-handed away, will he not?

I think so.

Then it must produce at home not only enough for itself, but also articles of the right kind and quantity to accommodate those whose services it needs.

It must.

Then our city requires larger numbers both of farmers and other craftsmen.

Yes, it does.

And among the rest it will need more of those agents also, who are to export and import the several products, and these are merchants, are they not?

Yes.

Then we shall require merchants also.

Certainly.

And if the commerce is carried on by sea, there will be a further demand for a considerable number of other persons, who are skilled in the practice of navigation.

A considerable number, undoubtedly.

But now tell me. In the city itself how are they to exchange their several productions? For it was to promote this exchange, you know, that we formed the community, and so founded our city.

Clearly, by buying and selling.

Then this will give rise to a market and a currency, for the sake of exchange.

Undoubtedly.

Suppose then that the farmer, or one of the other craftsmen, should come with some of his produce into the market, at a time when none of those who wish to make an exchange with him are there, is he to leave his occupation and sit idle in the marketplace?

By no means, there are persons who, with an eye to this contingency, undertake the service required; and these in well-regulated cities are, generally speaking, persons of excessive physical weakness, who are of no use in other kinds of labor. Their business is to remain on the spot in the market, and give money for goods to those who want to sell, and goods for money to those who want to buy.

This demand, then, causes a class of tradesmen to spring up in our city. For do we not give the name of trademen to those who station themselves in the market, to minister to buying and selling, applying the term merchants to those who go about from city to city?

Exactly so.

In addition to these, I imagine, there is also another class of servants, consisting of those whose reasoning capacities do not recommend them as associates, but whose bodily strength is equal to hard labor. These, selling the use of their strength and calling the price of it wage, are thus named, I believe, wage-earners. Is it not so?

Precisely.

Then wage-earners also form, as it seems, a complementary portion of a city

I think so.

Shall we say then, Adeimantus, that our city has at length grown to its full stature?

Perhaps so. . . .

How then, said I, would you have them live, Glaucon?

In the customary manner, he replied. They ought to recline on couches. I should think, if they are not to have a hard life of it, and dine off tables, and have the usual dishes and dessert in the way we do now.

Very good. I understand. Apparently we are considering the growth not of a city merely, but of a luxurious city. 1 dare say it is not a bad plan, for by this extension of our inquiry we shall perhaps discover how it is that justice and injustice take root in cities. Now it appears to me that the city which we have described is the true and, so to speak, healthy city. But if you wish us to contemplate a city that is suffering from inflammation, there is nothing to hinder us. Some people will not be satisfied, it seems, with the fare or the mode of life which we have described, but must have, in addition, couches and tables and every other article of furniture, as well as seasonings and fragrant oils, and perfumes, and courtesans, and confectionery; and all these in plentiful variety. Moreover, we must not limit ourselves now to essentials in those articles which we specified at first. I mean houses and clothes and shoes, but we must set painting and embroidery to work, and acquire gold and ivory, and all similar valuables, must we not?

Yes.

Then we shall also have to enlarge our city, for our first or healthy city will not now be of sufficient size, but requires to be increased in bulk, and needs to be filled with a multitude of callings, which do not exist in cities to satisfy any natural want. For example, the whole class of hunters, and all who practice the art of imitation, including many who use forms and colors, and many who use music: and poets also—and their helpers, the rhapsodes, actors, dancers, contractors: and lastly, the craftsmen of all sorts of articles, and among others those who make parts of feminine adornments. We shall similarly require more personal servants. Shall we not? That is to say, teachers, wet-nurses, dry-nurses, beauticians, barbers, and cooks moreover and butchers? Swineherds again are among the additions we shall require, a class of persons not to be found, because not needed, in our former city, but needed among the rest in this. We shall also need great quantities of all kinds of cattle, for those who may wish to eat them, shall we not?

Of course we shall.

Then shall we not experience the need of medical men also, to a much greater extent under this than under the former lifestyle?

Yes, indeed.

The land too, I presume, which was formerly sufficient for the support of its then inhabitants will be now too small, and adequate no longer. Shall we say so?

Certainly.

Then must we not cut ourselves a slice of our neighbor's territory, if we are to have land enough both for pasture and tillage, while they will do the same to ours, if they, like us, permit themselves to overstep the limit of necessities, and plunge into the unbounded acquisition of wealth?

It must inevitably be so, Socrates.

Will our next step be to go to war, Glaucon, or how will it be?

As you say.

At this stage of our inquiry let us avoid asserting either that war does good or that it does harm, confining ourselves to this statement, that we have further traced the origin of war to causes which bring about whatever ills befall a city, either in its public capacity, or in its individual members.

Exactly so.

Once more then, my friend, our city must be larger and not just by a small extent, but by a whole army, which must go forth and do battle with all invaders in defense of its entire property, and of the things we were just now describing.

How so? He asked. Are not those persons sufficient of themselves?

They are not, if you and all the rest of us were right in the admissions which we made, when we were modeling our city. We admitted, I think, if you remember, that it was impossible for one man to work well at many crafts.

True.

Well then, is not the business of war looked upon as a craft in itself?

Undoubtedly.

And have we not as much reason to concern ourselves about the craft of war as the craft of shoemaking?

Quite as much.

But we cautioned the shoemaker, you know, against attempting to be a farmer or a weaver or a builder besides, with a view to our shoemaking work being well done; and to every other artisan we assigned in like manner one occupation, namely, that for which he was naturally fitted, and in which, if he let other things alone, and worked at it all his time without neglecting his opportunities, he was likely to prove a successful workman. Now is it not of the greatest moment that the work of war should be well done? Or is it so easy, that anyone can succeed in it and be at the same time a farmer or a shoemaker or a laborer at any other craft whatever, although there is no one in the world who could become a good checkers-player or dice-player by merely taking up the game at unoccupied moments, instead of pursuing it as his special study from his childhood? And will it be enough for a man merely to handle a shield or the other arms and implements of war? Will that make him competent to play his part well on that very day in an engagement of heavy troops or in any other military service—although the mere handling of any other instrument will never make anyone a true craftsman or athlete, nor will such instrument be even useful to one who has neither learnt its capabilities nor exercised himself sufficiently in its practical applications?

If it were so, these implements of war would be very valuable, he said.

In proportion, then, to the importance of the work which these guardians have to do, it will require more leisure than most, as well as extraordinary skill and attention. I quite think so.

Will it not also require natural endowments suited to this particular occupation

Undoubtedly. . . .

BOOK III

Very good; then what will be the next point for us to settle? Is it not this, which of the persons so educated are to be the rulers, and which the ruled?

Unquestionably it is.

There can be no doubt that the rulers must be the elderly men, and the subjects would be the younger.

True.

And also that the rulers must be the best men among them.

True again.

Are not the best farmers those who are most skilled in farming?

Yes.

In the present case, as we require the best guardians, shall we not find them in those who are most capable of guarding a city?

Yes.

Then for this purpose must they not be prudent and powerful, and, moreover, care for the city?

They must.

And a man will care most for that which he loves?

Of course.

And assuredly he will love that most whose interests he regards as identical with his own, and in whose prosperity or adversity he believes his own fortunes to be involved.

Just so.

Then we must select from the whole body of guardians those men who appear to us, after due observation, to be remarkable above others for the zeal with which, through their whole life, they have done what they have thought advantageous to the city, and inflexibly refused to do what they thought the reverse.

Yes, these are the suitable persons, he said.

Then I think we must watch them at every stage of their life, to see if they are tenacious guardians of this conviction, and never bewitched or forced into a forgetful banishment of the opinion that they ought to do what is best for the city. . . .

We must also appoint them labors, and pains, and contests, in which we must watch for the same symptoms of character.

Rightly so. . . .

And, just as young horses are taken into the presence of noise and tumult, to see whether they are timid, so must we bring our men, while still young, into the midst of objects of terror, and soon transfer them to scenes of pleasure, testing them much more thoroughly than gold is tried in the fire, to find whether they show themselves under all circumstances . . . proper in their bearing, good guardians of themselves and . . . acting in such a way as would render them most useful to themselves and the city. And whoever, from time to time, after being put to the test as a child, as a youth, and as a man, comes forth uninjured from the trial, must be appointed a ruler and guardian of the city, and must receive honors in life and in death, and be admitted to the highest privileges, in the way of funeral rites and other tributes to his memory. And all who are the reverse of this character must be rejected. Such appears to me, Glaucon, to be the true method of selecting and appointing our rulers and guardians, described simply as a sketch, without accuracy in detail.

I am pretty much of your mind.

Is it not then entirely correct to give them the name of complete guardians, as being qualified to take care that their friends at home shall not wish, and their enemies abroad not be able, to do any harm, and to call the young men, whom up to this time we called "guardians," "auxiliaries" and helpers with the decrees of the rulers?

I think so, he said.

This being the case, I continued, can we contrive any ingenious mode of. . . propounding a single noble lie . . . persuading even the rulers themselves, if possible, to believe it, or if not them, the rest of the city?

What kind of a lie?

Nothing new, but a Phoenician story, which has happened often before now, as the poets tell and mankind believe, but which in our time has not been, nor, so far as I know, is likely to happen, and which would require great powers of persuasion.

You seem very reluctant to tell it.

You will think my reluctance very natural when I have told it.

Speak out boldly and without fear.

Well I will; and yet I hardly know where I shall find the courage or where the words to express myself. I shall try, I say, to persuade first the rulers themselves and the military class, and after them the rest of the city, that when we were training and instructing them, they only thought, as in dreams, that all this was happening to them and about them, while in truth they were in course of formation and training in the bowels of the earth, where they themselves, their armor, and the rest of their equipments were manufactured. As soon as they were finished, the earth, their real mother, sent them up to its surface; and, consequently, that they ought now to take thought for the land in which they dwell, as their mother and nurse, and repel all attacks upon it, and to feel towards their fellow-citizens as brothers born of the earth.

It was not without reason that you were so long ashamed to tell us your lie.

I dare say; nevertheless, hear the rest of the story. We shall tell our people, in mythical language: You are doubtless all brothers, as many as inhabit the city, but the god who created you mixed gold in the composition of such of you as are qualified to rule, which is why they are most honored, while in the auxiliaries he made silver an ingredient, assigning iron and bronze to the farmers and the other workmen. Therefore, inasmuch as you are all related to one another, although your children will generally resemble their parents, yet sometimes a golden parent will produce a silver child, and a silver parent a golden child, and so on, each producing any. The rulers therefore have received this charge first and above all from the gods, to observe nothing more closely, as good guardians, than the children that are born, to see which of these metals is mixed in their souls. And if a child be born in their class with an alloy of bronze or iron, they are to have no manner of pity upon it, but giving it the value that belongs to its nature, they are to thrust it among artisans or farmers; and if again among these latter a child be born with any admixture of gold or silver, they will honour it, and they are to raise it either to the class of guardians, or to that of auxiliaries, because there is an oracle which declares that the city shall then perish when it is guarded by iron or bronze. Can you suggest any device by which we can make them believe this story?

None at all by which we could persuade the men with whom we begin our new city; but I think there could be such a device for their sons, and the next generation, and all subsequent generations.

Well, I said, even this might have a good effect towards making them care more for the city and for one another: for I think I understand what you mean. . . .

BOOK IV

Here Adeimantus interposed, inquiring, Then what defense will you make, Socrates, if anyone protests that you are not making these men particularly happy? And that it is their own fault, too, if they are not? For the city really belongs to them, and yet they derive nothing good from it, as others do, who own lands and build fine large houses, and furnish them in corresponding style, and perform private sacrifices to the gods, and entertain their strangers, and, in fact, as you said just now, possess gold and silver, and everything that is usually necessary to be considered blessed. On the contrary, they appear to be posted in the city, as it might be said, precisely like mercenary troops, wholly occupied keeping watch. . . .

What defense then shall we make, you ask?

By traveling the same road as before, we shall find, I think, what to say. We shall reply that, though it would not surprise us if, in the given circumstances, they too were very happy, yet that our object in the construction of our city is not to make any one class preeminently happy, but to make the whole city as happy as it can be made. For we thought that in such a city we should be most likely to discover justice, as, on the other hand, in the worst-regulated city we should be most likely to discover injustice, and that after having observed them we might decide the question we have been so long investigating. At present, we believe we are forming the happy city, not by selecting a few of its members and making them happy, but by making the whole so. Soon we shall examine a city of the opposite kind. Now, if someone came up to us while we were painting statues, and blamed us for not putting the most beautiful colors on the most beautiful parts of the body, because the eyes, being the most beautiful part, were not painted purple, but black, we should think it a sufficient defense to reply. Please, sir, do not suppose that we ought to make the eyes so beautiful as not to look like eyes, nor the other parts in like manner, but observe whether, by giving to every part what properly belongs to it, we make the whole beautiful. In the same way do not, in the present instance, compel us to attach to our guardians such a kind of happiness as shall make them anything but guardians. For we are well aware that we might, on the same principle, clothe our farmers in long robes, and put gold on their heads, and tell them to till the land at their pleasure; and that we might stretch our potters at their ease on couches before the fire, to drink and make merry, placing the wheel by their side, with directions to ply their trade just so far as they should feel it agreeable; and that we might dispense this kind of bliss to all the rest, so that the entire city might thus be happy. But give not such advice to us, since, if we comply with your recommendation, the farmer will be no farmer, the potter no potter; nor will any of those professions, which make up a city, maintain its proper character. For the other occupations it matters less—cobblers who become careless and corrupt and pretend to be what they are not, are not dangerous to a city; but when guardians of the laws and of the city are such in appearance only, and not in reality, you see that they utterly destroy the whole city, as, on the other hand, they alone can make them well-governed and happy. If then, while we aim at making genuine guardians, who shall be as far as possible from doing harm to the city, the person speaking in opposition makes a class of farmers and, as it were, jovial feasters at a holiday gathering, rather than citizens of a city: he will be describing something which is not a city. We should examine then whether our object in constituting our guardians should be to secure to them the greatest possible amount of happiness, or whether our duty, as regards happiness, is to see if our city as a whole enjoys it, persuading or compelling our auxiliaries and guardians to study only how to make themselves the best possible workmen at their own occupation, and treating all the rest in like manner, and thus, while the whole city grows and, being beautifully founded, we must let nature apportion happiness to each group.

I think, he replied, that what you say is quite right. . . .

Then the organization of our city is now complete, son of Ariston; and the next thing for you to do is to examine it, furnishing yourself with the necessary light from any quarter you can, and calling to your aid your brother and Polemarchus and the rest, in order to try, if we can, to see where justice may be found in it, and where injustice, and wherein they differ the one from the other. . . .

Now observe whether you hold the same opinion that I do. If a carpenter should undertake to execute the work of a shoemaker, or a shoemaker that of a carpenter, either by interchanging their tools and honors, or by the same person undertaking both trades, with all the changes involved in it, do you think it would greatly damage the city?

Not very greatly.

But when one whom nature has made an craftsman, or a producer of any other kind, is so elated by wealth, or a large connection, or bodily strength, or any similar advantages, as to intrude himself into the class of the warriors; or when a warrior intrudes himself into the class of the counselors and guardians, of which he is unworthy, and when these interchange their tools and their distinctions, or when one and the same person attempts to discharge all these duties at once, then, I imagine, you will agree with me, that such change and meddling among these will be ruinous to the city.

Most assuredly they will.

Then any intermeddling in the three parts, or change from one to another, would inflict great damage on the city, and may properly be described, as doing the most extreme harm.

Quite so.

And will you not admit that the greatest harm towards one's own city is injustice?

Unquestionably.

This then is injustice. On the other hand, let us state that, conversely, adherence to their own business on the part of the moneymakers, the military, and the guardians, each of these doing its own work in the city, is justice, and will render the city just.

I fully agree, he said. . . .

BOOK V

I must return, then, to a portion of our subject which perhaps I ought to have discussed before in its proper place. But after all, the present order may be the best; the male drama having been played out; we proceed then with the performance of the women. . . .

Do we think that the females of watchdogs ought to guard the flock along with the males, and hunt with them, and share in all their other duties; or that the females ought to stay at home, because they are disabled by having to breed and rear the puppies, while the males are to labor and be charged with all the care of the flocks?

We expect them to share in whatever is to be done: only we treat the females as the weaker, and the males as the stronger.

Is it possible to use animals for the same work, if you do not give them the same training and education?

It is not.

If then we are to employ the women in the same duties as the men, we must give them the same instructions . . . giving them a military education, and treating them in the same way as the men.

It follows naturally from what you say. . . .

Must we not . . . first come to an agreement as to whether the regulations proposed are possible or not, and give to any one . . . an opportunity of raising the question, whether the nature of the human female is such as to enable her to share in all the deeds of the male. . . .

Yes, quite so.

Would you like, then, that we should argue against ourselves in behalf of an objector, that the opposition may not be attacked without a defense?

There is no reason why we should not.

Then let us say in his behalf: "Socrates and Glaucon, there is no need for others to advance anything against you; for you yourselves, at the beginning of your scheme for constructing a city, admitted that every individual therein ought, in accordance with nature, to do the one work which belongs to him."

"We did admit this. I imagine; how could we do otherwise?"

"Can you deny that there is a very marked difference between the nature of woman and that of man?"

"Of course there is a difference."

"Then is it not fitting to assign to each sex a different work, appropriate to its peculiar nature?"

"Undoubtedly."

"Then if so, you must be in error now, and be contradicting yourselves when you go on to say, that men and women ought to engage in the same occupations, when their natures are so widely diverse?" Do you have any answer to that objection, my clever friend? . . .

Come then, I continued, let us see if we can find the way out. We admitted, you say, that different natures ought to have different occupations, and that the natures of men and women are different; but now we maintain that these different natures ought to engage in the same occupations. Is this your charge against us?

Precisely. . . .

But we did not in any way consider what form of sameness and difference of nature and what that referred to, and what we were distinguishing when we assigned different pursuits to different natures, and the same pursuits to the same natures.

It is true we have not considered that.

That being the case, it is open to us apparently to ask ourselves whether bald men and long-haired men are of the same or of opposite natures, and after admitting the latter to be the case, we may say that if bald men make shoes, long-haired men must not be allowed to make them, or if the long-haired men make them, the others must be forbidden to do so.

No, that would be ridiculous.

It is ridiculous for any other reason that that we did not agree on "the same" and "different nature" in every respect, being engaged only with that form of likeness and difference which applied directly to the pursuits in question? For example, we said that a male and female physician have the same nature and soul. Or do you not think so?

I do.

And that a man who would make a good physician had a different nature from one who would make a good carpenter.

Of course he has.

If, then, the class of men and women appear to differ in reference to any art, or other occupation, we shall say that such occupation must be assigned to the one or the other. But if we find the difference to consist simply in the fact that the female bears and the male mounts, we shall assert that it has not yet been by any means demonstrated that the difference between man and woman touches our purpose; on the contrary, we shall still think it proper for our guardians and their wives to engage in the same pursuits.

And rightly.

Shall we not proceed to call upon our opponents to inform us what is that particular art or occupation connected with the organization of a city, in reference to which the nature of a man and a woman are not the same, but different?

We certainly are entitled to do so. . . .

Would you, then, like us to beg the man who voices such objections to accompany us, to see if we can show him that no occupation which belongs to the ordering of a city is peculiar to women?

By all means.

Well then, we will address him thus: "Tell us whether, when you say that one man is well-suited for a particular study, and that another is not, you mean that the former learns it easily, the latter with difficulty; and that the one with little instruction can find out much for himself in the subject he has studied, whereas the other after much teaching and practice cannot even retain what he has learned; and that the reasoning of the one is duly aided, that of the other thwarted, by the bodily powers? Are not these the only marks by which you define the possession and the want of natural talents for any pursuit?"

I conclude then, my friend, that none of the occupations concerned with ordering a city belong to woman as woman, nor yet to man as man; but natural gifts are to be found here and there, in both animals alike; and, so far as her nature is concerned, the woman is admissible to all pursuits as well as the man. . . . Precisely so.

Shall we then appropriate all duties to men, and none to women?

How can we?

On the contrary, we shall hold, I imagine, that one woman may have talents for medicine, and another be without them; and that one may be musical, and another unmusical.

Undoubtedly.

And shall we not also say, that one woman may have qualifications for gymnastic exercises, and for war, and another be unwarlike, and without a taste for gymnastics?

I think we shall.

Again, may there not be a lover of wisdom in one, and a hatred of it in another? And may not one be spirited, and another without spirit?

True again.

If that be so, there are some women who are fit, and others who are unfit, for the office of guardians. For were not those the qualities that we selected, in the case of the men, as marking their fitness for that office?

Yes, they were.

Then as far as the guardianship of a city is concerned, there is no difference between the natures of the man and of the woman, but only various degrees of weakness and strength.

Apparently there is none.

Then we shall have to select duly qualified women also, to share in the life and guardianship with the duly qualified men; since we find that they are competent, and of kindred nature with the men.

Just so.

And must we not assign the same pursuit to the same natures?

We must. . . .

Then our next step apparently must be, to try to search out and demonstrate what there is now amiss in the working of our cities, preventing their being governed in the manner described, and what is the smallest change that would enable a city to assume this form of regime, confining ourselves, if possible, to a single change; if not, to two; or else, to such as are fewest in number and least important in their influence.

Let us by all means endeavor so to do.

Well, I proceeded, there is one change by which, as I think we might show, the required transformation would be secured; but it is certainly neither a small nor an easy change, though it is a possible one.

What is it?

Unless it happen either that philosophers acquire the kingly power in cities, or that those who are now called kings and rulers be genuinely and adequately philosophical, that is to say, unless political power and philosophy be united in the same place, most of those who at present pursue one to the exclusion of the other being necessarily excluded from either, there will be no deliverance, my dear Glaucon, for cities, nor yet, I believe, for the human race. . . .

How can it be right to assert that the miseries of our cities will find no relief, until those philosophers who, on our own admission, are useless to them, become their rulers?

You are asking a question, I replied, which I must answer by the help of an image. . . .

Think of a fleet, or a single ship, in which the state of affairs on board is as follows. The owner, you are to suppose, is taller and stronger than any of the crew, but rather deaf, and rather nearsighted, and correspondingly deficient in nautical skill; and the sailors are quarreling together about piloting, each of them thinking he has a right to steer the vessel, although up to that moment he has never studied the art, and cannot name his instructor, or the time when he served his apprenticeship. More than this, they assert that it is a thing which positively cannot be taught, and are even ready to tear in pieces the person who affirms that it can. Meanwhile they crowd incessantly round the person of the ship-owner, begging and beseeching him with every importunity to entrust the helm to them; and occasionally, failing to persuade him, while others succeed better, these disappointed candidates kill their successful rivals, or fling them overboard, and, after binding the noble ship-owner hand and foot with drugs or strong drink, or disabling him by some other contrivance, they rule the ship, and apply its contents to their own purposes, and pass their time at sea in drinking and feasting, as you might expect with such a crew. And besides all this, they compliment with the title of "able seaman," "pilot," "skillful navigator," any sailor that can second them cleverly in either persuading or forcing the ship-owner into installing them in command of the ship, while they condemn as useless everyone whose talents are of a different order, they don't know that the true pilot must devote his attention to the year and its seasons, to the sky, and the stars, and the winds, and all that concerns his art, if he intends to be really fit to command a ship; and thinking it impossible to acquire and practice, along with the pilot's art, the art of maintaining the pilot's authority whether some of the crew like it or not. Such being the state of things on board, do you not think that the pilot who is really master of his craft is sure to be called a useless, stargazing babbler by those who form the crews of ships run like this?

Yes, that he will, replied Adeimantus.

Well, said I, I suppose you do not need to scrutinize my image, to remind you that it is a true picture of our cities insofar as their disposition towards philosophers is concerned; on the contrary, I think you understand my meaning.

Yes, quite.

That being the case, when a person expresses his astonishment that philosophers are not respected in our cities, begin by telling him our illustration, and try to persuade him that it would be far more astonishing if they were respected.

Well, I will.

And go on to tell him that he is right in saying that those most suitable for philosophy are considered most useless by the many; only recommend him to lay the blame for it not on these good people themselves, but upon those who decline their services. For it is not in the nature of things that a pilot should petition the sailors to submit to his authority, or that the wise should wait at the rich man's door. No, the author of that bit of cleverness was wrong. For the real truth is, that, just as a sick man, whether he be rich or poor, must attend at the physician's door, so all who require to be ruled must attend at the gate of him who is able to rule, it being against nature that the ruler, supposing him to be really good for anything, should have to beg his subjects to submit to his rule. In fact, you will not be wrong, if you compare the statesmen of our time to the sailors whom we were just now describing, and the useless visionary talkers, as they are called by our politicians, you can compare to those who are truly pilots.

You are perfectly right. . . .

BOOK VIII

It is indeed difficult for a city thus constituted, to be shaken. But since everything that has come into being must one day perish, even a construction like ours will not endure for all time, but must suffer dissolution. . . .

Democracy arises, whenever the poor win the day, killing some of the opposite party, expelling others, and admitting the remainder to an equal participation in regime and ruling, and most commonly the offices in such a city are given by lot.

Yes, you have correctly described the establishment of democracy, whether it be brought about by resorting to arms, or by the terrified withdrawal of the other party.

And now tell me, I continued, in what style these persons administer the city. . . . First of all, are they not free, and does not liberty of act and speech abound in the city, and has not a man license therein to do what he wants?

Yes, so we are told.

And clearly, where such license is permitted, every citizen will arrange his own manner of life as suits his pleasure.

Clearly he will.

Hence I should suppose, that in this regime there will be the greatest diversity of human beings.

Unquestionably there will.

Possibly, I proceeded, this regime may be the prettiest of all. Embroidered as it is with every kind of character, it may be thought as beautiful as a colored dress embroidered with every kind of flower. And perhaps, I added, as children and women admire dresses of many colors, so many persons will judge it to be the most beautiful.

No doubt many will.

Yes, my excellent friend, and it would be a good plan to explore it, if we were in search of a regime.

Why so?

Because it contains within it every kind of regime in consequence of that license of which I spoke; and perhaps a person wishing to found a city, as we were just now doing, ought to go into a democratic city, as a bazaar of regimes, and pick out whatever sort pleases him, and then found his regime according to the choice he has made.

We may safely say that he is not likely to be at a loss for patterns.

Again, consider that, in this city, you are not obliged to rule, though your talents may be equal to the task; and that you need not submit to being ruled, if you dislike it, or go to war when your fellow citizens are at war, or keep peace when they are doing so, if you do not want peace; and again, consider that, though a law forbids your holding office or sitting on a jury, you may nevertheless do both the one and the other, should it occur to you to do so. And now tell me, is not such a course of life divinely pleasant for the moment?

Yes perhaps it is, he replied, for the moment.

Once more. Is not the leniency regarding some who have been tried in a court of law exquisite? Or have you failed to notice in such a regime how men who have been condemned to death or exile, stay all the same, and walk about the streets, and parade like heroes, as if no one saw or cared?

I have seen many instances of it, he replied.

And is there not something splendid in the sympathy of such a regime, lacking pettiness? It positively scorns what we were saying when we were founding our city, to the effect that no one who is not endowed with a transcendent nature, can ever become a good man, unless from his earliest childhood he plays among beautiful objects and studies all beautiful things. How magnificently it tramples all this underfoot, without troubling itself in the least about the previous pursuits of those who enter on a political course, whom it raises to honor, if they only assert to the multitude that they wish well.

Yes, he said, it behaves very grandly.

These, then, will be some of the features of democracy, to which we might add others of the same family; and it will be, in all likelihood, an agreeable, anarchic, many-colored regime, dealing with all alike on a footing of equality, whether they be really equal or not.

The facts you mention are well known. . . .

Come then, my dear friend, tell me in what way tyranny arises. That it is a transformation of democracy, is all but obvious.

It is. . . .

Then may we say that democracy is destroyed by its insatiable craving for that which it defines as supremely good?

And what, according to you, is that?

Freedom, I replied; for I imagine that in a democratic city you will be told that it has, in freedom, the most beautiful of possessions, and that therefore such a city is the only fit abode for the man who is free by nature. . . .

Whenever a democratic city which is thirsting for freedom has fallen under the leadership of wicked wine-bearers, and has drunk the unmixed wine of liberty far beyond due measure, it proceeds, I should imagine, to arraign its rulers as accursed oligarchs, and punishes them, unless they become very gentle, and supply it with freedom in copious draughts.

Yes, that is what is done.

And likewise it insults those who are obedient to the rulers with the titles of willing slaves and worthless fellows; while it commends and honors, both privately and publicly, the rulers who carry themselves like subjects, and the subjects who carry themselves like rulers. Must it not follow that in such a city freedom goes to all lengths?

Of course it must.

Yes, my friend, and does not the prevailing anarchy steal into private houses, and spread on every side, until at last it takes root even among the beasts?

What are we to understand by this?

I mean, for example, that a father accustoms himself to behave like a child, and stands in awe of his sons, and that a son behaves himself like a father, and ceases to respect or fear his parents, in order to prove his freedom. And I mean that citizens, and resident aliens, and foreigners, are all perfectly equal.

Yes, that is how it happens.

I have told you some of the results: let me tell you a few more trifles of the kind. The schoolmaster, in these circumstances, fears and flatters his pupils, and the pupils despise their masters and also their tutors. And, speaking generally, the young copy their elders, and compete with them both in speech and deed; and the old men condescend so far as to abound in wit and pleasantry, in imitation of the young, in order, by their own account, to avoid the reputation of being odious or despotic.

Exactly so. . . .

Now putting all these things together, I proceeded, do you perceive that they amount to this, that the soul of the citizens is rendered so sensitive as to be indignant and impatient at the smallest symptom of slavery? For surely you are aware that they end by making light of the laws themselves, whether written or unwritten, in order that, as they say, they may not have any master at all.

I am very well aware of it.

This then, my friend, if I am not mistaken, is the beginning, so fair and vigorous, out of which tyranny naturally grows.

Vigorous, indeed! But what is the next step?

And is it not always the practice of the people to select a special leader of their cause, whom they maintain and exalt to greatness?

Yes, it is their practice.

Then, obviously, whenever a tyrant grows up naturally, his origin may be traced wholly to this leadership, which is the root from which he shoots.

That is quite obvious.

And what are the first steps in the transformation of the leader into a tyrant? Can we doubt that the change dates from the time when the leader has begun to act like the man in that legend which is told in reference to the temple of Lycaean Zeus in Arcadia?

What legend?

According to it, the man who tasted one piece of human entrails, which was minced up with the other entrails of other victims, was inevitably turned into a wolf. Have you never heard the story?

Yes, I have.

In like manner, should the people's leader find the populace so very compliant that he need make no scruple of shedding kindred blood; should he bring unjust charges against a man, as such persons love to do, prosecute his victim, and murder him, making away with human life, and tasting the blood of his fellows with unholy tongue and lips; should he banish, and kill, and give the signal for canceling debts and redistributing the land; is it not the inevitable destiny of such a man either to be destroyed by his enemies, or to become a tyrant, and be turned from a man into a wolf?

There is no escape from it—necessarily so. Such is the fate of the man who stirs up faction against the propertied class.

It is.

And if he is banished, and afterwards restored in despite of his enemies, does he not return a complete tyrant? Obviously he does.

And if his enemies find themselves unable to expel him, or to put him to death, by accusing him before the city, in that case they take measures to remove him secretly by a violent end.

Yes, that is what usually happens.

In order to prevent this, those who have gone so far always adopt that notorious device of the tyrant, which consists in asking the people for a body-guard, in order that the people's friend may not be lost to them.

Just so.

And the people, I imagine, grant the request, for they are alarmed on his account, while they are confident on their own.

Just so.

But as for that leader himself, it is quite clear that far from being laid "great in his greatness," he has overthrown many others, and stands in the chariot of the city, turned from a leader into a perfected tyrant.

Yes, there is no help for it.

Chapter 4

Politics

Aristotle

Aristotle (384–322 B.C.E.), a student of Plato, made extraordinary contributions in virtually every area of philosophy. He argues that the purpose of a state is to encourage the goodness of its citizens. Indeed, he holds that individuals are not self-sufficient; they need a social arrangement in order to function properly. But which social arrangement best promotes human flourishing? Aristotle argues that, in some cases, having the many rule is best. He reasons that just as a meal composed of a collection of dishes might be tastier than any individual dish by itself, a group of people might be collectively better at ruling than any one individual ruling alone.

Aristotle, *Politics: A New Translation*, trans. C. D. C. Reeve (Indianapolis: Hackett Publishing Company, 2017).

BOOK II, CHAPTER 2

. . . [W]hat each thing is when its coming to be has been completed, this we say is the nature of each—for example, of a human, of a horse, or of a household. Further, its for-the-sake-of-which—namely, its end—is best, and self-sufficiency is both end and best.

From these considerations, then, it is evident that a city is among the things that exist by nature, that a human is by nature a political animal, and that anyone who is without a city, not by luck but by nature, is either a wretch or else better than human, and, like the one Homer condemns, he is "clanless, lawless, and homeless." For someone with such a nature has at the same time an appetite for war, like an isolated piece in a game of checkers.

It is also clear why a human is more of a political animal than any bee or any other gregarious animal. For nature does nothing pointlessly, as we say, and a human being alone among the animals has speech. Now, the voice is a signifier of what is pleasant or painful, which is why it is also possessed by the other animals (for their nature does extend this far, namely, to having the perception of pleasure and pain and signifying them to each other). But speech is for making clear what is advantageous or harmful, and so too what is just or unjust. For this is special to humans, in comparison to the other animals, that they alone have perception of the good and the bad, the just and the unjust, and the rest. And it is community in these that makes a household and a city.

Also the city is prior in nature to the household and to each of us individually. For it is necessary for the whole to be prior to the part. For if the whole body is put to death, there will no longer be a foot or a hand. . . . It is clear, then, that the city both exists by nature and is prior in nature to the individual. For if an individual is not self-sufficient when separated, he will be in a similar state to that of the other parts in relation to the whole. And anyone who cannot live in a community with others, or who does not need to because of his self-sufficiency, is no part of a city, so that he is either a wild beast or a god.

Now, although the impulse toward this sort of community exists by nature in everyone, the person who first put one together was also the cause of very great goods. For just as when completed a human is the best of the animals, so when separated from law and judicial proceeding he is worst of all. For injustice is harshest when it possesses weapons, and a human grows up possessed of weapons for practical wisdom and virtue to use, which may be used for absolutely contrary purposes. That is why he is the most unrestrained and most savage of animals when he lacks virtue, as well as the worst as regards sex and food. But justice is something political. For justice is a political community's order, and justice is judgment of what is just

. . . [T]he view that the majority rather than those who are the best people, albeit few, should be in control would seem to be well stated, and to involve some puzzles, though perhaps also some truth. For the many, each of whom individually is not an excellent man, nevertheless may, when they have come together, be better than the few best people, not individually but collectively, just as dinners to which many contribute are better than dinners provided at one person's expense. For, being many, each can have some part of virtue and practical wisdom, and when they come together, the multitude is just like one human being, with many feet, hands, and senses, and so too for their characters and thought. That is why the many are also better judges of works of music and of the poets. For distinct ones are better judges of distinct parts, and all of them are better judges of the whole thing.

Indeed, it is in this respect that excellent men differ from each of the many, just as noble people are said to differ from those who are not noble, and the things in paintings produced by craft knowledge from real things, namely, by bringing together what is scattered and separate into one—even though, if taken separately at any rate, this person's eye and some other feature of someone else will be more noble than the painted ones.

Now whether it is in the case of every people and every multitude that this superiority of the majority to the few excellent people can exist is not clear. Although, by Zeus, it presumably is clear that in some of them it cannot possibly do so, since the same argument would apply to wild beasts. And yet what difference is there (one might ask) between some people and wild beasts? But of some multitude there is nothing to prevent what has been said from being true.

That is why, by means of these considerations, one might also resolve . . . what the free and the multitude of citizens—those who are not rich and have no claim whatsoever to virtue—should be in control of, since to have them share in the most important offices is not safe. For, because of their lack of justice and lack of practical wisdom, they would of necessity act unjustly in some instances and make errors in others. On the other hand, neither to give a share nor have a share is a fearful thing. For when a large number of poor people are deprived of honors in this way the city is necessarily full of enemies. The remaining alternative, then, is to have them share in deliberation and judgment. That is why Solon and some other legislators arrange to have them elect and inspect officials, but do not allow them to hold office individually. For when they all come together their perception is adequate, and, when mixed with their betters, they benefit their cities, just as a mixture of impure food mixed with the pure sort makes the whole thing more useful than a little [of the latter]. Taken separately, however, each of them is incomplete where judging is concerned.

But this order characteristic of the constitution itself raises puzzles, in the first place, it might seem that it belongs to the very same person to judge whether someone has treated a patient correctly, and to treat patients, that is, to cure them of their present disease—namely, the doctor. And the same would also seem to hold in other areas of experience and other crafts. Hence, just as a doctor should be inspected by doctors, so others should also be inspected by their peers. A doctor, however, may be either an ordinary practitioner of the craft, an architectonic one, or thirdly, someone well educated in the craft. For there are people of this third sort in (one might almost say) all crafts. And we assign the task of judging to well-educated people no less than to those who know the craft.

It might seem, therefore, that election [of officials] is the same way, since choosing correctly is also a function of those who know the craft—for example, choosing a geometer is a function of geometers, and choosing a ship's captain of ship's captains. For even if, in the case of some functions and crafts, certain private individuals also have a share in choosing, they do not have a greater share than those who know the craft. According to this argument, then, the multitude should not be put in control of the election or inspection of officials.

But presumably not all of these things are stated correctly, both because of the argument just given, provided that the multitude is not too slavish (for each individually may be a worse judge than those who know the craft, but a better or no worse one when they all come together), and also because there are some crafts in which the maker might not be either the only or the best judge—the ones where those who lack the craft nevertheless know its products. For example, knowing about a house does not belong only to the maker—instead, the one who uses it is an even better judge (and the one who uses it is the household manager). A ship's captain, too, is a better judge of a rudder than a carpenter is, and a dinner guest, rather than the cook, a better judge of a feast. This puzzle, then, might seem to be adequately solved in this way.

There is another, however, connected with it. For it seems to be absurd for base people to control more important matters than decent ones do. But inspections and elections of officials are a most important thing. And in some constitutions, as we said, these are assigned to the people, since the assembly controls all such matters. And although those who share in the assembly, in deliberation, and in judging, are drawn from those with low property assessments, whatever their age, the treasurers and generals and those who hold the most important offices are drawn from those with high property assessments.

But one can, of course, also solve this puzzle in the same way, since this way of doing things does seem to have something correct about it. For the official is neither the individual juror, nor the individual councilor, nor the individual assemblyman, but rather the court, the council, and the people, whereas each of the individuals mentioned (I mean the individual councilor, assemblyman, and juror) is only a part of these. So it is just for the majority to have control of the more important matters. For the people, the council, and the court consist of many individuals. Also, their collective property assessment is greater than the assessment of those who, whether individually or in small groups, hold the important offices. These matters, then, should be determined in this way.

BOOK IV, CHAPTER 11

What is the best constitution, and what is the best life for most cities and most human beings, comparing it neither to a virtue that is beyond the reach of private individuals, nor to an education that requires natural gifts and resources that depend on luck, nor to the constitution that is in accord with our prayers, but to a life that most people can share and a constitution in which most cities can share? . . .

But now the judgment about all these matters depends on the same elements. For if what is said in the *Ethics* is correct, and a happy life is the unimpeded life that is in accord with virtue, and virtue is a medial state, then the middle life is best, the mean that admits of being aimed at by each sort of person. These same defining marks must also define the virtue and vice of a city or constitution. For the constitution is a sort of life of a city.

In all cities, you see, there are three things that are parts of the city, the very rich, the very poor, and third those who are in the middle between these. Therefore, since it is agreed that the moderate and the middle is best, it is evident that possessing a middling amount of the goods of luck is also best of all. For that makes it easiest to obey reason, whereas whatever is hypernoble, hyper-strong, hyper-well bred, or hyper-rich, or the contraries of these, hyper-poor, hyper-weak, or exceedingly without honor has difficulty in obeying reason. For the first lot tend more toward committing wanton aggression and major vice, whereas the second lot tend too much to become malicious and pettily wicked. And injustices are caused in the one case by wanton aggression and in the other by evildoing. Further, those in the middle are least inclined either to avoid rule or to be eager to rule, both of which things are harmful to cities.

In addition, those who are superior in the goods of luck (strength, wealth, friends, and other things of that sort) neither wish to be ruled nor know how to be ruled. And this characteristic they acquire right from the start at home while they are still children. For because of their luxurious living they are not accustomed to being ruled even in school. Those, on the other hand, who are excessively deprived of such goods are too humble. So the latter do not have the scientific knowledge of how to rule, but only how to be ruled in the way slaves are ruled, whereas the former do not have it of how to be ruled in any way, but only how to rule with the rule of a master.

What comes into being, then, is a city consisting of slaves and masters, but not of free people, the one group envious, the other contemptuous—which is the furthest thing from political friendship and community. For community is fitted to friendship, since enemies do not wish to share even a road in common. But a city tends at any rate to consist as much as possible of people who are equal and similar, and this especially holds of those in the middle. So it is necessary for this city—the one that is composed of those we say a city is by nature composed of—to be governed in the best way.

Also, of all the citizens, those in the middle are the ones that preserve themselves most in cities. For they neither desire other people's property, as the poor do, nor do other people desire theirs, as the poor desire that of the rich. And because they are neither plotted against nor plot, they pass their time free from danger. That is why Phocylides did well to pray: "Many things are best for those in the middle. In the middle is where I want to be in a city."

It is clear, therefore, that the political community that is due to those in the middle is best too, and that cities can be well governed where the middle class is numerous and stronger—especially if it is stronger than both of the others, or, failing that, than one of them. For it will tip the balance when added to either and prevent opposing excesses from arising. That is why it is the height of good luck if those in the governing body own a middling and adequate amount of property, because when some people own an excessive amount and the rest own nothing, either extreme democracy arises or unmixed oligarchy or—as a result of both excesses—tyranny. For tyranny arises from the most vigorous sort of democracy and from [unmixed] oligarchy, but much less often from middle constitutions or those close to them. . . .

It is evident that the middle constitution is best, then, since it alone is free from factional conflict. For where there are many people in the middle, conflicts and disagreements least occur among the citizens. And large cities are freer from factional conflict due to the same cause, namely, that the middle class is numerous. In small cities, on the other hand, it is easy to divide all the citizens into two, so that no middle class is left and pretty much everyone is either poor or rich. And democracies are more stable and longer lasting than oligarchies because of those in the middle (for they are more numerous in democracies than oligarchies and share in office more), since when, without these, the poor are predominant in number, failure comes about and the democracy is quickly ruined.

BOOK VI, CHAPTER 2

The hypothesis of the democratic constitution is freedom. For people usually say that they share in freedom only in this constitution, since all democracies, they say, aim at this. One sort of freedom is ruling and being ruled in turn. For democratic justice is equality in accord with number, not in accord with worth. But if this is what is just, then the multitude must be in control, and whatever seems so to the majority, this must be the end and this must be what is just. For they say that each of the citizens should have an equal share, with the result that in democracies the poor happen to have more control than the rich. For they are the majority, and what seems [to be the case] to the majority is in control. This, then, is one sign of freedom, which all democrats take as a defining mark of their constitution. Another one is to live as one wishes. For this, they say, is the result of freedom, since indeed that of slavery is not to live as one wishes. This, then, is the second defining mark of democracy. From it arises the demand not to be ruled, best of all to be ruled by no one, or, failing that, to rule and be ruled in turn. In this way the second goal contributes to freedom in accord with equality.

When these things are presupposed and the starting-point is of this sort, the following features are democratic: [1] Having all choose officials from all. [2] Having all rule each and each in turn rule all. [3] Having all offices, or all that do not require experience or craft knowledge, filled by lot. [4] Having no property assessment for the offices or as low a one as possible. [5] Having no office, or few besides military ones, held twice or more than a few times by the same person. [6] Having all offices or as many as possible be short-term. [7] Having all, or bodies chosen from all, judge all cases, or most of them and the ones that are most important and involve the most control, such as those having to do with the inspection of officials, the constitution, or private transactions. [8] Having the assembly control everything or all the important things, but having no office control any or as few as possible. Of the offices, the most democratic is the council, when there is ample pay for no one, since where there is ample pay, even this office is stripped of its power. For when the people are well paid, they take all judgments into their own hands (as we said in the methodical inquiry preceding this one). [9] Having pay provided, preferably for all, for the assembly, courts, and public offices, or, failing that, for service in the offices, courts, council, and the controlling assemblies, or for those offices that require their holders to share a communal mess. [10] Further, since oligarchy is defined by family, wealth, and education, their contraries (lack of breeding, poverty, and vulgarity) are held to be characteristically democratic. [11] Further, it is democratic to have no office be permanent; and if such an office happens to survive an ancient change of constitution, at any rate to strip it of its power and make it be filled by lot instead of election.

These, then, are the features common to democracies. And from the justice that is agreed to be democratic, which consists in everyone having equality in accord with number, comes what is believed to be most of all democracy and rule by the people. For equality consists in the poor neither ruling more than the rich nor being alone in control, but in all ruling equally on the basis of equality in accord with number, since in that way they would acknowledge that equality and freedom are present in the constitution.

Chapter 5

The Works of Mencius

Mencius

Mencius (371–289 B.C.E.) was a Confucian philosopher who claims that authority is granted by Heaven through the people. Thus the acceptance of the people is necessary for legitimacy and is a sign that Heaven has granted authority to this ruler.

Mencius, *Mencius*, ed. Philip J. Ivanhoe, trans. Irene Bloom (New York: Columbia University Press, 2009).

Mencius said, "Jie and Zhou lost the world because they lost the people, and they lost the people because they lost the hearts of the people. There is a Way to obtain the world: one gains the world by gaining the people; when one gains the people, one gains the world. There is a Way of gaining the people: by gaining their hearts one gains the people. There is a Way to gain their hearts: gather for them the things that you desire; do not impose on them the things that you dislike. The people's turning to humaneness is like water flowing downward or wild animals heading for the wilds. Thus, as the otter drives the fish toward the deep and the sparrow hawk drives the smaller birds toward the thicket, Jie and Zhou drove the people toward Tang and Wu. If, in the world today, there were a ruler who loved humaneness, the lords would all drive the people to him, and, though he might wish not to become a king, he could not help but do so.

"Those in the world today who wish to become a true king are like the case of needing to find an herb requiring three years of drying and preparation to treat an illness of seven years' duration. If it has not been stored up, to the end of his life, the patient will never have an adequate supply. If rulers do not commit themselves to humaneness, they will endure a lifetime of grief and disgrace and finally sink into death and destruction.

"This is what is meant when the ode says,

How can they become good?

They only lead one another toward drowning.". . .

Wan Zhang said, "Did it happen that Yao gave the realm to Shun?"

Mencius said, "No. The Son of Heaven cannot give the realm to someone."

"But Shun did possess the realm. Who gave it to him?"

"Heaven gave it to him."

"When Heaven gave it to him, did it ordain this through repeated instructions?"

"No. Heaven does not speak. This was manifested simply through Shun's actions and his conduct of affairs."

"In what way was this manifested through his actions and his conduct of affairs?"

"The Son of Heaven can present a man to Heaven, but he cannot cause Heaven to give him the realm. The lords can present a man to the Son of Heaven, but they cannot cause the Son of Heaven to make him a lord. A great officer can present a man to the lords, but he cannot cause the lords to make him a great officer. In antiquity Yao presented Shun to Heaven, and it was Heaven that accepted him. He displayed him to the people, and the people accepted him. This is why I said that 'Heaven does not speak.' This was manifested solely through his actions and his conduct of affairs."

"I venture to ask how it was that Yao presented him to Heaven and Heaven accepted him, and he showed him to the people and the people accepted him?"

"He caused him to preside over the sacrifices, and the hundred spirits enjoyed them. This shows that Heaven accepted him. He put him in charge of affairs, and affairs were well ordered, and the hundred surnames were at peace. This shows that the people accepted him. Heaven gave it to him; the people gave it to him. This is why I said that 'the Son of Heaven cannot give the realm to someone.' Shun assisted Yao for twenty-eight years. This is not something that could have been brought about by a human being. It was Heaven. After Yao died, and the three years' mourning was completed, Shun withdrew from Yao's son and went south of the South River. But the lords of the realm, when they went to court, went not to Yao's son but to Shun. Litigants went not to Yao's son but to Shun. Singers sang not of Yao's son but of Shun. This is why I said, 'It was Heaven.' It was after all this that he went to the central states and ascended to the position of the Son of Heaven. If he had just taken up residence in Yao's palace and ousted Yao's son, this would have been usurpation and not Heaven's gift. The 'Great Declaration' says,

Heaven sees as my people see,

Heaven hears as my people hear.

This is what was meant."

Chapter 6

The Discourses

Niccolò Machiavelli

Niccolò Machiavelli (1469–1527) was a leading Italian Renaissance figure. When the Medici returned to power in Florence, he was forced into exile where he wrote a commentary on the work of the Roman historian Titus Livy. Machiavelli argues that it is usually better to have the many rule, rather than a single individual. The populace makes surprisingly accurate predictions about potential benefits and burdens, and, as a group, the many can determine which of two disputants presents the better argument. By contrast, single individuals are cognitively limited and passions often distort their judgment.

Niccolò Machiavelli, *The Discourses*, trans. Leslie J. Walker, S. J., revised by Brian Richardson (London: Penguin Books).

CHAPTER FIFTY-THREE

On how the populace often seeks its own ruin, taken in by some plan with a misleading appearance of being in its interests; and on how great hopes and cheerful promises easily influence it

When the city of Yeii had been conquered, the populace of Rome persuaded itself that the city of Rome would benefit if half the Romans went to live in Yeii. It argued that since that city was in a fertile region, had fine buildings, and was close to Rome, half the citizens of Rome could be made better off, while, since they would still be nearby, they could continue to play their part in Roman politics. The senate and the more sensible citizens thought that this plan was pointless and potentially damaging. They openly said that they would rather be put to death than agree to such a proposal. The result was that, as the debate on the question became heated, the populace became so furious with the senate it was on the point of resorting to arms, which would have led to bloodshed. But the senate took refuge behind a number of old and revered citizens; respect for them made the populace pause, and it went no further in their disobedience towards the authorities.

Here there are two things we need to note. The first is that the populace is often taken in by some plan with a misleading appearance of being in its interests, and seeks its own ruin. Unless someone who has its confidence makes it understand why the plan is a bad one and what policy ought to be followed instead, the republic will run into an infinity of dangers and suffer innumerable losses. Of course, there are times when nobody has the confidence of the populace, for it may have already been disillusioned either by events or by its leaders. Then you are unlucky; your city is bound to be destroyed. Dante remarks on this subject, in his discourse *On Monarchy*, that the populace often cries out: "Kill us quick! Off with our heads!" This popular scepticism with regard to good advice means that republics often fail to reach sound decisions. [. . . T]he Venetians who, when under attack by so many enemies, could not agree to save something before all was lost by returning the territory they had taken from their neighbors (which was the reason why they were under attack, and the cause of the alliance of powers against them).

However, if you ask yourself what decisions it is easy to persuade a populace to take, and what decisions it is difficult, these categories are helpful: Either the policy you propose appears at first sight to involve gains or losses; alternatively, it either appears brave or cowardly. When you propose something to the populace that appears to involve gain, even if hidden behind the appearance of gain there is a real loss, and when you propose something that seems courageous, even if the real consequence is likely to be the destruction of the republic, then it is easy to persuade the masses to agree with you. On the other hand, it is always difficult to persuade them to adopt policies that seem to involve cowardice or loss, even if they are likely to lead, in fact, to security and to gain.

Innumerable examples could be cited to confirm this, both Roman and non-Roman, both ancient and modern. Thus, this is the explanation of the hostility with which Fabius Maximus came to be regarded in Rome. He could not persuade the Roman populace that the republic would benefit by drawing the war out and by allowing Hannibal to advance without meeting him in battle. The populace thought this policy was cowardly, and did not understand the real benefits that would come from it. Fabius could not find arguments strong enough to convince it. The populace is often blinded by its sense of honor. Thus, the people of Rome not only made the mistake of giving Fabius's commander of the cavalry permission to engage the enemy, even though Fabius disapproved, and even though there was a danger that the resulting conflict of authority would tear the Roman army apart unless Fabius was astute enough to find a way of resolving the problem; they did not learn their lesson, but went on to make Varro consul, not because of any good qualities he had, but simply because he had gone around Rome telling everyone he met in the streets and squares that he would defeat Hannibal as soon as he was given permission to engage him in battle. This led straight to the Battle of Cannae and the rout of the Roman army, and it very nearly caused the defeat of Rome.

On this subject I want to introduce one more example from Roman history. Hannibal had been in Italy for eight or ten years. He had slaughtered Romans from one end of the peninsula to the other. Then Marcus Centenius Penula, a man of contemptible family background (although he had risen to a senior rank in the army), stood up in the senate and said that if they gave him permission to form an army of volunteers wherever he wanted in Italy he would either capture or kill Hannibal in no time at all. The senate thought that his proposal was reckless; but they also feared that if they turned it down, and the populace later got to hear of Penula's offer, then there might be a riot, for the populace would be provoked to hatred and ill-will towards the senatorial class. So they accepted his proposal, preferring to endanger the lives of all those who enrolled under Penula than to risk provoking new hostility towards themselves within the populace. For they understood how easy it would be to persuade the populace to approve of a proposal of this sort, and how difficult it would be to persuade it to reject it. So Penula set out with a disorderly and undisciplined mob to confront Hannibal. The battle was no sooner begun than it was over, and he and all his followers were defeated and killed.

Let us turn to Greece, and in particular to Athens. There Nicias, a man of remarkable wisdom and good sense, could never persuade the populace that it was a bad idea to set out to attack Sicily. They voted for it, despite the opposition of those who were sensible, and the result was the complete defeat of Athens. Again, Scipio, when he became consul, wanted to have command in Africa, claiming he would be able to destroy the Carthaginians. Fabius Maximus persuaded the senate that this was a bad idea; but Scipio threatened to propose it to the populace, knowing perfectly well that proposals of this sort appeal to the common sort.

There are relevant examples to be found in the history of our own city. For instance, there was the occasion when Mr. Ercole Bentivoglio, commander, along with Antonio Giacomini, of the Florentine armies, defeated Bartolommeo d'Alviano at San Vincenti, and so went on to attack Pisa. The populace

voted in favor of this campaign on the basis of the optimistic promises made
by Mr. Ercole, although many wise citizens criticized it. Nevertheless, there
was nothing they could do to stop it, for the vast majority were all in favor
of it, having taken at face value the optimistic promises of the commander. I
conclude that there is no easier way to destroy a republic where the populace
holds power than to encourage it to engage in bold enterprises. For where
the populace have any influence, such proposals will always be adopted; and
those who are opposed to it will find themselves marginalized. But if the
outcome is often the destruction of the city, it is even more often the ruin of
the individual citizens who put forward such enterprises. For the populace
is led to expect victory; when it faces defeat it does not blame fortune, nor
does it excuse its military commander on the grounds that he had insufficient
resources at his disposal. It concludes he was stupid or malicious. Usually, he
is either assassinated, or imprisoned, or put under house arrest; this was the
fate of innumerable Carthaginian commanders and of many Athenian ones.
Any victories they had in the past are discounted; today's defeat cancels them
out. This is what happened to our Antonio Giacomini who, having failed to
take Pisa as the populace expected and as he had promised, became the object
of such contempt among the people that, despite the fact that he had done
innumerable good deeds in the past, he was allowed to live only because the
political authorities took pity on him, and not because the populace could see
any reason why he should be pardon. . . .

CHAPTER FIFTY-EIGHT

On how the masses are wiser and more loyal than any monarch

There is nothing more worthless and more unreliable than the masses. So says
our Titus Livy, and all the other historians agree with him. For it often happens that, as one follows a political narrative, one sees the masses condemn
someone to death, and then next moment lament his death, and long for his
return. . . .

I am not sure if I want to embark on an undertaking that is so hard and
full of so many difficulties that I will either have to give up in disgrace or,
if I carry on, be made to pay dearly for my persistence. I am not sure if I
want to defend a view that, as I have said, is rejected by all the authorities.
Nevertheless, I do not think, and never will think, that one should be blamed
for putting forward an argument, so long as one relies on reason and has no
intention of resorting to citing authorities or to force. In my view, then, the
defect for which authors criticize the masses is a defect to be found in all
men, considered as individuals, and, above all, in rulers. For anyone who

is not constrained by the laws will make exactly the same errors as will the unbridled masses. One can easily recognize the truth of this, for there are and have been plenty of rulers but there are few who have been good and wise. . . .

I conclude, therefore, that the common opinion, which holds that the populace, when they are in power, are unreliable, changeable, and disloyal is wrong. I maintain that they are no more guilty of these vices than are individual rulers. If someone were to criticize both multitudes and individuals who hold power, he might be right; but if he makes an exception of the individuals, then he makes a mistake. For a populace in power, if it is well ordered, will be as reliable, prudent, and loyal as an individual, or rather it will be even better than an individual, even one who is thought wise. On the other hand, an individual who is not restrained by the laws will be even more disloyal, unreliable, and imprudent than a populace. The difference in their behavior would be a consequence, not of a difference in their natures, for all men are alike, and if any type of person is better than the rest, it is the common man who is; but would reflect whether they had more or less respect for the laws under which both prince and populace are supposed to live. . . .

But as far as prudence and predictability are concerned, I say that the populace is generally more prudent, more predictable, and has better judgment than a monarch. It is with good reason that people compare the voice of the populace to the voice of God, for one can see that there is a widespread belief that the predictions of a populace are uncannily accurate; indeed, it seems as if it has an inexplicable capacity to foresee what will bring it good fortune and what bad. As far as exercising their judgment is concerned, one sees that it is rare indeed that the people hear two speeches upholding different policies, and do not, if the speeches are equally effective, choose the better policy. They are almost always able to understand those truths that are explained to them. I have already admitted they sometimes make mistakes in matters involving their pride or what they take to be their interests. But monarchs often make mistakes when their passions are aroused, which happens much more often with a single ruler than it does with the populace. One also sees that, when it comes to making appointments to government offices, the populace makes much better choices than rulers do. You will never persuade the populace that it is a good idea to promote to an office a man who has a bad reputation and lives a decadent life. But rulers are easily persuaded to do this for all sorts of reasons. One sees a populace begin to be committed to opposing something, and then not change its mind for several centuries; the same cannot be said for rulers. . . .

One may also note, in addition, that cities where the populace is in power are capable of making immense territorial gains in very short periods of time, much greater than any that have been made by an individual ruler. . . . The only possible reason for this is that the populace is better at ruling than individuals are. . . . For if you go over all the cases of bad government by the populace, and all those by monarchs, all the achievements of the populace, and all those of monarchs, you will find the populace to be much superior in both goodness and glory. If individuals are superior to the populace in drawing up laws, establishing civic forms of life, creating constitutions and institutions, then the populace is equally superior to an individual when it comes to maintaining the institutions once they have been established. No doubt its achievements in this respect get credited to the original legislators.

So finally, to conclude my discussion, I say that just as some states based on one-man rule have endured over time, so have some republics. Both monarchies and republics need to be regulated by laws, for a king who can do whatever he wants is a madman on the loose, and a populace that can do what it wants is never wise. However, if we were to discuss the relative merits of a monarch who is obliged to obey the law and a populace restrained by legislation, you would find that the populace made a better ruler than the monarch. If we were to discuss both types of government unconstrained by the law, you would find that the populace makes fewer mistakes than a monarch, and the ones it makes are less significant and easier to put right. For a populace that is licentious and disorderly needs only to be talked to by someone who is good, and he will find it easy to set it on the right path. A bad monarch will not listen to anyone, and the only way to correct him is to kill him. This enables one to judge the relative importance of the faults of the two types of government. To cure the faults of the people, you need only words; to cure those of a monarch, you need cold steel. Now it is obvious that a disease that is hard to cure is worse than one that is easy.

When a populace breaks free from restraint, there is no need to fear the foolish things it may do. It is not the present evil one has to worry about but the evil that may develop out of popular government, for a tyrant may seize power in the midst of the confusion. But the opposite is the case with bad monarchs. With them, one fears the present evil and hopes for some future improvement, for men persuade themselves that the evil deeds of their ruler may provoke people to lay claim to their freedom. So you can see that the difference between them is that under one type of government you fear what exists, under the other what might come to pass.

The cruel deeds of the multitude are directed at those whom it fears will endanger the common good; those of a monarch are directed at those whom he fears will endanger his own interests. Why then do people think ill of the populace? Because everyone freely speaks ill of them; they can do so without fear even when they are in power. But about monarchs one always speaks with great caution, and one is always fearful of the consequences.

Chapter 7

Leviathan

Thomas Hobbes

Thomas Hobbes (1588–1679) was an English philosopher who played a crucial role in the history of social thought. He develops a moral and political theory that views justice and other ethical ideals as resting on an implied agreement among individuals. Outside the social order, the good is whatever anyone desires, the evil whatever anyone hates, and each human life is, as Hobbes famously puts it, "solitary, poor, nasty, brutish, and short." Thus he argues that reason requires that we should relinquish the right to do whatever we please in exchange for all others limiting their own rights in a similar manner, thus achieving security for all. In order to guard against collapsing back into the disastrous state of nature, a monarchy should be established rather than an aristocracy or democracy, for multiple rulers invite instability, jeopardizing the security sovereignty affords.

———

PART I: OF MAN
CHAPTER XIII

Of the natural condition of mankind as concerning their felicity, and misery

Nature hath made men so equal, in the faculties of the body, and mind; as that though there be found one man sometimes manifestly stronger in body, or of quicker mind than another; yet when all is reckoned together, the difference between man, and man, is not so considerable, as that one man can thereupon claim to himself any benefit, to which another may not pretend, as well as he. For as to the strength of body, the weakest has strength enough to kill the strongest, either by secret machination, or by confederacy with others, that are in the same danger with himself.

And as to the faculties of the mind, setting aside the arts grounded upon words, and especially that skill of proceeding upon general, and infallible rules, called science: which very few have, and but in few things; as being not a native faculty, born with us: nor attained, as prudence, while we look after somewhat else. I find yet a greater equality amongst men, than that of strength. For prudence, is but experience; which equal time, equally bestows on all men, in those things they equally apply themselves unto. That which may perhaps make such equality incredible, is but a vain conceit of one's own wisdom, which almost all men think they have in a greater degree, than the vulgar: that is, than all men but themselves, and a few others, whom by fame, or for concurring with themselves, they approve. For such is the nature of men, that howsoever they may acknowledge many others to be more witty, or more eloquent, or more learned: yet they will hardly believe there be many so wise as themselves: for they see their own wit at hand, and other men's at a distance. But this proveth rather that men are in that point equal, than unequal. For there is not ordinarily a greater sign of the equal distribution of any thing, than that every man is contented with his share.

From this equality of ability, ariseth equality of hope in the attaining of our ends. And therefore if any two men desire the same thing, which nevertheless they cannot both enjoy, they become enemies; and in the way to their end, which is principally their own conservation, and sometimes their delectation only, endeavour to destroy, or subdue one another. And from hence it comes to pass, that where an invader hath no more to fear, than another man's single power; if one plant, sow, build, or possess a convenient seat, others may probably be expected to come prepared with forces united, to dispossess, and deprive him, not only of the fruit of his labour, but also of his life, or liberty. And the invader again is in the like danger of another.

And from this diffidence of one another, there is no way for any man to secure himself, so reasonable, as anticipation; that is, by force, or wiles, to master the persons of all men he can, so long, till he see no other power great enough to endanger him: and this is no more than his own conservation requireth, and is generally allowed. Also because there be some, that taking pleasure in contemplating their own power in the acts of conquest, which they pursue farther than their security requires; if others, that otherwise would be glad to be at case within modest bounds, should not by invasion increase their power, they would not be able, long time, by standing only on their defence, to subsist. And by consequence, such augmentation of dominion over men being necessary to a man's conservation, it ought to be allowed him.

Again, men have no pleasure, but on the contrary a great deal of grief, in keeping company, where there is no power able to over-awe them all. For every man looketh that his companion should value him, at the same rate he sets upon himself: and upon all signs of contempt, or undervaluing, naturally endeavours, as far as he dares, (which amongst them that have no common power to keep them in quiet, is far enough to make them destroy each other), to extort a greater value from his contemners, by damage; and from others, by the example.

So that in the nature of man, we find three principal causes of quarrel. First, competition; secondly, diffidence; thirdly, glory.

The first, maketh man invade for gain; the second, for safety; and the third, for reputation. The first use violence, to make themselves masters of other men's persons, wives, children, and cattle; the second, to defend them; the third, for trifles, as a word, a smile, a different opinion, and any other sign of undervalue, either direct in their persons, or by reflection in their kindred, their friends, their nation, their profession, or their name.

Hereby it is manifest, that during the time men live without a common power to keep them all in awe, they are in that condition which is called war; and such a war, as is of every man, against every man. For war, consisteth not in battle only, or the act of fighting; but in a tract of time, wherein the will to contend by battle is sufficiently known; and therefore the notion of *time*, is to be considered in the nature of war; as it is in the nature of weather. For as the nature of foul weather, lieth not in a shower or two of rain; but in an inclination thereto of many days together; so the nature of war, consisteth not in actual fighting; but in the known disposition thereto, during all the time there is no assurance to the contrary. All other time is peace.

Whatsoever therefore is consequent to a time of war, where every man is enemy to every man; the same is consequent to the time, wherein men live without other security, than what their own strength, and their own invention shall furnish them withal. In such condition, there is no place for industry; because the fruit thereof is uncertain; and consequently no culture of the earth; no navigation nor use of the commodities that may be imported by sea; no commodious building; no instruments of moving, and removing, such things as require much force; no knowledge of the face of the earth; no account of time; no arts: no letters: no society; and which is worst of all, continual fear, and danger of violent death; and the life of man, solitary, poor, nasty, brutish, and short.

It may seem strange to some man, that has not well weighed these things; that nature should thus dissociate, and render men apt to invade, and destroy one another; and he may therefore, not trusting to this inference, made from the passions, desire perhaps to have the same confirmed by experience. Let him therefore consider with himself, when taking a journey, he arms himself, and seeks to go well accompanied; when going to sleep, he locks his doors; when even in his house he locks his chests; and this when he knows there be laws, and public offices, armed, to revenge all injuries shall be done him; what opinion he has of his fellow subjects, when he rides armed; of his fellow citizens, when he locks his doors; and of his children, and servants, when he locks his chests. Does he not there as much accuse mankind by his actions, as I do by my words? But neither of us accuse man's nature in it. The desires, and other passions of man, are in themselves no sin. No more are the actions, that proceed from those passions, till they know a law that forbids them; which till laws be made they cannot know; nor can any law be made, till they have agreed upon the person that shall make it.

It may peradventure be thought, there was never such a time, nor condition of war as this; and I believe it was never generally so, over all the world; but there are many places, where they live so now. For the savage people in many places of America, except the government of small families, the concord whereof dependeth on natural lust, have no government at all; and live at this day in that brutish manner, as I said before. Howsoever, it may be perceived what manner of life there would be, where there were no common power to fear, by the manner of life, which men that have formerly lived under a peaceful government, use to degenerate into, in a civil war.

But though there had never been any time, wherein particular men were in a condition of war one against another; yet in all times, kings, and persons of sovereign authority, because of their independency, are in continual jealousies, and in the state and posture of gladiators; having their weapons pointing, and their eyes fixed on one another; that is, their forts, garrisons, and guns upon the frontiers of their kingdoms; and continual spies upon their neighbours; which is a posture of war. But because they uphold thereby, the industry of their subjects; there does not follow from it, that misery, which accompanies the liberty of particular men.

To this war of every man, against even man, this also is consequent; that nothing can be unjust. The notions of right and wrong, justice and injustice have there no place, where there is no common power, there is no law; where no law, no injustice. Force, and fraud, are in war the two cardinal virtues. Justice, and injustice are none of the faculties neither of the body, nor mind. If they were, they might be in a man that were alone in the world, as well as his senses, and passions. They are qualities, that relate to men in society, not in solitude. It is consequent also to the same condition, that there be no propriety, no dominion, no *mine* and *thine* distinct; but only that to be every man's, that he can get; and for so long, as he can keep it. And thus much for the ill condition, which man by mere nature is actually placed in; though with a possibility to come out of it, consisting partly in the passions, partly in his reason.

The passions that incline men to peace, are fear of death; desire of such things as are necessary to commodious living; and a hope by their industry to obtain them. And reason suggesteth convenient articles of peace, upon which men may be drawn to agreement. These articles, are they, which otherwise are called the Laws of Nature; whereof I shall speak more particularly, in the two following chapters.

CHAPTER XIV

Of the first and second natural laws, and of contracts

The right of nature, which writers commonly call *jus naturale*, is the liberty each man hath, to use his own power, as he will himself, for the preservation of his own nature; that is to say, of his own life; and consequently, of doing any thing, which in his own judgment, and reason, he shall conceive to be the aptest means thereunto.

By LIBERTY, is understood, according to the proper signification of the word, the absence of external impediments; which impediments, may oft take away part of a man's power to do what he would; but cannot hinder him from using the power left him, according as his judgment, and reason shall dictate to him.

A LAW OF NATURE, *lex naturalis*, is a precept or general rule, found out by reason, by which a man is forbidden to do that, which is destructive of his life, or taketh away the means of preserving the same; and to omit that, by which he thinketh it may be best preserved. For though they that speak of this subject, use to confound *jus*, and *lex*, *right* and *law*; yet they ought to be distinguished; because right, consisteth in liberty to do, or to forbear; whereas LAW, determineth, and bindeth to one of them; so that law, and right, differ as much, as obligation, and liberty; which in one and the same matter are inconsistent.

And because the condition of man, as hath been declared in the precedent chapter, is a condition of war of every one against every one; in which case every one is governed by his own reason; and there is nothing he can make use of, that may not be a help unto him, in preserving his life against his enemies; it followeth, that in such a condition, every man has a right to every thing; even to one another's body. And therefore, as long as this natural right of every man to every thing endureth, there can be no security to any man, how strong or wise soever he be, of living out the time, which nature ordinarily alloweth men to live. And consequently it is a precept, or general rule of reason, *that every man, ought to endeavour peace, as far as he has hope of obtaining it; and when he cannot obtain it, that he may seek, and use, all helps, and advantages of war.* The first branch of which rule, containeth the first, and fundamental law of nature; which is, to seek *peace, and follow it.* The second, the sum of the right of nature; which is, *by all means we can, to defend ourselves.*

From this fundamental law of nature, by which men are commanded to endeavour peace, is derived this second law; *that a man be willing, when others are so too, as far-forth, as for peace, and defence of himself he shall think it necessary, to lay down this right to all things; and be contented with so much liberty against other men; as he would allow other men against himself.* For as long as every man holdeth this right, of doing any thing he liketh; so long are all men in the condition of war. But if other men will not lay down their right, as well as he; then there is no reason for any one, to divest himself of his; for that were to expose himself to prey, which no man is bound to, rather than to dispose himself to peace. This is that law of the Gospel; *whatsoever you require that others should do to you, that do yet to them.* . . .

To *lay down* a man's *right* to any thing, is to *divest* himself of the *liberty*, of hinderianother of the benefit of his own right to the same. For he that renounceth, or passeth away his right, giveth not to any other man a right which he had not before; because there is nothing to which every man had not right by nature; but only standeth out of his way, that he may enjoy his own original right, without hindrance from him: not without hindrance from another. So that the effect which redoundeth to one man, by another man's defect of right, is but so much diminution of impediments to the use of his own right original. Right is laid aside, either by simply renouncing it; or by transferring it to another. By *simply* RENOUNCING; when he cares not to whom the benefit thereof redoundeth. By transferring; when he intendeth the benefit thereof to some certain person, or persons. And when a man hath in either manner abandoned, or granted away his right; then he is said to be OBLIGED, or BOUND, not to hinder those, to whom such right is granted, or abandoned, from the benefit of it; and that he *ought*, and it is his DUTY, not to make void that voluntary act of his own; and that such hindrance is INJUSTICE, and INJURY, as being *sine jure*; the right being before renounced, or transferred. So that *injury*, or *injustice*, in the controversies of the world, is somewhat like to that, which in the disputations of scholars is called absurdity. For as it is there called an *absurdity*, to contradict what one maintained in the beginning; so in the world, it is called injustice, and injury, voluntarily to undo that, which from the beginning he had voluntarily done. The way by which a man either simply renounceth, or transferred his right, is a declaration, or signification, by some voluntary and sufficient sign, or signs, that he doth so renounce, or transfer; or hath so renounced, or transferred the same, to him that accepteth it. And these signs are either words only, or actions only; or, as it happeneth most often, both words, and actions. And the same are the BONDS, by which men are bound, and obliged; bonds, that have their strength, not from their own nature, for nothing is more easily broken than a man's word, but from fear of some evil consequences upon the rupture.

Whensoever, a man transferreth his right, or renounceth it; it is either in consideration of some right reciprocally transferred to himself; or for some other good he hopeth for thereby. For it is a voluntary act; and of the voluntary acts of every man, the object is some *good to himself*. And therefore there be some rights, which no man can be understood by any words, or other signs, to have abandoned, or transferred. As first a man cannot lay down the right of resisting them, that assault him by force, to take away his life; because he cannot be understood to aim thereby, at any good to himself. The same may be said of wounds, and chains, and imprisonment; both because there is no benefit consequent to such patience; as there is to the patience of suffering another to be wounded, or imprisoned; as also because a man cannot tell, when he seeth men proceed against him by violence, whether they intend his death or not. And lastly the motive, and end for which this renouncing, and transferring of right is introduced, is nothing else but the security of a man's person, in his life, and in the means of so preserving life, as not to be weary of it. And therefore if a man by words, or other signs, seem to despoil himself of the end, for which those signs were intended; he is not to be understood as if he meant it, or that it was his will; but that he was ignorant of how such words and actions were to be interpreted.

The mutual transferring of right, is that which men call CONTRACT. . . .

CHAPTER XV

Of other laws of nature

From that law of nature, by which we are obliged to transfer to another, such rights, as being retained, hinder the peace of mankind, there followeth a third; which is this, *that men perform their covenants made*; without which, covenants are in vain, and but empty words; and the right of all men to all things remaining, we are still in the condition of war.

And in this law of nature, consisteth the fountain and original of JUSTICE. For where no covenant hath preceded, there hath no right been transferred, and every man has right to every thing; and consequently, no action can be unjust. But when a covenant is made, then to break it is *unjust*; and the definition of INJUSTICE, is no other than *the not performance of covenant*. And whatsoever is not unjust, is *just*.

But because covenants of mutual trust, where there is a fear of not performance on either part, as hath been said in the former chapter, are invalid; though the original of justice be the making of covenants; yet injustice actually there can be none, till the cause of such fear be taken away; which while men are in the natural condition of war, cannot be done. Therefore before the names of just, and unjust can have place, there must be some coercive power, to compel men equally to the performance of their covenants, by the terror of some punishment, greater than the benefit they expect by the breach of their covenant; and to make good that propriety, which by mutual contract men acquire, in recompense of the universal right they abandon; and such power there is none before the erection of a commonwealth. And this is also to be gathered out of the ordinary definition of justice in the Schools; for they say, that *justice is the constant will of giving to every man his own*. And therefore where there is no *own*, that is no propriety, there is no injustice; and where there is no coercive power erected, that is, where there is no commonwealth, there is no propriety; all men having right to all things: therefore where there is no commonwealth, there nothing is unjust. So that the nature of justice, consisteth in keeping of valid covenants: but the validity of covenants begins not but with the constitution of a civil power, sufficient to compel men to keep them: and then it is also that propriety begins.

The fool hath said in his heart, there is no such thing as justice; and sometimes also with his tongue; seriously alleging, that every man's conservation, and contentment, being committed to his own care, there could be no reason, why every man might not do what he thought conduced thereunto; and therefore also to make, or not make; keep, or not keep covenants, was not against reason, when it conduced to one's benefit. He does not therein deny, that there be covenants; and that they are sometimes broken, sometimes kept; and that such breach of them may be called injustice, and the observance of them justice; but he questioneth, whether injustice, taking away the fear of God, (for the same fool hath said in his heart there is no God) may not sometimes stand with that reason, which dictateth to every man his own good; and particularly then, when it conduceth to such a benefit, as shall put a man in a condition, to neglect not only the dispraise, and revilings, but also the power of other men. The kingdom of God is gotten by violence; but what if it could be gotten by unjust violence? were it against reason so to get it, when it is impossible to receive hurt by it? and if it be not against reason, it is not against justice; or else justice is not to be approved for good. From such reasoning as this, successful wickedness hath obtained the name of virtue; and some that in all other things have disallowed the violation of faith; yet have allowed it, when it is for the getting of a kingdom. . . . This specious reasoning is nevertheless false.

For the question is not of promises mutual, where there is no security of performance on either side; as when there is no civil power erected over the parties promising; for such promises are no covenants: but either where one of the parties has performed already; or where there is a power to make him perform; there is the question whether it be against reason, that is, against the benefit of the other to perform, or not. And I say it is not against reason. For the manifestation whereof, we are to consider; first, that when a man doth a thing, which notwithstanding any thing can be foreseen, and reckoned on, tendeth to his own destruction, howsoever some accident which he could not expect, arriving may turn it to his benefit; yet such events do not make it reasonably or wisely done. Secondly, that in a condition of war, wherein every man to every man, for want of a common power to keep them all in awe, is an enemy, there is no man can hope by his own strength, or wit, to defend himself from destruction, without the help of confederates; where every one expects the same defence by the confederation, that any one else does: and therefore he which declares he thinks it reason to deceive those that help him, can in reason expect no other means of safety, than what can be had from his own single power. He therefore that breaketh his covenant, and consequently declareth that he thinks he may with reason do so, cannot be received into any society, that unite themselves for peace and defence, but by the error of them that receive him; nor when he is received, be retained in it, without seeing the danger of their error; which errors a man cannot reasonably reckon upon as the means of his security; and therefore if he be left, or cast out of society, he perisheth; and if he live in society, it is by the errors of other men, which he could not foresee, nor reckon upon; and consequently against the reason of his preservation; and so, as all men that contribute not to his destruction, forbear him only out of ignorance of what is good for themselves.

PART II: OF COMMONWEALTH
CHAPTER XVII

Of the causes, generation, and definition of a commonwealth

The final cause, end, or design of men, (who naturally love liberty, and dominion over others,) in the introduction of that restraint upon themselves, (in which we see them live in commonwealths,) is the foresight of their own preservation, and of a more contented life thereby; that is to say, of getting themselves out from that miserable condition of war, which is necessarily consequent (as hath been shown), to, the natural passions of men, when there is no visible power to keep them in awe, and tie them by fear of punishment to the performance of their covenants, and observation of those laws of nature set down in the fourteenth and fifteenth chapters.

For the laws of nature (as *justice, equity, modesty, mercy,* and (in sum) *doing to others, as we would be done to.*) of themselves, without the terror of some power, to cause them to be observed, are contrary to our natural passions, that carry us to partiality, pride, revenge, and the like. And covenants, without the sword, are but words, and of no strength to secure a man at all. Therefore notwithstanding the laws of nature, (which every one hath then kept, when he has the will to keep them, when he can do it safely,) if there be no power erected, or not great enough for our security; every man will, and may lawfully rely on his own strength and art, for caution against all other men. And in all places, where men have lived by small families, to rob and spoil one another, has been a trade, and so far from being reputed against the law of nature, that the greater spoils they gained, the greater was their honour; and men observed no other laws therein, but the laws of honour; that is, to abstain from cruelty, leaving to men their lives, and instruments of husbandry. And as small families did then; so now do cities and kingdoms which are but greater families (for their own security) enlarge their dominions, upon all pretences of danger, and fear of invasion, or assistance that may be given to invaders, endeavour as much as they can, to subdue, or weaken their neighbours, by open force, and secret arts, for want of other caution, justly; and are remembered for it in after ages with honour.

Nor is it the joining together of a small number of men that gives them this security; because in small numbers, small additions on the one side or the other make the advantage of strength so great as is sufficient to carry the victory, and therefore gives encouragement to an invasion. The multitude sufficient to confide in for our security is not determined by any certain number, but by comparison with the enemy we fear; and is then sufficient when the odds of the enemy is not of so visible and conspicuous moment to determine the event of war, as to move him to attempt.

And be there never so great a multitude; yet if their actions be directed according to their particular judgements, and particular appetites, they can expect thereby no defence, nor protection, neither against a common enemy, nor against the injuries of one another. For being distracted in opinions concerning the best use and application of their strength, they do not help, but hinder one another, and reduce their strength by mutual opposition to nothing: whereby they are easily, not only subdued by a very few that agree together, but also, when there is no common enemy, they make war upon each other for their particular interests. For if we could suppose a great multitude of men to consent in the observation of justice, and other laws of nature, without a common power to keep them all in awe, we might as well suppose all mankind to do the same; and then there neither would be, nor need to be, any civil government or Commonwealth at all, because there would be peace without subjection.

Nor is it enough for the security, which men desire should last all the time of their life, that they be governed, and directed by one judgment, for a limited time; as in one battle, or one war. For though they obtain a victory by their unanimous endeavour against a foreign enemy; yet afterwards, when either they have no common enemy, or he that by one part is held for an enemy, is by another part held for a friend, they must needs by the difference of their interests dissolve, and fall again into a war amongst themselves.

It is true, that certain living creatures, as bees, and ants, live sociably one with another, (which are therefore by Aristotle numbered amongst political creatures;) and yet have no other direction, than their particular judgments and appetites; nor speech, whereby one of them can signify to another, what he thinks expedient for the common benefit; and therefore some man may perhaps desire to know, why mankind cannot do the same. To which I answer.

First, that men are continually in competition for honour and dignity, which these creatures are not; and consequently amongst men there ariseth on that ground, envy and hatred, and finally war; but amongst these not so.

Secondly, that amongst these creatures, the common good differeth not from the private; and being by nature inclined to their private, they procure thereby the common benefit. But man, whose joy consisteth in comparing himself with other men, can relish nothing but what is eminent.

Thirdly, that these creatures, having not, (as man) the use of reason, do not see, nor think they see any fault, in the administration of their common business; whereas amongst men, there are very many, that think themselves wiser, and abler to govern the public, better than the rest; and these strive to reform and innovate, one this way, another that way; and thereby bring it into distraction and civil war.

Fourthly, that these creatures, though they have some use of voice, in making known to one another their desires, and other affections: yet they want that art of words, by which some men can represent to others, that which is good, in the likeness of evil; and evil, in the likeness of good; and augment, or diminish the apparent greatness of good and evil: discontenting men, and troubling their peace at their pleasure.

Fifthly, irrational creatures cannot distinguish between *injury*, and *damage*: and therefore as long as they be at ease, they are not offended with their fellows: whereas man is then most troublesome, when he is most at ease; for then it is that he loves to show his wisdom, and control the actions of them that govern the commonwealth.

Lastly, the agreement of these creatures is natural; that of men, is by covenant only, which is artificial; and therefore it is no wonder if there be somewhat else required, (besides covenant) to make their agreement constant and lasting; which is a common power, to keep them in awe, and to direct their actions to the common benefit.

The only way to erect such a common power, as may be able to defend them from the invasion of foreigners, and the injuries of one another, and thereby to secure them in such sort, as that by their own industry, and by the fruits of the earth, they may nourish themselves and live contentedly; is, to confer all their power and strength upon one man, or upon one assembly of men, that may reduce all their wills, by plurality of voices, unto one will; which is as much as to say, to appoint one man, or assembly of men, to bear their person; and even one to own, and acknowledge himself to be author of whatsoever he that so beareth their person, shall act, or cause to be acted, in those things which concern the common peace and safety; and therein to submit their wills, every one to his will, and their judgments, to his judgment. This is more than consent, or concord: it is a real unity of them all, in one and the same person, made by covenant of every man with every man, in such manner, as if every man should say to every man. *I authorise and give up my right of governing myself, to this man, or to this assembly of men, on this condition, that thou give up thy right to him, and authorise all his actions in like manner.* This done, the multitude so united in one person, is called a COMMONWEALTH, in Latin CIVITAS. This is the generation of that great LEVIATHAN, or rather (to speak more reverently) of that mortal god, to which we owe under the immortal God, our peace and defence. For by this authority, given him by every particular man in the commonwealth, he hath the use of so much power and strength conferred on him, that by terror thereof, he is enabled to form the wills of them all, to peace at home, and mutual aid against their enemies abroad. And in him consisteth the essence of the commonwealth; which (to define it) *is one person, of whose acts a great multitude, by mutual covenants one with another, have made themselves every one the author, to the end he may use the strength and means of them all, as he shall think expedient, for their peace and common defence.*

And he that carrieth this person, is called SOVEREIGN, and said to have sovereign power; and every one besides, his SUBJECT.

CHAPTER XIX

Of the several kinds of commonwealth by institution, and of succession to the sovereign power

The difference of commonwealths, consisteth in the difference of the sovereign, or the person representative of all and every one of the multitude. And because the sovereignty is either in one man, or in an assembly of more than one; and into that assembly either every man hath right to enter, or not every one, but certain men distinguished from the rest; it is manifest, there can be but three kinds of commonwealth. For the representative must needs be one man, or more; and if more, then it is the assembly of all, or but of a part. When the representative is one man, then is the commonwealth a MONARCHY; when an assembly of all that will come together, then it is a DEMOCRACY, or popular commonwealth; when an assembly of a part only, then it is called an ARISTOCRACY. Other kind of commonwealth there can be none; for either one, or more, or all, must have the sovereign power (which I have shown to be indivisible) entire. . . .

The difference between these three kinds of commonwealth, consisteth not in the difference of power; but in the difference of convenience, or aptitude to produce the peace, and security of the people; for which end they were instituted. And to compare monarchy with the other two, we may observe: first, that whosoever beareth the person of the people, or is one of that assembly that bears it, beareth also his own natural person. And though he be careful in his politic person to procure the common interest; yet he is more, or no less careful to procure the private good of himself, his family, kindred and friends; and for the most part, if the public interest chance to cross the private, he prefers the private; for the passions of men, are commonly more potent than their reason. From whence it follows, that where the public and private interest are most closely united, there is the public most advanced. Now in monarchy, the private interest is the same with the public. The riches, power, and honour of a monarch arise only from the riches, strength and reputation of his subjects. For no king can be rich, nor glorious, nor secure, whose subjects are either poor, or contemptible, or too weak through want, or dissention, to maintain a war against their enemies; whereas in a democracy, or aristocracy, the public prosperity confers not so much to the private fortune of one that is corrupt, or ambitious, as doth many times a perfidious advice, a treacherous action, or a civil war.

Secondly, that a monarch receiveth counsel of whom, when, and where he pleaseth; and consequently may hear the opinion of men versed in the matter about which he deliberates, of what rank or quality soever, and as long before the time of action, and with as much secrecy, as he will. But when a sovereign assembly has need of counsel, none are admitted but such as have a right thereto from the beginning; which for the most part are of those who have been versed more in the acquisition of wealth than of knowledge; and are to give their advice in long discourses, which may, and do commonly excite men to action, but not govern them in it. For the *understanding* is by the flame of the passions, never enlightened, but dazzled: Nor is there any place, or time, wherein an assembly can receive counsel with secrecy, because of their own multitude.

Thirdly, that the resolutions of a monarch, are subject to no other inconstancy, than that of human nature; but in assemblies, besides that of nature, there ariseth an inconstancy from the number. For the absence of a few, that would have the resolution once taken, continue firm (which may happen by security, negligence, or private impediments) or the diligent appearance of a few of the contrary opinion, undoes to day, all that was concluded yesterday.

Fourthly, that a monarch cannot disagree with himself, out of envy, or interest; but an assembly may; and that to such a height, as may produce a civil war.

Fifthly, that in monarchy there is this inconvenience; that any subject, by the power of one man, for the enriching of a favourite or flatterer, may be deprived of all he possesseth; which I confess is a great and inevitable inconvenience. But the same may as well happen, where the sovereign power is in an assembly: for their power is the same; and they are as subject to evil counsel, and to be seduced by orators, as a monarch by flatterers; and becoming one another's flatterers, serve one another's covetousness and ambition by turns. And whereas the favourites of monarchs, are few, and they have none else to advance but their own kindred; the favourites of an assembly, are many; and the kindred much more numerous, than of any monarch. Besides, there is no favourite of a monarch, which cannot as well succour his friends, as hurt his enemies: but orators, that is to say, favourites of sovereign assemblies, though they have great power to hurt, have little to save. For to accuse, requires less eloquence (such is man's nature) than to excuse; and condemnation, than absolution more resembles justice.

Chapter 8

Theologico-Political Treatise

Baruch Spinoza

Baruch Spinoza (1632–1677) was a leading figure in early modern philosophy. He argues that, in the absence of a state, all persons are free and equal. Each is free because all have a right to exist and act in accordance with their nature. All are equal because everyone enjoys this right. A state's legitimacy is the product of the good consequences it secures; in their absence, those that continue to obey are merely fools. Democracy lays the best claim to legitimacy because it preserves better than any other arrangement the natural liberty and equality of each individual.

Baruch Spinoza, *The Chief Works of Baruch Spinoza*, vol. 1., trans. R. H. M. Elwes (New York: Dover, 1951).

⸻❀❀❀⸻

CHAPTER XVI

Of the Foundations of a State; Of the Natural and Civil Rights of Individuals; and Of the Rights of the Sovereign Power

Hitherto our care has been to separate philosophy from theology, and to show the freedom of thought which such separation insures to both. It is now time to determine the limits to which such freedom of thought and discussion may extend itself in the ideal state. For the due consideration of this question we must examine the foundations of a state, first turning our attention to the natural rights of individuals, and afterwards to religion and the state as a whole.

By the right and ordinance of nature, I merely mean those natural laws wherewith we conceive every individual to be conditioned by nature, so as to live and act in a given way. For instance, fishes are naturally conditioned for swimming, and the greater for devouring the less; therefore fishes enjoy the water, and the greater devour the less by sovereign natural right. For it is certain that nature, taken in the abstract, has sovereign right to do anything, she can; in other words, her right is co-extensive with her power. The power of nature is the power of God, which has sovereign right over all things; and, inasmuch as the power of nature is simply the aggregate of the powers of all her individual components, it follows that every individual has sovereign right to do all that he can; in other words, the rights of an individual extend to the utmost limits of his power as it has been conditioned. Now it is the sovereign law and right of nature that each individual should endeavour to preserve itself as it is, without regard to anything but itself; therefore this sovereign law and right belongs to every individual, namely, to exist and act according to its natural conditions. We do not here acknowledge any difference between mankind and other individual natural entities, nor between men endowed with reason and those to whom reason is unknown; nor between fools, madmen, and sane men. Whatsoever an individual does by the laws of its nature it has a sovereign right to do, inasmuch as it acts as it was conditioned by nature, and cannot act otherwise. Wherefore among men, so long as they are considered as living under the sway of nature, he who does not yet know reason, or who has not yet acquired the habit of virtue, acts solely according to the laws of his desire with as sovereign a right as he who orders his life entirely by the laws of reason.

That is, as the wise man has sovereign right to do all that reason dictates, or to live according to the laws of reason, so also the ignorant and foolish man has sovereign right to do all that desire dictates, or to live according to the laws of desire. This is identical with the teaching of Paul, who acknowledges that previous to the law—that is, so long as men are considered of as living under the sway of nature, there is no sin.

The natural right of the individual man is thus determined, not by sound reason, but by desire and power. All are not naturally conditioned so as to act according to the laws and rules of reason; nay, on the contrary, all men are born ignorant, and before they can learn the right way of life and acquire the habit of virtue, the greater part of their life, even if they have been well brought up, has passed away. Nevertheless, they are in the meanwhile bound to live and preserve themselves as far as they can by the unaided impulses of desire. Nature has given them no other guide, and has denied them the present power of living according to sound reason; so that they are no more bound to live by the dictates of an enlightened mind, than a cat is bound to live by the laws of the nature of a lion.

Whatsoever, therefore, an individual (considered as under the sway of nature) thinks useful for himself, whether led by sound reason or impelled by the passions, that he has a sovereign right to seek and to take for himself as he best can, whether by force, cunning, entreaty, or any other means; consequently he may regard as an enemy anyone who hinders the accomplishment of his purpose.

It follows from what we have said that the right and ordinance of nature, under which all men are born, and under which they mostly live, only prohibits such things as no one desires, and no one can attain; it does not forbid strife, nor hatred, nor anger, nor deceit, nor, indeed, any of the means suggested by desire.

This we need not wonder at, for nature is not bounded by the laws of human reason, which aims only at man's true benefit and preservation; her limits are infinitely wider, and have reference to the eternal order of nature, wherein man is but a speck; it is by the necessity of this alone that all individuals are conditioned for living and acting in a particular way. If anything, therefore, in nature seems to us ridiculous, absurd, or evil, it is because we only know in part, and are almost entirely ignorant of the order and interdependence of nature as a whole, and also because we want everything to be arranged according to the dictates of our human reason; in reality that which reason considers evil, is not evil in respect to the order and laws of nature as a whole, but only in respect to the laws of our reason.

Nevertheless, no one can doubt that it is much better for us to live according to the laws and assured dictates of reason, for, as we said, they have men's true good for their object. Moreover, everyone wishes to live as far as possible securely beyond the reach of fear, and this would be quite impossible so long as everyone did everything he liked, and reason's claim was lowered to a par with those of hatred and anger; there is no one who is not ill at ease in the midst of enmity, hatred, anger, and deceit, and who does not seek to avoid them as much as he can. When we reflect that men without mutual help, or the aid of reason, must needs live most miserably, we shall plainly see that men must necessarily come to an agreement to live together as securely and well as possible if they are to enjoy as a whole the rights which naturally belong to them as individuals, and their life should be no more conditioned by the force and desire of individuals, but by the power and will of the whole body. This end they will be unable to attain if desire be their only guide (for by the laws of desire each man is drawn in a different direction); they must, therefore, most firmly decree and establish that they will be guided in everything by reason (which nobody will dare openly to repudiate lest he should be taken for a madman), and will restrain any desire which is injurious to a man's fellows, that they will do to all as they would be done by, and that they will defend their neighbor's rights as their own.

How such a compact as this should be entered into, how ratified and established, we will now inquire.

Now it is a universal law of human nature that no one ever neglects anything which he judges to be good, except with the hope of gaining a greater good, or from the fear of a greater evil; nor does anyone endure an evil except for the sake of avoiding a greater evil, or gaining a greater good. That is, everyone will, of two goods, choose that which he thinks the greatest; and, of two evils, that which he thinks the least. I say advisedly that which he thinks the greatest or the least, for it does not necessarily follow that he judges right. This law is so deeply implanted in the human mind that it ought to be counted among eternal truths and axioms.

As a necessary consequence of the principle just enunciated, no one can honestly promise to forego the right which he has over all things, and in general no one will abide by his promises, unless under the fear of a greater evil, or the hope of a greater good. An example will make the matter clearer. Suppose that a robber forces me to promise that I will give him my goods at his will and pleasure. It is plain (inasmuch as my natural right is, as I have shown, co-extensive with my power) that if I can free myself from this robber by stratagem, by assenting to his demands, I have the natural right to do so, and to pretend to accept his conditions. Or again, suppose I have genuinely promised someone that for the space of twenty days I will not taste food or any nourishment; and suppose I afterwards find that my promise was foolish, and cannot be kept without very great injury to myself; as I am bound by natural law and right to choose the least of two evils, I have complete right to break my compact, and act as if my promise had never been uttered. I say that I should have perfect natural right to do so, whether I was actuated by true and evident reason, or whether I was actuated by mere opinion in thinking I had promised rashly; whether my reasons were true or false, I should be in fear of a greater evil, which, by the ordinance of nature, I should strive to avoid by every means in my power.

We may, therefore, conclude that a compact is only made valid by its utility, without which it becomes null and void. It is, therefore, foolish to ask a man to keep his faith with us for ever, unless we also endeavour that the violation of the compact we enter into shall involve for the violator more harm than good. This consideration should have very great weight in forming a state. However, if all men could be easily led by reason alone, and could recognize what is best and most useful for a state, there would be no one who would not forswear deceit, for every one would keep most religiously to their compact in their desire for the chief good, namely, the preservation of the state, and would cherish good faith above all things as the shield and buckler of the commonwealth. However, it is far from being the case that all men can always be easily led by reason alone; everyone is drawn away by his pleasure. While avarice, ambition, envy, hatred, and the like so engross the mind that reason has no place therein. Hence, though men make promises with all the appearances of good faith, and agree that they will keep to their engagement, no one can absolutely rely on another man's promise unless there is something behind it. Everyone has by nature a right to act deceitfully, and to break his compacts, unless he be restrained by the hope of some greater good, or the fear of some greater evil.

However, as we have shown that the natural right of the individual is only limited by his power, it is clear that by transferring, either willingly or under compulsion, this power into the hands of another, he in so doing necessarily cedes also a part of his right; and further, that the sovereign right over all men belongs to him who has sovereign power, wherewith he can compel men by force, or restrain them by threats of the universally feared punishment of death; such sovereign right he will retain only so long as he can maintain his power of enforcing his will; otherwise he will totter on his throne, and no one who is stronger than he will be bound unwillingly to obey him.

In this manner a society can be formed without any violation of natural right, and the covenant can always be strictly kept—that is, if each individual hands over the whole of his power to the body politic, the latter will then possess sovereign natural right over all things: that is, it will have sole and unquestioned dominion, and everyone will be bound to obey, under pain of the severest punishment. A body politic of this kind is called a Democracy, which may be defined as a society which wields all its power as a whole. The sovereign power is not restrained by any laws, but everyone is bound to obey it in all things; such is the state of things implied when men either tacitly or expressly handed over to it all their power of self-defence, or in other words, all their right. For if they had wished to retain any right for themselves, they ought to have taken precautions for its defence and preservation; as they have not done so, and indeed could not have done so without dividing and consequently ruining the state, they placed themselves absolutely at the mercy of the sovereign power; and, therefore, having acted (as we have shown) as reason and necessity demanded, they are obliged to fulfil the commands of the sovereign power, however absurd these may be, else they will be public enemies, and will act against reason, which urges the preservation of the state as a primary duty. For reason bids us choose the least of two evils.

Furthermore, this danger of submitting absolutely to the dominion and will of another, is one which may be incurred with a light heart: for we have shown that sovereigns only possess this right of imposing their will, so long as they have the full power to enforce it; if such power be lost their right to command is lost also, or lapses to those who have assumed it and can keep it. Thus it is very rare for sovereigns to impose thoroughly irrational commands, for they are bound to consult their own interests, and retain their power by consulting the public good and acting according to the dictates of reason, as Seneca says, "violenta imperia nemo continuit dia." No one can long retain a tyrant's sway.

In a democracy, irrational commands are still less to be feared: for it is almost impossible that the majority of a people, especially if it be a large one, should agree in an irrational design; and, moreover, the basis and aim of a democracy is to avoid the desires as irrational, and to bring men as far as possible under the control of reason, so that they may live in peace and harmony; if this basis be removed the whole fabric falls to ruin.

Such being the ends in view for the sovereign power, the duty of subjects is, as I have said, to obey its commands, and to recognize no right save that which it sanctions.

It will, perhaps, be thought that we are turning subjects into slaves: for slaves obey commands and free men live as they like; but this idea is based on a misconception, for the true slave is he who is led away by his pleasures and can neither see what is good for him nor act accordingly; he alone is free who lives with free consent under the entire guidance of reason.

Action in obedience to orders does take away freedom in a certain sense, but it does not, therefore, make a man a slave, all depends on the object of the action. If the object of the action be the good of the state, and not the good of the agent, the latter is a slave and does himself no good. But in a state or kingdom where the weal of the whole people, and not that of the ruler, is the supreme law, obedience to the sovereign power does not make a man a slave, of no use to himself, but a subject. Therefore, that state is the freest whose laws are founded on sound reason, so that every member of it may, if he will, be free; that is, live with full consent under the entire guidance of reason.

Children, though they are bound to obey all the commands of their parents, are yet not slaves; for the commands of parents look generally to the children's benefit.

We must, therefore, acknowledge a great difference between a slave, a son, and a subject; their positions may be thus defined. A slave is one who is bound to obey his master's orders, though they are given solely in the master's interest; a son is one who obeys his father's orders, given in his own interest; a subject obeys the orders of the sovereign power, given for the common interest, wherein he is included.

I think I have now shown sufficiently clearly the basis of a democracy: I have especially desired to do so, for I believe it to be of all forms of government the most natural, and the most consonant with individual liberty. In it no one transfers his natural right so absolutely that he has no further voice in affairs, he only hands it over to the majority of a society, whereof he is a unit. Thus all men remain, as they were in the state of nature, equals.

Chapter 9

Second Treatise of Government
John Locke

John Locke (1632–1704) was a key figure in modern philosophy. He argues that all persons are naturally in a state of perfect freedom and equality because no one has natural authority over anyone else. This freedom, however, is restricted by the laws of nature. In particular, no one is permitted to harm others by taking away their lives, liberty, or possessions. Despite the state of nature being governed by morality, due to human fragility political institutions are required. People are too emotional, leading to improper enforcement of the laws of nature. Furthermore, people are too ignorant, leading to controversies over the precise interpretation of the laws of nature. A government's main function is to correct these deficiencies, interpreting, judging, and punishing in accord with the law of nature. Locke maintains that because all individuals need to give up their natural rights, only by majority rule is the government entitled to act.

CHAPTER II

Of the State of Nature

4. To understand political power, right, and derive it from its original, we must consider what state all men are naturally in, and that is, a state of perfect freedom to order their actions, and dispose of their possessions and persons, as they think fit, within the bounds of the law of nature, without asking leave, or depending upon the will of any other man.

A state also of equality, wherein all the power and jurisdiction is reciprocal, no one having more than another; there being nothing more evident, than that creatures of the same species and rank, promiscuously born to all the same advantages of nature, and the use of the same faculties, should also be equal one amongst another without subordination or subjection; unless the lord and master of them all should, by any manifest declaration of his will, set one above another, and confer on him, by an evident and clear appointment, an undoubted right to dominion and sovereignty. . . .

6. But though this be a state of liberty, yet it is not a state of licence; though man in that state have an uncontrollable liberty to dispose of his person or possessions, yet he has not liberty to destroy himself, or so much as any creature in his possession, but where some nobler use than its bare preservation calls for it. The state of nature has a law of nature to govern it, which obliges every one: And reason, which is that law, teaches all mankind, who will but consult it, that being all equal and independent, no one ought to harm another in his life, health, liberty, or possessions. For men being all the workmanship of one omnipotent and infinitely wise Maker: all the servants of one sovereign master, sent into the world by his order, and about his business; they are his property, whose workmanship they are, made to last during his, not another's pleasure. And being furnished with like faculties, sharing all in one community of nature, there cannot be supposed any such subordination among us, that may authorize us to destroy another, as if we were made for one another's uses, as the inferior ranks of creatures are for ours. Everyone, as he is bound to preserve himself, and not to quit his station willfully, so by the like reason, when his own preservation comes not in competition, ought he, as much as he can, to preserve the rest of mankind, and may not, unless it be to do justice to an offender, take away or impair the life, or what tends to the preservation of life, the liberty, health, limb, or goods of another.

7. And that all men may be restrained from invading others rights, and from doing hurt to one another, and the law of nature be observed, which willeth the peace and preservation of all mankind, the execution of the law of nature is, in that state, put into every man's hands, whereby everyone has a right to punish the transgressors of that law to such a degree as may hinder its violation. For the law of nature would, as all other laws that concern men in this world, be in vain, if there were nobody that in the state of nature had a power to execute that law, and thereby preserve the innocent and restrain offenders. And if anyone in the state of nature may punish another for any evil he has done, everyone may do so. For in that state of perfect equality, where naturally there is no superiority or jurisdiction of one over another, what any may do in prosecution of that law, everyone must needs have a right to do.

13. To this strange doctrine, viz. That in the state of nature every one has the executive power of the law of nature. I doubt not but it will be objected, that it is unreasonable for men to be judges in their own cases, that self-love will make men partial to themselves and their friends: And on the other side, that ill nature, passion and revenge will carry them too far in punishing others; and hence nothing but confusion and disorder will follow, and that therefore God has certainly appointed government to restrain the partiality and violence of men. I easily grant, that civil government is the proper remedy for the inconveniencies of the state of nature, which must certainly be great, where men may be judges in their own case, since it is easy to be imagined, that he who was so unjust as to do his brother an injury, will scarce be so just as to condemn himself for it; but I shall desire those who make this objection to remember, that absolute monarchs are but men, and if government is to be the remedy of those evils, which necessarily follow from men's being judges in their own cases, and the state of nature is therefore not to be endured. I desire to know what kind of government that is, and how much better it is than the state of nature, where one man commanding a multitude, has the liberty to be judge in his own case, and may do to all his subjects whatever he pleases, without the least liberty to anyone to question or control those who execute his pleasure? and in whatsoever he doth, whether led by reason, mistake or passion, must be submitted to? Much better it is in the state of nature, wherein men are not bound to submit to the unjust will of another: And if he that judges, judges amiss in his own, or any other case, he is answerable for it to the rest of mankind.

14. It is often asked as a mighty objection, where are, or ever were, there any men in such a state of nature? To which it may suffice as an answer at present: That since all princes and rulers of independent governments, all through the world, are in a state of nature, it is plain the world never was, nor ever will be, without numbers of men in that state. I have named all governors of independent communities, whether they are, or are not, in league with others. For it is not every compact that puts an end to the state of nature between men, but only this one of agreeing together mutually to enter into one community, and make one body politic; other promises and compacts men may make one with another, and yet still be in the state of nature. The promises and bargains for truck, &c. between the two men in the desert island, mentioned by Garcilasso de la Vega, in his history of Peru: or between a Swiss and an Indian, in the woods of America, are binding to them, though they are perfectly in a state of nature, in reference to one another. For truth and keeping of faith belongs to men as men, and not as members of society. . . .

CHAPTER V

Of Property

27. Though the earth, and all inferior creatures, be common to all men, yet every man has a property in his own person: this nobody has any right to but himself. The labour of his body, and the work of his hands, we may say, are properly his. Whatsoever then he removes out of the state that nature has provided, and left it in, he has mixed his labour with, and joined to it something that is his own, and thereby makes it his property. It being by him removed from the common state nature has placed it in, it has by this labour something annexed to it, that excludes the common right of other men. For this labour being the unquestionable property of the labourer, no man but he can have a right to what that is once joined to, at least where there is enough, and as good, left in common for others.

28. He that is nourished by the acorns he picked up under an oak, or the apples he gathered from the trees in the wood, has certainly appropriated them to himself. Nobody can deny but the nourishment is his. I ask then, when did they begin to be his? When he digested? Or when he eat? Or when he boiled? Or when he brought them home? Or when he picked them up? And it is plain, if the first gathering made them not his, nothing else could. That labour put a distinction between them and common: that added something to them more than nature, the common mother of all, had done; and so they became his private right. And will anyone say he had no right to those acorns or apples he thus appropriated, because he had not the consent of all mankind to make them his? Was it a robbery thus to assume to himself what belonged to all in common? If such a consent as that was necessary, man had starved, notwithstanding the plenty God had given him. We see in commons, which remain so by compact, that it is the taking any part of what is common, and removing it out of the state nature leaves it in, which begins the property; without which the common is of no use. And the taking of this or that part does not depend on the express consent of all the commoners. Thus the grass my horse has bit; the turfs my servant has cut; and the ore I have digged in any place, where I have a right to them in common with others, become my property, without the assignation or consent of anybody. The labour that was mine, removing them out of that common state they were in. has fixed my property in them. . . .

31. It will perhaps be objected to this, that "if gathering the acorns, or other fruits of the earth, &c. makes a right to them, then anyone may engross as much as he will." To which I answer. Not so. The same law of nature, that does by this means give us property, does also bound that property too. "God has given us all things richly." 1 Tim; vi. 17. is the voice of reason confirmed

by inspiration. But how far has he given it us? To enjoy. As much as anyone can make use of to any advantage of life before it spoils, so much he may by his labour fix a property in; whatever is beyond this, is more than his share, and belongs to others. Nothing was made by God for man to spoil or destroy. And thus, considering the plenty of natural provisions there was a long time in the world, and the few spenders; and to how small a part of that provision the industry of one man could extend itself, and engross it to the prejudice of others; especially keeping within the bounds, set by reason, of what might serve for his use; there could be then little room for quarrels or contentions about property so established. . . .

CHAPTER VIII

Of the Beginning of Political Societies

95. Men being . . . by nature, all free, equal, and independent, no one can be put out of this estate, and subjected to the political power of another, without his own consent. The only way whereby any one divests himself of his natural liberty, and puts on the bonds of civil society, is by agreeing with other men to join and unite into a community, for their comfortable, safe, and peaceable living one amongst another, in a secure enjoyment of their properties, and a greater security against any, that are not of it. This any number of men may do, because it injures not the freedom of the rest; they are left as they were in the liberty of the state of nature. When any number of men have so consented to make one community or government, they are thereby presently incorporated, and make one body politic, wherein the majority have a right to act and conclude the rest.

96. For when any number of men have, by the consent of every individual, made a community, they have thereby made that community one body, with a power to act as one body, which is only by the will and determination of the majority. . . .

97. And thus every man, by consenting with others to make one body politic under one government, puts himself under an obligation, to everyone of that society, to submit to the determination of the majority . . . or else this original compact, whereby he with others incorporate into one society, would signify nothing, and be no compact, if he be left free, and under no other ties than he was in before in the state of nature. . . .

99. Whosoever therefore out of a state of nature unite into a community, must be understood to give up all the power, necessary to the ends for which they unite into society, to the majority of the community, unless they expressly agreed in any number greater than the majority. And this is done by

barely agreeing to unite into one political society, which is all the compact
that is, or needs be, between the individuals, that enter into, or make up a
commonwealth. And thus, that which begins and actually constitutes any political society, is nothing, but the consent of any number of freemen capable
of a majority, to unite and incorporate into such a society. And this is that,
and that only, which did, or could give beginning to any lawful government
in the world. . . .

119. Every man that has any possessions, or enjoyment of any part of the
dominions of any government, doth thereby give his tacit consent, and is as
far forth obliged to obedience to the laws of that government, during such
enjoyment, as anyone under it; whether this his possession be of land, to him
and his heirs for ever, or a lodging only for a week; or whether it be barely
travelling freely on the highway; and, in effect, it reaches as far as the very
being of anyone within the territories of that government.

120. To understand this the better, it is fit to consider, that every man,
when he at first incorporates himself into any commonwealth, he, by his
uniting himself thereunto, annexed also, and submits to the community, those
possessions which he has, or shall acquire, that do not already belong to any
other government. For it would be a direct contradiction, for anyone to enter
into society with others for the securing and regulating of property, and yet
to suppose, his land, whose property is to be regulated by the laws of the
society, should be exempt from the jurisdiction of that government, to which
he himself, the proprietor of the land, is a subject. By the same act therefore,
whereby anyone unites his person, which was before free, to any commonwealth; by the same he unites his possessions, which were before free, to it
also; and they become, both of them, person and possession, subject to the
government and dominion of that commonwealth, as long as it has a being.
Whoever therefore, from thenceforth, by inheritance, purchase, permission,
or otherways, enjoys any part of the land so annexed to, and under the government of that commonwealth, must take it with the condition it is under;
that is, of submitting to the government of the commonwealth, under whose
jurisdiction it is, as far forth as any subject of it.

121. But since the government has a direct jurisdiction only over the land,
and reaches the possessor of it, (before he has actually incorporated himself in
the society) only as he dwells upon, and enjoys that; the obligation anyone is
under, by virtue of such enjoyment, to submit to the government, begins and
ends with the enjoyment: so that whenever the owner, who has given nothing
but such a tacit consent to the government, will, by donation, sale, or otherwise, quit the said possession, he is at liberty to go and incorporate himself
into any other commonwealth; or to agree with others to begin a new one,
in vacuis locis, in any part of the world they can find free and unpossessed:

whereas he, that has once, by actual agreement, and any express declaration, given his consent to be of any commonwealth, is perpetually and indispensably obliged to be, and remain unalterably a subject to it, and can never be again in the liberty of the state of nature; unless, by any calamity, the government he was under comes to be dissolved, or else by some public act cuts him off from being any longer a member of it.

122. But submitting to the laws of any country, living quietly, and enjoying privileges and protection under them, makes not a man a member of that society: this is only a local protection and homage due to and from all those, who, not being in a state of war, come within the territories belonging to any government, to all parts whereof the force of its laws extends. But this no more makes a man a member of that society, a perpetual subject of that commonwealth, than it would make a man a subject to another, in whose family he found it convenient to abide for some time, though, whilst he continued in it, he were obliged to comply with the laws, and submit to the government he found there. And thus we see, that foreigners, by living all their lives under another government, and enjoying the privileges and protection of it, though they are bound, even in conscience, to submit to its administration, as far forth as any denison; yet do not thereby come to be subjects or members of that commonwealth. Nothing can make any man so, but his actually entering into it by positive engagement, and express promise and compact. . . .

CHAPTER IX

Of the Ends of Political Society and Government

123. If man in the state of nature be so free, as has been said; if he be absolute lord of his own person and possessions, equal to the greatest, and subject to nobody, why will he part with his freedom? why will he give up his empire, and subject himself to the dominion and control of any other power? To which it is obvious to answer, that though in the state of nature he has such a right, yet the enjoyment of it is very uncertain, and constantly exposed to the invasion of others. For all being kings as much as he, every man his equal, and the greater part no strict observers of equity and justice, the enjoyment of the property he has in this state is very unsafe, very unsecure. This makes him willing to quit this condition, which, however free, is full of fears and continual dangers: and it is not without reason, that he seeks out, and is willing to join in society with others, who are already united, or have a mind to unite, for the mutual preservation of their lives, liberties, and estates, which I call by the general name, property.

124. The great and chief end, therefore, of men's uniting into commonwealths, and putting themselves under government, is the preservation of their property. To which in the state of nature there are many things wanting.

First. There wants an established, settled, known law, received and allowed by common consent to be the standard of right and wrong, and the common measure to decide all controversies between them. For though the law of nature be plain and intelligible to all rational creatures; yet men being biased by their interest, as well as ignorant for want of studying it, are not apt to allow of it as a law binding to them in the application of it to their particular cases.

125. Secondly. In the state of nature there wants a known and indifferent judge, with authority to determine all differences according to the established law. For everyone in that state being both judge and executioner of the law of nature, men being partial to themselves, passion and revenge is very apt to carry them too far, and with too much heat, in their own cases; as well as negligence, and unconcernedness, to make them too remiss in other men's.

126. Thirdly. In the state of nature, there often wants power to back and support the sentence when right, and to give it due execution. They who by any injustice offended, will seldom fail, where they are able, by force to make good their injustice; such resistance many times makes the punishment dangerous, and frequently destructive, to those who attempt it.

127. Thus mankind, notwithstanding all the privileges of the state of nature; being but in an ill condition, while they remain in it, are quickly driven into society. Hence it comes to pass that we seldom find any number of men live any time together in this state. The inconveniencies that they are therein exposed to, by the irregular and uncertain exercise of the power every man has of punishing the transgressions of others, make them take sanctuary under the established laws of government, and therein seek the preservation of their property. It is this makes them so willingly give up every one his single power of punishing, to be exercised by such alone, as shall be appointed to it amongst them; and by such rules as the community, or those authorized by them to that purpose, shall agree on. And in this we have the original right and rise of both the legislative and executive power, as well as of the governments and societies themselves.

128. For in the state of nature, to omit the liberty he has of innocent delights, a man has two powers.

The first is to do whatsoever he thinks fit for the preservation of himself and others within the permission of the law of nature: by which law, common to them all, he and all the rest of mankind are one community, make up one society, distinct from all I other creatures. And, were it not for the corruption and viciousness of degenerate men, there would be no need of any other; no necessity that men should separate from this great and natural community, and by positive agreements combine into smaller and divided associations.

The other power a man has in the state of nature, is the power to punish the crimes committed against that law. Both these he gives up, when he joins in a private, if I may so call it, or particular politic society, and incorporates into any commonwealth, separate from the rest of mankind.

129. The first power, viz. of doing whatsoever, he thought fit for the preservation of himself, and the rest of mankind, he gives up to be regulated by laws made by the society, so far forth as the preservation of himself and the rest of that society shall require; which laws of the society in many things confine the liberty he had by the law of nature.

130. Secondly, The power of punishing he wholly gives up, and engages his natural force, (which he might before employ in the execution of the law of nature, by his own single authority, as he thought fit) to assist the executive power of the society, as the law thereof shall require. For being now in a new state, wherein he is to enjoy many conveniencies, from the labour, assistance, and society of others in the same community, as well as protection from its whole strength; he is to part also, with as much of his natural liberty, in providing for himself, as the good, prosperity, and safety of the society shall require; which is not only necessary, but just, since the other members of the society do the like.

131. But though men, when they enter into society, give up the equality, liberty, and executive power they had in the state of nature, into the hands of the society, to be so far disposed of by the legislative, as the good of the society shall require; yet it being only with an intention in everyone the better to preserve himself, his liberty and property; (for no rational creature can be supposed to change his condition with an intention to be worse) the power of the society, or legislative constituted by them, can never be supposed to extend farther, than the common good; but is obliged to secure everyone's property, by providing against those three defects above mentioned, that made the state of nature so unsafe and uneasy. And so whoever has the legislative or supreme power of any commonwealth, is bound to govern by established standing laws, promulgated and known to the people, and not by extemporary decrees; by indifferent and upright judges, who are to decide controversies by those laws; and to employ the force of the community at home, only in the execution of such laws; or abroad to prevent or redress foreign injuries, and secure the community from inroads and invasion. And all this to be directed to no other end, but the peace, safety, and public good of the people.

CHAPTER XI

Of the Extent of the Legislative Power

134. The great end of men's entering into society being the enjoyment of their properties in peace and safety, and the great instrument and means of that being the laws established in that society; the first and fundamental positive law of all commonwealths is the establishing of the legislative power; as the first and fundamental natural law, which is to govern even the legislative itself, is the preservation of the society, and (as far as will consist with the public good) of every person in it. This legislative is not only the supreme power of the commonwealth, but sacred and unalterable in the hands where the community have once placed it; nor can any edict of anybody else, in what form soever conceived, or by what power soever backed, have the force and obligation of a law, which has not its sanction from that legislative which the public has chosen and appointed; for without this the law could not have that, which is absolutely necessary to its being a law, the consent of the society; over whom nobody can have a power to make laws, but by their own consent, and by authority received from them; and therefore all the obedience, which by the most solemn ties any one can be obliged to pay, ultimately terminates in this supreme power, and is directed by those laws which it enacts; nor can any oaths to any foreign power whatsoever, or any domestic subordinate power, discharge any member of the society from his obedience to the legislative, acting pursuant to their trust; nor oblige him to any obedience contrary to the laws so enacted, or farther than they do allow; it being ridiculous to imagine one can be tied ultimately to obey any power in the society, which is not the supreme.

135. Though the legislative, whether placed in one or more, whether it be always in being, or only by intervals, though it be the supreme power in every commonwealth; yet:

First, it is not, nor can possibly be absolutely arbitrary over the lives and fortunes of the people. For it being but the joint power of every member of the society given up to that person, or assembly, which is legislator, it can be no more than those persons had in a state of nature before they entered into society, and gave up to the community. For nobody can transfer to another more power than he has in himself; and nobody has an absolute arbitrary power over himself, or over any other, to destroy his own life, or take away the life or property of another. A man, as has been proved, cannot subject himself to the arbitrary power of another; and having in the state of nature no arbitrary power over the life, liberty, or possession of another, but only so much as the law of nature gave him for the preservation of himself and the rest of mankind; this is all he doth, or can give up to the commonwealth, and by it to the legislative power, so that the legislative can have no more than this. Their power, in the utmost bounds of it, is limited to the public good of the society. It is a power, that has no other end but preservation, and therefore can never have a right to destroy, enslave, or designedly to impoverish the subjects. The obligations of the law of nature cease not in society, but only in many cases are drawn closer, and have by human laws known penalties annexed to them, to enforce their observation. Thus the law of nature stands as an eternal rule to all men, legislators as well as others. The rules that they make for other men's actions, must, as well as their own and other men's actions, be conformable to the law of nature, i.e. to the will of God, of which that is a declaration; and the fundamental law of nature being the preservation of mankind, no human sanction can be good or valid against it.

136. Secondly, the legislative or supreme authority cannot assume to itself a power to rule, by extemporary, arbitrary decrees, but is bound to dispense justice, and decide the rights of the subject, by promulgated, standing laws, and known authorised judges. For the law of nature being unwritten, and so nowhere to be found, but in the minds of men; they who through passion, or interest, shall miscite, or misapply it, cannot so easily be convinced of their mistake, where there is no established judge; and so it serves not, as it ought, to determine the rights, and fence the properties of those that live under it; especially where everyone is judge, interpreter, and executioner of it too, and that in his own case; and he that has right on his side having ordinarily but his own single strength, has not force enough to defend himself from injuries, or to punish delinquents. To avoid these inconveniencies, which disorder men's properties in the state of nature, men unite into societies, that they may have the united strength of the whole society to secure and defend their properties, and may have standing rules to bound it, by which everyone may know what is his. To this end it is that men give up all their natural power to the society which they enter into, and the community put the legislative power into such hands as they think fit, with this trust, that they shall be governed by declared laws, or else their peace, quiet, and property will still be at the same uncertainty, as it was in the state of nature.

137. Absolute arbitrary power, or governing without settled standing laws, can neither of them consist with the ends of society and government, which men would not quit the freedom of the state of nature for, and tie themselves up under, were it not to preserve their lives, liberties, and fortunes, and by stated rules of right and property to secure their peace and quiet. It cannot be supposed that they should intend, had they a power so to do, to give to anyone, or more, an absolute arbitrary power over their persons and estates, and put a force into the magistrate's hand to execute his unlimited will arbitrarily upon them. This were to put themselves into a worse condition than the state

of nature, wherein they had a liberty to defend their right against the injuries of others, and were upon equal terms of force to maintain it, whether invaded by a single man, or many in combination. Whereas by supposing they have given up themselves to the absolute arbitrary power and will of a legislator, they have disarmed themselves, and armed him, to make a prey of them when he pleases. He being in a much worse condition, who is exposed to the arbitrary power of one man, who has the command of 100,000 than he that is exposed to the arbitrary power of 100,000 single men; nobody being secure, that his will, who has such a command, is better than that of other men, though his force be 100,000 times stronger. And therefore, whatever form the commonwealth is under, the ruling power ought to govern by declared and received laws, and not by extemporary dictates and undetermined resolutions. For then mankind will be in a far worse condition than in the state of nature, if they shall have armed one or a few men with the joint power of a multitude, to force them to obey at pleasure the exorbitant and unlimited decrees of their sudden thoughts, or unrestrained, and till that moment unknown wills, without having any measures set down which may guide and justify their actions; for all the power the government has, being only for the good of the society, as it ought not to be arbitrary and at pleasure, so it ought to be exercised by established and promulgated laws; that both the people may know their duty, and be safe and secure within the limits of the law, and the rulers too kept within their bounds, and not to be tempted, by the power they have in their hands, to employ it to such purposes, and by such measures, as they would not have known, and own not willingly.

138. Thirdly, the supreme power cannot take from any man part of his property without his own consent. For the preservation of property being the end of government, and that for which men enter into society, it necessarily supposes and requires, that the people should have property, without which they must be supposed to lose that, by entering into society, which was the end for which they entered into it; too gross an absurdity for any man to own. Men therefore in society having property, they have such right to the goods, which by the law of the community are theirs, that nobody has a right to take their substance or any part of it from them, without their own consent; without this they have no property at all. For I have truly no property in that, which another can by right take from me, when he pleases, against my consent. Hence it is a mistake to think, that the supreme or legislative power of any commonwealth can do what it will, and dispose of the estates of the subject arbitrarily, or take any part of them at pleasure. This is not much to be feared in governments where the legislative consists, wholly or in part, in assemblies which are variable, whose members, upon the dissolution of the assembly, are subjects under the common laws of their country, equally with

the rest. But in governments, where the legislative is in one lasting assembly always in being, or in one man, as in absolute monarchies, there is danger still, that they will think themselves to have a distinct interest from the rest of the community; and so will be apt to increase their own riches and power by taking what they think fit from the people. For a man's property is not at all secure, though there be good and equitable laws to set the bounds of it between him and his fellow subjects, if he who commands those subjects, have power to take from any private man, what part he pleases of his property, and use and dispose of it as he thinks good. . . .

140. It is true, governments cannot be supported without great charge, and it is fit everyone who enjoys his share of the protection, should pay out of his estate his proportion for the maintenance of it. But still it must be with his own consent, i.e. the consent of the majority, giving it either by themselves, or their representatives chosen by them. For if anyone shall claim a power to lay and levy taxes on the people, by his own authority, and without such consent of the people, he thereby invades the fundamental law of property, and subverts the end of government. For what property have I in that, which another may by right take when he pleases, to himself?

141. Fourthly, the legislative cannot transfer the power of making laws to any other hands. For it being but a delegated power from the people, they who have it cannot pass it over to others. The people alone can appoint the form of the commonwealth, which is by constituting the legislative, and appointing in whose hands that shall be. And when the people have said, we will submit to rules, and be governed by laws made by such men. and in such forms, nobody else can say other men shall make laws for them; nor can the people be bound by any laws, but such as are enacted by those whom they have chosen, and authorized to make laws for them. The power of the legislative being derived from the people by a positive voluntary grant and institution, can be no other than what that positive grant conveyed, which being only to make laws, and not to make legislators, the legislative can have no power to transfer their authority of making laws and place it in other hands. . . .

CHAPTER XII

Of the Legislative, Executive, and Federative Power of the Commonwealth

143. The legislative power is that which has a right to direct how the force of the commonwealth shall be employed for preserving the community and the members of it. But because those laws which are constantly to be executed, and whose force is always to continue, may be made in a little time; therefore

there is no need, that the legislative should be always in being, not having always business to do. And because it may be too great a temptation to human frailty, apt to grasp at power, for the same persons, who have the power of making laws, to have also in their hands the power to execute them, whereby they may exempt themselves from obedience to the laws they make, and suit the law, both in its making and execution, to their own private advantage, and thereby come to have a distinct interest from the rest of the community, contrary to the end of society and government: therefore in well ordered commonwealths, where the good of the whole is so considered, as it ought, the legislative power is put into the hands of diverse persons, who, duly assembled, have by themselves, or jointly with others, a power to make laws; which is a new and near tie upon them, to take care that they make them for the public good.

144. But because the laws, that are at once, and in a short time made, have a constant and lasting force, and need a perpetual execution, or an attendance thereunto: therefore it is necessary there should be a power always in being, which should see to the execution of the laws that are made, and remain in force. And thus the legislative and executive power come often to be separated.

145. There is another power in every commonwealth, which one may call natural, because it is that which answers to the power every man naturally had before he entered into society. For though in a commonwealth, the members of it are distinct persons still in reference to one another, and as such are governed by the laws of the society; yet in reference to the rest of mankind, they make one body, which is, as every member of it before was, still in the state of nature with the rest of mankind. Hence it is, that the controversies that happen between any man of the society with those that are out of it, are managed by the public; and an injury done to a member of their body engages the whole in the reparation of it. So that, under this consideration, the whole community is one body in the state of nature, in respect of all other states or persons out of its community.

146. This therefore contains the power of war and peace, leagues and alliances, and all the transactions, with all persons and communities without the commonwealth; and may be called federative, if anyone pleases. So the thing be understood, I am indifferent as to the name.

147. These two powers, executive and federative, though they be really distinct in themselves, yet one comprehending the execution of the municipal laws of the society within itself, upon all that are parts of it; the other the management of the security and interest of the public without, with all those that it may receive benefit or damage from; yet they are always almost united. And though this federative power in the well or ill management of it

be of great moment to the commonwealth, yet it is much less capable to be directed by antecedent, standing, positive laws, than the executive; and so must necessarily be left to the prudence and wisdom of those whose hands it is in, to be managed for the public good. For the laws that concern subjects one amongst another, being to direct their actions, may well enough precede them. But what is to be done in reference to foreigners, depending much upon their actions, and the variation of designs, and interests, must be left in great part to the prudence of those who have this power committed to them, to be managed by the best of their skill, for the advantage of the commonwealth.

CHAPTER XIX

Of the Dissolution of Government

222. The reason why men enter into society is the preservation of their property; and the end why they choose and authorize a legislative is that there may be laws made and rules set as guards and fences to the properties of all the members of the society to limit the power and moderate the dominion or every part and member of the society, for since it can never be supposed to be the will of the society that the legislative should have a power to destroy that which every one designs to secure by entering into society, and for which the people submitted themselves to legislators of their own making. Whenever the legislators endeavour to take away and destroy the property of the people, or to reduce them to slavery under arbitrary power, they put themselves into a state of war with the people who are thereupon absolved from any further obedience, and are left to the common refuge which God has provided for all men against force and violence. Whensoever, therefore, the legislative shall transgress this fundamental rule of society, and either by ambition, fear, folly, or corruption, endeavour to grasp themselves, or put into the hands of any other, an absolute power over the lives, liberties and estates of the people, by this breach of trust they forfeit the power the people had put into their hands for quite contrary ends, and it devolves to the people, who have a right to resume their original liberty and, by the establishment of a new legislative, such as they shall think fit, provide for their own safety and security, which is the end for which they are in society. What I have said here concerning the legislative in general holds true also concerning the supreme executor, who having a double trust put in him—both to have a part in the legislative and the supreme execution of the law—acts against both when he goes about to set up his own arbitrary will as the law of the society. . . .

240. Here, it is like, the common question will be made: Who shall be judge whether the prince or legislative act contrary to their trust? This, perhaps,

ill affected and factious men may spread amongst the people, when the prince only makes use of his due prerogative. To this I reply: The people shall be judge; for who shall be judge whether his trustee or deputy acts well and according to the trust reposed in him but he who deputes him and must, by having deputed him, have still a power to discard him when he tails in his trust? If this be reasonable in particular cases of private men, why should it be otherwise in that of the greatest moment where the welfare of millions is concerned, and also where the evil, if not prevented, is greater and the redress very difficult, dear, and dangerous? . . .

243. To conclude, the power that every individual gave the society when he entered into it, can never revert to the individuals again as long as the society lasts, but will always remain in the community, because without this there can be no community, no commonwealth, which is contrary to the original agreement; so also when the society hath placed the legislative in any assembly of men to continue in them and their successors, with direction and authority for providing such successors, the legislative can never revert to the people whilst that government lasts, because having provided a legislative with power to continue for ever, they have given up their political power to the legislative and cannot resume it. But if they have set limits to the duration of their legislative, and made this supreme power in any person or assembly only temporary; or else when by the miscarriages of those in authority it is forfeited; upon the forfeiture, or at the determination of the time set, it reverts to the society, and the people have a right to act as supreme, and continue the legislative in themselves; or place it in a new form, or new hands as they think good.

Chapter 10

Letter Concerning Toleration

John Locke

John Locke argues that governments are created to protect life, liberty, and property; thus their legitimate exercise of power is restricted accordingly. The promotion or preservation of a particular religion therefore falls outside a state's authority. Moreover, Locke contends that the use of external coercion is misplaced, given that religion concerns one's internal beliefs.

The commonwealth seems to me to be a society of men constituted only for the procuring, preserving, and advancing their own civil interests.

Civil interests I call life, liberty, health, and indolency of body; and the possession of outward things, such as money, lands, houses, furniture, and the like.

It is the duty of the civil magistrate, by the impartial execution of equal laws, to secure unto all the people in general, and to every one of his subjects in particular, the just possession of these things belonging to this life. If anyone presume to violate the laws of public justice and equity, established for the preservation of those things, his presumption is to be checked by the fear of punishment consisting of the deprivation or diminution of those civil interests or goods which otherwise he might and ought to enjoy. But seeing no man does willingly suffer himself to be punished by the deprivation of any part of his goods, and much less of his liberty or life, therefore is the magistrate armed with the force and strength of all his subjects, in order to the punishment of those that violate any other man's rights.

Now that the whole jurisdiction of the magistrate reaches only to these civil concernments; and that all civil power, right and dominion is bounded and confined to the only care of promoting these things; and that it neither can nor ought in any manner to be extended to the salvation of souls, these following considerations seem unto me abundantly to demonstrate.

First, because the care of souls is not committed to the civil magistrate any more than to other men. It is not committed unto him. I say, by God; because it appears not that God has ever given any such authority to one man over another, as to compel anyone to his religion. Nor can any such power be vested in the magistrate by the consent of the people, because no man can so far abandon the care of his own salvation as blindly to leave to the choice of any other, whether prince or subject, to prescribe to him what faith or worship he shall embrace. For no man can, if he would, conform his faith to the dictates of another. All the life and power of true religion consist in the inward and full persuasion of the mind; and faith is not faith without believing. Whatever profession we make, to whatever outward worship we conform, if we are not fully satisfied in our own mind that the one is true, and the other well pleasing unto God, such profession and such practice, far from being any furtherance, are indeed great obstacles to our salvation. For in this manner, instead of expiating other sins by the exercise of religion. I say, in offering thus unto God Almighty such a worship as we esteem to be displeasing unto Him, we add unto the number of our other sins those also of hypocrisy and contempt of His Divine Majesty.

In the second place, the care of souls cannot belong to the civil magistrate because his power consists only in outward force; but true and saving religion consists in the inward persuasion of the mind, without which nothing can be acceptable to God. And such is the nature of the understanding that it cannot be compelled to the belief of anything by outward force, Confiscation of estate, imprisonment, torments, nothing of that nature can have any such efficacy as to make men change the inward judgment that they have framed of things.

It may indeed be alleged that the magistrate may make use of arguments, and thereby draw the heterodox into the way of truth and procure their salvation. I grant it; but this is common to him with other men. In teaching, instructing, and redressing the erroneous by reason, he may certainly do what becomes any good man to do. Magistracy does not oblige him to put off either humanity or Christianity; but it is one thing to persuade, another to command; one thing to press with arguments, another with penalties. This civil power alone has a right to do; to the other, goodwill is authority enough. Every man has commission to admonish, exhort, convince another of error, and by reasoning, to draw him into truth; but to give laws, receive obedience, and compel with the sword, belongs to none but the magistrate. And upon this ground I affirm that the magistrate's power extends not to the establishing of any articles of faith or forms of worship by the force of his laws. For laws are

of no force at all without penalties, and penalties in this case are absolutely impertinent, because they are not proper to convince the mind. Neither the profession of any articles of faith, nor the conformity to any outward form of worship (as has been already said), can be available to the salvation of souls unless the truth of the one, and the acceptableness of the other unto God, be thoroughly believed by those that so profess and practice. But penalties are no way capable to produce such belief. It is only light and evidence that can work a change in men's opinions; which light can in no manner proceed from corporal sufferings or any other outward penalties.

In the third place, the care of the salvation of men's souls cannot belong to the magistrate; because, though the rigor of laws and the force of penalties were capable to convince and change men's minds, yet would not that help at all to the salvation of their souls. For there being but one truth, one way to heaven, what hope is there that more men would be led into it if they had no rule but the religion of the court, and were put under the necessity to quit the light of their own reason, and oppose the dictates of their own consciences, and blindly to resign themselves up to the will of their governors and to the religion which either ignorance, ambition, or superstition had chanced to establish in the countries where they were born? In the variety and contradiction of opinions in religion, wherein the princes of the world are as much divided as in their secular interests, the narrow way would be much straitened; one country alone would be in the right, and all the rest of the world put under an obligation of following their princes in the ways that lead to destruction; and that which heightens the absurdity, and very ill suits the notion of a Deity, men would owe their eternal happiness or misery to the places of their nativity.

These considerations, to omit many others that might have been urged to the same purpose, seem unto me sufficient to conclude that all the power of civil government relates only to men's civil interests, is confined to the care of the things of this world, and hath nothing to do with the world to come.

Chapter 11

Of the Social Contract

Jean-Jacques Rousseau

Jean-Jacques Rousseau (1712–1778) was an influential figure in modern thought. He sets out to answer this question: What social arrangement allows one to bind oneself with others but to obey oneself alone and so remain as free as before any such arrangement? His answer is that legitimate political power is exercised only in accordance with the "general will." According to Rousseau, the general will always promotes the good on the whole. Although it can conflict with an individual's good, it does not diminish the freedom of each person because, by dint of a social contract, all have transferred to the community their individual natural rights. In this way, a collection of private wills transforms into an irreducible collection so that if the general will is contrary to one's private will, this difference shows that one's private will is mistaken.

Jean-Jacques Rousseau, *The Social Contract*, trans. Charles M. Sherover (New York: New American Library, 1974).

———⌒⌒⌒———

BOOK I

I. Subject of This First Book

Man is born free, and everywhere he is in chains. One believes himself the master of others, and yet he is a greater slave than they. How has this change come about? I do not know. What can render it legitimate? I believe that I can settle this question. . . .

VI. Of the Social Pact

I suppose that men have reached a point at which the obstacles that endanger their preservation in the state of nature prevail by their resistance over the forces which each individual can exert in order to maintain himself in that state. Then this primitive condition can no longer subsist, and the human race would perish unless it changed its manner of being.

Now as men cannot create any new forces, but only unite and direct those that exist, they have no other means of self-preservation than to form by aggregation a sum of forces which may overcome the resistance, to put them in action by a single motive power, and to make them work in concert.

This sum of forces can be produced only by the combination of many; but the strength and freedom of each man being the primary instruments of his preservation, how can he pledge them without injuring himself, and without neglecting the care which he owes to himself? This difficulty, applied to my subject, may be stated in these terms:

"To find a form of association which defends and protects with the whole force of the community the person and goods of every associate, and by means of which each, uniting with all, nevertheless obeys only himself, and remains as free as before." Such is the fundamental problem to which the social contract gives the solution.

The clauses of this contract are so determined by the nature of the act that the slightest modification would render them vain and ineffectual: so that, although perhaps they have never been formally enunciated, they are everywhere the same, everywhere tacitly admitted and recognized, until, the social pact being violated, each man regains his initial rights and recovers his natural liberty, while losing the conventional liberty for which he renounced it.

These clauses, rightly understood, are all reducible to one only, namely the total alienation of each associate, with all of his rights, to the whole community: For, in the first place, as each gives himself up entirely, the condition is equal for all, and, the condition being equal for all, no one has any interest in making it burdensome to others.

Further, the alienation being made without reserve, the union is as perfect as it can be, and no associate has anything more to claim. For if some rights were left to individuals, since there would be no common superior who could judge between them and the public, each, being on some point his own judge, would soon claim to be so on all; the state of nature would still subsist, and the association would necessarily become tyrannical or useless.

Finally, each, in giving himself to all, gives himself to nobody; and as there is not one associate over whom we do not acquire the same rights which we concede to him over ourselves, we gain the equivalent of all that we lose, and more power to preserve what we have.

If, then, everything which is not of the essence of the social pact is set aside, one finds that it reduces itself to the following terms: *Each of us puts in common his person and his whole power under the supreme direction of the general will; and in return we receive in a body every member as an indivisible part of the whole.*

VII. Of the Sovereign

One sees by this formula that the act of association includes a reciprocal engagement between the public and the individual, and that each individual, contracting so to speak with himself, is engaged in a double relation: namely, as a member of the Sovereign toward individuals, and as a member of the State toward the Sovereign. But we cannot apply here the maxim of civil right that no one is bound by engagements made with himself; for there is a great difference between being obligated to oneself and to a whole of which one forms a part.

It is necessary to note further that the public deliberation which can obligate all subjects to the Sovereign in consequence of the two different relations under which each of them is regarded cannot, for a contrary reason, bind the Sovereign to itself; and that accordingly it is contrary to the nature of the body politic for the Sovereign to impose on itself a law which it cannot transgress. As it can only be considered under one and the same relation, it is in the position of an individual contracting with himself; thus we see that there is not, nor can there be, any kind of fundamental law obligatory for the body of the people, not even the social contract. This does not imply that such a body cannot perfectly well enter into engagements with others in what does not derogate from this contract; for, with regard to foreigners, it becomes a simple being, an individual.

But the body politic or Sovereign, deriving its existence only from the sanctity of the contract, can never bind itself, even to others, in anything that derogates from the original act, such as to alienate some portion of itself, or submission to another Sovereign. To violate the act by which it exists would be to annihilate itself; and what is nothing produces nothing.

As soon as this multitude is thus united into one body, it is impossible to injure one of the members without attacking the body; still less to injure the body without the members feeling the effects. Thus duty and interest equally obligate the two contracting parties to give mutual assistance; and the same men should seek to combine in this twofold relationship all the advantages which are attendant on it.

Now the Sovereign, being formed only of the individuals who compose it, neither has nor can have any interest contrary to theirs; consequently the

Sovereign power needs no guarantee toward its subjects, because it is impossible that the body should wish to injure all its members; and we shall see hereafter that it can injure no one in particular. The Sovereign, for the simple reason that it is, is always everything that it ought to be.

But this is not the case with respect to the relation of subjects to the Sovereign, which, notwithstanding the common interest, would have no security for the performance of their engagements, unless it found means to ensure their fidelity.

Indeed, each individual may, as a man, have a particular will contrary to, or divergent from, the general will which he has as a Citizen. His private interest may speak to him quite differently from the common interest; his absolute and naturally independent existence may make him regard what he owes to the common cause as a gratuitous contribution, the loss of which will be less harmful to others than will the payment of it be onerous to him; and viewing the moral person that constitutes the State as a being of reason because it is not a man, he would be willing to enjoy the rights of a citizen without being willing to fulfill the duties of a subject; an injustice, the progress of which would bring about the ruin of the body politic.

In order, then, that the social pact may not be a vain formula, it tacitly includes this engagement, which can alone give force to the others—that whoever refuses to obey the general will shall be constrained to do so by the whole body; which means nothing else than that he shall be forced to be free; for such is the condition which, giving each Citizen to his Fatherland, guarantees him from all personal dependence, a condition that makes up the spark and interplay of the political mechanism, and alone renders legitimate civil engagements, which, without it, would be absurd and tyrannical, and subject to the most enormous abuse.

VIII. Of the Civil State

This passage from the state of nature to the civil state produces in man a very remarkable change, by substituting in his conduct justice for instinct, and by giving his actions the morality that they previously lacked. It is only when the voice of duty succeeds physical impulsion, and right succeeds appetite, that man, who till then had only looked after himself, sees that he is forced to act on other principles, and to consult his reason before listening to his inclinations. Although, in this state, he is deprived of many advantages he holds from nature, he gains such great ones in return, that his faculties are exercised and developed; his ideas are expanded; his feelings are ennobled: his whole soul is exalted to such a degree that, if the abuses of this new condition did not often degrade him below that from which he has emerged, he should ceaselessly bless the happy moment that removed him from it forever, and transformed him from a stupid and ignorant animal into an intelligent being and a man.

Let us reduce this whole balance to terms easy to compare. What man loses by the social contract is his natural liberty and an unlimited right to anything which tempts him and which he is able to attain; what he gains is civil liberty and the ownership of all that he possesses. In order not to be mistaken about these compensations, we must clearly distinguish natural liberty, which is limited only by the force of the individual, from civil liberty, which is limited by the general will; and possession, which is only the result of force or the right of the first occupant, from ownership, which can only be based on a positive title.

Besides the preceding, one can add to the acquisitions of the civil state the moral freedom which alone renders man truly master of himself; for the impulsion of mere appetite is slavery, and obedience to the law one prescribes to oneself is freedom. . . .

BOOK II

I. That Sovereignty Is Inalienable

The first and most important consequence of the principles established above is that the general will can only direct the forces of the State in keeping with the end for which it was instituted, which is the common good; for if the opposition of private interests has made the establishment of societies necessary, the harmony of these same interests has made it possible. That which is common to these different interests forms the social bond; and if there were not some point in which all interests agree, no society could exist. Now it is only on this common interest that the society should be governed.

I say, then, that sovereignty, being only the exercise of the general will, can never be alienated, and that the Sovereign, which is only a collective being, can be represented only by itself; power can well be transmitted, but will cannot.

In fact, if it is not impossible that a private will agree on some point with the general will, it is at least impossible that this agreement should be lasting and constant, for the private will naturally tends to preferences, and the general will to equality. It is still more impossible to have a guarantee for this agreement; even though it should always exist, it would be an effect not of art but of chance. The Sovereign may indeed say: I now will what a certain man wills, or at least what he says that he wills; but it cannot say: what that man wills tomorrow, I shall also will; since it is absurd that the will should bind itself for the future and since it is not incumbent on any will to consent to anything contrary to the good of the being that wills. If, then, the people promises simply to obey, it dissolves itself by that act, it loses its quality as a people; at the instant that there is a master, there is no longer a Sovereign, and forthwith the body politic is destroyed.

This is not to say that the orders of the chiefs cannot pass for expressions of the general will, so long as the Sovereign, free to oppose them, does not do so. In such case, from the universal silence one should presume the consent of the people. This will be explained at greater length.

II. That Sovereignty Is Indivisible

For the same reason that sovereignty is inalienable, it is indivisible. For either the will is general or it is not; it is the will either of the body of the people, or only of a part. In the first case, this declared will is an act of sovereignty and constitutes law. In the second case, it is only a private will, or an act of magistracy; it is at most a decree.

But our political men, not being able to divide sovereignty in its principles, divide it in its object: they divide it into force and will, into legislative power and executive power; into rights of taxation, of justice, and of war; into internal administration and power of treating with foreigners: sometimes they confound all these parts and sometimes separate them. They make the Sovereign to be a fantastic being formed of borrowed pieces; it is as if they composed a man from several bodies, one having eyes, another having arms, another having feet, and nothing more. Charlatans of Japan, it is said, cut up a child before the eyes of the spectators; then, throwing all its limbs, one after another, into the air, they make the child come back down alive and whole. Such almost are the juggler's tricks of our politicians; after dismembering the social body by a deception worthy of a carnival, they recombine the parts, one knows not how.

This error comes from not having formed exact notions of sovereign authority, and from having taken as parts of this authority what are only emanations from it. Thus, for example, the act of declaring war and that of making peace have been looked at as acts of sovereignty; but this is not the case, since each of these acts is not a law, but only an application of the law, a particular act which determines the case of the law, as will be clearly seen when the idea attached to the word *law* will be fixed.

In following out the other divisions in the same way, one would find that whenever sovereignty appears divided, a mistake has been made; that the rights which are taken as parts of that sovereignty are all subordinate to it, and always suppose supreme wills of which these rights are merely the execution.

III. Whether the General Will Can Err

It follows from what precedes that the general will is always upright and always tends toward the public utility; but it does not follow that the deliberations of the people always have the same rectitude. One wishes always his own good, but does not always discern it. The people is never corrupted, though often deceived, and then only does it seem to will that which is bad.

There is often a great difference between the will of all and the general will; the latter regards only the common interest, the other regards private interests and is only the sum of particular wills; but remove from these wills the pluses and minuses which cancel each other out and the general will remains as the sum of the differences.

If, when an adequately informed people deliberates, the Citizens having no communication among themselves, from the large number of small differences the general will would always result, and the deliberation would always be good. But when factions are formed, partial associations at the expense of the whole, the will of each of these associations becomes general with regard to its members, and particular with regard to the State; one is then able to say that there are no longer as many voters as there are men, but only as many as there are associations. The differences become less numerous and yield a less general result. Finally, when one of these associations is so large that it overcomes the rest, you no longer have a sum of small differences as the result, but a unique difference; then there no longer is a general will, and the opinion which dominates is only a private opinion.

BOOK III

III. Division of Governments

. . . In all times, there has been much dispute about the best form of Government, without considering that each of them is the best in certain cases, and the worst in others.

If in different States the number of supreme magistrates should be in an inverse ratio to that of the Citizens, it follows that generally Democratic Government suits small states, Aristocratic medium sized, and Monarchical large ones. This rule is immediately derived from the principle, but how count the multitude of circumstances which can furnish exceptions?

IV. Of Democracy

He who makes the law knows better than anyone how it ought to be executed and interpreted. It seems then that there could be no better constitution than the one in which the executive power is joined to the legislative. But it is just that which renders this Government insufficient in certain regards, because things that ought to be distinguished are not, and the prince and the Sovereign, being the same person, only form as it were a Government without a Government.

It is not good that he who makes the laws execute them, nor that the body of the people turn their attention away from general considerations in order to give it to particular objects. Nothing is more dangerous than the influence of private interests in public affairs, and the abuse of laws by the Government is a lesser evil than the corruption of the Legislator, the inevitable result of private considerations. Then, the State having been corrupted in its substance, all reform becomes impossible. A people who would never abuse the Government would not abuse independence either; a people who would always govern well would have no need of being governed.

To take the term in a rigorous sense, there has never existed a true Democracy, and it will never exist. It is contrary to the natural order that the greater number should govern and that the lesser number should be governed. One cannot imagine the people remaining constantly assembled in order to attend to public affairs, and one readily sees that it would not know how to establish commissions for this purpose without the form of the administration changing.

In fact, I think it possible to lay down as a principle that when the functions of the government are divided among several tribunals, sooner or later those with the fewest members acquire the greatest authority, if only because of the facility in expediting the public business which naturally brings this about.

Besides, how many things difficult to unite does this Government presume! First, a very small State where the people are easily assembled and where each citizen can easily know all the others; second, a great simplicity of moral customs, which prevents a multitude of public matters and thorny discussions; next, a great equality of rank and fortune, without which equality in rights and authority would not long subsist; finally, little or no luxury because luxury either is the result of wealth or renders it necessary; it corrupts both the rich and the poor, the one by possession, the other by covetousness; it sells the fatherland to indolence and vanity; it deprives the State of all its citizens in order to enslave some to others, and all to opinion.

That is why a celebrated author has named virtue as the principle of the Republic, for all these conditions could not subsist without virtue; but failing to make the necessary distinctions, this great genius often lacked accuracy and sometimes clarity, and did not see that the Sovereign authority being everywhere the same, the same principle ought to function in every well-constituted State, more or less, it is true, according to the form of Government.

Let us add that there is no Government so subject to civil wars and internal agitations as the Democratic or popular, because there is none which tends so strongly and continually to change its form, nor demands more vigilance and courage in order to be maintained in its own form. It is especially in this constitution that the Citizen ought to arm himself with force and steadfastness and to say each day of his life from his heart what a virtuous Palatine said in the Diet of Poland: "Malo periculosam libertatem quam quietum servitium." [I prefer liberty with danger to peace with slavery.]

If there were a people of Gods, it would govern itself democratically. A Government so perfect is not suited to men.

BOOK IV

I. That the General Will Is Indestructible

As long as several men together consider themselves as a single body, they have only one will which relates to the common preservation and to the general well-being. Then all the activities of the State are vigorous and simple, its maxims are clear and luminous, it has no entangled and conflicting interests, the common good is clearly apparent everywhere and only good sense is needed to perceive it. Peace, union, equality, are enemies of political subtleties. Upright and simple men are hard to deceive because of their simplicity: snares and refined pretexts do not impose upon them; they are not even clever enough to be duped. When one sees among the happiest people in the world groups of peasants regulating the affairs of State under an oak tree and always conducting themselves wisely, can one keep from scorning the refinement of other nations, who render themselves illustrious and miserable with so much art and mystery?

A State thus governed has need of very few Laws, and to the extent that it becomes necessary to promulgate new ones, this necessity is universally seen. The first man who proposes them does no more than say what all have already felt, and there is no question of intrigues or eloquence in order to pass into law what each has already resolved to do, as soon as he is sure that the others will do likewise.

What deceives those who reason is that seeing only States badly constituted from their origin, they are impressed by the impossibility of maintaining a similar polity in such States. They laugh on imagining all the follies to which a cunning knave, an insinuating speaker, could persuade the people of Paris or London. . . .

But when the social bond begins to loosen and the State to weaken; when private interests begin to make themselves felt and the small societies to influence the great one, the common interest degenerates and finds opponents; unanimity reigns no more in the votes, the general will is no longer the will of all, contradictions, debates arise, and the best advice does not pass without disputes.

Finally, when the State, near its ruin, subsists only as a vain and illusory form, when the social bond is broken in all hearts, when the vilest interest impudently takes on the sacred name of the public good, then the general will becomes mute; all, guided by secret motives, no longer express their opinions as Citizens, as if the State had never existed; and they falsely pass under the name of Laws iniquitous decrees which have only private interest as their goal.

Does it follow from this that the general will is annihilated or corrupted? No, it is always constant, unalterable, and pure; but it is subordinated to others that prevail over it. Each, detaching his own interest from the common interest, sees clearly that he cannot completely separate himself from it, but his part in the public evil does not seem anything to him compared with the exclusive good he intends to appropriate. This private good excepted, he wishes the general good for his own interest as strongly as anyone else. Even in selling his vote for money he does not extinguish the general will in himself; he eludes it. The fault he commits is to change the status of the question and to answer another than what he has been asked; so that instead of saying by his vote. "It is advantageous to the State," he says. "It is advantageous to a certain man or a certain party that such or such a motion passes." Thus the law of public order in the assemblies is not so much to maintain the general will as to make sure that it always is questioned and that it always responds. . . .

II. Of Voting

From the preceding chapter one sees that the manner in which general affairs are managed gives a sufficiently accurate indication of the actual state of the habitual conduct, and the health of the body politic. The more harmony reigns in the assemblies, that is to say the closer opinions approach unanimity, the more dominant is the general will: but long debates, dissensions, tumult, indicate the ascendancy of private interests and the decline of the State. . . .

At the other extremity of the circle unanimity returns. It is when the citizens, having fallen into slavery, no longer have either liberty or will. Then fright and flattery change votes into acclamations; one no longer deliberates, but adores or curses. . . .

From these diverse considerations arise the maxims by which one ought to regulate the manner of counting the votes and comparing opinions, according to whether the general will is more or less easy to know, and the State more or less declining.

There is only one single law which by its nature requires unanimous consent. It is the social pact: for civil association is the most voluntary act in the world; every man being born free and master of himself, no one can, under any pretext whatever, subjugate him without his assent. To decide that the son of a slave is born a slave is to decide that he is not born a man.

If, then, at the time of the social pact, there are found some opponents of it, their opposition does not invalidate the contract, it only prevents them from being included in it: they are foreigners among citizens. When the State is instituted, consent is in residence; to live in a territory is to submit oneself to sovereignty.

Outside of this basic contract, the voice of the greater number always obliges all the others; it is a consequence of the contract itself. But one asks how a man can be free and forced to conform to wills that are not his own. How are opponents free and yet subject to laws to which they have not consented?

I respond that the question is poorly posed. The citizen consents to all the laws, even those which are passed despite him, and even to those that punish him when he dares to violate any of them. The constant will of all the members of the State is the general will: by it they are citizens and free. When a law is proposed in the assembly of the People, what is asked of them is not precisely whether they approve the proposition or reject it, but whether or not it conforms to the general will which is their own: each in giving his vote states his opinion on that question, and from the counting of the votes is taken the declaration of the general will. When the opinion contrary to mine prevails, that only proves that I was mistaken, and that what I had considered to be the general will was not. If my private opinion had prevailed, I would have done something other than I had wanted to do, and then I would not have been free.

This supposes, it is true, that all the characteristics of the general will are still in the majority; when they cease to be there, whichever side one takes, there is no longer any liberty.

Chapter 12

Speech to the Electors of Bristol

Edmund Burke

Edmund Burke (1729–1797) was an influential thinker and member of Parliament. He argues that representatives are not obliged to vote in line with the preferences of their constituents, for Parliament is a deliberative body designed to make decisions that best promote the country's interest on the whole. After debate and careful consideration, each representative should rely on that individual's own best judgment.

——⋯——

I cannot conclude without saying a word on a topic touched upon by my worthy colleague. I wish that topic had been passed by at a time when I have so little leisure to discuss it. But since he has thought proper to throw it out, I owe you a clear explanation of my poor sentiments on that subject.

He tells you that "the topic of instructions has occasioned much altercation and uneasiness in this city"; and he expresses himself (if I understand him rightly) in favor of the coercive authority of such instructions.

Certainly, Gentlemen, it ought to be the happiness and glory of a representative to live in the strictest union, the closest correspondence, and the most unreserved communication with his constituents. Their wishes ought to have great weight with him; their opinions high respect; their business unremitted attention. It is his duty to sacrifice his repose, his pleasure, his satisfactions, to theirs,—and above all, ever, and in all cases, to prefer their interest to his own.

But his unbiased opinion, his mature judgment, his enlightened conscience, he ought not to sacrifice to you, to any man, or to any set of men living. These he does not derive from your pleasure,—no, nor from the law and the Constitution. They are a trust from Providence, for the abuse of which he is deeply answerable. Your representative owes you, not his industry only, but his judgment; and he betrays, instead of serving you, if he sacrifices it to your opinion.

My worthy colleague says, his will ought to be subservient to yours. If that be all, the thing is innocent. If government were a matter of will upon any side, yours, without question, ought to be superior. But government and legislation are matters of reason and judgment, and not of inclination; and what sort of Reason is that in which the determination precedes the discussion, in which one set of men deliberate and another decide, and where those who form the conclusion are perhaps three hundred miles distant from those who hear the arguments?

To deliver an opinion is the right of all men; that of constituents is a weighty and respectable opinion, which a representative ought always to rejoice to hear, and which he ought always most seriously to consider. But authoritative instructions, mandates issued, which the member is bound blindly and implicitly to obey, to vote, and to argue for, though contrary to the clearest conviction of his judgment and conscience—these are things utterly unknown to the laws of this land, and which arise from a fundamental mistake of the whole order and tenor of our Constitution.

Parliament is not a *congress* of ambassadors from different and hostile interests, which interests each must maintain, as an agent and advocate, against other agents and advocates; but Parliament is a *deliberate* assembly of *one* nation, with *one* interest, that of the whole—where not local purposes, not local prejudices, ought to guide, but the general good, resulting from the general reason of the whole. You choose a member, indeed; but when you have chosen him, he is not a member of Bristol, but he is a member of *Parliament*. If the local constituent should have an interest or should form an hasty opinion evidently opposite to the real good of the rest of the community, the member for that place ought to be as far as any other from any endeavor to give it effect. I beg pardon for saying so much on this subject; I have been unwillingly drawn into it; but I shall ever use a respectful frankness of communication with you. Your faithful friend, your devoted servant, I shall be to the end of my life: a flatterer you do not wish for. On this point of instructions, however, I think it scarcely possible we ever can have any sort of difference. Perhaps I may give you too much, rather than too little, trouble.

From the first hour I was encouraged to court your favor, to this happy day of obtaining it, I have never promised you anything but humble and persevering endeavors to do my duty. The weight of that duty, I confess, makes me tremble; and whoever well considers what it is, of all things in the world, will fly from what has the least likeness to a positive and precipitate engagement. To be a good member of Parliament is, let me tell you, no easy task,—

especially at this time, when there is so strong a disposition to run into the perilous extremes of servile compliance or wild popularity. To unite circumspection with vigor is absolutely necessary, but it is extremely difficult. We are now members for a rich commercial *city*; this city, however, is but a part of a rich commercial *nation*, the interests of which are various, multiform, and intricate. We are members for that great nation, which, however, is itself but part of a great *empire*, extended by our virtue and our fortune to the farthest limits of the East and of the West. All these widespread interests must be considered,—must be compared,—must be reconciled, if possible. We are members for a free country; and surely we all know that the machine of a free constitution is no simple thing, but as intricate and as delicate as it is valuable. We are members in a great and ancient *monarchy*; and we must preserve religiously the true, legal rights of the sovereign, which form the keystone that binds together the noble and well-constructed arch of our empire and our Constitution. A constitution made up of balanced powers must ever be a critical thing. As such I mean to touch that part of it which comes within my reach, I know my in inability, and I wish for support from every quarter.

Chapter 13

The Declaration of Independence

Thomas Jefferson (1743–1826) was the primary author of this foundational statement of American principles.

IN CONGRESS, JULY 4, 1776

The unanimous Declaration of the thirteen united States of America

When in the Course of human events it becomes necessary for one people to dissolve the political bands which have connected them with another and to assume among the powers of the earth, the separate and equal station to which the Laws of Nature and of Nature's God entitle them, a decent respect to the opinions of mankind requires that they should declare the causes which impel them to the separation.

We hold these truths to be self-evident, that all men are created equal, that they are endowed by their Creator with certain unalienable Rights, that among these are Life, Liberty and the pursuit of Happiness. — That to secure these rights, Governments are instituted among Men, deriving their just powers from the consent of the governed, — That whenever any Form of Government becomes destructive of these ends, it is the Right of the People to alter or to abolish it, and to institute new Government, laying its foundation on such principles and organizing its powers in such form, as to them shall seem most likely to effect their Safety and Happiness. Prudence, indeed, will dictate that Governments long established should not be changed for light and transient causes; and accordingly all experience hath shewn that mankind are more disposed to suffer, while evils are sufferable than to right themselves by abolishing the forms to which they are accustomed. But when a long train of abuses and usurpations, pursuing invariably the same Object evinces a design to reduce them under absolute Despotism, it is their right, it is their duty, to throw off such Government, and to provide new Guards for their future security. — Such has been the patient sufferance of these Colonies; and such is now the necessity which constrains them to alter their former Systems of Government. The history of the present King of Great Britain is a history of repeated injuries and usurpations, all having in direct object the establishment of an absolute Tyranny over these States. To prove this, let Facts be submitted to a candid world.

He has refused his Assent to Laws, the most wholesome and necessary for the public good.

He has forbidden his Governors to pass Laws of immediate and pressing importance, unless suspended in their operation till his Assent should be obtained; and when so suspended, he has utterly neglected to attend to them.

He has refused to pass other Laws for the accommodation of large districts of people, unless those people would relinquish the right of Representation in the Legislature, a right inestimable to them and formidable to tyrants only.

He has called together legislative bodies at places unusual, uncomfortable, and distant from the depository of their Public Records, for the sole purpose of fatiguing them into compliance with his measures.

He has dissolved Representative Houses repeatedly, for opposing with manly firmness his invasions on the rights of the people.

He has refused for a long time, after such dissolutions, to cause others to be elected, whereby the Legislative Powers, incapable of Annihilation, have returned to the People at large for their exercise; the State remaining in the mean time exposed to all the dangers of invasion from without, and convulsions within.

He has endeavoured to prevent the population of these States; for that purpose obstructing the Laws for Naturalization of Foreigners; refusing to pass others to encourage their migrations hither, and raising the conditions of new Appropriations of Lands.

He has obstructed the Administration of Justice by refusing his Assent to Laws for establishing Judiciary Powers.

He has made Judges dependent on his Will alone for the tenure of their offices, and the amount and payment of their salaries.

He has erected a multitude of New Offices, and sent hither swarms of Officers to harass our people and eat out their substance.

He has kept among us, in times of peace, Standing Armies without the Consent of our legislatures.

He has affected to render the Military independent of and superior to the Civil Power.

He has combined with others to subject us to a jurisdiction foreign to our constitution, and unacknowledged by our laws; giving his Assent to their Acts of pretended Legislation:

For quartering large bodies of armed troops among us:

For protecting them, by a mock Trial from punishment for any Murders which they should commit on the Inhabitants of these States:

For cutting off our Trade with all parts of the world:

For imposing Taxes on us without our Consent:

For depriving us in many cases, of the benefit of Trial by Jury:

For transporting us beyond Seas to be tried for pretended offences:

For abolishing the free System of English Laws in a neighbouring Province, establishing therein an Arbitrary government, and enlarging its Boundaries so as to render it at once an example and fit instrument for introducing the same absolute rule into these Colonies

For taking away our Charters, abolishing our most valuable Laws and altering fundamentally the Forms of our Governments:

For suspending our own Legislatures, and declaring themselves invested with power to legislate for us in all cases whatsoever.

He has abdicated Government here, by declaring us out of his Protection and waging War against us.

He has plundered our seas, ravaged our coasts, burnt our towns, and destroyed the lives of our people.

He is at this time transporting large Armies of foreign Mercenaries to complete the works of death, desolation, and tyranny, already begun with circumstances of Cruelty & Perfidy scarcely paralleled in the most barbarous ages, and totally unworthy the Head of a civilized nation.

He has constrained our fellow Citizens taken Captive on the high Seas to bear Arms against their Country, to become the executioners of their friends and Brethren, or to fall themselves by their Hands.

He has excited domestic insurrections amongst us, and has endeavoured to bring on the inhabitants of our frontiers, the merciless Indian Savages whose known rule of warfare, is an undistinguished destruction of all ages, sexes and conditions.

In every stage of these Oppressions We have Petitioned for Redress in the most humble terms: Our repeated Petitions have been answered only by repeated injury. A Prince, whose character is thus marked by every act which may define a Tyrant, is unfit to be the ruler of a free people.

Nor have We been wanting in attentions to our British brethren. We have warned them from time to time of attempts by their legislature to extend an unwarrantable jurisdiction over us. We have reminded them of the circumstances of our emigration and settlement here. We have appealed to their native justice and magnanimity, and we have conjured them by the ties of our common kindred to disavow these usurpations, which would inevitably interrupt our connections and correspondence. They too have been deaf to the voice of justice and of consanguinity. We must, therefore, acquiesce in the necessity, which denounces our Separation, and hold them, as we hold the rest of mankind, Enemies in War, in Peace Friends.

We, therefore, the Representatives of the united States of America, in General Congress, Assembled, appealing to the Supreme Judge of the world for the rectitude of our intentions, do, in the Name, and by Authority of the good People of these Colonies, solemnly publish and declare, That these united Colonies are, and of Right ought to be Free and Independent States, that they are Absolved from all Allegiance to the British Crown, and that all political connection between them and the State of Great Britain, is and ought to be totally dissolved; and that as Free and Independent States, they have full Power to levy War, conclude Peace, contract Alliances, establish Commerce, and to do all other Acts and Things which Independent States may of right do. — And for the support of this Declaration, with a firm reliance on the protection of Divine Providence, we mutually pledge to each other our Lives, our Fortunes, and our sacred Honor.

New Hampshire:
Josiah Bartlett, William Whipple, Matthew Thornton

Massachusetts:
John Hancock, Samuel Adams, John Adams, Robert Treat Paine, Elbridge Gerry

Rhode Island:
Stephen Hopkins, William Ellery

Connecticut:
Roger Sherman, Samuel Huntington, William Williams, Oliver Wolcott

New York:
William Floyd, Philip Livingston, Francis Lewis, Lewis Morris

New Jersey:
Richard Stockton, John Witherspoon, Francis Hopkinson, John Hart, Abraham Clark

Pennsylvania:
Robert Morris, Benjamin Rush, Benjamin Franklin, John Morton, George Clymer, James Smith, George Taylor, James Wilson, George Ross

Delaware:
Caesar Rodney, George Read, Thomas McKean

Maryland:
Samuel Chase, William Paca, Thomas Stone, Charles Carroll of Carrollton

Virginia:
George Wythe, Richard Henry Lee, Thomas Jefferson, Benjamin Harrison, Thomas Nelson, Jr., Francis Lightfoot Lee, Carter Braxton

North Carolina:
William Hooper, Joseph Hewes, John Penn

South Carolina:
Edward Rutledge, Thomas Heyward, Jr., Thomas Lynch, Jr., Arthur Middleton

Georgia:
Button Gwinnett, Lyman Hall, George Walton

Chapter 14

The Constitution of the United States

The Constitution of the United States was drawn up at the Constitutional Convention in Philadelphia in 1787 and went into effect in 1789.

We the People of the United States, in Order to form a more perfect Union, establish Justice, insure domestic Tranquility, provide for the common defence, promote the general Welfare, and secure the Blessings of Liberty to ourselves and our Posterity, do ordain and establish this Constitution for the United States of America.

ARTICLE. I.

Section. 1.

All legislative Powers herein granted shall be vested in a Congress of the United States, which shall consist of a Senate and House of Representatives.

Section. 2.

The House of Representatives shall be composed of Members chosen every second Year by the People of the several States, and the Electors in each State shall have the Qualifications requisite for Electors of the most numerous Branch of the State Legislature.

No Person shall be a Representative who shall not have attained to the Age of twenty five Years, and been seven Years a Citizen of the United States, and who shall not, when elected, be an Inhabitant of that State in which he shall be chosen.

Representatives and direct Taxes shall be apportioned among the several States which may be included within this Union, according to their respective Numbers, which shall be determined by adding to the whole Number of free Persons, including those bound to Service for a Term of Years, and excluding Indians not taxed, three fifths of all other Persons. The actual Enumeration shall be made within three Years after the first Meeting of the Congress of the United States, and within every subsequent Term of ten Years, in such Manner as they shall by Law direct. The Number of Representatives shall not exceed one for every thirty Thousand, but each State shall have at Least one Representative; and until such enumeration shall be made, the State of New Hampshire shall be entitled to chuse three, Massachusetts eight, Rhode-Island and Providence Plantations one, Connecticut five, New-York six, New Jersey four, Pennsylvania eight, Delaware one, Maryland six, Virginia ten, North Carolina five, South Carolina five, and Georgia three.

When vacancies happen in the Representation from any State, the Executive Authority thereof shall issue Writs of Election to fill such Vacancies.

The House of Representatives shall chuse their Speaker and other Officers; and shall have the sole Power of Impeachment.

Section. 3.

The Senate of the United States shall be composed of two Senators from each State, chosen by the Legislature thereof, for six Years; and each Senator shall have one Vote.

Immediately after they shall be assembled in Consequence of the first Election, they shall be divided as equally as may be into three Classes. The Seats of the Senators of the first Class shall be vacated at the Expiration of the second Year, of the second Class at the Expiration of the fourth Year, and of the third Class at the Expiration of the sixth Year, so that one third may be chosen every second Year; and if Vacancies happen by Resignation, or otherwise, during the Recess of the Legislature of any State, the Executive thereof may make temporary Appointments until the next Meeting of the Legislature, which shall then fill such Vacancies.

No Person shall be a Senator who shall not have attained to the Age of thirty Years, and been nine Years a Citizen of the United States, and who shall not, when elected, be an Inhabitant of that State for which he shall be chosen.

The Vice President of the United States shall be President of the Senate, but shall have no Vote, unless they be equally divided.

The Senate shall chuse their other Officers, and also a President pro tempore, in the Absence of the Vice President, or when he shall exercise the Office of President of the United States.

The Senate shall have the sole Power to try all Impeachments. When sitting for that Purpose, they shall be on Oath or Affirmation. When the President of the United States is tried, the Chief Justice shall preside: And no Person shall be convicted without the Concurrence of two thirds of the Members present.

Judgment in Cases of Impeachment shall not extend further than to removal from Office, and disqualification to hold and enjoy any Office of honor, Trust or Profit under the United States: but the Party convicted shall nevertheless be liable and subject to Indictment, Trial, Judgment and Punishment, according to Law.

Section. 4.

The Times, Places and Manner of holding Elections for Senators and Representatives, shall be prescribed in each State by the Legislature thereof; but the Congress may at any time by Law make or alter such Regulations, except as to the Places of chusing Senators.

The Congress shall assemble at least once in every Year, and such Meeting shall be on the first Monday in December, unless they shall by Law appoint a different Day.

Section. 5.

Each House shall be the Judge of the Elections, Returns and Qualifications of its own Members, and a Majority of each shall constitute a Quorum to do Business; but a smaller Number may adjourn from day to day, and may be authorized to compel the Attendance of absent Members, in such Manner, and under such Penalties as each House may provide.

Each House may determine the Rules of its Proceedings, punish its Members for disorderly Behaviour, and, with the Concurrence of two thirds, expel a Member.

Each House shall keep a Journal of its Proceedings, and from time to time publish the same, excepting such Parts as may in their Judgment require Secrecy; and the Yeas and Nays of the Members of either House on any question shall, at the Desire of one fifth of those Present, be entered on the Journal.

Neither House, during the Session of Congress, shall, without the Consent of the other, adjourn for more than three days, nor to any other Place than that in which the two Houses shall be sitting.

Section. 6.

The Senators and Representatives shall receive a Compensation for their Services, to be ascertained by Law, and paid out of the Treasury of the United States. They shall in all Cases, except Treason, Felony and Breach of the Peace, be privileged from Arrest during their Attendance at the Session of their respective Houses, and in going to and returning from the same; and for any Speech or Debate in either House, they shall not be questioned in any other Place.

No Senator or Representative shall, during the Time for which he was elected, be appointed to any civil Office under the Authority of the United States, which shall have been created, or the Emoluments whereof shall have been encreased during such time; and no Person holding any Office under the United States, shall be a Member of either House during his Continuance in Office.

Section. 7.

All Bills for raising Revenue shall originate in the House of Representatives; but the Senate may propose or concur with Amendments as on other Bills.

Every Bill which shall have passed the House of Representatives and the Senate, shall, before it become a Law, be presented to the President of the United States; If he approve he shall sign it, but if not he shall return it, with his Objections to that House in which it shall have originated, who shall enter the Objections at large on their Journal, and proceed to reconsider it. If after such Reconsideration two thirds of that House shall agree to pass the Bill, it shall be sent, together with the Objections, to the other House, by which it shall likewise be reconsidered, and if approved by two thirds of that House, it shall become a Law. But in all such Cases the Votes of both Houses shall be determined by yeas and Nays, and the Names of the Persons voting for and against the Bill shall be entered on the Journal of each House respectively. If any Bill shall not be returned by the President within ten Days (Sundays excepted) after it shall have been presented to him, the Same shall be a Law, in like Manner as if he had signed it, unless the Congress by their Adjournment prevent its Return, in which Case it shall not be a Law.

Every Order, Resolution, or Vote to which the Concurrence of the Senate and House of Representatives may be necessary (except on a question of Adjournment) shall be presented to the President of the United States; and before the Same shall take Effect, shall be approved by him, or being disapproved by him, shall be repassed by two thirds of the Senate and House of Representatives, according to the Rules and Limitations prescribed in the Case of a Bill.

Section. 8.

The Congress shall have Power To lay and collect Taxes, Duties, Imposts and Excises, to pay the Debts and provide for the common Defence and general Welfare of the United States; but all Duties, Imposts and Excises shall be uniform throughout the United States;

To borrow Money on the credit of the United States;

To regulate Commerce with foreign Nations, and among the several States, and with the Indian Tribes;

To establish an uniform Rule of Naturalization, and uniform Laws on the subject of Bankruptcies throughout the United States;

To coin Money, regulate the Value thereof, and of foreign Coin, and fix the Standard of Weights and Measures;

To provide for the Punishment of counterfeiting the Securities and current Coin of the United States;

To establish Post Offices and post Roads;

To promote the Progress of Science and useful Arts, by securing for limited Times to Authors and Inventors the exclusive Right to their respective Writings and Discoveries;

To constitute Tribunals inferior to the supreme Court;

To define and punish Piracies and Felonies committed on the high Seas, and Offences against the Law of Nations;

To declare War, grant Letters of Marque and Reprisal, and make Rules concerning Captures on Land and Water;

To raise and support Armies, but no Appropriation of Money to that Use shall be for a longer Term than two Years;

To provide and maintain a Navy;

To make Rules for the Government and Regulation of the land and naval Forces;

To provide for calling forth the Militia to execute the Laws of the Union, suppress Insurrections and repel Invasions;

To provide for organizing, arming, and disciplining, the Militia, and for governing such Part of them as may be employed in the Service of the United States, reserving to the States respectively, the Appointment of the Officers, and the Authority of training the Militia according to the discipline prescribed by Congress;

To exercise exclusive Legislation in all Cases whatsoever, over such District (not exceeding ten Miles square) as may, by Cession of particular States, and the Acceptance of Congress, become the Seat of the Government of the United States, and to exercise like Authority over all Places purchased by the Consent of the Legislature of the State in which the Same shall be, for the Erection of Forts, Magazines, Arsenals, dock-Yards, and other needful Buildings;—And

To make all Laws which shall be necessary and proper for carrying into Execution the foregoing Powers, and all other Powers vested by this Constitution in the Government of the United States, or in any Department or Officer thereof.

Section. 9.

The Migration or Importation of such Persons as any of the States now existing shall think proper to admit, shall not be prohibited by the Congress prior to the Year one thousand eight hundred and eight, but a Tax or duty may be imposed on such Importation, not exceeding ten dollars for each Person.

The Privilege of the Writ of Habeas Corpus shall not be suspended, unless when in Cases of Rebellion or Invasion the public Safety may require it.

No Bill of Attainder or ex post facto Law shall be passed.

No Capitation, or other direct, Tax shall be laid, unless in Proportion to the Census or enumeration herein before directed to be taken.

No Tax or Duty shall be laid on Articles exported from any State.

No Preference shall be given by any Regulation of Commerce or Revenue to the Ports of one State over those of another: nor shall Vessels bound to, or from, one State, be obliged to enter, clear, or pay Duties in another.

No Money shall be drawn from the Treasury, but in Consequence of Appropriations made by Law; and a regular Statement and Account of the Receipts and Expenditures of all public Money shall be published from time to time.

No Title of Nobility shall be granted by the United States: And no Person holding any Office of Profit or Trust under them, shall, without the Consent of the Congress, accept of any present, Emolument, Office, or Title, of any kind whatever, from any King, Prince, or foreign State.

Section. 10.

No State shall enter into any Treaty, Alliance, or Confederation; grant Letters of Marque and Reprisal; coin Money; emit Bills of Credit; make any Thing but gold and silver Coin a Tender in Payment of Debts; pass any Bill of Attainder, ex post facto Law, or Law impairing the Obligation of Contracts, or grant any Title of Nobility.

No State shall, without the Consent of the Congress, lay any Imposts or Duties on Imports or Exports, except what may be absolutely necessary for executing it's inspection Laws: and the net Produce of all Duties and Imposts, laid by any State on Imports or Exports, shall be for the Use of the Treasury of the United States; and all such Laws shall be subject to the Revision and Control of the Congress.

No State shall, without the Consent of Congress, lay any Duty of Tonnage, keep Troops, or Ships of War in time of Peace, enter into any Agreement or Compact with another State, or with a foreign Power, or engage in War, unless actually invaded, or in such imminent Danger as will not admit of delay.

ARTICLE. II.

Section. 1.

The executive Power shall be vested in a President of the United States of America. He shall hold his Office during the Term of four Years, and, together with the Vice President, chosen for the same Term, be elected, as follows

Each State shall appoint, in such Manner as the Legislature thereof may direct, a Number of Electors, equal to the whole Number of Senators and Representatives to which the State may be entitled in the Congress: but no Senator or Representative, or Person holding an Office of Trust or Profit under the United States, shall be appointed an Elector.

The Electors shall meet in their respective States, and vote by Ballot for two Persons, of whom one at least shall not be an Inhabitant of the same State with themselves. And they shall make a List of all the Persons voted for, and of the Number of Votes for each; which List they shall sign and certify, and transmit sealed to the Seat of the Government of the United States, directed to the President of the Senate. The President of the Senate shall, in the Presence of the Senate and House of Representatives, open all the Certificates, and the Votes shall then be counted. The Person having the greatest Number of Votes shall be the President, if such Number be a Majority of the whole Number of Electors appointed; and if there be more than one who have such Majority, and have an equal Number of Votes, then the House of Representatives shall immediately chuse by Ballot one of them for President; and if no Person have a Majority, then from the five highest on the List the said House shall in like Manner chuse the President. But in chusing the President, the Votes shall be taken by States, the Representation from each State having one Vote; A quorum for this Purpose shall consist of a Member or Members from two thirds of the States, and a Majority of all the States shall be necessary to a Choice. In every Case, after the Choice of the President, the Person having the greatest Number of Votes of the Electors shall be the Vice President. But if there should remain two or more who have equal Votes, the Senate shall chuse from them by Ballot the Vice President.

The Congress may determine the Time of chusing the Electors, and the Day on which they shall give their Votes; which Day shall be the same throughout the United States.

No Person except a natural born Citizen, or a Citizen of the United States, at the time of the Adoption of this Constitution, shall be eligible to the Office of President; neither shall any Person be eligible to that Office who shall not have attained to the Age of thirty five Years, and been fourteen Years a Resident within the United States.

In Case of the Removal of the President from Office, or of his Death, Resignation, or Inability to discharge the Powers and Duties of the said Office, the Same shall devolve on the Vice President, and the Congress may by Law provide for the Case of Removal, Death, Resignation or Inability, both of the President and Vice President, declaring what Officer shall then act as President, and such Officer shall act accordingly, until the Disability be removed, or a President shall be elected.

The President shall, at stated Times, receive for his Services, a Compensation, which shall neither be encreased nor diminished during the Period for which he shall have been elected, and he shall not receive within that Period any other Emolument from the United States, or any of them.

Before he enter on the Execution of his Office, he shall take the following Oath or Affirmation:—"I do solemnly swear (or affirm) that I will faithfully execute the Office of President of the United States, and will to the best of my Ability, preserve, protect and defend the Constitution of the United States."

Section. 2.

The President shall be Commander in Chief of the Army and Navy of the United States, and of the Militia of the several States, when called into the actual Service of the United States; he may require the Opinion, in writing, of the principal Officer in each of the executive Departments, upon any Subject relating to the Duties of their respective Offices, and he shall have Power to grant Reprieves and Pardons for Offences against the United States, except in Cases of Impeachment.

He shall have Power, by and with the Advice and Consent of the Senate, to make Treaties, provided two thirds of the Senators present concur; and he shall nominate, and by and with the Advice and Consent of the Senate, shall appoint Ambassadors, other public Ministers and Consuls, Judges of the supreme Court, and all other Officers of the United States, whose Appointments are not herein otherwise provided for, and which shall be established by Law: but the Congress may by Law vest the Appointment of such inferior Officers, as they think proper, in the President alone, in the Courts of Law, or in the Heads of Departments.

The President shall have Power to fill up all Vacancies that may happen during the Recess of the Senate, by granting Commissions which shall expire at the End of their next Session.

Section. 3.

He shall from time to time give to the Congress Information of the State of the Union, and recommend to their Consideration such Measures as he shall judge necessary and expedient; he may, on extraordinary Occasions, convene both Houses, or either of them, and in Case of Disagreement between them, with Respect to the Time of Adjournment, he may adjourn them to such Time as he shall think proper; he shall receive Ambassadors and other public Ministers; he shall take Care that the Laws be faithfully executed, and shall Commission all the Officers of the United States.

Section. 4.

The President, Vice President and all civil Officers of the United States, shall be removed from Office on Impeachment for, and Conviction of, Treason, Bribery, or other high Crimes and Misdemeanors.

ARTICLE III.

Section. 1.

The judicial Power of the United States, shall be vested in one supreme Court, and in such inferior Courts as the Congress may from time to time ordain and establish. The Judges, both of the supreme and inferior Courts, shall hold their Offices during good Behaviour, and shall, at stated Times, receive for their Services, a Compensation, which shall not be diminished during their Continuance in Office.

Section. 2.

The judicial Power shall extend to all Cases, in Law and Equity, arising under this Constitution, the Laws of the United States, and Treaties made, or which shall be made, under their Authority;—to all Cases affecting Ambassadors, other public Ministers and Consuls;—to all Cases of admiralty and maritime Jurisdiction;—to Controversies to which the United States shall be a Party;— to Controversies between two or more States;—between a State and Citizens of another State,—between Citizens of different States,—between Citizens of the same State claiming Lands under Grants of different States, and between a State, or the Citizens thereof, and foreign States, Citizens or Subjects.

In all Cases affecting Ambassadors, other public Ministers and Consuls, and those in which a State shall be Party, the supreme Court shall have original Jurisdiction. In all the other Cases before mentioned, the supreme Court shall have appellate Jurisdiction, both as to Law and Fact, with such Exceptions, and under such Regulations as the Congress shall make.

The Trial of all Crimes, except in Cases of Impeachment, shall be by Jury; and such Trial shall be held in the State where the said Crimes shall have been committed; but when not committed within any State, the Trial shall be at such Place or Places as the Congress may by Law have directed.

Section. 3.

Treason against the United States, shall consist only in levying War against them, or in adhering to their Enemies, giving them Aid and Comfort. No Person shall be convicted of Treason unless on the Testimony of two Witnesses to the same overt Act, or on Confession in open Court.

The Congress shall have Power to declare the Punishment of Treason, but no Attainder of Treason shall work Corruption of Blood, or Forfeiture except during the Life of the Person attainted.

ARTICLE. IV.

Section. 1.

Full Faith and Credit shall be given in each State to the public Acts, Records, and judicial Proceedings of every other State. And the Congress may by general Laws prescribe the Manner in which such Acts, Records and Proceedings shall be proved, and the Effect thereof.

Section. 2.

The Citizens of each State shall be entitled to all Privileges and Immunities of Citizens in the several States.

A Person charged in any State with Treason, Felony, or other Crime, who shall flee from Justice, and be found in another State, shall on Demand of the executive Authority of the State from which he fled, be delivered up, to be removed to the State having Jurisdiction of the Crime.

No Person held to Service or Labour in one State, under the Laws thereof, escaping into another, shall, in Consequence of any Law or Regulation therein, be discharged from such Service or Labour, but shall be delivered up on Claim of the Party to whom such Service or Labour may be due.

Section. 3.

New States may be admitted by the Congress into this Union; but no new State shall be formed or erected within the Jurisdiction of any other State; nor any State be formed by the Junction of two or more States, or Parts of States, without the Consent of the Legislatures of the States concerned as well as of the Congress.

The Congress shall have Power to dispose of and make all needful Rules and Regulations respecting the Territory or other Property belonging to the United States; and nothing in this Constitution shall be so construed as to Prejudice any Claims of the United States, or of any particular State.

Section. 4.

The United States shall guarantee to every State in this Union a Republican Form of Government, and shall protect each of them against Invasion; and on Application of the Legislature, or of the Executive (when the Legislature cannot be convened), against domestic Violence.

ARTICLE. V.

The Congress, whenever two thirds of both Houses shall deem it necessary, shall propose Amendments to this Constitution, or, on the Application of the Legislatures of two thirds of the several States, shall call a Convention for proposing Amendments, which, in either Case, shall be valid to all Intents and Purposes, as Part of this Constitution, when ratified by the Legislatures of three fourths of the several States, or by Conventions in three fourths thereof, as the one or the other Mode of Ratification may be proposed by the Congress; Provided that no Amendment which may be made prior to the Year One thousand eight hundred and eight shall in any Manner affect the first and fourth Clauses in the Ninth Section of the first Article; and that no State, without its Consent, shall be deprived of its equal Suffrage in the Senate.

ARTICLE. VI.

All Debts contracted and Engagements entered into, before the Adoption of this Constitution, shall be as valid against the United States under this Constitution, as under the Confederation.

This Constitution, and the Laws of the United States which shall be made in Pursuance thereof; and all Treaties made, or which shall be made, under the Authority of the United States, shall be the supreme Law of the Land; and the Judges in every State shall be bound thereby, any Thing in the Constitution or Laws of any State to the Contrary notwithstanding.

The Senators and Representatives before mentioned, and the Members of the several State Legislatures, and all executive and judicial Officers, both of the United States and of the several States, shall be bound by Oath or Affirmation, to support this Constitution; but no religious Test shall ever be required as a Qualification to any Office or public Trust under the United States.

ARTICLE. VII.

The Ratification of the Conventions of nine States, shall be sufficient for the Establishment of this Constitution between the States so ratifying the Same.

Done in Convention by the Unanimous Consent of the States present the Seventeenth Day of September in the Year of our Lord one thousand seven hundred and Eighty seven and of the Independence of the United States of America the Twelfth In witness whereof We have hereunto subscribed our Names,

Attest William Jackson Secretary
Geo. Washington—Presidt and deputy from Virginia

Delaware

Geo: Read
Gunning Bedford jun
John Dickinson
Richard Bassett
Jaco: Broom

Maryland

James McHenry
Dan of St Thos. Jenifer
Danl. Carroll

Virginia

John Blair
James Madison Jr.

North Carolina

Wm. Blount
Richd. Dobbs Spaight
Hu Williamson

South Carolina

J. Rutledge
Charles Cotesworth Pinckney
Charles Pinckney
Pierce Butler

Georgia

William Few
Abr Baldwin

New Hampshire

John Langdon
Nicholas Gilman

Massachusetts

Nathaniel Gorham
Rufus King

Connecticut

Wm. Saml. Johnson
Roger Sherman

New York

Alexander Hamilton

New Jersey

Wil: Livingston
David Brearley
Wm. Paterson
Jona: Dayton

Pennsylvania

B Franklin
Thomas Mifflin
Robt. Morris
Geo. Clymer
Thos. FitzSimons
Jared Ingersoll
James Wilson
Gouv Morris

ARTICLES in addition to, and Amendment of the Constitution of the United States of America, proposed by Congress, and ratified by the Legislatures of the several States, pursuant to the fifth Article of the original Constitution.

AMENDMENT I

Congress shall make no law respecting an establishment of religion, or prohibiting the free exercise thereof; or abridging the freedom of speech, or of the press; or the right of the people peaceably to assemble, and to petition the Government for a redress of grievances.

AMENDMENT II

A well regulated Militia, being necessary to the security of a free State, the right of the people to keep and bear Arms, shall not be infringed.

AMENDMENT III

No Soldier shall, in time of peace be quartered in any house, without the consent of the Owner, nor in time of war, but in a manner to be prescribed by law.

AMENDMENT IV

The right of the people to be secure in their persons, houses, papers, and effects, against unreasonable searches and seizures, shall not be violated, and no Warrants shall issue, but upon probable cause, supported by Oath or affirmation, and particularly describing the place to be searched, and the persons or things to be seized.

AMENDMENT V

No person shall be held to answer for a capital, or otherwise infamous crime, unless on a presentment or indictment of a Grand Jury, except in cases arising in the land or naval forces, or in the Militia, when in actual service in time of War or public danger; nor shall any person be subject for the same offence to be twice put in jeopardy of life or limb; nor shall be compelled in any criminal case to be a witness against himself, nor be deprived of life, liberty, or property, without due process of law; nor shall private property be taken for public use, without just compensation.

AMENDMENT VI

In all criminal prosecutions, the accused shall enjoy the right to a speedy and public trial, by an impartial jury of the State and district wherein the crime shall have been committed, which district shall have been previously ascertained by law, and to be informed of the nature and cause of the accusation; to be confronted with the witnesses against him; to have compulsory process for obtaining witnesses in his favor, and to have the Assistance of Counsel for his defence.

AMENDMENT VII

In Suits at common law, where the value in controversy shall exceed twenty dollars, the right of trial by jury shall be preserved, and no fact tried by a jury, shall be otherwise re-examined in any Court of the United States, than according to the rules of the common law.

AMENDMENT VIII

Excessive bail shall not be required, nor excessive fines imposed, nor cruel and unusual punishments inflicted.

AMENDMENT IX

The enumeration in the Constitution, of certain rights, shall not be construed to deny or disparage others retained by the people.

AMENDMENT X

The powers not delegated to the United States by the Constitution, nor prohibited by it to the States, are reserved to the States respectively, or to the people.

AMENDMENT XI

The Judicial power of the United States shall not be construed to extend to any suit in law or equity, commenced or prosecuted against one of the United States by Citizens of another State, or by Citizens or Subjects of any Foreign State.

AMENDMENT XII

The Electors shall meet in their respective states and vote by ballot for President and Vice-President, one of whom, at least, shall not be an inhabitant of the same state with themselves; they shall name in their ballots the person voted for as President, and in distinct ballots the person voted for as Vice-President, and they shall make distinct lists of all persons voted for as President, and of all persons voted for as Vice-President, and of the number of votes for each, which lists they shall sign and certify, and transmit sealed to the seat of the government of the United States, directed to the President of the Senate; — the President of the Senate shall, in the presence of the Senate and House of Representatives, open all the certificates and the votes shall then be counted; — The person having the greatest number of votes for President, shall be the President, if such number be a majority of the whole number of Electors appointed; and if no person have such majority, then from the persons having the highest numbers not exceeding three on the list of those voted for as President, the House of Representatives shall choose immediately, by ballot, the President. But in choosing the President, the votes shall be taken by states, the representation from each state having one vote; a quorum for this purpose shall consist of a member or members from two-thirds of the states, and a majority of all the states shall be necessary to a choice. [And if the House of Representatives shall not choose a President whenever the right of choice shall devolve upon them, before the fourth day of March next following, then the Vice-President shall act as President, as in case of the death or other constitutional disability of the President. — ¹] The person having the greatest number of votes as Vice-President, shall be the Vice-President, if such number be a majority of the whole number of Electors appointed, and if no person have a majority, then from the two highest numbers on the list, the Senate shall choose the Vice-President; a quorum for the purpose shall consist of two-thirds of the whole number of Senators, and a majority of the whole number shall be necessary to a choice. But no person constitutionally ineligible to the office of President shall be eligible to that of Vice-President of the United States.

AMENDMENT XIII

Section 1.

Neither slavery nor involuntary servitude, except as a punishment for crime whereof the party shall have been duly convicted, shall exist within the United States, or any place subject to their jurisdiction.

Section 2.

Congress shall have power to enforce this article by appropriate legislation.

AMENDMENT XIV

Section 1.

All persons born or naturalized in the United States, and subject to the jurisdiction thereof, are citizens of the United States and of the State wherein they reside. No State shall make or enforce any law which shall abridge the privileges or immunities of citizens of the United States; nor shall any State deprive any person of life, liberty, or property, without due process of law; nor deny to any person within its jurisdiction the equal protection of the laws.

Section 2.

Representatives shall be apportioned among the several States according to their respective numbers, counting the whole number of persons in each State, excluding Indians not taxed. But when the right to vote at any election for the choice of electors for President and Vice-President of the United States, Representatives in Congress, the Executive and Judicial officers of a State, or the members of the Legislature thereof, is denied to any of the male inhabitants of such State, being twenty-one years of age,[2] and citizens of the United States, or in any way abridged, except for participation in rebellion, or other crime, the basis of representation therein shall be reduced in the proportion which the number of such male citizens shall bear to the whole number of male citizens twenty-one years of age in such State.

Section 3.

No person shall be a Senator or Representative in Congress, or elector of President and Vice-President, or hold any office, civil or military, under the United States, or under any State, who, having previously taken an oath, as a member of Congress, or as an officer of the United States, or as a member of any State legislature, or as an executive or judicial officer of any State, to support the Constitution of the United States, shall have engaged in insurrection or rebellion against the same, or given aid or comfort to the enemies thereof. But Congress may by a vote of two-thirds of each House, remove such disability.

Section 4.

The validity of the public debt of the United States, authorized by law, including debts incurred for payment of pensions and bounties for services in suppressing insurrection or rebellion, shall not be questioned. But neither the United States nor any State shall assume or pay any debt or obligation incurred in aid of insurrection or rebellion against the United States, or any claim for the loss or emancipation of any slave; but all such debts, obligations and claims shall be held illegal and void.

Section 5.

The Congress shall have the power to enforce, by appropriate legislation, the provisions of this article.

AMENDMENT XV

Section 1.

The right of citizens of the United States to vote shall not be denied or abridged by the United States or by any State on account of race, color, or previous condition of servitude—

Section 2.

The Congress shall have the power to enforce this article by appropriate legislation.

AMENDMENT XVI

The Congress shall have power to lay and collect taxes on incomes, from whatever source derived, without apportionment among the several States, and without regard to any census or enumeration.

AMENDMENT XVII

The Senate of the United States shall be composed of two Senators from each State, elected by the people thereof, for six years; and each Senator shall have one vote. The electors in each State shall have the qualifications requisite for electors of the most numerous branch of the State legislatures.

When vacancies happen in the representation of any State in the Senate, the executive authority of such State shall issue writs of election to fill such vacancies: Provided, That the legislature of any State may empower the executive thereof to make temporary appointments until the people fill the vacancies by election as the legislature may direct.

This amendment shall not be so construed as to affect the election or term of any Senator chosen before it becomes valid as part of the Constitution.

AMENDMENT XVIII

Section 1.

After one year from the ratification of this article the manufacture, sale, or transportation of intoxicating liquors within, the importation thereof into, or the exportation thereof from the United States and all territory subject to the jurisdiction thereof for beverage purposes is hereby prohibited.

Section 2.

The Congress and the several States shall have concurrent power to enforce this article by appropriate legislation.

Section 3.

This article shall be inoperative unless it shall have been ratified as an amendment to the Constitution by the legislatures of the several States, as provided in the Constitution, within seven years from the date of the submission hereof to the States by the Congress.

AMENDMENT XIX

The right of citizens of the United States to vote shall not be denied or abridged by the United States or by any State on account of sex.

Congress shall have power to enforce this article by appropriate legislation.

AMENDMENT XX

Section 1.

The terms of the President and the Vice President shall end at noon on the 20th day of January, and the terms of Senators and Representatives at noon on the 3d day of January, of the years in which such terms would have ended if this article had not been ratified; and the terms of their successors shall then begin.

Section 2.

The Congress shall assemble at least once in every year, and such meeting shall begin at noon on the 3d day of January, unless they shall by law appoint a different day.

Section 3.

If, at the time fixed for the beginning of the term of the President, the President elect shall have died, the Vice President elect shall become President. If a President shall not have been chosen before the time fixed for the beginning of his term, or if the President elect shall have failed to qualify, then the Vice President elect shall act as President until a President shall have qualified; and the Congress may by law provide for the case wherein neither a President elect nor a Vice President elect shall have qualified, declaring who shall then act as President, or the manner in which one who is to act shall be selected, and such person shall act accordingly until a President or Vice President shall have qualified.

Section 4.

The Congress may by law provide for the case of the death of any of the persons from whom the House of Representatives may choose a President whenever the right of choice shall have devolved upon them, and for the case of the death of any of the persons from whom the Senate may choose a Vice President whenever the right of choice shall have devolved upon them.

Section 5.

Sections 1 and 2 shall take effect on the 15th day of October following the ratification of this article.

Section 6.

This article shall be inoperative unless it shall have been ratified as an amendment to the Constitution by the legislatures of three-fourths of the several States within seven years from the date of its submission.

AMENDMENT XXI

Section 1.

The eighteenth article of amendment to the Constitution of the United States is hereby repealed.

Section 2.

The transportation or importation into any State, Territory, or possession of the United States for delivery or use therein of intoxicating liquors, in violation of the laws thereof, is hereby prohibited.

Section 3.

This article shall be inoperative unless it shall have been ratified as an amendment to the Constitution by conventions in the several States, as provided in the Constitution, within seven years from the date of the submission hereof to the States by the Congress.

AMENDMENT XXII

Section 1.

No person shall be elected to the office of the President more than twice, and no person who has held the office of President, or acted as President, for more than two years of a term to which some other person was elected President shall be elected to the office of the President more than once. But this Article shall not apply to any person holding the office of President when this Article was proposed by the Congress, and shall not prevent any person who may be holding the office of President, or acting as President, during the term within which this Article becomes operative from holding the office of President or acting as President during the remainder of such term.

Section 2.

This article shall be inoperative unless it shall have been ratified as an amendment to the Constitution by the legislatures of three-fourths of the several States within seven years from the date of its submission to the States by the Congress.

AMENDMENT XXIII

Section 1.

The District constituting the seat of Government of the United States shall appoint in such manner as the Congress may direct:

A number of electors of President and Vice President equal to the whole number of Senators and Representatives in Congress to which the District would be entitled if it were a State, but in no event more than the least populous State; they shall be in addition to those appointed by the States, but they shall be considered, for the purposes of the election of President and Vice President, to be electors appointed by a State; and they shall meet in the District and perform such duties as provided by the twelfth article of amendment.

Section 2.

The Congress shall have power to enforce this article by appropriate legislation.

AMENDMENT XXIV

Section 1.

The right of citizens of the United States to vote in any primary or other election for President or Vice President, for electors for President or Vice President, or for Senator or Representative in Congress, shall not be denied or abridged by the United States or any State by reason of failure to pay any poll tax or other tax.

Section 2.

The Congress shall have power to enforce this article by appropriate legislation.

AMENDMENT XXV

Section 1.

In case of the removal of the President from office or of his death or resignation, the Vice President shall become President.

Section 2.

Whenever there is a vacancy in the office of the Vice President, the President shall nominate a Vice President who shall take office upon confirmation by a majority vote of both Houses of Congress.

Section 3.

Whenever the President transmits to the President pro tempore of the Senate and the Speaker of the House of Representatives his written declaration that he is unable to discharge the powers and duties of his office, and until he transmits to them a written declaration to the contrary, such powers and duties shall be discharged by the Vice President as Acting President.

Section 4.

Whenever the Vice President and a majority of either the principal officers of the executive departments or of such other body as Congress may by law provide, transmit to the President pro tempore of the Senate and the Speaker of the House of Representatives their written declaration that the President is unable to discharge the powers and duties of his office, the Vice President shall immediately assume the powers and duties of the office as Acting President.

Thereafter, when the President transmits to the President pro tempore of the Senate and the Speaker of the House of Representatives his written declaration that no inability exists, he shall resume the powers and duties of his office unless the Vice President and a majority of either the principal officers of the executive department or of such other body as Congress may by law provide, transmit within four days to the President pro tempore of the Senate and the Speaker of the House of Representatives their written declaration that the President is unable to discharge the powers and duties of his office. Thereupon Congress shall decide the issue, assembling within forty-eight hours for that purpose if not in session. If the Congress, within twenty-one days after receipt of the latter written declaration, or, if Congress is not in session, within twenty-one days after Congress is required to assemble, determines by two-thirds vote of both Houses that the President is unable to discharge the powers and duties of his office, the Vice President shall continue to discharge the same as Acting President; otherwise, the President shall resume the powers and duties of his office.

AMENDMENT XXVI

Section 1.

The right of citizens of the United States, who are eighteen years of age or older, to vote shall not be denied or abridged by the United States or by any State on account of age.

Section 2.

The Congress shall have power to enforce this article by appropriate legislation.

AMENDMENT XXVII

No law, varying the compensation for the services of the Senators and Representatives, shall take effect, until an election of Representatives shall have intervened.

Chapter 15

The Federalist Papers

James Madison and Alexander Hamilton

The Federalist Papers, written by Alexander Hamilton (1755–1804), James Madison (1751–1836), and John Jay (1745–1829), aimed to convince the people of New York State to ratify the proposed Constitution. These writers argue that representative government is superior to direct democracy. The masses are easily swayed by their passions, and the use of representatives empowers those who possess the time and commitment to reflect on complex issues. Moreover, by separating the powers of government into different branches—legislative, executive, and judiciary—specific functions can more efficiently be carried out, each branch preventing abuses of power by the others.

—⚬⚬⚬—

NUMBER 10

Among the numerous advantages promised by a well-constructed Union, none deserves to be more accurately developed than its tendency to break and control the violence of faction. The friend of popular governments never finds himself so much alarmed for their character and fate, as when he contemplates their propensity to this dangerous vice. He will not fail, therefore, to set a due value on any plan which, without violating the principles to which he is attached, provides a proper cure for it. The instability, injustice, and confusion introduced into the public councils, have, in truth, been the mortal diseases under which popular governments have everywhere perished; as they continue to be the favorite and fruitful topics from which the adversaries to liberty derive their most specious declamations. The valuable improvements made by the American constitutions on the popular models, both ancient and modern, cannot certainly be too much admired; but it would be an unwarrantable partiality, to contend that they have as effectually obviated the danger on this side, as was wished and expected. Complaints are everywhere heard from our most considerate and virtuous citizens, equally the friends of public and private faith, and of public and personal liberty, that our governments are too unstable, that the public good is disregarded in the conflicts of rival parties, and that measures are too often decided, not according to the rules of justice and the rights of the minor party, but by the superior force of an interested and overbearing majority. However anxiously we may wish that these complaints had no foundation, the evidence of known facts will not permit us to deny that they are in some degree true. It will be found, indeed, on a candid review of our situation, that some of the distresses under which we labor have been erroneously charged on the operation of our governments; but it will be found, at the same time, that other causes will not alone account for many of our heaviest misfortunes; and, particularly, for that prevailing and increasing distrust of public engagements, and alarm for private rights, which are echoed from one end of the continent to the other. These must be chiefly, if not wholly, effects of the unsteadiness and injustice with which a factious spirit has tainted our public administrations.

By a faction, I understand a number of citizens, whether amounting to a majority or minority of the whole, who are united and actuated by some common impulse of passion, or of interest, adverse to the rights of other citizens, or to the permanent and aggregate interests of the community.

There are two methods of curing the mischiefs of faction: the one, by removing its causes; the other, by controlling its effects.

There are again two methods of removing the causes of faction: the one, by destroying the liberty which is essential to its existence; the other, by giving to every citizen the same opinions, the same passions, and the same interests.

It could never be more truly said than of the first remedy, that it was worse than the disease. Liberty is to faction what air is to fire, an aliment without which it instantly expires. But it could not be less folly to abolish liberty, which is essential to political life, because it nourishes faction, than it would be to wish the annihilation of air, which is essential to animal life, because it imparts to fire its destructive agency.

The second expedient is as impracticable as the first would be unwise. As long as the reason of man continues fallible, and he is at liberty to exercise it; different opinions will be formed. As long as the connection subsists between his reason and his self-love, his opinions and his passions will have a reciprocal influence on each other; and the former will be objects to which the latter will attach themselves. The diversity in the faculties of men, from which the rights of property originate, is not less an insuperable obstacle to a uniformity of interests. The protection of these faculties is the first object of government. From the protection of different and unequal faculties of acquiring property, the possession of different degrees and kinds of property immediately results; and from the influence of these on the sentiments and views of the respective proprietors, ensues a division of the society into different interests and parties.

The latent causes of faction are thus sown in the nature of man; and we see them everywhere brought into different degrees of activity, according to the different circumstances of civil society. A zeal for different opinions concerning religion, concerning government, and many other points, as well of speculation as of practice; an attachment to different leaders ambitiously contending for pre-eminence and power; or to persons of other descriptions whose I fortunes have been interesting to the human passions, have, in turn, divided mankind into parties, inflamed them with mutual animosity, and rendered them much more disposed to vex and oppress each other than to co-operate for their common good. So strong is this propensity of mankind to fall into mutual animosities, that where no substantial occasion presents itself, the most frivolous and fanciful distinctions have been sufficient to kindle their unfriendly passions and excite their most violent conflicts. But the most common and durable source of factions has been the various and unequal distribution of property. Those who hold and those who are without property have ever formed distinct interests in society. Those who are creditors, and those who are debtors, fall under a like discrimination. A landed interest, a manufacturing interest, a mercantile interest, a moneyed interest, with many lesser interests, grow up of necessity in civilized nations, and divide them into different classes, actuated by different sentiments and views. The regulation of these various and interfering interests forms the principal task of modern legislation, and involves the spirit of party and faction in the necessary and ordinary operations of the government.

No man is allowed to be a judge in his own cause, because his interest would certainly bias his judgment, and, not improbably, corrupt his integrity. With equal, nay with greater reason, a body of men are unfit to be both judges and parties at the same time; yet what are many of the most important acts of legislation, but so many judicial determinations, not indeed concerning the rights of single persons, but concerning the rights of large bodies of citizens? And what are the different classes of legislators but advocates and parties to the causes which they determine? Is a law proposed concerning private debts? It is a question to which the creditors are parties on one side and the debtors on the other. Justice ought to hold the balance between them. Yet the parties are, and must be, themselves the judges; and the most numerous party, or, in other words, the most powerful faction must be expected to prevail. Shall domestic manufactures be encouraged, and in what degree, by restrictions on foreign manufactures? are questions which would be differently decided by the landed and the manufacturing classes, and probably by neither with a sole regard to justice and the public good. The apportionment of taxes on the various descriptions of property is an act which seems to require the most exact impartiality; yet there is, perhaps, no legislative act in which greater opportunity and temptation are given to a predominant party to trample on the rules of justice. Every shilling with which they overburden the inferior number, is a shilling saved to their own pockets.

It is in vain to say that enlightened statesmen will be able to adjust these clashing interests, and render them all subservient to the public good. Enlightened statesmen will not always be at the helm. Nor, in many cases, can such an adjustment be made at all without taking into view indirect and remote considerations, which will rarely prevail over the immediate interest which one party may find in disregarding the rights of another or the good of the whole.

The inference to which we are brought is, that the *causes* of faction cannot be removed, and that relief is only to be sought in the means of controlling its *effects*.

If a faction consists of less than a majority, relief is supplied by the republican principle, which enables the majority to defeat its sinister views by regular vote. It may clog the administration, it may convulse the society; but it will be unable to execute and mask its violence under the forms of the Constitution. When a majority is included in a faction, the form of popular government, on the other hand, enables it to sacrifice to its ruling passion or interest both the public good and the rights of other citizens. To secure the public good and private rights against the danger of such a faction, and at the same time to preserve the spirit and the form of popular government, is then the great object to which our inquiries are directed. Let me add that it is the great desideratum by which this form of government can be rescued from the opprobrium under which it has so long labored, and be recommended to the esteem and adoption of mankind.

By what means is this object attainable? Evidently by one of two only. Either the existence of the same passion or interest in a majority at the same time must be prevented, or the majority, having such coexistent passion or interest, must be rendered, by their number and local situation, unable to concert and carry into effect schemes of oppression. If the impulse and the opportunity be suffered to coincide, we well know that neither moral nor religious motives can be relied on as an adequate control. They are not found to be such on the injustice and violence of individuals, and lose their efficacy in proportion to the number combined together, that is, in proportion as their efficacy becomes needful.

From this view of the subject it may be concluded that a pure democracy, by which I mean a society consisting of a small number of citizens, who assemble and administer the government in person, can admit of no cure for the mischiefs of faction. A common passion or interest will, in almost every case, be felt by a majority of the whole: a communication and concert result from the form of government itself; and there is nothing to check the inducements to sacrifice the weaker party or an obnoxious individual. Hence it is that such democracies have ever been spectacles of turbulence and contention; have ever been found incompatible with personal security or the rights of property; and have in general been as short in their lives as they have been violent in their deaths. Theoretic politicians, who have patronized this species of government, have erroneously supposed that by reducing mankind to a perfect equality in their political rights, they would, at the same time, be perfectly equalized and assimilated in their possessions, their opinions, and their passions.

A republic, by which I mean a government in which the scheme of representation takes place, opens a different prospect, and promises the cure for which we are seeking. Let us examine the points in which it varies from pure democracy, and we shall comprehend both the nature of the cure and the efficacy which it must derive from the Union.

The two great points of difference between a democracy and a republic are: first, the delegation of the government, in the latter, to a small number of citizens elected by the rest; secondly, the greater number of citizens, and greater sphere of country, over which the latter may be extended.

The effect of the first difference is, on the one hand, to refine and enlarge the public views, by passing them through the medium of a chosen body of citizens, whose wisdom may best discern the true interest of their country, and whose patriotism and love of justice will be least likely to sacrifice it to temporary or partial considerations. Under such a regulation, it may well happen that the public voice, pronounced by the representatives of the people, will be more consonant to the public good than if pronounced by the people themselves, convened for the purpose. On the other hand, the effect may be inverted. Men of factious tempers, of local prejudices, or of sinister designs, may, by intrigue, by corruption, or by other means, first obtain the suffrages, and then betray the interests, of the people. The question resulting is, whether small or extensive republics are more favorable to the election of proper guardians of the public weal; and it is clearly decided in favor of the latter by two obvious considerations:

In the first place, it is to be remarked that, however small the republic may be, the representatives must be raised to a certain number, in order to guard against the cabals of a few; and that, however large it may be, they must be limited to a certain number, in order to guard against the confusion of a multitude. Hence, the number of representatives in the two cases not being in proportion to that of the two constituents, and being proportionally greater in the small republic, it follows that, if the proportion of fit characters be not less in the large than in the small republic, the former will present a greater option, and consequently a greater probability of a fit choice.

In the next place, as each representative will be chosen by a greater number of citizens in the large than in the small republic, it will be more difficult for unworthy candidates to practice with success the vicious arts by which elections are too often carried; and the suffrages of the people being more free, will be more likely to centre in men who possess the most attractive merit and the most diffusive and established characters.

It must be confessed that in this, as in most other cases, there is a mean, on both sides of which inconveniences will be found to lie. By enlarging too much the number of electors, you render the representative too little acquainted with all their local circumstances and lesser interests; as by reducing it too much, you render him unduly attached to these, and too little fit to comprehend and pursue great and national objects. The federal Constitution forms a happy combination in this respect; the great and aggregate interests being referred to the national, the local and particular to the State legislatures.

The other point of difference is, the greater number of citizens and extent of territory which may be brought within the compass of republican than of democratic government; and it is this circumstance principally which renders factious combinations less to be dreaded in the former than in the latter. The smaller the society, the fewer probably will be the distinct parties and interests composing it; the fewer the distinct parties and interests, the more frequently will a majority be found of the same party; and the smaller the number of individuals composing a majority, and the smaller the compass within which they are placed, the more easily will they concert and execute their plans of oppression. Extend the sphere and you take in a greater variety of parties and interests; you make it less probable that a majority of the whole will have a common motive to invade the rights of other citizens; or if such a common motive exists, it will be more difficult for all who feel it to discover their own strength, and to act in unison with each other. Besides other impediments, it may be remarked that, where there is a consciousness of unjust or dishonorable purposes, communication is always checked by distrust in proportion to the number whose concurrence is necessary.

Hence, it clearly appears, that the same advantage which a republic has over a democracy, in controlling the effects of faction, is enjoyed by a large over a small republic—is enjoyed by the Union over the States composing it. Does the advantage consist in the substitution of representatives whose enlightened views and virtuous sentiments render them superior to local prejudices and to schemes of injustice? It will not be denied that the representation of the Union will be most likely to possess these requisite endowments. Does it consist in the greater security afforded by a greater variety of parties, against the event of any one party being able to outnumber and oppress the rest? In an equal degree does the increased variety of parties comprised within the Union, increase this security. Does it, in fine, consist in the greater obstacles opposed to the concert and accomplishment of the secret wishes of an unjust and interested majority? Here, again, the extent of the Union gives it the most palpable advantage.

The influence of factious leaders may kindle a flame within their particular States, but will be unable to spread a general conflagration through the other States. A religious sect may degenerate into a political faction in a part of the Confederacy; but the variety of sects dispersed over the entire face of it must secure the national councils against any danger from that source. A rage for paper money, for an abolition of debts, for an equal division of property, or for any other improper or wicked project, will be less apt to pervade the whole body of the Union than a particular member of it; in the same proportion as such a malady is more likely to taint a particular county or district, than an entire State.

In the extent and proper structure of the Union, therefore, we behold a republican remedy for the diseases most incident to republican government. And according to the degree of pleasure and pride we feel in being republicans, ought to be our zeal in cherishing the spirit and supporting the character of Federalists.

Publius [Madison]

NUMBER 51

To what expedient, then, shall we finally resort, for maintaining in practice the necessary partition of power among the several departments, as laid down in the Constitution? The only answer that can be given is, that as all these exterior provisions are found to be inadequate the defect must be supplied, by so contriving the interior structure of the government as that its several constituent parts may, by their mutual relations, be the means of keeping each other in their proper places. Without presuming to undertake a full development of this important idea, I will hazard a few general observations, which may perhaps place it in a clearer light, and enable us to form a more correct judgment of the principles and structure of the government planned by the convention.

In order to lay a due foundation for that separate and distinct exercise of the different powers of government, which to a certain extent is admitted on all hands to be essential to the preservation of liberty, it is evident that each department should have a will of its own; and consequently should be so constituted that the members of each should have as little agency as possible in the appointment of the members of the others. Were this principle rigorously adhered to, it would require that all the appointments for the supreme executive, legislative, and judiciary magistracies should be drawn from the same fountain of authority, the people, through channels having no communication whatever with one another. Perhaps such a plan of constructing the several departments would be less difficult in practice than it may in contemplation appear. Some difficulties, however, and some additional expense would attend the execution of it. Some deviations, therefore, from the principle must be admitted. In the constitution of the judiciary department in particular, it might be inexpedient to insist rigorously on the principle; first, because peculiar qualifications being essential in the members, the primary consideration ought to be to select that mode of choice which best secures these qualifications; secondly, because the permanent tenure by which the appointments are held in that department, must soon destroy all sense of dependence on the authority conferring them.

It is equally evident, that the members of each department should be as little dependent as possible on those of the others, for the emoluments annexed to their offices. Were the executive magistrate, or the judges, not independent of the legislature in this particular, their independence in every other would be merely nominal.

But the great security against a gradual concentration of the several powers in the same department, consists in giving to those who administer each department the necessary constitutional means and personal motives to resist encroachments of the others. The provision for defence must in this, as in all other cases, be made commensurate to the danger of attack. Ambition must be made to counteract ambition. The interest of the man must be connected with the constitutional rights of the place. It may be a reflection on human nature, that such devices should be necessary to control the abuses of government. But what is government itself, but the greatest of all reflections on human nature? If men were angels, no government would be necessary. If angels were to govern men, neither external nor internal controls on government would be necessary. In framing a government which is to be administered by men over men, the great difficulty lies in this: you must first enable the government to control the governed; and in the next place oblige it to control itself. A dependence on the people is, no doubt, the primary control on the government; but experience has taught mankind the necessity of auxiliary precautions.

This policy of supplying, by opposite and rival interests, the defect of better motives, might be traced through the whole system of human affairs, private as well as public. We see it particularly displayed in all the subordinate distributions of power, where the constant aim is to divide and arrange the several offices in such a manner as that each may be a check on the other—that the private interest of every individual may be a sentinel over the public rights. These inventions of prudence cannot be less requisite in the distribution of the supreme powers of the State.

But it is not possible to give to each department an equal power of self-defence. In republican government, the legislative authority necessarily predominates. The remedy for this inconveniency is to divide the legislature into different branches; and to render them, by different modes of election and different principles of action, as little connected with each other as the nature of their common functions and their common dependence on the society will admit. It may even be necessary to guard against dangerous encroachments by still further precautions. As the weight of the legislative authority requires that it should be thus divided, the weakness of the executive may require, on the other hand, that it should be fortified. An absolute negative on the legislature appears, at first view, to be the natural defence with which the executive magistrate should be armed. But perhaps it would be neither altogether safe nor alone sufficient. On ordinary occasions it might not be exerted with the requisite firmness, and on extraordinary occasions it might be perfidiously abused. May not this defect of an absolute negative be supplied by some qualified connection between this weaker department and the weaker branch of the stronger department, by which the latter may be led to support the constitutional rights of the former, without being too much detached from the rights of its own department?

If the principles on which these observations are founded be just, as I persuade myself they are, and they be applied as a criterion to the several State constitutions, and to the federal Constitution, it will be found that if the latter does not perfectly correspond with them, the former are infinitely less able to bear such a test.

There are, moreover, two considerations particularly applicable to the federal system of America, which place that system in a very interesting point of view.

First. In a single republic, all the power surrendered by the people is submitted to the administration of a single government; and the usurpations are guarded against by a division of the government into distinct and separate departments. In the compound republic of America, the power surrendered by the people is first divided between two distinct governments, and then the portion allotted to each subdivided among distinct and separate departments. Hence a double security arises to the rights of the people. The different governments will control each other, at the same time that each will be controlled by itself.

Second. It is of great importance in a republic not only to guard the society against the oppression of its rulers, but to guard one part of the society against the injustice of the other part. Different interests necessarily exist in different classes of citizens. If a majority be united by a common interest, the rights of the minority will be insecure. There are but two methods of providing against this evil: the one by creating a will in the community independent of the majority—that is, of the society itself; the other, by comprehending in the society so many separate descriptions of citizens as will render an unjust combination of a majority of the whole very improbable, if not impracticable. The first method prevails in all governments possessing an hereditary or self-appointed authority. This, at best, is but a precarious security; because a power independent of the society may as well espouse the unjust views of the major, as the rightful interests of the minor party, and may possibly be turned against both parties. The second method will be exemplified in the federal republic of the United States. Whilst all authority in it will be derived from and dependent on the society, the society itself will be broken into so many parts, interests and classes of citizens, that the rights of individuals, or of the minority, will be in little danger from interested combinations of the majority. In a free government the security for civil rights must be the same as that for religious rights. It consists in the one case in the multiplicity of interests, and in the other in the multiplicity of sects. The degree of security in both cases will depend on the number of interests and sects; and this may be presumed to depend on the extent of country and number of people comprehended under the same government. This view of the subject must particularly recommend a proper federal system to all the sincere and considerate friends of republican government, since it shows that in exact proportion as the territory of the Union may be formed into more circumscribed Confederacies, or States, oppressive combinations of a majority will be facilitated; the best security, under the republican forms, for the rights of every class of citizens, will be diminished; and consequently the stability and independence of some member of the government, the only other security, must be proportionally increased. Justice is the end of government. It is the end of civil society. It ever has been and ever will be pursued until it be obtained, or until liberty be lost in the pursuit. In a society under the forms of which the stronger faction can readily unite and oppress the weaker, anarchy may as truly be said to reign as in a state of nature, where the weaker individual is not secured against the violence of the stronger; and as, in the latter state, even the stronger individuals are prompted, by the uncertainty of their condition, to submit to a government which may protect the weak as well as themselves; so, in the former state, will the more powerful factions or parties be gradually induced, by a like motive, to wish for a government which will protect all parties, the weaker as well as the more powerful. It can be little doubted that if the State of Rhode Island was separated from the Confederacy and left to itself, the insecurity of rights under the popular form of government within such narrow limits would be displayed by such reiterated oppressions of factious majorities that some power altogether independent of the people would soon be called for by the voice of the very factions whose misrule had proved the necessity of it. In the extended republic of the United States, and among the great variety of interests, parties, and sects which it embraces, a coalition of a majority of the whole society could seldom take place on any other principles than those of justice and the general good; whilst there being thus less danger to a minor from the will of a major party, there must be less pretext, also, to provide for the security of the former, by introducing into the government a will not dependent on the latter, or, in other words, a will independent of the society itself. It is no less certain than it is important, notwithstanding the contrary opinions which have been entertained, that the larger the society, provided it lie within a practical sphere, the more duly capable it will be of self-government. And happily for the *republican cause*, the practicable sphere may be carried to a very great extent, by a judicious modification and mixture of the *federal principle*.

Publius [Madison]

NUMBER 70

There is an idea, which is not without its advocates, that a vigorous Executive is inconsistent with the genius of republican government. The enlightened well-wishers to this species of government must at least hope that the supposition is destitute of foundation; since they can never admit its truth, without at the same time admitting the condemnation of their own principles. Energy in the Executive is a leading character in the definition of good government. It is essential to the protection of the community against foreign attacks; it is not less essential to the steady administration of the laws; to the protection of property against those irregular and high-handed combinations which sometimes interrupt the ordinary course of justice; to the security of liberty against the enterprises and assault of ambition, of faction, and of anarchy.

Every man the least conversant in Roman history, knows how often that republic was obliged to take refuge in the absolute power of a single man, under the formidable title of Dictator, as well against the intrigues of ambitious individuals who aspired to the tyranny, and the seditions, of whole classes of the community whose conduct threatened the existence of all government, as against the invasions of external enemies who menaced the conquest and destruction of Rome.

There can be no need, however, to multiply arguments or examples on this head. A feeble Executive implies a feeble execution of the government. A feeble execution is but another phrase for a bad execution; and a government ill executed, whatever it may be in theory, must be, in practice, a bad government.

Taking it for granted, therefore, that all men of sense will agree in the necessity of an energetic Executive, it will only remain to inquire, what are the ingredients which constitute this energy? How far can they be combined with those other ingredients which constitute safety in the republican sense? And how far does this combination characterize the plan which has been reported by the convention?

The ingredients which constitute energy in the Executive are, first, unity; secondly, duration; thirdly, an adequate provision for its support; fourthly, competent powers.

The ingredients which constitute safety in the republican sense are, first, a due dependence on the people; secondly, a due responsibility.

Those politicians and statesmen who have been the most celebrated for the soundness of their principles and for the justice of their views, have declared in favor of a single Executive and a numerous legislature. They have, with great propriety, considered energy as the most necessary qualification of the former, and have regarded this as most applicable to power in a single hand; while they have, with equal propriety, considered the latter as best adapted to deliberation and wisdom, and best calculated to conciliate the confidence of the people and to secure their privileges and interests.

That unity is conducive to energy will not be disputed. Decision, activity, secrecy, and despatch will generally characterize the proceedings of one man in a much more eminent degree than the proceedings of any greater number; and in proportion as the number is increased, these qualities will be diminished. . . .

Wherever two or more persons are engaged in any common enterprise or pursuit, there is always danger of difference of opinion. If it be a public trust or office, in which they are clothed with equal dignity and authority, there is peculiar danger of personal emulation and even animosity. From either, and especially from all these causes, the most bitter dissensions are apt to spring.

Whenever these happen, they lessen the respectability, weaken the authority, and distract the plans and operations of those whom they divide. If they should unfortunately assail the supreme executive magistracy of a country, consisting of a plurality of persons, they might impede or frustrate the most important measures of the government, in the most critical emergencies of the state. And what is still worse, they might split the community into the most violent and irreconcilable factions, adhering differently to the different individuals who composed the magistracy.

Men often oppose a thing, merely because they have had no agency in planning it, or because it may have been planned by those whom they dislike. But if they have been consulted, and have happened to disapprove, opposition then becomes, in their estimation, an indispensable duty of self-love. They seem to think themselves bound in honor, and by all the motives of personal infallibility, to defeat the success of what has been resolved upon contrary to their sentiments. Men of upright, benevolent tempers have too many opportunities of remarking, with horror, to what desperate lengths this disposition is sometimes carried, and how often the great interests of society are sacrificed to the vanity, to the conceit, and to the obstinacy of individuals, who have credit enough to make their passions and their caprices interesting to mankind. Perhaps the question now before the public may, in its consequences, afford melancholy proofs of the effects of this despicable frailty, or rather detestable vice, in the human character.

Upon the principles of a free government, inconveniences from the source just mentioned must necessarily be submitted to in the formation of the legislature; but it is unnecessary, and therefore unwise, to introduce them into the constitution of the Executive. It is here too that they may be most pernicious. In the legislature, promptitude of decision is oftener an evil than a benefit. The differences of opinion, and the jarrings of parties in that department of the government, though they may sometimes obstruct salutary plans, yet often promote deliberation and circumspection, and serve to check excesses in the majority. When a resolution too is once taken, the opposition must be at an end. That resolution is a law, and resistance to it punishable. But no favorable circumstances palliate or atone for the disadvantages of dissension in the executive department. Here, they are pure and unmixed. There is no point at which they cease to operate. They serve to embarrass and weaken the execution of the plan or measure to which they relate, from the first step to the final conclusion of it. They constantly counteract those qualities in the Executive which are the most necessary ingredients in its composition—vigor and expedition, and this without any counterbalancing good. In the conduct of war, in which the energy of the Executive is the bulwark of the national security, every thing would be to be apprehended from its plurality. . . .

But one of the weightiest objections to a plurality in the Executive . . . is, that it tends to conceal faults and destroy responsibility. Responsibility is of two kinds—to censure and to punishment. The first is the more important of the two, especially in an elective office. Man, in public trust, will much oftener act in such a manner as to render him unworthy of being any longer trusted, than in such a manner as to make him obnoxious to legal punishment. But the multiplication of the Executive adds to the difficulty of detection in either case. It often becomes impossible, amidst mutual accusations, to determine on whom the blame or the punishment of a pernicious measure, or series of pernicious measures, ought really to fall. It is shifted from one to another with so much dexterity, and under such plausible appearances, that the public opinion is left in suspense about the real author. The circumstances which may have led to any national miscarriage of misfortune are sometimes so complicated that, where there are a number of actors who may have had different degrees and kinds of agency, though we may clearly see upon the whole that there has been mismanagement, yet it may be impracticable to pronounce to whose account the evil which may have been incurred is truly chargeable. . . .

It is evident from these considerations, that the plurality of the Executive tends to deprive the people of the two greatest securities they can have for the faithful exercise of any delegated power, *first*, the restraints of public opinion, which lose their efficacy, as well on account of the division of the censure attendant on bad measures among a number, as on account of the uncertainty on whom it ought to fall; and, *secondly*, the opportunity of discovering with facility and clearness the misconduct of the persons they trust, in order either to their removal from office, or to their actual punishment in cases which admit of it. . . .

I will only add that, prior to the appearance of the Constitution, I rarely met with an intelligent man from any of the States, who did not admit, as the result of experience, that the UNITY of the executive of this State was one of the best of the distinguishing features of our constitution.

Publius [Hamilton]

Chapter 16

The Declaration of the Rights of Man and of the Citizen

The Declaration was adopted August 26, 1789, by the French Constituent Assembly and served as a preamble to the French constitution of 1791.

The representatives of the people of France, formed into a National Assembly, considering that ignorance, neglect, or contempt of human rights, are the sole causes of public misfortunes and corruptions of Government, have resolved to set forth in a solemn declaration, these natural, imprescriptible, and inalienable rights: that this declaration being constantly present to the minds of the members of the body social, they may be forever kept attentive to their rights and their duties; that the acts of the legislative and executive powers of Government, being capable of being every moment compared with the end of political institutions, may be more respected; and also, that the future claims of the citizens, being directed by simple and incontestable principles, may always tend to the maintenance of the Constitution, and the general happiness.

For these reasons the National Assembly doth recognize and declare, in the presence of the Supreme Being, and with the hope of his blessing and favour, the following sacred rights of men and of citizens:

ONE:

Men are born, and always continue, free and equal in respect of their rights. Civil distinctions, therefore, can be founded only on public utility.

TWO:

The end of all political associations is the preservation of the natural and imprescriptible rights of man; and these rights are liberty, property, security, and resistance of oppression.

THREE:

The nation is essentially the source of all sovereignty; nor can any individual, or any body of men, be entitled to any authority which is not expressly derived from it.

FOUR:

Political liberty consists in the power of doing whatever does not injure another. The exercise of the natural rights of every man, has no other limits than those which are necessary to secure to every other man the free exercise of the same rights; and these limits are determinable only by the law.

FIVE:

The law ought to prohibit only actions hurtful to society. What is not prohibited by the law should not be hindered; nor should anyone be compelled to that which the law does not require.

SIX:

The law is an expression of the will of the community. All citizens have a right to concur, either personally or by their representatives, in its formation. It should be the same to all, whether it protects or punishes; and all being equal in its sight, are equally eligible to all honours, places, and employments, according to their different abilities, without any other distinction than that created by their virtues and talents.

SEVEN:

No man should be accused, arrested, or held in confinement, except in cases determined by the law, and according to the forms which it has prescribed. All who promote, solicit, execute, or cause to be executed, arbitrary orders, ought to be punished, and every citizen called upon, or apprehended by virtue of the law, ought immediately to obey, and renders himself culpable by resistance.

EIGHT:

The law ought to impose no other penalties but such as are absolutely and evidently necessary; and no one ought to be punished, but in virtue of a law promulgated before the offence, and legally applied.

NINE:

Every man being presumed innocent till he has been convicted, whenever his detention becomes indispensable, all rigour to him, more than is necessary to secure his person, ought to be provided against by the law.

TEN:

No man ought to be molested on account of his opinions, not even on account of his religious opinions, provided his avowal of them does not disturb the public order established by the law.

ELEVEN:

The unrestrained communication of thoughts and opinions being one of the most precious rights of man, every citizen may speak, write, and publish freely, provided he is responsible for the abuse of this liberty, in cases determined by the law.

TWELVE:

A public force being necessary to give security to the rights of men and of citizens, that force is instituted for the benefit of the community and not for the particular benefit of the persons to whom it is intrusted.

THIRTEEN:

A common contribution being necessary for the support of the public force, and for defraying the other expenses of government, it ought to be divided equally among the members of the community, according to their abilities.

FOURTEEN:

Every citizen has a right, either by himself or his representative, to a free voice in determining the necessity of public contributions, the appropriation of them, and their amount, mode of assessment, and duration.

FIFTEEN:

Every community has a right to demand of all its agents an account of their conduct.

SIXTEEN:

Every community in which a separation of powers and a security of rights is not provided for, wants a constitution.

SEVENTEEN:

The right to property being inviolable and sacred, no one ought to be deprived of it, except in cases of evident public necessity, legally ascertained, and on condition of a previous just indemnity.

Chapter 17

Democracy in America

Alexis de Tocqueville

Alexis de Tocqueville (1805–1859) was a French aristocrat who traveled to the United States in order to study the prison system. He stayed less than a year, then wrote two remarkably insightful and prescient volumes focusing on America's democratic society and the egalitarianism it embodied. Despite the many virtues of Americans that Tocqueville highlights—such as a respect for rights and a willingness to participate in government—a serious problem looms: the tyranny of the majority. Tocqueville argues that what is particularly insidious about this form of tyranny is that, unlike non-egalitarian social arrangements, it does not take an overt legal form. Rather, it is a power wielded over private opinions that covertly urges the conformity of thought from the minority. As Tocqueville concludes, "I know of no country in which there is so little independence of mind and freedom of discussion as in America."

Alexis de Tocqueville, *Democracy in America*, trans. Henry Reeve and Francis Bowen, revised by the editors.

—◦◦◦—

CHAPTER XIV: *WHAT ARE THE REAL ADVANTAGES WHICH AMERICAN SOCIETY DERIVES FROM A DEMOCRATIC GOVERNMENT*

Before I enter on the present chapter I must remind the reader of what I have more than once observed in this book. The political institutions of the United

States appear to me to be one of the forms of government that a democracy may adopt, but I do not regard the American Constitution as the best, or as the only one, that a democratic people may establish. In showing the advantages which the Americans derive from the government of democracy, I am therefore very far from affirming, or believing, that similar advantages can only be obtained from the same laws.

General Tendency Of The Laws Under American Democracy, And Instincts Of Those Who Apply Them

The defects and weaknesses of a democratic government may readily be discovered; they can be proved by obvious facts, whereas their healthy influence is evident in less obvious ways. A single glance suffices to detect its faults, but its good qualities can only be discerned by long observation. The laws of the American democracy are frequently defective or incomplete; they sometimes attack vested rights, or sanction others which are dangerous to the community; but even if they were good, their frequency would still be evil. How comes it, then, that the American republics prosper and continue?

In the consideration of laws a distinction must be carefully observed between the end at which they aim and the means by which they pursue that end, between their absolute and their relative excellence. If it be the intention of the legislator to favor the interests of the minority at the expense of the majority, and if the measures he takes are so combined as to accomplish the object he has in view with the least possible expense of time and exertion, the law may be well drawn up although its purpose be bad; and the more efficacious it is, the greater the mischief it will cause.

Democratic laws generally tend to promote the welfare of the greatest possible number, for they emanate from the majority of the citizens, who are subject to error but cannot have an interest opposed to their own advantage. The laws of an aristocracy tend, on the contrary, to concentrate wealth and power in the hands of the minority, because an aristocracy, by its very nature, constitutes a minority. It may therefore be asserted, as a general proposition, that the purpose of a democracy in its legislation is more useful to humanity than that of an aristocracy. This, however, is the sum total of its advantages.

Aristocracies are infinitely more expert in the science of legislation than democracies ever can be. They are possessed of a self-control that protects them from the errors of temporary excitement, and they form lasting designs which they mature with the assistance of favorable opportunities. Aristocratic government proceeds with the dexterity of art; it understands how to make the collective force of all its laws converge at the same time to a given point. Such is not the case with democracies, whose laws are almost always ineffective or inopportune. The means of democracy are therefore more imperfect than those of aristocracy, and the measures that it unwittingly adopts are frequently opposed to its own cause, but the object it has in view is more useful.

Let us now imagine a community so organized by nature or by its constitution that it can support the transitory action of bad laws, and that it can await, without destruction, the general tendency of its legislation: we shall then be able to conceive that a democratic government, notwithstanding its defects, will be most fitted to produce the prosperity of this community. This is precisely what has occurred in the United States, and I repeat what I have before remarked that the great advantage of the Americans consists in their being able to commit faults which they may afterwards repair.

An analogous observation may be made respecting public officers. It is easy to perceive that the American democracy frequently errs in the choice of the individuals to whom it entrusts the power of the administration, but it is more difficult to say why the state prospers under their rule. In the first place it is to be remarked that if in a democratic state the governors have less honesty and less capacity than elsewhere, the governed are more enlightened and more attentive to their interests. As the people in democracies are more incessantly vigilant in their affairs and more jealous of their rights, they prevent their representatives from abandoning that general line of conduct which their own interest prescribes. In the second place, it must be remembered that if the democratic magistrate is more apt to misuse his power, he possesses it for a shorter time. But there is yet another reason which is still more general and conclusive. It is no doubt of importance to the welfare of nations that they should be governed by men of talents and virtue, but it is perhaps still more important that the interests of those men should not differ from the interests of the community at large, for if such were the case, their virtues might become useless and their talents turned to bad account. I have said that it is important that the interests of the persons in authority should not conflict with or oppose the interests of the community at large, but I do not insist upon their having the same interests as the whole population, because I am not aware that such a state of things ever existed in any country.

No political form has hitherto been discovered that is equally favorable to the prosperity and the development of all the classes into which society is divided. These classes continue to form, as it were, so many distinct communities in the same nation, and experience has shown that it is no less dangerous to place the fate of these classes exclusively in the hands of any one of them than it is to make one people the arbiter of the destiny of another. When the rich alone govern, the interest of the poor is always endangered, and when the poor make the laws, that of the rich incurs very serious risks. The advantage of democracy does not consist, therefore, as has sometimes been asserted, in favoring the prosperity of all, but simply in contributing to the well-being of the greatest number.

The men who are entrusted with the direction of public affairs in the United States are frequently inferior, in both capacity and morality, to those whom aristocratic institutions would raise to power. But their interest is identified and mingled with that of the majority of their fellow citizens. They may frequently be faithless and frequently mistaken, but they will never systematically adopt a line of conduct opposed to the will of the majority, and it is impossible that they give a dangerous or exclusive tendency to the government.

The maladministration of a democratic magistrate is an isolated fact, which has influence only during the short period for which the individual is elected. Corruption and incapacity do not act as common interests which may connect the people permanently with one another. A corrupt or incapable magistrate will not combine his measures with another magistrate simply because that individual is equally corrupt and incapable as himself, and these two men will never unite their endeavors to promote the corruption and inaptitude of their remote posterity. The ambition and the maneuvers of the one will serve, on the contrary, to unmask the other. The vices of a magistrate in democratic states are usually wholly personal.

But under aristocratic governments public men are swayed by the interest of their order, which, if it is sometimes confounded with the interests of the majority, is very frequently distinct from them. This interest is the common and lasting bond which unites them; it induces them to coalesce and combine their efforts in order to attain an end which does not always ensure the greatest happiness of the greatest number; and it serves not only to connect the persons in authority but to unite them to a considerable portion of the community, since a numerous body of citizens belongs to the aristocracy without being invested with official functions. The aristocratic magistrate is therefore constantly supported by a portion of the community as well as by the government of which he is a member.

The common purpose which in aristocracies connects the interest of the magistrates with that of a portion of their contemporaries identifies it also with that of future generations; they labor for the future as much as for the present. Aristocratic magistrates are urged at the same time toward the same point by the passions of their community, by his own, and, I may almost add, by those of his posterity. Is it, then, wonderful that he does not resist such repeated impulses? And, indeed, aristocracies are often carried away by their class spirit without being corrupted by it; and they unconsciously fashion society to their own ends and prepare it for their own descendants.

The English aristocracy is perhaps the most liberal that has ever existed, and no body of men has ever, uninterruptedly, furnished so many honorable and enlightened individuals to the government of a country. It cannot escape observation, however, that in the legislation of England the interests of the poor have often been sacrificed to the advantage of the rich, and the rights of the majority to the privileges of a few. The consequence is that England at the present day combines the extremes of good and evil fortune in the bosom of her society, and the miseries and privations calamities of her poor almost equal her power and renown.

In the United States, where the public officers have no class interests to promote, the general and constant influence of the government is beneficial, although the individuals who conduct it are frequently unskilful and sometimes contemptible. There is, indeed, a secret tendency in democratic institutions to render the exertions of the citizens subservient to the prosperity of the community, notwithstanding their private vices and mistakes, while in aristocratic institutions there is a secret propensity which, notwithstanding the talents and the virtues of those who conduct the government, leads them to contribute to the evils that oppress their fellow-creatures. In aristocratic governments public men may frequently do injuries that they do not intend, and in democratic states they produce advantages of which they have never thought.

Public Spirit In The United States

There is one sort of patriotic attachment which principally arises from that instinctive, disinterested, and undefinable feeling which connects the affections of individuals with their birthplace. This natural fondness is united with a taste for ancient customs and a reverence for ancient traditions; those who cherish them love their country as they love the mansions of their fathers. They enjoy the tranquillity that it affords them; they cling to the peaceful habits that they have contracted within its bosom; they are attached to the reminiscences that it awakens, and they are even pleased by the state of obedience in which they are placed. This patriotism is sometimes stimulated by religious enthusiasm, and then it is capable of making prodigious efforts. It is in itself a kind of religion; it does not reason, but it acts from the impulse of faith and sentiment. In some nations the monarch has been regarded as a personification of the country, and the fervor of patriotism being converted into the fervor of loyalty, they took a sympathetic pride in his conquests, and glory in his power. At one time, under the ancient monarchy, the French felt a sort of satisfaction in the sense of their dependence upon the arbitrary pleasure of their king, and they were wont to say with pride, "We are the subjects of the most powerful king in the world."

But, like all instinctive passions, this kind of patriotism is more apt to prompt transient exertion than supply the motives of continuous endeavor.

It may save the state in critical circumstances but often allows it to decline in times of peace. While the manners of a people are simple and its faith unshaken, while society is steadily based upon traditional institutions whose legitimacy has never been contested, this instinctive patriotism is wont to endure.

But there is another species of attachment to a country which is more rational than the one I have been describing. It is perhaps less generous and less ardent, but it is more fruitful and more lasting; it springs from knowledge, it is nurtured by the laws, it grows by the exercise of civil rights, and, in the end, it is confounded with the personal interest of the citizen. A man comprehends the influence which the prosperity of his country has upon his own; he is aware that the laws authorize him to contribute to that prosperity, and he labors to promote it because it benefits him and because it is in part his own work.

But epochs sometimes occur in the life of a nation when the ancient customs of a people are changed, public morality destroyed, religious belief disturbed, and the spell of tradition broken, while the diffusion of knowledge is yet imperfect, and the civil rights of the community are ill secured, or confined within very narrow limits. The country then assumes a dim and dubious shape in the eyes of the citizens; they no longer behold it in the soil which they inhabit, for that soil is to them a dull inanimate clod; nor in the usages of their ancestors, which they have been taught to look upon as a debasing yoke; nor in religion, for of that they doubt; nor in the laws, which do not originate in their own authority; nor in the legislator, whom they fear and despise. The country is lost to their senses; they can discover it neither under its own nor under borrowed features, and they retire within a narrow and unenlightened egotism. They are emancipated from prejudice without having acknowledged the empire of reason; they are neither animated by the instinctive patriotism of monarchical subjects nor by the thinking patriotism of republican citizens; they have stopped halfway between the two, in the midst of confusion and distress.

In this predicament, to retreat is impossible, for a people cannot restore the vivacity of its earlier times, any more than a man can return to the innocence of childhood; such things may be regretted, but they cannot be renewed. The only thing, then, that remains to be done is to proceed, and accelerate the union of private with public interests, since the period of disinterested patriotism is gone forever.

I am certainly far from affirming that, in order to obtain this result, the exercise of political rights should be immediately granted to all men. But I maintain that the most powerful and perhaps the only means of interesting men in the welfare of their country is to make them partakers in the government. At the present time civic zeal seems to me inseparable from the exercise of political rights, and I believe that the number of citizens will be found to augment or to decrease in Europe in proportion as those rights are extended.

In the United States the inhabitants have only recently immigrated to the land they now occupy, and brought neither customs nor traditions with them; they meet each other for the first time with no previous acquaintance; in short, the instinctive love of their country can scarcely exist in their minds; but everyone takes as zealous an interest in the affairs of his township, his county, and of the whole state, as if they were his own, because all, in their sphere, take an active part in the government of society.

The lower orders in the United States understand the influence exercised by the general prosperity upon their own welfare; simple as this observation is, it is too rarely made by the people. But in America the people regard this prosperity as the result of their own exertions; the citizen look upon the fortune of the public as his own, and he cooperates in its success, not so much from a sense of pride or of duty, but from what I term *cupidity*.

It is unnecessary to study the institutions and the history of the Americans in order to discover the truth of this remark, for their manners render it sufficiently evident. As the American participates in all that is done in his country, he thinks himself obliged to defend whatever may be censured; for it is not only his country that is then attacked, it is himself. The consequence is that their national pride resorts to a thousand artifices and all the petty tricks of individual vanity.

Nothing is more embarrassing in the ordinary intercourse of life than this irritable patriotism of the Americans. A stranger may be inclined to praise many of the institutions of their country, but he begs permission to blame some things in it, a permission which is, however, inexorably refused. America is therefore a free country, in which, lest anybody should be hurt by your remarks, you are not allowed to speak freely of private individuals, or of the state, of the citizens or of the authorities, of public or of private undertakings, or, in short, of anything at all, except perhaps the climate and the soil; and even then Americans will be found ready to defend both as if they had cooperated in producing them.

In our times we must choose between the patriotism of all and the government of a few; for the social force and activity which the first confers are irreconcilable with the guarantees of tranquillity which the second furnishes.

The Idea Of Rights In The United States

After the idea of virtue, I know no higher principle than that of right, or, to speak more accurately, these two ideas are united in one. The idea of right is simply that of virtue introduced into the political world. It is the idea of right that enabled men to define anarchy and tyranny, and that taught them to remain independent without arrogance and obey without servility. The man who submits to violence is debased by his compliance; but when he obeys the mandate of one who possesses that right of authority which he acknowledges in a fellow creature, he rises in some measure above the person who delivers the command. There are no great men without virtue, and there are no great nations—it may almost be added, there would be no society—without the notion of rights, for what is the condition of a mass of rational and intelligent beings who are united only by the bond of force?

I am persuaded that the only means which we possess at the present time of inculcating the notion of rights, and of rendering it, as it were, palpable to the senses, is to endow all the members of the community with the peaceful exercise of certain rights: this is very clearly seen in children, who are men without the strength and the experience of manhood. When a child begins to move in the midst of the objects which surround him, he is instinctively led to turn everything that he can lay their hands on to his own purposes; he has no notion of the property of others, but as he gradually learns the value of things and begins to perceive that he may in turn be deprived of their possessions, he becomes more circumspect and observes those rights in others which he wishes to have respected in himself. The principle which the child derives from the possession of his toys is taught by the objects of his own. In America those complaints against property in general which are so frequent in Europe are never heard, because in America there are no paupers, and as everyone has property of his own to defend, everyone recognizes the principle upon which he holds it.

The same thing occurs in the political world. In America the lowest classes have conceived a very high notion of political rights, because they exercise those rights, and they refrain from attacking those of other people in order to ensure their own from attack. While in Europe the same classes sometimes resist the supreme power, the American submits without a murmur to the authority of the pettiest magistrate.

This truth is exemplified by the most trivial details of national peculiarities. In France very few pleasures are exclusively reserved for the higher classes; the poor are admitted wherever the rich are received, and they consequently behave with propriety and respect whatever contributes to the enjoyments in which they themselves participate. In England, where wealth has a monopoly of amusement as well as of power, complaints are made that whenever the poor happen to enter the places reserved for the pleasures of the rich, they commit acts of wanton mischief: can this be wondered at, since care has been taken that they should have nothing to lose?

The government of democracy brings the notion of political rights to the level of the humblest citizens, just as the dissemination of wealth brings the notion of property within the reach of all men; to my mind, this is one of its greatest advantages. I do not assert that it is easy to teach men to exercise political rights, but I maintain that, when it is possible, the effects which result from it are highly important, and if there ever was a time at which such an attempt ought to be made, that time is our own. It is clear that the influence of religious belief is shaken and the notion of divine rights declining, that public morality is vitiated and the notion of moral rights disappearing: these are general symptoms of the substitution of argument for faith, and of calculation for the impulses of sentiment. If, in the midst of this general disruption, you do not succeed in connecting the notion of rights with that of private interest, which is the only immutable point in the human heart, what means will you have of governing the world except by fear? When I am told that no measures must be taken to increase the rights of the democracy because the laws are weak and the populace wild, passions excited and the authority of virtue paralyzed, I reply that for these very reasons some measures of the kind must be taken, and I am persuaded that governments are still more interested in taking them than society at large, because governments may perish but society cannot die.

I am not inclined, however, to exaggerate the example that America furnishes. There the people are invested with political rights at a time when they could not be abused, for the inhabitants were few in number and simple in their manners. As they have increased, the Americans have not augmented the power of the democracy; they have rather extended its domain.

It cannot be doubted that the moment at which political rights are granted to a people that had before been without them is a critical though necessary one. A child may kill before he is aware of the value of life; and he may deprive another person of property before he is aware that his own may be taken away. The lower orders, when first they are invested with political rights, stand in relation to those rights in the same position as the child does to the whole of nature, and the celebrated adage may then be applied to them, *Homo puer robustus* [A man is a strong boy]. This truth may be perceived even in America. The states in which the citizens have enjoyed their rights longest are those in which they make the best use of them.

It cannot be repeated too often that nothing is more fertile in prodigies than the art of being free, but there is nothing more arduous than the apprenticeship of liberty. Such is not the case with despotic institutions: despotism often promises to make amends for a thousand previous ills; it supports the right, it protects the oppressed, and it maintains public order. The nation is lulled by the temporary prosperity that it produces, until it is roused to a sense of its own misery. Liberty, on the contrary, is generally established in the midst of agitation, it is perfected by civil discord, and its benefits cannot be appreciated until it is already old.

Respect For The Law In The United States

It is not always feasible to consult the whole people, either directly or indirectly, in the formation of law, but it cannot be denied that, when this is possible, the authority of the law is much augmented. This popular origin, which impairs the excellence and the wisdom of legislation, contributes prodigiously to increase its power. There is an amazing strength in the expression of the will of a whole people, and when it declares itself, even the imagination of those who are most inclined to contest it is overawed. The truth of this fact is well known by parties, and they consequently strive to make out a majority whenever they can. If they have not the greater number of voters on their side, they assert that the true majority abstained from voting; and if they are foiled even there, they have recourse to those persons who had no right to vote.

In the United States, except slaves, servants, and paupers in the receipt of relief from the townships, there is no class of persons who do not exercise the elective franchise and who do not indirectly contribute to make the laws. Those who wish to attack the laws must consequently either modify the opinion of the nation or trample upon its decision.

A second reason, which is still more weighty, may be adduced: in the United States everyone is personally interested in enforcing the obedience of the whole community to the law, for as the minority may shortly rally the majority to its principles, it is interested in professing that respect for the decrees of the legislator which it may soon have occasion to claim for its own. However irksome an enactment may be, the citizens of the United States comply with it, not only because it is the work of the majority but because it originates in his own authority, and he regards it as a contract to which he is himself a party.

In the United States, then, that numerous and turbulent multitude does not exist who, regarding the law as their natural enemy, look upon it with fear and distrust. It is impossible, on the other hand, not to perceive that all classes display the utmost reliance upon the legislation of their country and are attached to it by a kind of parental affection.

I am wrong, however, in saying all classes, for as in America the European scale of authority is inverted; there the wealthy are placed in a position analogous to that of the poor in the Old World, and it is the opulent classes who frequently look upon the law with suspicion. I have already observed that the advantage of democracy is not, as has been sometimes asserted, that it protects the interests of the whole community, but simply that it protects those of the majority. In the United States, where the poor rule, the rich always have something to fear from the abuse of their power. This natural anxiety of the rich may produce a secret dissatisfaction, but society is not disturbed by it, for the same reason that withholds the confidence of the rich from the legislative authority makes them obey its mandates: their wealth, which prevents them from making the law, prevents them from withstanding it. Among civilized nations, only those who have nothing to lose ever revolt, and if the laws of a democracy are not always worthy of respect, at least they are always respected; for those who usually infringe the laws have no excuse for not complying with the enactments they have themselves made and by which they are benefited, while the citizens whose interests might be promoted by the infraction of them are induced, by their character and station, to submit to the decisions of the legislature, whatever they may be. Besides, the people in America obey the law not only because it emanates from the popular authority but because that authority may modify it in any points which may prove harmful; a law is observed because, first, it is a self-imposed evil, and, second, it is an evil of transient duration.

Activity That Pervades All Branches Of The Body Politic In The United States; Influence That It Exercises Upon Society

On passing from a free country into one which is not free, the traveller is struck by the change; in the former all is bustle and activity, in the latter everything is calm and motionless. In the one, amelioration and progress are the topics of inquiry; in the other, it seems as if the community aspired only to repose in the enjoyment of advantages already acquired. Nevertheless, the country which exerts itself so strenuously to promote its welfare is generally more wealthy and more prosperous than that which appears to be so contented with its lot; and when we compare them, we can scarcely conceive how so many new wants are daily felt in the former, while so few seem to occur in the latter.

If this remark is applicable to those free countries which have preserved monarchical forms and aristocratic institutions, it is still more striking in democratic republics. In these states it is not a portion only of the people who endeavor to improve the social conditions but the whole community is engaged in the task; and it is not the exigencies and convenience of a single class for which a provision is to be made, but the exigencies and the convenience of all classes at once.

It is not impossible to conceive the surpassing liberty that the Americans enjoy; some idea may likewise be formed of their extreme equality; but the political activity that pervades the United States must be seen in order to be understood. No sooner do you set foot upon American soil than you are stunned by a kind of tumult; a confused clamor is heard on every side, and a thousand simultaneous voices demand the immediate satisfaction of their social wants. Everything is in motion around you; here, the people of one quarter of a town are met to decide upon the building of a church; there, the election of a representative is going on; a little further the delegates of a district are hastening to the town in order to consult upon some local improvements; or in another place the laborers of a village quit their ploughs to deliberate upon the project of a road or a public school. Meetings are called for the sole purpose of declaring their disapprobation of the conduct pursued by the Government, while in other assemblies the citizens salute the authorities of the day as the fathers of their country. Societies are formed which regard drunkenness as the principal cause of the evils of the state and solemnly bind themselves to give a constant example of temperance.

The great political agitation of the American legislative bodies, which is the only kind of excitement that attracts the attention of foreigners, is a mere episode or a sort of continuation of that universal movement which originates in the lowest classes of the people and extends successively to all the ranks of society. It is impossible to spend more effort in the pursuit of happiness.

It is difficult to say what place is taken up in the life of an inhabitant of the United States by his concern for politics. To take a hand in the regulation of society and to discuss it his biggest concern. This feeling pervades the most trifling habits of life; even the women frequently take relief from their household labors to attend public meetings and listen to political harangues. Debating clubs are to a certain extent a substitute for theatrical entertainments: an American cannot converse, but he can discuss, and his talk falls into a dissertation. He speaks to you as if he was a addressing a meeting, and if he should chance to warm in the course of the discussion, he will infallibly say, "Gentlemen," to the person with whom he is conversing.

In some countries the inhabitants display a certain repugnance to avail themselves of the political privileges which the law gives them; it would seem that they set too high a value upon their time to spend it on the interests of the community, and they prefer to withdraw within a narrow selfishness, marked out by four sunk fences and a quickset hedge. But if an American was condemned to confine his activity to his own affairs, he would be robbed of one half of his existence; he would feel an immense void in the life which he is accustomed to lead, and his wretchedness would be unbearable. I am persuaded that if ever a despotic government is established in America, it will find it more difficult to surmount the habits that free institutions have formed than to conquer the attachment of the citizens to freedom.

This ceaseless agitation which democratic government has introduced into the political world influences all social intercourse. I am not sure that upon the whole this is not the greatest advantage of democracy; and I am much less inclined to applaud it for what it does than for what it causes to be done.

It is incontestable that the people frequently conduct public business badly, but it is impossible that the lower orders should take a part in public business without extending the circle of their ideas and quitting the ordinary routine of their thoughts. The humblest individual who is called upon to cooperate in the government of society acquires a certain degree of self-respect; and as he possesses authority, he can command the services of minds much more enlightened than his own. He is canvassed by a multitude of applicants who seek to deceive him in a thousand different ways, but they instruct him by deceit. He takes part in political undertakings which he did not originate but which give him a taste for undertakings of that kind. New improvements are daily pointed out to him in the property which he holds in common with others, and this gives him the desire of improving that property which is his own. He is perhaps neither happier nor better than those who came before him, but better informed and more active. I have no doubt that the democratic institutions of the United States, joined to the physical constitution of the country, are the cause (not the direct, as is so often asserted, but the indirect cause) of the prodigious commercial activity of the inhabitants. It is not created by the laws, but the people learn how to promote it by the experience derived from legislation.

When the opponents of democracy assert that a single man performs his duties much better than the government of the community, it appears to me that they are right. The government of an individual, supposing an equality of knowledge on either side, is more consistent, more persevering, more uniform, and more accurate in details than that of a multitude, and it selects more judiciously the men it employs. If any deny this, they have never seen a democratic government or have formed their opinion upon partial evidence. It is true that even when local circumstances and the disposition of the people allow democratic institutions to exist, they never display a regular and methodical system of government. Democratic liberty is far from accomplishing all its projects with the skill of an adroit despotism. It frequently abandons them before they have borne their fruits, or risks them when the consequences may prove dangerous, but in the end it produces more than any absolute government, and if it does fewer things well, it does a greater number of things. Under its sway the transactions of the public administration are not nearly so important as what is done by private exertion. Democracy does not confer the most skillful kind of government upon the people, but it produces that which the most skillful governments are frequently unable to awaken, namely, an all-pervading and restless activity, a superabundant force, and an energy which is inseparable from it, and which may, under favorable circumstances, produce the most amazing benefits. These are the true advantages of democracy.

In the present age, when the destinies of Christendom seem to be in suspense, some hasten to assail democracy as its foe while it is yet in its early growth, and others are ready with their vows of adoration for this new deity which is springing forth from chaos. But both parties are imperfectly acquainted with the object of their hatred or of their worship; they strike in the dark and distribute their blows by mere chance.

We must first understand what is wanted of society and its government. Is it your intention to confer a certain elevation upon the human mind, and to teach it to regard the things of this world with generous feelings, to inspire men with a scorn of mere temporal advantage, to give birth to living convictions, and to keep alive the spirit of honorable devotedness? Do you hold it to be a good thing to refine the habits, to embellish the manners, to cultivate the arts of a nation, and to promote the love of poetry, of beauty, and of renown? Would you constitute a people fitted to act with power upon all other nations, prepared for those high enterprises which, whatever be the result of its efforts, will leave a name forever famous in history? If you believe such to be the principal object of society, you must avoid the government of democracy, which would be a very uncertain guide to the end you have in view.

But if you hold it to be expedient to divert moral and intellectual activity of men to the production of comfort and the acquirement of the necessities of life; if a clear understanding be more profitable than genius; if your object is not to stimulate the virtues of heroism, but to create habits of peace; if you had rather witness vices than crimes and are content to meet with fewer noble deeds, provided offenses be diminished in the same proportion; if, instead of living in the midst of a brilliant state of society, you are contented to have prosperity around you; if, in short, you are of the opinion that the principal object of a government is not to confer the greatest possible power and glory upon the body of the nation but to ensure the greatest enjoyment and the least misery to each of the individuals who compose it—if such be your desires, you can have no surer means of satisfying them than by equalizing the conditions of all and establishing democratic institutions.

But if the time is passed at which such a choice was possible, and if some superhuman power impel us towards one or the other of these two governments without consulting our wishes, let us at least endeavor to make the best of that which is allotted to us and, by finding out its good and evil tendencies, be able to foster the former and repress the latter to the utmost.

CHAPTER XV: UNLIMITED POWER OF THE MAJORITY IN THE UNITED STATES, AND ITS CONSEQUENCES

The very essence of democratic government consists in the absolute sovereignty of the majority, for there is nothing in democratic states that is capable of resisting it. Most of the American constitutions have sought to increase this natural strength of the majority by artificial means.

Of all political institutions, the legislature is the one most easily swayed by the will of the majority. The Americans determined that the members of the legislature should be elected by the people directly, and for a very brief term, in order to subject them not only to the general convictions but even to the daily passions of their constituents. The members of both houses are taken from the same classes in society, and are nominated in the same manner, so that the movements of the legislative bodies are almost as rapid and quite as irresistible as those of a single assembly. It is to a legislature thus constituted that almost all the authority of the government has been entrusted.

While the law increased the strength of those authorities which of themselves were strong, it enfeebled more and more those which were naturally weak. It deprived the representatives of the executive power of all stability and independence, and by subjecting them completely to the caprices of the legislature, it robbed them of the slender influence that the nature of a democratic government might have allowed them to retain. In several states the judicial power was also submitted to the elective discretion of the majority, and in all of them its existence was made to depend on the pleasure of the legislative authority, since the representatives were empowered annually to regulate the stipend of the judges.

Custom, however, has done even more than law. A proceeding is becoming more and more general in the United States that will in the end do away with all the guarantees of representative government; it frequently happens that the voters, who choose a delegate, point out a certain line of conduct to him and impose upon him certain positive obligations that he is pledged to fulfill. With the exception of the tumult, this comes to the same thing as if the majority held its deliberations in the market-place.

Several other circumstances combine in rendering the power of the majority in America not only preponderant but irresistible. The moral authority of the majority is partly based upon the notion that there is more intelligence and wisdom in a great number of men united than in a single individual, and that the quantity of legislators is more important than their quality. The theory of equality is thus applied to the intellect of man, and human pride is thus assailed in its last retreat by a doctrine which the minority hesitate to admit and in which they very slowly concur. Like all other powers, and perhaps more than all other, the authority of the many requires the sanction of time; at first it enforces obedience by constraint, but its laws are not respected until they have been long maintained.

The right of governing society, which the majority supposes itself to derive from its superior intelligence, was introduced into the United States by the first settlers, and this idea, which by itself would be sufficient to create a free nation, has now been amalgamated with the manners of the people and the minor incidents of social life.

The French, under the old monarchy, held it for a maxim (which is still a fundamental principle of the English Constitution) that the King could do no wrong; and if he did do wrong, the blame was imputed to his advisers. This notion was highly favorable to habits of obedience, and it enabled the subject to complain of the law without ceasing to love and honor the lawgiver. The Americans entertain the same opinion with respect to the majority.

The moral power of the majority is founded upon yet another principle, which is that the interests of the many are to be preferred to those of the few. It will readily be perceived that the respect here professed for the rights of the majority must naturally increase or diminish according to the state of parties. When a nation is divided into several irreconcilable factions, the privilege of the majority is often overlooked, because it is intolerable to comply with its demands.

If there existed in America a class of citizens whom the legislating majority sought to deprive of exclusive privileges which they had possessed for ages and to bring down from an elevated station to the level of the multitude, it is probable that the minority would be less ready to comply with its laws. But as the United States were colonized by men holding equal rank among themselves, there is as yet no natural or permanent source of dissension between the interests of its different inhabitants.

There are certain communities in which the persons who constitute the minority can never hope to draw the majority over to their side, because they must then give up the very point that is at issue between them. Thus an aristocracy can never become a majority while it retains its exclusive privileges, and it cannot cede its privileges without ceasing to be an aristocracy.

In the United States political questions cannot be taken up in so general and absolute a manner, and all parties are willing to recognize the right of the majority, because they all hope at some future time to turn those rights to their own advantage. The majority in that country, therefore, exercises a prodigious actual authority, and a moral influence which is nearly as great; no obstacles exist which can impede or even retard its progress, or which can induce it to heed the complaints of those whom it crushes in its path. This state of things is harmful in itself and dangerous for the future.

How The Unlimited Power Of The Majority Increases In America The Instability Of Legislation And Administration Inherent In Democracy

I have already spoken of the natural defects of democratic institutions, all of which increase at the same ratio as the power of the majority. To begin with the most evident of them all, the mutability of the laws is an evil inherent in democratic government, because it is natural to democracies to raise new men to power in rapid succession. But this evil is more or less perceptible in proportion to the authority and the means of action which the legislature possesses.

In America the authority exercised by the legislative bodies is supreme; nothing prevents them from accomplishing their wishes with celerity and with irresistible power, and they are supplied with new representatives every year. That is to say, the circumstances which contribute most powerfully to democratic instability, and which admit of the free application of caprice to every object in the state, are here in full operation. Hence America is, at the present day, the country in the world where laws last the shortest time. Almost all the American constitutions have been amended within thirty years: there is therefore not a single American state which has not modified the principles of its legislation in that time. As for the laws themselves, a single glance upon the archives of the different states of the Union suffices to convince one that in America the activity of the legislator never slackens. Not that the American democracy is naturally less stable than any other, but that it is allowed to follow, in the formulation of its laws, its capricious propensities.

The omnipotence of the majority, and the rapid as well as absolute manner in which its decisions are executed in the United States, not only render the law unstable but exercise the same influence upon the execution of the law and the conduct of the public administration. As the majority is the only power that is important to court, all its projects are taken up with the greatest ardor, but no sooner is its attention distracted than all this ardor ceases; while in the free States of Europe the administration is at once independent and secure, so that the projects of the legislature are executed even when its immediate attention may be directed to other objects.

In America certain improvements are undertaken with much more zeal and activity than elsewhere; in Europe the same ends are promoted by much less social effort, more continuously applied.

Some years ago several pious individuals undertook to ameliorate the condition of the prisons. The public was excited by their statements, and the reform of criminals became a popular undertaking. New prisons were built, and for the first time the idea of reforming as well as of punishing the delinquent formed a part of prison discipline.

But this happy change, in which the public had taken so hearty an interest, and which the exertions of the citizens had irresistibly accelerated, could not be completed in a moment. While the new penitentiaries were being erected (and it was the pleasure of the majority that they should be finished with all possible celerity), the old prisons existed and contained a great number of offenders. These jails became more unwholesome and more corrupt in proportion as the new establishments were beautified and improved, forming a contrast that may readily be understood. The majority was so eagerly employed in founding the new prisons that those which already existed were forgotten, and as the general attention was diverted to a novel object, the care which had hitherto been bestowed upon the others ceased. The salutary regulations of discipline were first relaxed and afterwards broken, so that in the immediate neighborhood of a prison which bore witness to the mild and enlightened spirit of our time, dungeons existed that reminded the visitor of the barbarity of the Middle Ages.

Tyranny Of The Majority

I hold it to be an impious and detestable maxim that, politically speaking, a people has a right to do whatsoever it pleases, and yet I have asserted that all authority originates in the will of the majority. Am I then, in contradiction with myself?

A general law—which bears the name of justice—has been made and sanctioned, not only by a majority of this or that people but by a majority of mankind. The rights of every people are consequently confined within the limits of what is just. A nation may be considered as a jury which is empowered to represent society at large and apply the great and general law of justice. Ought such a jury, which represents society, to have more power than the society in which the laws it applies?

When I refuse to obey an unjust law, I do not contest the right which the majority has of commanding, but I simply appeal from the sovereignty of the people to the sovereignty of mankind. It has been asserted that a people can never entirely outstep the boundaries of justice and reason in those affairs which are more peculiarly its own, and that consequently, full power may fearlessly be given to the majority by which it is represented. But this language is that of a slave.

A majority taken collectively may be regarded as a being whose opinions, and most frequently whose interests, are opposed to those of another being, which is styled a minority. If it be admitted that a man, possessing absolute power, may misuse that power by wronging his adversaries, why should a majority not be liable to the same reproach? Men are not apt to change their characters by uniting, nor does their patience in the presence of obstacles increase with the consciousness of their strength. And for these reasons I can never willingly invest any number of my fellow-creatures with that unlimited authority which I should refuse to any one of them.

I do not think that it is possible, for the sake of preserving liberty, to combine several principles in the same government so as to oppose them to one another. The form of government that is usually termed *mixed* has always appeared to me to be a mere chimera. Accurately speaking there is no such thing as a mixed government (with the meaning usually given to that word), because in all communities some one principle of action may be discovered which preponderates over the others. England in the last century, which has been more especially cited as an example of this form of government, was an essentially aristocratic state, although it comprised very powerful elements of democracy, for the laws and customs of the country were such that the aristocracy could not but preponderate in the end and direct public affairs to its own will. The error arose from too much attention being paid to the actual struggle which was going on between the nobles and the people, without considering the probable issue of the contest, which was in reality the important point. When a community really has a mixed government, that is to say, when it is equally divided between two adverse principles, it must either pass through a revolution or fall into complete dissolution.

I am therefore of the opinion that some one social power must always be made to predominate over the others, but I think that liberty is endangered when this power is checked by no obstacles which may retard its course and force it to moderate its own vehemence.

Unlimited power is in itself a bad and dangerous thing; human beings are not competent to exercise it with discretion, and God alone can be omnipotent, because His wisdom and His justice are always equal to His power. But no power upon earth is so worthy of honor in itself, or of reverential obedience to the rights which it represents, that I would consent to admit its uncontrolled and all-predominant authority. When I see that the right and the means of absolute command are conferred on a people or upon a king, upon an aristocracy or a democracy, a monarchy or a republic, I recognize the germ of tyranny, and I journey onward to a land of more hopeful institutions.

In my opinion the main evil of the present democratic institutions of the United States does not arise, as is often asserted in Europe, from their weakness, but from their overpowering strength, and I am not so much alarmed at the excessive liberty which reigns in that country as at the very inadequate securities which exist against tyranny.

When an individual or a party is wronged in the United States, to whom can he apply for redress? If to public opinion, public opinion constitutes the majority; if to the legislature, it represents the majority, and implicitly obeys its injunctions; if to the executive power, it is appointed by the majority, and remains a passive tool in its hands; the public troops consist of the majority under arms; the jury is the majority invested with the right of hearing judicial cases; and in certain states even the judges are elected by the majority. However iniquitous or absurd may be the evil of which you complain, you must submit to it as well as you can.

If, on the other hand, a legislative power could be so constituted as to represent the majority without necessarily being the slave of its passions, an executive, so as to retain a certain degree of uncontrolled authority; and a judiciary, so as to remain independent of the two other powers; a government would be formed which would still be democratic without incurring any risk of tyrannical abuse.

I do not say that tyrannical abuses frequently occur in America at the present day, but I maintain that no sure barrier is established against them, and that the causes which mitigate the government are to be found in the circumstances and the manners of the country more than in its laws.

Effects Of The Unlimited Power Of The Majority Upon The Arbitrary Authority Of American Public Officers

A distinction must be drawn between tyranny and arbitrary power. Tyranny may be exercised by means of the law, and in that case it is not arbitrary; arbitrary power may be exercised for the good of the community at large, in which case it is not tyrannical. Tyranny usually employs arbitrary means, but, if necessary, it can rule without them.

In the United States the unbounded power of the majority, which is favorable to the legal despotism of the legislature, is likewise favorable to the arbitrary authority of the magistrate. The majority has control over making the law and executing it; and as it possesses an equal authority over those who are in power and the community at large, it considers public officers as its passive agents and readily confides to them the task of serving its designs. The details of their office and the privileges that they are to enjoy are rarely defined beforehand, but the majority treats them as a master does his servants, since they are always at work in his sight, and he has the power of directing or reprimanding them at every instant.

In general the American functionaries are far more independent within the sphere that is prescribed to them than the French civil officers. Sometimes, even, they are allowed by the popular authority to exceed those bounds, and as they are protected by the opinion and backed by the cooperation of the majority, they manifest their power in ways that astonish a European. By this means habits are formed in the heart of a free country which may some day prove fatal to its liberties.

Power Exercised By The Majority In America Upon Opinion

It is in the examination of the display of public opinion in the United States that we clearly perceive how far the power of the majority surpasses all the powers with which we are acquainted in Europe. Intellectual principles exercise an invisible and subtle power that mocks all the efforts of tyranny. At the present time the most absolute monarchs in Europe are unable to prevent certain opinions, opposed to their authority, from circulating in secret throughout their dominions and even in their courts. Such is not the case in America; as long as the majority is still undecided, discussion is carried on, but as soon as its decision is irrevocably pronounced, a submissive silence is observed, and the friends, as well as the opponents, of the measure unite in assenting to its propriety. The reason for this is perfectly clear: no monarch is so absolute as to combine all the powers of society in his own hands, and to conquer all opposition with the energy of a majority which is invested with the right of making and of executing the laws.

The authority of a king is purely physical, and it controls the actions of the subject without subduing his private will; but the majority possesses a power which is physical and moral at the same time; it acts upon the will as well as upon the actions of men, and it represses not only all contest, but all controversy.

I know of no country in which there is so little independence of mind and freedom of discussion as in America. In any constitutional state in Europe every sort of religious and political theory may be advocated and propagated abroad, for there is no country in Europe so subdued by any single authority as not to protect from the consequences of his hardihood the man who raises his voice in the cause of truth. If he is unfortunate enough to live under an absolute government, the people is upon his side; if he inhabits a free country, he can, if necessary, find a shelter behind the authority of the throne. The aristocratic part of society supports him in some countries, and the democracy in others. But in a nation where democratic institutions exist, organized like those of the United States, there is but one sole authority, one single element of strength and of success, with nothing beyond it.

In America the majority raises formidable barriers to the liberty of opinion: within these barriers an author may write whatever he pleases, but he will regret it if he ever steps beyond them. Not that he is exposed to the terrors of an auto-da-fé, but he is tormented by continued obloquy and persecution. His political career is closed forever, since he has offended the only authority which is able to promote his success. Every sort of compensation, even that of celebrity, is refused to him. Before he published his opinions he imagined that he held them in common with many others, but no sooner has he declared them openly than he is loudly censured by his overbearing opponents, while those who think like him without having the courage to speak abandon him in silence. He yields at length, oppressed by the daily efforts he has been making, and he subsides into silence, as if he was tormented by remorse for having spoken the truth.

Fetters and headsmen were the coarse instruments that tyranny formerly employed, but the civilization of our age has refined the arts of despotism which seem, however, to have been sufficiently perfected before. The excesses of monarchical power had devised a variety of physical means of oppression; the democratic republics of the present day have rendered it as entirely an affair of the mind as the will which it is intended to coerce. Under the absolute sway of an individual despot the body was attacked in order to subdue the soul, and the soul escaped the blows which were directed against it and rose superior to the attempt; but such is not the course adopted by tyranny in democratic republics; there the body is left free, and the soul is enslaved. The sovereign can no longer say, "You shall think as I do on pain of death;" but he says, "You are free to think differently from me, and to retain your life, your property, and all that you possess, but you are henceforth an alien among your people. You may retain your civil rights, but they will be useless to you, for you will never be chosen by your fellow-citizens if you solicit their suffrages, and they will affect to scorn you if you ask for their esteem. You will remain among men, but you will be deprived of the rights of mankind. Your fellow creatures will shun you like an impure being, and those who believe in your innocence will abandon you, lest they should be shunned in their turn. Go in peace! I have given you your life, but it is an existence worse than death."

Monarchical institutions have dishonored despotism; let us beware lest democratic republics should restore oppression and render it less odious and degrading in the eyes of the many by making it still more onerous to the few.

Works have been published in the proudest nations of the Old World expressly intended to censure the vices and deride the follies of the times; Labruyère inhabited the palace of Louis XIV when he composed his chapter upon the Great, and Molière criticized the courtiers in the very pieces which were acted before the Court. But the ruling power in the United States is not to be made game of; the smallest reproach irritates its sensibility, and the slightest joke that has any foundation in truth renders it indignant; from the style of its language to the more solid virtues of its character, everything must be made the subject of encomium. No writer, whatever be his eminence, can escape from this tribute of adulation to his fellow citizens. The majority lives in the perpetual practice of self-applause, and there are certain truths which the Americans can only learn from strangers or from experience.

If great writers have not at present existed in America, the reason is given in these facts; there can be no literary genius without freedom of opinion, and freedom of opinion does not exist in America. The Inquisition has never been able to prevent a vast number of anti-religious books from circulating in Spain. The empire of the majority succeeds much better in the United States, since it actually removes the wish to publish them. Unbelievers are to be met with in America, but there is no public organ of infidelity. Attempts have been made by some governments to protect the morality of nations by prohibiting licentious books. In the United States no one is punished for this sort of works, but no one is induced to write them; not because all the citizens are immaculate in their manners, but because the majority of the community is decent and orderly.

In these cases the advantages derived from the exercise of this power are unquestionable, and I am simply discussing the nature of the power itself. This irresistible authority is a constant fact, and its judicious exercise is only an accident.

Effects Of The Tyranny Of The Majority Upon The National Character Of The Americans

The tendencies to which I have just alluded are as yet only slightly perceptible in political society, but they already begin to exercise an unfavorable influence upon the national character of the Americans. I am inclined to attribute the singular paucity of distinguished political characters to the ever-increasing activity of the despotism of the majority in the United States.

When the American Revolution broke out they arose in great numbers, for public opinion then served, not to tyrannize over, but to direct the exertions of individuals. Those celebrated men took a full part in the general agitation of mind common at that period, and they attained a high degree of personal fame, which was reflected back upon the nation, but which was by no means borrowed from it.

In absolute governments the great nobles who are nearest to the throne flatter the passions of the sovereign, and voluntarily truckle to his caprices. But the mass of the nation does not degrade itself by servitude: it often submits from weakness, from habit, or from ignorance, and sometimes from loyalty. Some nations have been known to sacrifice their own desires to those of the sovereign with pleasure and pride, thus exhibiting a sort of independence in the very act of submission. These peoples are miserable, but they are not degraded. There is a great difference between doing what one does not approve and feigning to approve what one does; the one is the necessary case of a weak person, the other befits the temper of a lackey.

In free countries, where everyone is more or less called upon to give his opinion on the affairs of state; in democratic republics, where public life is incessantly mingled with domestic affairs, where the sovereign authority is accessible on every side, and where its attention can almost always be attracted by vociferation, more persons are to be met with who speculate upon its weaknesses and live ministering to its passions than in absolute monarchies. Not because men are naturally worse in these states than elsewhere, but the temptation is stronger, and at the same time of easier access. The result is a far more extensive debasement of the characters of citizens.

Democratic republics extend the practice of currying favor with the many and introduce it into a greater number of classes at once; this is one of the most serious reproaches that can be addressed to them. This is especially true in democratic states organized on the principles of the American republics, where the authority of the majority is so absolute and irresistible that one must give up one's rights as a citizen and almost abjure one's quality as a human being, if one intends to stray from the track which it prescribes.

In that immense crowd which throngs the avenues to power in the United States, I found very few men who displayed any of that manly candor and masculine independence of opinion which frequently distinguished the Americans in former times, and which constitutes the leading feature in distinguished characters, wherever they may be found. It seems at first sight as if all the minds of the Americans were formed upon one model, so accurately do they correspond in their manner of judging. A stranger does, indeed, sometimes meet with Americans who dissent from these rigorous formulas, with men who deplore the defects of the laws, the mutability and the ignorance of democracy, who even go so far as to observe the evil tendencies which impair the national character, and to point out such remedies as it might be possible to apply, but no one is there to hear these things besides yourself, and you, to whom these secret reflections are confided, are a stranger and a bird of passage. They are very ready to communicate truths which are useless to you, but they continue to hold a different language in public.

If these lines are ever read in America, I am well assured of two things: in the first place, that all who peruse them will raise their voices to condemn me; and in the second place, that many of them will acquit me at the bottom of their conscience.

I have heard of patriotism in the United States, and I have found it among the people, but never among the leaders of the people. This may be explained by analogy; despotism debases the oppressed much more than the oppressor: in absolute monarchies the king has often great virtues, but the courtiers are invariably servile. It is true that the American courtiers do not say "Sire," or "Your Majesty," a distinction without a difference. They are forever talking of the natural intelligence of the populace they serve; they do not debate the question as to which of the virtues of their master is preeminently worthy of admiration, for they assure him that he possesses all the virtues under heaven without having acquired them or without caring to acquire them; they do not give him their daughters and their wives to be raised at his pleasure to the rank of his concubines, but, by sacrificing their opinions, they prostitute themselves. Moralists and philosophers in America are not obliged to conceal their opinions under the veil of allegory, but before they venture upon a harsh truth, they say, "We are aware that the people which we are addressing are too superior to all the weaknesses of human nature to lose the command of their temper for an instant; and we should not hold this language if we were not speaking to men whom their virtues and their intelligence render more worthy of freedom than all the rest of the world." It would have been impossible for the sycophants of Louis XIV to flatter more dexterously.

For my part, I am persuaded that in all governments, whatever their nature may be, servility will cower to force, and adulation will follow power. The only means of preventing men from degrading themselves is to invest no one with that unlimited authority which is the surest method of debasing them.

The Greatest Dangers Of The American Republics Proceed From The Unlimited Power Of The Majority

Governments usually perish from impotence or tyranny. In the former case their power escapes from them; in the latter it is wrested from their grasp. Many observers who have witnessed the anarchy of democratic states have imagined that the government of those states was naturally weak and impotent. The truth is that when once hostilities are begun between parties, the government loses its control over society. But I do not think that a democratic power is naturally without force or resources: say, rather, that it is almost always by the abuse of its force and the misemployment of its resources that a democratic government fails. Anarchy is almost always produced by its tyranny or its mistakes but not by its want of strength.

It is important not to confound stability with force, or the greatness of a thing with its duration. In democratic republics, the power that directs society is not stable, for it often changes hands and assumes a new direction. But whichever way it turns, its force is almost irresistible. The governments of the American republics appear to me to be as much centralized as those of the absolute monarchies of Europe, and more energetic than they are. I do not, therefore, imagine that they will perish from weakness.

If ever the free institutions of America are destroyed, that event may be attributed to the unlimited authority of the majority, which may at some future time urge the minorities to desperation and oblige them to have recourse to physical force. Anarchy will then be the result, but it will have been brought about by despotism.

Mr. Madison expresses the same opinion in *The Federalist*, No. 51. "It is of great importance in a republic not only to guard the society against the oppression of its rulers, but to guard one part of the society against the injustice of the other part. . . . Justice is the end of government. It is the end of civil society. It ever has been and ever will be pursued until it be obtained, or until liberty be lost in the pursuit. In a society under the forms of which the stronger faction can readily unite and oppress the weaker, anarchy may as truly be said to reign as in a state of nature, where the weaker individual is not secured against the violence of the stronger: and as, in the latter state, even the stronger individuals are prompted by the uncertainty of their condition to submit to a government which may protect the weak as well as themselves, so, in the former state, will the more powerful factions or parties be gradually induced, by a like motive, to wish for a government which will protect all parties, the weaker as well as the more powerful. It can be little doubted that if the State of Rhode Island was separated from the Confederacy and left to itself, the insecurity of rights under the popular form of government within such narrow limits would be displayed by such reiterated oppressions of factious majorities that some power altogether independent of the people would soon be called for by the voice of the very factions whose misrule had proved the necessity of it."

Jefferson has also thus expressed himself in a letter to Madison: "The executive power in our Government is not the only, perhaps not even the principal, object of my solicitude. The tyranny of the legislature is really the danger most to be feared, and will continue to be so for many years to come. The tyranny of the executive power will come in its turn, but at a more distant period."

I am glad to cite the opinion of Jefferson upon this subject rather than that of another, because I consider him to be the most powerful advocate democracy has ever had.

Chapter 18

Economic and Philosophic Manuscripts of 1844

Karl Marx

Karl Marx (1818–1883), a journalist, political economist, and philosopher, was a powerful proponent of communism. He argues that under capitalism the humanity of workers, rather than expressing their creativity, is separated from them and then comes back in an oppressive, alien form. Workers make goods that they lack the resources to own or even fully understand. Division of labor ensures that they perform repetitive, uncooperative tasks that use none of their rational capacities. These conditions put a distance between workers and their essence such that they feel most fully human when away from work. Thus, in capitalist societies, Marx maintains, "What is animal becomes human and what is human becomes animal."

Karl Marx, *Economic and Philosophic Manuscripts of 1844*, trans. Martin Milligan (New York: International Publishers, 1964).

We have proceeded from the premises of political economy. We have accepted its language and its laws. We presupposed private property, the separation of labor, capital and land, and of wages, profit of capital and rent of land—likewise division of labor, competition, the concept of exchange value, etc. On the basis of political economy itself, in its own words, we have shown that the worker sinks to the level of a commodity and becomes indeed the most wretched of commodities; that the wretchedness of the worker is in inverse proportion to the power and magnitude of his production; that the necessary result of competition is the accumulation of capital in a few hands, and thus the restoration of monopoly in a more terrible form; and that finally the distinction between capitalist and land rentier, like that between the tiller of the soil and the factory worker, disappears and that the whole of society must fall apart into the two classes—property owners and propertyless workers.

Political economy starts with the fact of private property; it does not explain it to us. It expresses in general, abstract formulas the *material* process through which private property actually passes, and these formulas it then takes for *laws*. It does not *comprehend* these laws—i.e., it does not demonstrate how they arise from the very nature of private property. Political economy throws no light on the cause of the division between labor and capital, and between capital and land. When, for example, it defines the relationship of wages to profit, it takes the interest of the capitalists to be the ultimate cause, i.e., it takes for granted what it is supposed to explain. Similarly, competition comes in everywhere. It is explained from external circumstances. As to how far these external and apparently accidental circumstances are but the expression of a necessary course of development, political economy teaches us nothing. We have seen how exchange itself appears to it as an accidental fact. The only wheels which political economy sets in motion are *greed*, and the *war amongst the greedy—competition.*

Precisely because political economy does not grasp the way the movement is connected, it was possible to oppose, for instance, the doctrine of competition to the doctrine of monopoly, the doctrine of the freedom of the crafts to the doctrine of the guild, the doctrine of the division of landed property to the doctrine of the big estate—for competition, freedom of the crafts and the division of landed property were explained and comprehended only as accidental, premeditated and violent consequences of monopoly, of the guild system, and of feudal property, not as their necessary, inevitable and natural consequences.

Now, therefore, we have to grasp the intrinsic connection between private property, greed, the separation of labor, capital and landed property; the connection of exchange and competition, of value and the devaluation of man, of monopoly and competition, etc.—the connection between this whole estrangement and the *money* system.

Do not let us go back to a fictitious primordial condition as the political economist does, when he tries to explain. Such a primordial condition explains nothing; it merely pushes the question away into a grey nebulous distance. The economist assumes in the form of a fact, of an event, what he is supposed to deduce—namely, the necessary relationship between two things—between, for example, division of labor and exchange. Thus the theologian explains the origin of evil by the fall of man—that is, he assumes as a fact, in historical form, what has to be explained.

We proceed from an *actual* economic fact.

The worker becomes all the poorer the more wealth he produces, the more his production increases in power and size. The worker becomes an ever cheaper commodity the more commodities he creates. The *devaluation* of the world of men is in direct proportion to the *increasing value* of the world of things. Labor produces not only commodities; it produces itself and the worker as a *commodity*—and this at the same rate at which it produces commodities in general.

This fact expresses merely that the object which labor produces—labor's product—confronts it as *something alien*, as a *power independent* of the producer. The product of labor is labor which has been embodied in an object, which has become material: it is the *objectification* of labor. Labor's realization is its objectification. Under these economic conditions this realization of labor appears as *loss of realization* for the workers; objectification as *loss of the object and bondage to it*; appropriation as *estrangement*, as *alienation*.

So much does labor's realization appear as loss of realization that the worker loses realization to the point of starving to death. So much does objectification appear as loss of the object that the worker is robbed of the objects most necessary not only for his life but for his work. Indeed, labor itself becomes an object which he can obtain only with the greatest effort and with the most irregular interruptions. So much does the appropriation of the object appear as estrangement that the more objects the worker produces the less he can possess and the more he falls under the sway of his product, capital.

All these consequences are implied in the statement that the worker is related to the *product of his labor* as to an alien object. For on this premise it is clear that the more the worker spends himself, the more powerful becomes the alien world of objects which he creates over and against himself, the poorer he himself—his inner world—becomes, the less belongs to him as his own. It is the same in religion. The more man puts into God, the less he retains in himself. The worker puts his life into the object; but now his life no longer belongs to him but to the object. Hence, the greater this activity, the more the worker lacks objects. Whatever the product of his labor is, he is not. Therefore, the greater this product, the less is he himself. The *alienation* of the worker in his product means not only that his labor becomes an object, an *external* existence, but that it exists *outside him*, independently, as something alien to him, and that it becomes a power on its own confronting him. It means that the life which he has conferred on the object confronts him as something hostile and alien.

Let us now look more closely at the *objectification*, at the production of the worker; and in it at the *estrangement*, the *loss* of the object, of his product.

The worker can create nothing without *nature*, without the *sensuous external world.* It is the material on which his labor is realized, in which it is active, from which, and by means of which it produces.

But just as nature provides labor with [the] *means of life* in the sense that labor cannot *live* without objects on which to operate, on the other hand, it also provides the *means of life* in the more restricted sense, i.e., the means for the physical subsistence of the *worker* himself.

Thus the more the worker by his labor *appropriates* the external world, sensuous nature, the more he deprives himself of *means of life* in two respects: first, in that the sensuous external world more and more ceases to be an object belonging to his labor—to be his labor's *means of life;* and, second, in that it more and more ceases to be *means of life* in the immediate sense, means for the physical subsistence of the worker.

In both respects, therefore, the worker becomes a servant of his object, first, in that he receives an *object of labor*, i.e., in that he receives *work*, and, secondly, in that he receives *means of subsistence.* This enables him to exist, first as a *worker;* and second, as a *physical subject.* The height of this servitude is that it is only as a *worker* that he can maintain himself as a *physical subject* and that it is only as a *physical subject* that he is a worker.

(According to the economic laws the estrangement of the worker in his object is expressed thus: the more the worker produces, the less he has to consume; the more values he creates, the more valueless, the more unworthy he becomes; the better formed his product, the more deformed becomes the worker; the more civilized his object, the more barbarous becomes the worker; the more powerful labor becomes, the more powerless becomes the worker; the more ingenious labor becomes, the less ingenious becomes the worker and the more he becomes nature's servant.)

Political economy conceals the estrangement inherent in the nature of labor by not considering the direct *relationship between the* worker (labor) *and production.* It is true that labor produces for the rich wonderful things—but for the worker it produces privation. It produces palaces—but for the worker, hovels. It produces beauty—but for the worker, deformity. It replaces labor by machines, but it throws one section of the workers back into barbarous types of labor and it turns the other section into a machine. It produces intelligence—but for the worker, stupidity, cretinism.

The direct relationship of labor to its products is the relationship of the worker to the objects of his production. The relationship of the man of means to the objects of production and to production itself is only a *consequence* of this first relationship—and confirms it. We shall consider this other aspect later. When we ask, then, what is the essential relationship of labor we are asking about the relationship of the *worker* to production.

Till now we have been considering the estrangement, the alienation of the worker only in one of its aspects, i.e., the worker's relationship to the products of his labor. But the estrangement is manifested not only in the result but in the act of production, within the producing activity, itself. How could the worker come to face the product of his activity as a stranger, were it not that in the very act of production he was estranging himself from himself? The product is after all but the summary of the activity, of production. If then the product of labor is alienation, production itself must be active alienation, the alienation of activity, the activity of alienation. In the estrangement of the object of labor is merely summarized the estrangement, the alienation, in the activity of labor itself.

What, then, constitutes the alienation of labor?

First, the fact that labor is *external* to the worker, i.e., it does not belong to his intrinsic nature; that in his work, therefore, he does not affirm himself but denies himself, does not feel content but unhappy, does not develop freely his physical and mental energy but mortifies his body and ruins his mind. The worker therefore only feels himself outside his work, and in his work feels outside himself. He feels at home when he is not working, and when he is working he does not feel at home. His labor is therefore not voluntary, but coerced; it is *forced labor.* It is therefore not the satisfaction of a need; it is merely a *means* to satisfy needs external to it. Its alien character emerges clearly in the fact that as soon as no physical or other compulsion exists, labor is shunned like the plague. External labor, labor in which man alienates himself, is a labor of self-sacrifice, of mortification. Lastly, the external character of labor for the worker appears in the fact that it is not his own, but someone else's, that it does not belong to him, that in it he belongs, not to himself, but to another. Just as in religion the spontaneous activity of the human imagination, of the human brain and the human heart, operates on the individual independently of him—that is, operates as an alien, divine or diabolical activity—so is the worker's activity not his spontaneous activity. It belongs to another; it is the loss of his self.

As a result, therefore, man (the worker) only feels himself freely active in his animal functions—eating, drinking, procreating, or at most in his dwelling and in dressing-up, etc.; and in his human functions he no longer feels himself to be anything but an animal. What is animal becomes human and what is human becomes animal.

Certainly eating, drinking, procreating, etc., are also genuinely human functions. But taken abstractly, separated from the sphere of all other human activity and turned into sole and ultimate ends, they are animal functions.

We have considered the act of estranging practical human activity, labor, in two of its aspects. (1) The relation of the worker to the *product of labor* as an alien object exercising power over him. This relation is at the same time the relation to the sensuous external world, to the objects of nature, as an alien world inimically opposed to him. (2) The relation of labor to the *act of production* within the *labor* process. This relation is the relation of the worker to his own activity as an alien activity not belonging to him; it is activity as suffering, strength as weakness, begetting as emasculating, the worker's *own* physical and mental energy, his personal life—for what is life but activity?—as an activity which is turned against him, independent of him and not belonging to him. Here we have *self-estrangement*, as previously we had the estrangement of the *thing.*

We have still a third aspect of *estranged labor* to deduce from the two already considered.

Man is a species-being, not only because in practice and in theory he adopts the species (his own as well as those of other things) as his object, but—and this is only another way of expressing it—also because he treats himself as the actual, living species; because he treats himself as a *universal* and therefore a free being.

The life of the species, both in man and in animals, consists physically in the fact that man (like the animal) lives on organic nature; and the more universal man (or the animal) is, the more universal is the sphere of inorganic nature on which he lives. Just as plants, animals, stones, air, light, etc., constitute theoretically a part of human consciousness, partly as objects of natural science, partly as objects of art—his spiritual inorganic nature, spiritual nourishment which he must first prepare to make palatable and digestible—so also in the realm of practice they constitute a part of human life and human activity. Physically man lives only on these products of nature, whether they appear in the form of food, heating, clothes, a dwelling, etc. The universality of man appears in practice precisely in the universality which makes all nature his *inorganic* body—both inasmuch as nature is (1) his direct means of life, and (2) the material, the object, and the instrument of his life activity. Nature is man's *inorganic body*—nature, that is, insofar as it is not itself human body. Man *lives* on nature—means that nature is his *body*, with which he must remain in continuous interchange if he is not to die. That man's physical and spiritual life is linked to nature means simply that nature is linked to itself, for man is a part of nature.

In estranging from man (1) nature, and (2) himself, his own active functions, his life activity, estranged labor estranges the *species* from man. It changes for him the *life of the species* into a means of individual life. First it estranges the life of the species and individual life, and secondly it makes individual life in its abstract form the purpose of the life of the species, likewise in its abstract and estranged form.

For labor, *life activity, productive life* itself, appears to man in the first place merely as a *means* of satisfying a need—the need to maintain physical existence. Yet the productive life is the life of the species. It is life-engendering life. The whole character of a species, its species-character, is contained in the character of its life activity; and free, conscious activity is man's species-character. Life itself appears only as a *means to life.*

The animal is immediately one with its life activity. It does not distinguish itself from it. It is *its life activity.* Man makes his life activity itself the object of his will and of his consciousness. He has conscious life activity. It is not a determination with which he directly merges. Conscious life activity distinguishes man immediately from animal life activity. It is just because of this that he is a species-being. Or it is only because he is a species-being that he is a conscious being, i.e., that his own life is an object for him. Only because of that is his activity free activity. Estranged labor reverses the relationship, so that it is just because man is a conscious being that he makes his life activity, his *essential being*, a mere means to his *existence.*

In creating a *world of objects* by his personal activity, in his *work upon* inorganic nature, man proves himself a conscious species-being, i.e., as a being that treats the species as his own essential being, or that treats itself as a species-being. Admittedly animals also produce. They build themselves nests, dwellings, like the bees, beavers, ants, etc. But an animal only produces what it immediately needs for itself or its young. It produces one-sidedly, whilst man produces universally. It produces only under the dominion of immediate physical need, whilst man produces even when he is free from physical need and only truly produces in freedom therefrom. An animal produces only itself, whilst man reproduces the whole of nature. An animal's product belongs immediately to its physical body, whilst man freely confronts his product. An animal forms only in accordance with the standard and the need of the species to which it belongs, whilst man knows how to produce in accordance with the standard of every species, and knows how to apply everywhere the inherent standard to the object. Man therefore also forms objects in accordance with the laws of beauty.

It is just in his work upon the objective world, therefore, that man really proves himself to be a *species-being.* This production is his active species-life. Through this production, nature appears as *his* work and his reality. The object of labor is, therefore, the *objectification of man's species-life*: for he duplicates himself not only, as in consciousness, intellectually, but also actively, in reality, and therefore he sees himself in a world that he has created. In tearing away from man the object of his production, therefore, estranged labor tears from him his *species-life*, his real objectivity as a member of the species and transforms his advantage over animals into the disadvantage that his inorganic body, nature, is taken from him.

Similarly, in degrading spontaneous, free activity to a means, estranged labor makes man's species-life a means to his physical existence.

The consciousness which man has of his species is thus transformed by estrangement in such a way that species[-life] becomes for him a means.

Estranged labor turns thus:

(3) *Man's species-being*, both nature and his spiritual species-property, into a being *alien* to him, into a *means* of his *individual existence.* It estranges from man his own body, as well as external nature and his spiritual aspect, his *human* aspect.

(4) An immediate consequence of the fact that man is estranged from the product of his labor, from his life activity, from his species-being, is the *estrangement of man* from *man.* When man confronts himself, he confronts the *other* man. What applies to a man's relation to his work, to the product of his labor and to himself, also holds of a man's relation to the other man, and to the other man's labor and object of labor.

In fact, the proposition that man's species-nature is estranged from him means that one man is estranged from the other, as each of them is from man's essential nature.

The estrangement of man, and in fact every relationship in which man [stands] to himself, is realized and expressed only in the relationship in which a man stands to other men.

Hence within the relationship of estranged labor each man views the other in accordance with the standard and the relationship in which he finds himself as a worker.

We took our departure from a fact of political economy—the estrangement of the worker and his production. We have formulated this fact in conceptual terms as *estranged, alienated* labor. We have analyzed this concept—hence analyzing merely a fact of political economy.

Let us now see, further, how the concept of estranged, alienated labor must express and present itself in real life.

If the product of labor is alien to me, if it confronts me as an alien power, to whom, then, does it belong?

To a being *other* than myself.

Who is this being?

The *gods*? To be sure, in the earliest times the principal production (for example, the building of temples, etc., in Egypt, India and Mexico) appears to be in the service of the gods, and the product belongs to the gods. However, the gods on their own were never the lords of labor. No more was *nature.* And what a contradiction it would be if, the more man subjugated nature by his labor and the more the miracles of the gods were rendered superfluous by the miracles of industry, the more man were to renounce the joy of production and the enjoyment of the product to please these powers.

The *alien* being, to whom labor and the product of labor belongs, in whose service labor is done and for whose benefit the product of labor is provided, can only be *man* himself.

If the product of labor does not belong to the worker, if it confronts him as an alien power, then this can only be because it belongs to some *other man than the worker*. If the worker's activity is a torment to him, to another it must give *satisfaction* and pleasure. Not the gods, not nature, but only man himself can be this alien power over man.

We must bear in mind the previous proposition that man's relation to himself becomes for him *objective* and *actual* through his relation to the other man. Thus, if the product of his labor, his labor objectified, is for him an *alien*, *hostile*, powerful object independent of him, then his position towards it is such that someone else is master of this object, someone who is alien, hostile, powerful, and independent of him. If he treats his own activity as an unfree activity, then he treats it as an activity performed in the service, under the dominion, the coercion, and the yoke of another man.

Every self-estrangement of man, from himself and from nature, appears in the relation in which he places himself and nature to men other than and differentiated from himself. For this reason religious self-estrangement necessarily appears in the relationship of the layman to the priest, or again to a mediator, etc., since we are here dealing with the intellectual world. In the real practical world self-estrangement can only become manifest through the real practical relationship to other men. The medium through which estrangement takes place is itself *practical*. Thus through estranged labor man not only creates his relationship to the object and to the act of production as to powers that are alien and hostile to him; he also creates the relationship in which other men stand to his production and to his product, and the relationship in which he stands to these other men. Just as he creates his own production as the loss of his reality, as his punishment; his own product as a loss, as a product not belonging to him; so he creates the domination of the person who does not produce over production and over the product. Just as he estranges his own activity from himself, so he confers upon the stranger an activity which is not his own.

We have until now considered this relationship only from the standpoint of the worker and later on we shall be considering it also from the standpoint of the non-worker.

Through *estranged alienated labor*, then, the worker produces the relationship to this labor of a man alien to labor and standing outside it. The relationship of the worker to labor creates the relationship to it of the capitalist (or whatever one chooses to call the master of labor). *Private property* is thus the product, the result, the necessary consequence, of *alienated labor*, of the external relation of the worker to nature and to himself.

Private property thus results by analysis from the concept of *alienated labor*, i.e., of *alienated man*, of estranged labor, of estranged life, of *estranged man*.

True, it is as a result of the *movement of private property* that we have obtained the concept of *alienated labor (of alienated life)* in political economy. But on analysis of this concept it becomes clear that though private property appears to be the reason, the cause of alienated labor, it is rather its consequence, just as the gods are *originally* not the cause but the effect of man's intellectual confusion. Later this relationship becomes reciprocal.

Only at the culmination of the development of private property does this, its secret, appear again, namely, that on the one hand it is the *product* of alienated labor, and that on the other it is the *means* by which labor alienates itself, the *realization of this alienation.*

This exposition immediately sheds light on various hitherto unsolved conflicts.

(1) Political economy starts from labor as the real soul of production; yet to labor it gives nothing, and to private property everything. Confronting this contradiction, Proudhon has decided in favor of labor against private property. We understand, however, that this apparent contradiction is the contradiction of *estranged labor* with itself, and that political economy has merely formulated the laws of estranged labor.

We also understand, therefore, that *wages* and *private property* are identical. Indeed, where the product, as the object of labor, pays for labor itself, there the wage is but a necessary consequence of labor's estrangement. Likewise, in the wage of labor, labor does not appear as an end in itself but as the servant of the wage. We shall develop this point later, and meanwhile will only draw some conclusions.

An enforced *increase of wages* (disregarding all other difficulties, including the fact that it would only be by force, too, that such an increase, being an anomaly, could be maintained) would therefore be nothing but better *payment for the slave*, and would not win either for the worker or for labor their human status and dignity.

Indeed, even the *equality of wages*, as demanded by Proudhon, only transforms the relationship of the present-day worker to his labor into the relationship of all men to labor. Society is then conceived as an abstract capitalist.

Wages are a direct consequence of estranged labor, and estranged labor is the direct cause of private property. The downfall of the one must therefore involve the downfall of the other.

(2) From the relationship of estranged labor to private property it follows further that the emancipation of society from private property, etc., from

servitude, is expressed in the *political* form of the *emancipation of the workers'*, not that *their* emancipation alone is at stake, but because the emancipation of the workers contains universal human emancipation—and it contains this because the whole of human servitude is involved in the relation of the worker to production, and all relations of servitude are but modifications and consequences of this relation.

Just as we have derived the concept of *private property* from the concept of *estranged, alienated labor* by *analysis*, so we can develop every *category* of political economy with the help of these two factors; and we shall find again in each category, e.g., trade, competition, capital, money only a *particular* and *developed expression* of these first elements.

But before considering this phenomenon, however, let us try to solve two other problems.

(1) To define the general *nature of private property*, as it has arisen as a result of estranged labor, in its relation to *truly human* and *social property.*

(2) We have accepted the *estrangement of labor*, its *alienation*, as a fact, and we have analyzed this fact. How, we now ask, does *man* come to *alienate*, to estrange, his *labor?* How is this estrangement rooted in the nature of human development? We have already gone a long way to the solution of this problem by *transforming* the question of the *origin of private property* into the question of the relation of *alienated labor* to the course of humanity's development. For when one speaks of *private property*, one thinks of dealing with something external to man. When one speaks of labor, one is directly dealing with man himself. This new formulation of the question already contains its solution.

As to (1): The general nature of private property and its relation to truly human property.

Alienated labor has resolved itself for us into two components which depend on one another, or which are but different expressions of one and the same relationship. *Appropriation* appears as *estrangement*, as *alienation*; and *alienation* appears as *appropriation, estrangement* as truly *becoming a citizen?*

We have considered the one side—*alienated* labor in relation to the *worker* himself, i.e., the *relation of alienated labor to itself.* The product, the necessary outcome of this relationship, as we have seen, is the *property relation of the non-worker to the worker and to labor. Private property*, as the material, summary expression of alienated labor, embraces both relations—the *relation of the worker to work and to the product of his labor and to the non-worker*, and the relation of the *non-worker to the worker and to the product of his labor.*

Having seen that in relation to the worker who *appropriates* nature by means of his labor, this appropriation appears as estrangement, his own spontaneous activity as activity for another and as activity of another, vitality as a sacrifice of life, production of the object as loss of the object to an alien power, to an *alien* person—we shall now consider the relation to the worker, to labor and its object of this person who is *alien* to labor and the worker.

First it has to be noted that everything which appears in the worker as an *activity of alienation, of estrangement,* appears in the non-worker as a *state of alienation, of estrangement.*

Secondly, that the worker's *real, practical attitude* in production and to the product (as a state of mind) appears in the non-worker who confronting him as a *theoretical* attitude.

Thirdly, the non-worker does everything against the worker which the worker does against himself; but he does not do against himself what he does against the worker.

Let us look more closely at these three relations.

[At this point the manuscript breaks off unfinished.]

Chapter 19

What to the Slave Is the Fourth of July?

Frederick Douglass

Frederick Douglass (1818–1895) escaped from slavery and became a prominent leader of the abolitionist movement. The speech below, delivered to the
Ladies Anti-Slavery Society of Rochester on July 5, 1852, details the problems faced at that time by the United States of America and offers Douglass's
vision of its future.

⸺≈⟨⟩≈⸺

Mr. President, Friends and Fellow Citizens:

He who could address this audience without a quailing sensation, has
stronger nerves than I have. I do not remember ever to have appeared as a
speaker before any assembly more shrinkingly, nor with greater distrust of
my ability, than I do this day. A feeling has crept over me, quite unfavorable
to the exercise of my limited powers of speech. The task before me is one
which requires much previous thought and study for its proper performance. I
know that apologies of this sort are generally considered flat and unmeaning.
I trust, however, that mine will not be so considered. Should I seem at ease,
my appearance would much misrepresent me. The little experience I have had
in addressing public meetings, in country schoolhouses, avails me nothing on
the present occasion.

The papers and placards say, that I am to deliver a 4th [of] July oration.
This certainly sounds large, and out of the common way, for it is true that
I have often had the privilege to speak in this beautiful Hall, and to address
many who now honor me with their presence. But neither their familiar faces,
nor the perfect gage I think I have of Corinthian Hall, seems to free me from
embarrassment.

The fact is, ladies and gentlemen, the distance between this platform and the slave plantation, from which I escaped, is considerable—and the difficulties to be overcome in getting from the latter to the former, are by no means slight. That I am here to-day is, to me, a matter of astonishment as well as of gratitude. You will not, therefore, be surprised, if in what I have to say I evince no elaborate preparation, nor grace my speech with any high sounding exordium. With little experience and with less learning, I have been able to throw my thoughts hastily and imperfectly together; and trusting to your patient and generous indulgence, I will proceed to lay them before you.

This, for the purpose of this celebration, is the 4th of July. It is the birthday of your National Independence, and of your political freedom. This, to you, is what the Passover was to the emancipated people of God. It carries your minds back to the day, and to the act of your great deliverance; and to the signs, and to the wonders, associated with that act, and that day. This celebration also marks the beginning of another year of your national life; and reminds you that the Republic of America is now 76 years old. I am glad, fellow-citizens, that your nation is so young. Seventy-six years, though a good old age for a man, is but a mere speck in the life of a nation. Three score years and ten is the allotted time for individual men; but nations number their years by thousands. According to this fact, you are, even now, only in the beginning of your national career, still lingering in the period of childhood. I repeat, I am glad this is so. There is hope in the thought, and hope is much needed, under the dark clouds which lower above the horizon. The eye of the reformer is met with angry flashes, portending disastrous times; but his heart may well beat lighter at the thought that America is young, and that she is still in the impressible stage of her existence. May he not hope that high lessons of wisdom, of justice and of truth, will yet give direction to her destiny? Were the nation older, the patriot's heart might be sadder, and the reformer's brow heavier. Its future might be shrouded in gloom, and the hope of its prophets go out in sorrow. There is consolation in the thought that America is young. Great streams are not easily turned from channels, worn deep in the course of ages. They may sometimes rise in quiet and stately majesty, and inundate the land, refreshing and fertilizing the earth with their mysterious properties. They may also rise in wrath and fury, and bear away, on their angry waves, the accumulated wealth of years of toil and hardship. They, however, gradually flow back to the same old channel, and flow on as serenely as ever. But, while the river may not be turned aside, it may dry up, and leave nothing behind but the withered branch, and the unsightly rock, to howl in the abyss-sweeping wind, the sad tale of departed glory. As with rivers so with nations.

Fellow-citizens, I shall not presume to dwell at length on the associations that cluster about this day. The simple story of it is that, 76 years ago, the people of this country were British subjects. The style and title of your "sovereign people" (in which you now glory) was not then born. You were under the British Crown. Your fathers esteemed the English Government as the home government; and England as the fatherland. This home government, you know, although a considerable distance from your home, did, in the exercise of its parental prerogatives, impose upon its colonial children, such restraints, burdens and limitations, as, in its mature judgment, it deemed wise, right and proper.

But, your fathers, who had not adopted the fashionable idea of this day, of the infallibility of government, and the absolute character of its acts, presumed to differ from the home government in respect to the wisdom and the justice of some of those burdens and restraints. They went so far in their excitement as to pronounce the measures of government unjust, unreasonable, and oppressive, and altogether such as ought not to be quietly submitted to. I scarcely need say, fellow-citizens, that my opinion of those measures fully accords with that of your fathers. Such a declaration of agreement on my part would not be worth much to anybody. It would, certainly, prove nothing, as to what part I might have taken, had I lived during the great controversy of 1776. To say now that America was right, and England wrong, is exceedingly easy. Everybody can say it; the dastard, not less than the noble brave, can flippantly discant on the tyranny of England towards the American Colonies. It is fashionable to do so; but there was a time when to pronounce against England, and in favor of the cause of the colonies, tried men's souls. They who did so were accounted in their day, plotters of mischief, agitators and rebels, dangerous men. To side with the right, against the wrong, with the weak against the strong, and with the oppressed against the oppressor! here lies the merit, and the one which, of all others, seems unfashionable in our day. The cause of liberty may be stabbed by the men who glory in the deeds of your fathers. But, to proceed.

Feeling themselves harshly and unjustly treated by the home government, your fathers, like men of honesty, and men of spirit, earnestly sought redress. They petitioned and remonstrated; they did so in a decorous, respectful, and loyal manner. Their conduct was wholly unexceptionable. This, however, did not answer the purpose. They saw themselves treated with sovereign indifference, coldness and scorn. Yet they persevered. They were not the men to look back.

As the sheet anchor takes a firmer hold, when the ship is tossed by the storm, so did the cause of your fathers grow stronger, as it breasted the chilling blasts of kingly displeasure. The greatest and best of British statesmen admitted its justice, and the loftiest eloquence of the British Senate came to its support. But, with that blindness which seems to be the unvarying characteristic of tyrants, since Pharaoh and his hosts were drowned in the Red Sea, the British Government persisted in the exactions complained of.

The madness of this course, we believe, is admitted now, even by England; but we fear the lesson is wholly lost on our present ruler.

Oppression makes a wise man mad. Your fathers were wise men, and if they did not go mad, they became restive under this treatment. They felt themselves the victims of grievous wrongs, wholly incurable in their colonial capacity. With brave men there is always a remedy for oppression. Just here, the idea of a total separation of the colonies from the crown was born! It was a startling idea, much more so, than we, at this distance of time, regard it. The timid and the prudent (as has been intimated) of that day, were, of course, shocked and alarmed by it.

Such people lived then, had lived before, and will, probably, ever have a place on this planet; and their course, in respect to any great change, (no matter how great the good to be attained, or the wrong to be redressed by it), may be calculated with as much precision as can be the course of the stars. They hate all changes, but silver, gold and copper change! Of this sort of change they are always strongly in favor.

These people were called Tories in the days of your fathers; and the appellation, probably, conveyed the same idea that is meant by a more modern, though a somewhat less euphonious term, which we often find in our papers, applied to some of our old politicians.

Their opposition to the then dangerous thought was earnest and powerful; but, amid all their terror and affrighted vociferations against it, the alarming and revolutionary idea moved on, and the country with it.

On the 2nd of July, 1776, the old Continental Congress, to the dismay of the lovers of ease, and the worshipers of property, clothed that dreadful idea with all the authority of national sanction. They did so in the form of a resolution; and as we seldom hit upon resolutions, drawn up in our day whose transparency is at all equal to this, it may refresh your minds and help my story if I read it. "Resolved, That these united colonies are, and of right, ought to be free and Independent States; that they are absolved from all allegiance to the British Crown; and that all political connection between them and the State of Great Britain is, and ought to be, dissolved."

Citizens, your fathers made good that resolution. They succeeded; and to-day you reap the fruits of their success. The freedom gained is yours; and you, therefore, may properly celebrate this anniversary. The 4th of July is the first great fact in your nation's history—the very ring-bolt in the chain of your yet undeveloped destiny.

Pride and patriotism, not less than gratitude, prompt you to celebrate and to hold it in perpetual remembrance. I have said that the Declaration of Independence is the ring-bolt to the chain of your nation's destiny; so, indeed, I regard it. The principles contained in that instrument are saving principles. Stand by those principles, be true to them on all occasions, in all places, against all foes, and at whatever cost.

From the round top of your ship of state, dark and threatening clouds may be seen. Heavy billows, like mountains in the distance, disclose to the lee-ward huge forms of flinty rocks! That bolt drawn, that chain broken, and all is lost. Cling to this day—cling to it, and to its principles, with the grasp of a storm-tossed mariner to a spar at midnight.

The coming into being of a nation, in any circumstances, is an interesting event. But, besides general considerations, there were peculiar circumstances which make the advent of this republic an event of special attractiveness.

The whole scene, as I look back to it, was simple, dignified and sublime.

The population of the country, at the time, stood at the insignificant number of three millions. The country was poor in the munitions of war. The population was weak and scattered, and the country a wilderness unsubdued. There were then no means of concert and combination, such as exist now. Neither steam nor lightning had then been reduced to order and discipline. From the Potomac to the Delaware was a journey of many days. Under these, and innumerable other disadvantages, your fathers declared for liberty and independence and triumphed.

Fellow Citizens, I am not wanting in respect for the fathers of this republic. The signers of the Declaration of Independence were brave men. They were great men too—great enough to give fame to a great age. It does not often happen to a nation to raise, at one time, such a number of truly great men. The point from which I am compelled to view them is not, certainly, the most favorable; and yet I cannot contemplate their great deeds with less than admiration. They were statesmen, patriots and heroes, and for the good they did, and the principles they contended for, I will unite with you to honor their memory.

They loved their country better than their own private interests; and, though this is not the highest form of human excellence, all will concede that it is a rare virtue, and that when it is exhibited, it ought to command respect. He who will, intelligently, lay down his life for his country, is a man whom it is not in human nature to despise. Your fathers staked their lives, their fortunes, and their sacred honor, on the cause of their country. In their admiration of liberty, they lost sight of all other interests.

They were peace men; but they preferred revolution to peaceful submission to bondage. They were quiet men; but they did not shrink from agitating against oppression. They showed forbearance; but that they knew its limits. They believed in order; but not in the order of tyranny. With them, nothing was "settled" that was not right. With them, justice, liberty and humanity were "final"; not slavery and oppression. You may well cherish the memory of such men. They were great in their day and generation. Their solid manhood stands out the more as we contrast it with these degenerate times.

How circumspect, exact and proportionate were all their movements! How unlike the politicians of an hour! Their statesmanship looked beyond the passing moment, and stretched away in strength into the distant future. They seized upon eternal principles, and set a glorious example in their defense. Mark them!

Fully appreciating the hardship to be encountered, firmly believing in the right of their cause, honorably inviting the scrutiny of an on-looking world, reverently appealing to heaven to attest their sincerity, soundly comprehending the solemn responsibility they were about to assume, wisely measuring the terrible odds against them, your fathers, the fathers of this republic, did, most deliberately, under the inspiration of a glorious patriotism, and with a sublime faith in the great principles of justice and freedom, lay deep the corner-stone of the national superstructure, which has risen and still rises in grandeur around you.

Of this fundamental work, this day is the anniversary. Our eyes are met with demonstrations of joyous enthusiasm. Banners and pennants wave exultingly on the breeze. The din of business, too, is hushed. Even Mammon seems to have quitted his grasp on this day. The ear-piercing fife and the stirring drum unite their accents with the ascending peal of a thousand church bells. Prayers are made, hymns are sung, and sermons are preached in honor of this day; while the quick martial tramp of a great and multitudinous nation, echoed back by all the hills, valleys and mountains of a vast continent, bespeak the occasion one of thrilling and universal interest—a nation's jubilee.

Friends and citizens, I need not enter further into the causes which led to this anniversary. Many of you understand them better than I do. You could instruct me in regard to them. That is a branch of knowledge in which you feel, perhaps, a much deeper interest than your speaker. The causes which led to the separation of the colonies from the British crown have never lacked for a tongue. They have all been taught in your common schools, narrated at your firesides, unfolded from your pulpits, and thundered from your legislative halls, and are as familiar to you as household words. They form the staple of your national poetry and eloquence.

I remember, also, that, as a people, Americans are remarkably familiar with all facts which make in their own favor. This is esteemed by some as a national trait—perhaps a national weakness. It is a fact, that whatever makes for the wealth or for the reputation of Americans, and can be had cheap! will be found by Americans. I shall not be charged with slandering Americans, if I say I think the American side of any question may be safely left in American hands.

I leave, therefore, the great deeds of your fathers to other gentlemen whose claim to have been regularly descended will be less likely to be disputed than mine!

My business, if I have any here to-day, is with the present. The accepted time with God and his cause is the ever-living now.

> Trust no future, however pleasant,
> Let the dead past bury its dead;
> Act, act in the living present,
> Heart within, and God overhead.

We have to do with the past only as we can make it useful to the present and to the future. To all inspiring motives, to noble deeds which can be gained from the past, we are welcome. But now is the time, the important time. Your fathers have lived, died, and have done their work, and have done much of it well. You live and must die, and you must do your work. You have no right to enjoy a child's share in the labor of your fathers, unless your children are to be blest by your labors. You have no right to wear out and waste the hard-earned fame of your fathers to cover your indolence. Sydney Smith tells us that men seldom eulogize the wisdom and virtues of their fathers, but to excuse some folly or wickedness of their own. This truth is not a doubtful one. There are illustrations of it near and remote, ancient and modern. It was fashionable, hundreds of years ago, for the children of Jacob to boast, we have "Abraham to our father," when they had long lost Abraham's faith and spirit. That people contented themselves under the shadow of Abraham's great name, while they repudiated the deeds which made his name great. Need I remind you that a similar thing is being done all over this country to-day? Need I tell you that the Jews are not the only people who built the tombs of the prophets, and garnished the sepulchres of the righteous? Washington could not die till he had broken the chains of his slaves. Yet his monument is built up by the price of human blood, and the traders in the bodies and souls of men shout—"We have Washington to our father."—Alas! that it should be so; yet so it is.

> The evil that men do, lives after them,
> The good is oft-interred with their bones.

Fellow-citizens, pardon me, allow me to ask, why am I called upon to speak here to-day? What have I, or those I represent, to do with your national independence? Are the great principles of political freedom and of natural justice, embodied in that Declaration of Independence, extended to us? and am I, therefore, called upon to bring our humble offering to the national altar, and to confess the benefits and express devout gratitude for the blessings resulting from your independence to us?

Would to God, both for your sakes and ours, that an affirmative answer could be truthfully returned to these questions! Then would my task be light, and my burden easy and delightful. For who is there so cold, that a nation's sympathy could not warm him? Who so obdurate and dead to the claims of gratitude, that would not thankfully acknowledge such priceless benefits? Who so stolid and selfish, that would not give his voice to swell the hallelujahs of a nation's jubilee, when the chains of servitude had been torn from his limbs? I am not that man. In a case like that, the dumb might eloquently speak, and the "lame man leap as an hart."

But, such is not the state of the case. I say it with a sad sense of the disparity between us. I am not included within the pale of this glorious anniversary! Your high independence only reveals the immeasurable distance between us. The blessings in which you, this day, rejoice, are not enjoyed in common.—The rich inheritance of justice, liberty, prosperity and independence, bequeathed by your fathers, is shared by you, not by me. The sunlight that brought life and healing to you, has brought stripes and death to me. This Fourth [of] July is yours, not mine. You may rejoice, I must mourn. To drag a man in fetters into the grand illuminated temple of liberty, and call upon him to join you in joyous anthems, were inhuman mockery and sacrilegious irony. Do you mean, citizens, to mock me, by asking me to speak to-day? If so, there is a parallel to your conduct. And let me warn you that it is dangerous to copy the example of a nation whose crimes, lowering up to heaven, were thrown down by the breath of the Almighty, burying that nation in irrecoverable ruin! I can to-day take up the plaintive lament of a peeled and woe- smitten people!

"By the rivers of Babylon, there we sat down. Yea! we wept when we remembered Zion. We hanged our harps upon the willows in the midst thereof. For there, they that carried us away captive, required of us a song; and they who wasted us required of us mirth, saying, Sing us one of the songs of Zion. How can we sing the Lord's song in a strange land? If I forget thee, O Jerusalem, let my right hand forget her cunning. If I do not remember thee, let my tongue cleave to the roof of my mouth."

Fellow-citizens; above your national, tumultuous joy, I hear the mournful wail of millions! whose chains, heavy and grievous yesterday, are, to-day, rendered more intolerable by the jubilee shouts that reach them. If I do forget, if I do not faithfully remember those bleeding children of sorrow this day, "may my right hand forget her cunning, and may my tongue cleave to the roof of my mouth!" To forget them, to pass lightly over their wrongs, and to chime in with the popular theme, would be treason most scandalous and shocking, and would make me a reproach before God and the world. My subject, then fellow-citizens, is AMERICAN SLAVERY. I shall see, this day, and its popular characteristics, from the slave's point of view. Standing, there, identified with the American bondman, making his wrongs mine, I do not hesitate to declare, with all my soul, that the character and conduct of this nation never looked blacker to me than on this 4th of July! Whether we turn to the declarations of the past, or to the professions of the present, the conduct of the nation seems equally hideous and revolting. America is false to the past, false to the present, and solemnly binds herself to be false to the future. Standing with God and the crushed and bleeding slave on this occasion, I will, in the name of humanity which is outraged, in the name of liberty which is fettered, in the name of the constitution and the Bible, which are disregarded and trampled upon, dare to call in question and to denounce, with all the emphasis I can command, everything that serves to perpetuate slavery—the great sin and shame of America! "I will not equivocate; I will not excuse"; I will use the severest language I can command; and yet not one word shall escape me that any man, whose judgment is not blinded by prejudice, or who is not at heart a slaveholder, shall not confess to be right and just.

But I fancy I hear some one of my audience say, it is just in this circumstance that you and your brother abolitionists fail to make a favorable impression on the public mind. Would you argue more, and denounce less, would you persuade more, and rebuke less, your cause would be much more likely to succeed. But, I submit, where all is plain there is nothing to be argued. What point in the anti-slavery creed would you have me argue? On what branch of the subject do the people of this country need light? Must I undertake to prove that the slave is a man? That point is conceded already. Nobody doubts it. The slaveholders themselves acknowledge it in the enactment of laws for their government. They acknowledge it when they punish disobedience on the part of the slave. There are seventy-two crimes in the State of Virginia, which, if committed by a black man, (no matter how ignorant he be), subject him to the punishment of death; while only two of the same crimes will subject a white man to the like punishment. What is this but the acknowledgement that the slave is a moral, intellectual and responsible being? The manhood of the slave is conceded. It is admitted in the fact that Southern statute books are covered with enactments forbidding, under severe fines and penalties, the teaching of the slave to read or to write. When you can point to any such laws, in reference to the beasts of the field, then I may consent to argue the manhood of the slave. When the dogs in your streets, when the fowls of the air, when the cattle on your hills, when the fish of the sea, and the reptiles that crawl, shall be unable to distinguish the slave from a brute, then will I argue with you that the slave is a man!

For the present, it is enough to affirm the equal manhood of the Negro race. Is it not astonishing that, while we are ploughing, planting and reaping, using all kinds of mechanical tools, erecting houses, constructing bridges, building ships, working in metals of brass, iron, copper, silver and gold; that, while we are reading, writing and cyphering, acting as clerks, merchants and secretaries, having among us lawyers, doctors, ministers, poets, authors, editors, orators and teachers; that, while we are engaged in all manner of enterprises common to other men, digging gold in California, capturing the whale in the Pacific, feeding sheep and cattle on the hill-side, living, moving, acting, thinking, planning, living in families as husbands, wives and children, and, above all, confessing and worshipping the Christian's God, and looking hopefully for life and immortality beyond the grave, we are called upon to prove that we are men!

Would you have me argue that man is entitled to liberty? that he is the rightful owner of his own body? You have already declared it. Must I argue the wrongfulness of slavery? Is that a question for Republicans? Is it to be settled by the rules of logic and argumentation, as a matter beset with great difficulty, involving a doubtful application of the principle of justice, hard to be understood? How should I look to-day, in the presence of Americans, dividing, and subdividing a discourse, to show that men have a natural right to freedom? speaking of it relatively, and positively, negatively, and affirmatively. To do so, would be to make myself ridiculous, and to offer an insult to your understanding.—There is not a man beneath the canopy of heaven, that does not know that slavery is wrong for him.

What, am I to argue that it is wrong to make men brutes, to rob them of their liberty, to work them without wages, to keep them ignorant of their relations to their fellow men, to beat them with sticks, to flay their flesh with the lash, to load their limbs with irons, to hunt them with dogs, to sell them at auction, to sunder their families, to knock out their teeth, to burn their flesh, to starve them into obedience and submission to their masters? Must I argue that a system thus marked with blood, and stained with pollution, is wrong? No! I will not. I have better employments for my time and strength than such arguments would imply.

What, then, remains to be argued? Is it that slavery is not divine; that God did not establish it; that our doctors of divinity are mistaken? There is blasphemy in the thought. That which is inhuman, cannot be divine! Who can reason on such a proposition? They that can, may; I cannot. The time for such argument is passed.

At a time like this, scorching irony, not convincing argument, is needed. O! had I the ability, and could I reach the nation's ear, I would, to-day, pour out a fiery stream of biting ridicule, blasting reproach, withering sarcasm, and stern rebuke. For it is not light that is needed, but fire; it is not the gentle shower, but thunder. We need the storm, the whirlwind, and the earthquake. The feeling of the nation must be quickened; the conscience of the nation must be roused; the propriety of the nation must be startled; the hypocrisy of the nation must be exposed; and its crimes against God and man must be proclaimed and denounced.

What, to the American slave, is your 4th of July? I answer: a day that reveals to him, more than all other days in the year, the gross injustice and cruelty to which he is the constant victim. To him, your celebration is a sham; your boasted liberty, an unholy license; your national greatness, swelling vanity; your sounds of rejoicing are empty and heartless; your denunciations of tyrants, brass fronted impudence; your shouts of liberty and equality, hollow mockery; your prayers and hymns, your sermons and thanksgivings, with all your religious parade, and solemnity, are, to him, mere bombast, fraud, deception, impiety, and hypocrisy—a thin veil to cover up crimes which would disgrace a nation of savages. There is not a nation on the earth guilty of practices, more shocking and bloody, than are the people of these United States, at this very hour.

Go where you may, search where you will, roam through all the monarchies and despotisms of the old world, travel through South America, search out every abuse, and when you have found the last, lay your facts by the side of the everyday practices of this nation, and you will say with me, that, for revolting barbarity and shameless hypocrisy, America reigns without a rival.

Take the American slave-trade, which, we are told by the papers, is especially prosperous just now. Ex-Senator Benton tells us that the price of men was never higher than now. He mentions the fact to show that slavery is in no danger. This trade is one of the peculiarities of American institutions. It is carried on in all the large towns and cities in one-half of this confederacy; and millions are pocketed every year, by dealers in this horrid traffic. In several states, this trade is a chief source of wealth. It is called (in contradistinction to the foreign slave-trade) "the internal slave trade." It is, probably, called so, too, in order to divert from it the horror with which the foreign slave-trade is contemplated. That trade has long since been denounced by this government, as piracy. It has been denounced with burning words, from the high places of the nation, as an execrable traffic. To arrest it, to put an end to it, this nation keeps a squadron, at immense cost, on the coast of Africa. Everywhere, in this country, it is safe to speak of this foreign slave-trade, as a most inhuman traffic, opposed alike to the laws of God and of man. The duty to extirpate and destroy it, is admitted even by our DOCTORS OF DIVINITY. In order to put an end to it, some of these last have consented that their colored brethren (nominally free) should leave this country, and establish themselves on the western coast of Africa! It is, however, a notable fact that, while so much execration is poured out by Americans upon those engaged in the foreign slave-trade, the men engaged in the slave-trade between the states pass without condemnation, and their business is deemed honorable.

Behold the practical operation of this internal slave-trade, the American slave-trade, sustained by American politics and America religion. Here you will see men and women reared like swine for the market. You know what is a swine-drover? I will show you a man-drover. They inhabit all our Southern States. They perambulate the country, and crowd the highways of the nation, with droves of human stock. You will see one of these human flesh-jobbers, armed with pistol, whip and bowie-knife, driving a company of a hundred men, women, and children, from the Potomac to the slave market at New Orleans. These wretched people are to be sold singly, or in lots, to suit purchasers. They are food for the cotton-field, and the deadly sugar-mill. Mark the sad procession, as it moves wearily along, and the inhuman wretch who drives them. Hear his savage yells and his blood-chilling oaths, as he hurries on his affrighted captives! There, see the old man, with locks thinned and gray. Cast one glance, if you please, upon that young mother, whose shoulders are bare to the scorching sun, her briny tears falling on the brow of the babe in her arms. See, too, that girl of thirteen, weeping, yes! weeping, as she thinks of the mother from whom she has been torn! The drove moves tardily. Heat and sorrow have nearly consumed their strength; suddenly you hear a quick snap, like the discharge of a rifle; the fetters clank, and the chain rattles simultaneously; your ears are saluted with a scream, that seems to have torn its way to the center of your soul! The crack you heard, was the sound of the slave-whip; the scream you heard, was from the woman you saw with the babe. Her speed had faltered under the weight of her child and her chains! that gash on her shoulder tells her to move on. Follow the drove to New Orleans. Attend the auction; see men examined like horses; see the forms of women rudely and brutally exposed to the shocking gaze of American slave-buyers. See this drove sold and separated forever; and never forget the deep, sad sobs that arose from that scattered multitude. Tell me citizens, WHERE, under the sun, you can witness a spectacle more fiendish and shocking. Yet this is but a glance at the American slave-trade, as it exists, at this moment, in the ruling part of the United States.

I was born amid such sights and scenes. To me the American slave-trade is a terrible reality. When a child, my soul was often pierced with a sense of its horrors. I lived on Philpot Street, Fell's Point, Baltimore, and have watched from the wharves, the slave ships in the Basin, anchored from the shore, with their cargoes of human flesh, waiting for favorable winds to waft them down the Chesapeake. There was, at that time, a grand slave mart kept at the head of Pratt Street, by Austin Woldfolk. His agents were sent into every town and county in Maryland, announcing their arrival, through the papers, and on flaming "hand-bills," headed CASH FOR NEGROES. These men were generally well dressed men, and very captivating in their manners. Ever ready to drink, to treat, and to gamble. The fate of many a slave has depended upon the turn of a single card; and many a child has been snatched from the arms of its mother by bargains arranged in a state of brutal drunkenness.

The flesh-mongers gather up their victims by dozens, and drive them, chained, to the general depot at Baltimore. When a sufficient number have been collected here, a ship is chartered, for the purpose of conveying the forlorn crew to Mobile, or to New Orleans. From the slave prison to the ship, they are usually driven in the darkness of night; for since the antislavery agitation, a certain caution is observed.

In the deep still darkness of midnight, I have been often aroused by the dead heavy footsteps, and the piteous cries of the chained gangs that passed our door. The anguish of my boyish heart was intense; and I was often consoled, when speaking to my mistress in the morning, to hear her say that the custom was very wicked; that she hated to hear the rattle of the chains, and the heart-rending cries. I was glad to find one who sympathized with me in my horror.

Fellow-citizens, this murderous traffic is, to-day, in active operation in this boasted republic. In the solitude of my spirit, I see clouds of dust raised on the highways of the South; I see the bleeding footsteps; I hear the doleful wail of fettered humanity, on the way to the slave-markets, where the victims are to be sold like horses, sheep, and swine, knocked off to the highest bidder. There I see the tenderest ties ruthlessly broken, to gratify the lust, caprice and rapacity of the buyers and sellers of men. My soul sickens at the sight.

> Is this the land your Fathers loved,
> The freedom which they toiled to win?
> Is this the earth whereon they moved?
> Are these the graves they slumber in?

But a still more inhuman, disgraceful, and scandalous state of things remains to be presented. By an act of the American Congress, not yet two years old, slavery has been nationalized in its most horrible and revolting form. By that act, Mason and Dixon's line has been obliterated; New York has become as Virginia; and the power to hold, hunt, and sell men, women, and children as slaves remains no longer a mere state institution, but is now an institution of the whole United States. The power is co-extensive with the Star-Spangled Banner and American Christianity. Where these go, may also go the merciless slave-hunter. Where these are, man is not sacred. He is a bird for the sportsman's gun. By that most foul and fiendish of all human decrees, the liberty and person of every man are put in peril. Your broad republican domain is hunting ground for men. Not for thieves and robbers, enemies of society, merely, but for men guilty of no crime. Your lawmakers have commanded all good citizens to engage in this hellish sport. Your President, your Secretary of State, our lords, nobles, and ecclesiastics, enforce, as a duty you owe to your free and glorious country, and to your God, that you do this accursed thing. Not fewer than forty Americans have, within the past two years, been hunted down and, without a moment's warning, hurried away in chains, and consigned to slavery and excruciating torture. Some of these have had wives and children, dependent on them for bread; but of this, no account was made. The right of the hunter to his prey stands superior to the right of marriage, and to all rights in this republic, the rights of God included! For black men there are neither law, justice, humanity, not religion. The Fugitive Slave Law makes mercy to them a crime; and bribes the judge who tries them. An American judge gets ten dollars for every victim he consigns to slavery, and five, when he fails to do so. The oath of any two villains is sufficient, under this hell-black enactment, to send the most pious and exemplary black man into the remorseless jaws of slavery! His own testimony is nothing. He can bring no witnesses for himself. The minister of American justice is bound by the law to hear but one side; and that side, is the side of the oppressor. Let this damning fact be perpetually told. Let it be thundered around the world, that, in tyrant-killing, king-hating, people-loving, democratic, Christian America, the seats of justice are filled with judges, who hold their offices under an open and palpable bribe, and are bound, in deciding in the case of a man's liberty, hear only his accusers!

In glaring violation of justice, in shameless disregard of the forms of administering law, in cunning arrangement to entrap the defenseless, and in diabolical intent, this Fugitive Slave Law stands alone in the annals of tyrannical legislation. I doubt if there be another nation on the globe, having the brass and the baseness to put such a law on the statute-book. If any man in this assembly thinks differently from me in this matter, and feels able to disprove my statements, I will gladly confront him at any suitable time and place he may select.

I take this law to be one of the grossest infringements of Christian Liberty, and, if the churches and ministers of our country were not stupidly blind, or most wickedly indifferent, they, too, would so regard it.

At the very moment that they are thanking God for the enjoyment of civil and religious liberty, and for the right to worship God according to the dictates of their own consciences, they are utterly silent in respect to a law which robs religion of its chief significance, and makes it utterly worthless to a world lying in wickedness. Did this law concern the "mint, anise, and cumin"—abridge the right to sing psalms, to partake of the sacrament, or to engage in any of the ceremonies of religion, it would be smitten by the thunder of a thousand pulpits. A general shout would go up from the church, demanding repeal, repeal, instant repeal!—And it would go hard with that politician who presumed to solicit the votes of the people without inscribing this motto on his banner. Further, if this demand were not complied with, another Scotland would be added to the history of religious liberty, and the stern old Covenanters would be thrown into the shade. A John Knox would be seen at every church door, and heard from every pulpit, and Fillmore would have no more quarter than was shown by Knox, to the beautiful, but treacherous queen Mary of Scotland. The fact that the church of our country, (with fractional exceptions), does not esteem "the Fugitive Slave Law" as a declaration of war against religious liberty, implies that that church regards religion simply as a form of worship, an empty ceremony, and not a vital principle, requiring active benevolence, justice, love and good will towards man. It esteems sacrifice above mercy; psalm-singing above right doing; solemn meetings above practical righteousness. A worship that can be conducted by persons who refuse to give shelter to the houseless, to give bread to the hungry, clothing to the naked, and who enjoin obedience to a law forbidding these acts of mercy, is a curse, not a blessing to mankind. The Bible addresses all such persons as "scribes, Pharisees, hypocrites, who pay tithe of mint, anise, and cumin, and have omitted the weightier matters of the law, judgment, mercy and faith."

But the church of this country is not only indifferent to the wrongs of the slave, it actually takes sides with the oppressors. It has made itself the bulwark of American slavery, and the shield of American slave-hunters. Many of its most eloquent Divines. who stand as the very lights of the church, have shamelessly given the sanction of religion and the Bible to the whole slave system. They have taught that man may, properly, be a slave; that the relation of master and slave is ordained of God; that to send back an escaped bondman to his master is clearly the duty of all the followers of the Lord Jesus Christ; and this horrible blasphemy is palmed off upon the world for Christianity.

For my part, I would say, welcome infidelity! welcome atheism! welcome anything! in preference to the gospel, as preached by those Divines! They convert the very name of religion into an engine of tyranny, and barbarous cruelty, and serve to confirm more infidels, in this age, than all the infidel writings of Thomas Paine, Voltaire, and Bolingbroke, put together, have done! These ministers make religion a cold and flinty-hearted thing, having neither principles of right action, nor bowels of compassion. They strip the love of God of its beauty, and leave the throng of religion a huge, horrible, repulsive form. It is a religion for oppressors, tyrants, man-stealers, and thugs. It is not that "pure and undefiled religion" which is from above, and which is "first pure, then peaceable, easy to be entreated, full of mercy and good fruits, without partiality, and without hypocrisy." But a religion which favors the rich against the poor; which exalts the proud above the humble; which divides mankind into two classes, tyrants and slaves; which says to the man in chains, stay there; and to the oppressor, oppress on; it is a religion which may be professed and enjoyed by all the robbers and enslavers of mankind; it makes God a respecter of persons, denies his fatherhood of the race, and tramples in the dust the great truth of the brotherhood of man. All this we affirm to be true of the popular church, and the popular worship of our land and nation—a religion, a church, and a worship which, on the authority of inspired wisdom, we pronounce to be an abomination in the sight of God. In the language of Isaiah, the American church might be well addressed, "Bring no more vain ablations; incense is an abomination unto me: the new moons and Sabbaths, the calling of assemblies, I cannot away with; it is iniquity even the solemn meeting. Your new moons and your appointed feasts my soul hateth. They are a trouble to me; I am weary to bear them; and when ye spread forth your hands I will hide mine eyes from you. Yea! when ye make many prayers, I will not hear. YOUR HANDS ARE FULL OF BLOOD; cease to do evil, learn to do well; seek judgment; relieve the oppressed; judge for the fatherless; plead for the widow."

The American church is guilty, when viewed in connection with what it is doing to uphold slavery; but it is superlatively guilty when viewed in connection with its ability to abolish slavery. The sin of which it is guilty is one of omission as well as of commission. Albert Barnes but uttered what the common sense of every man at all observant of the actual state of the case will receive as truth, when he declared that "There is no power out of the church that could sustain slavery an hour, if it were not sustained in it."

Let the religious press, the pulpit, the Sunday school, the conference meeting, the great ecclesiastical, missionary, Bible and tract associations of the land array their immense powers against slavery and slave-holding; and the whole system of crime and blood would be scattered to the winds; and that they do not do this involves them in the most awful responsibility of which the mind can conceive.

In prosecuting the anti-slavery enterprise, we have been asked to spare the church, to spare the ministry; but how, we ask, could such a thing be done? We are met on the threshold of our efforts for the redemption of the slave, by the church and ministry of the country, in battle arrayed against us; and we are compelled to fight or flee. From what quarter, I beg to know, has proceeded a fire so deadly upon our ranks, during the last two years, as from the Northern pulpit? As the champions of oppressors, the chosen men of American theology have appeared—men, honored for their so-called piety, and their real learning. The Lords of Buffalo, the Springs of New York, the Lathrops of Auburn, the Coxes and Spencers of Brooklyn, the Gannets and Sharps of Boston, the Deweys of Washington, and other great religious lights of the land have, in utter denial of the authority of Him by whom they professed to be called to the ministry, deliberately taught us, against the example or the Hebrews and against the remonstrance of the Apostles, they teach that we ought to obey man's law before the law of God.

My spirit wearies of such blasphemy; and how such men can be supported, as the "standing types and representatives of Jesus Christ," is a mystery which I leave others to penetrate. In speaking of the American church, however, let it be distinctly understood that I mean the great mass of the religious organizations of our land. There are exceptions, and I thank God that there are. Noble men may be found, scattered all over these Northern States, of whom Henry Ward Beecher of Brooklyn, Samuel J. May of Syracuse, and my esteemed friend (Rev. R. R. Raymond) on the platform, are shining examples; and let me say further, that upon these men lies the duty to inspire our ranks with high religious faith and zeal, and to cheer us on in the great mission of the slave's redemption from his chains.

One is struck with the difference between the attitude of the American church towards the anti-slavery movement, and that occupied by the churches in England towards a similar movement in that country. There, the church, true to its mission of ameliorating, elevating, and improving the condition of mankind, came forward promptly, bound up the wounds of the West Indian slave, and restored him to his liberty. There, the question of emancipation was a high religious question. It was demanded, in the name of humanity, and according to the law of the living God. The Sharps, the Clarksons, the Wilberforces, the Buxtons, and Burchells and the Knibbs, were alike famous for their piety, and for their philanthropy. The anti-slavery movement there was not an anti-church movement, for the reason that the church took its full share in prosecuting that movement: and the anti-slavery movement in this country will cease to be an anti-church movement, when the church of this country shall assume a favorable, instead of a hostile position towards that movement. Americans! your republican politics, not less than your republican religion, are flagrantly inconsistent. You boast of your love of liberty, your superior civilization, and your pure Christianity, while the whole political power of the nation (as embodied in the two great political parties), is solemnly pledged to support and perpetuate the enslavement of three millions of your countrymen. You hurl your anathemas at the crowned headed tyrants of Russia and Austria, and pride yourselves on your Democratic institutions, while you yourselves consent to be the mere tools and body-guards of the tyrants of Virginia and Carolina. You invite to your shores fugitives of oppression from abroad, honor them with banquets, greet them with ovations, cheer them, toast them, salute them, protect them, and pour out your money to them like water; but the fugitives from your own land you advertise, hunt, arrest, shoot and kill. You glory in your refinement and your universal education yet you maintain a system as barbarous and dreadful as ever stained the character of a nation—a system begun in avarice, supported in pride, and perpetuated in cruelty. You shed tears over fallen Hungary, and make the sad story of her wrongs the theme of your poets, statesmen and orators, till your gallant sons are ready to fly to arms to vindicate her cause against her oppressors; but, in regard to the ten thousand wrongs of the American slave, you would enforce the strictest silence, and would hail him as an enemy of the nation who dares to make those wrongs the subject of public discourse! You are all on fire at the mention of liberty for France or for Ireland; but are as cold as an iceberg at the thought of liberty for the enslaved of America. You discourse eloquently on the dignity of labor; yet, you sustain a system which, in its very essence, casts a stigma upon labor. You can bare your bosom to the storm of British artillery to throw off a threepenny tax on tea; and yet wring the last hard-earned farthing from the grasp of the black laborers of your country. You profess to believe "that, of one blood, God made all nations of men to dwell on the face of all the earth," and hath commanded all men, everywhere to love one another; yet you notoriously hate, (and glory in your hatred), all men whose skins are not colored like your own. You declare, before the world, and are understood by the world to declare, that you "hold these truths to be self evident, that all men are created equal; and are endowed by their Creator with certain inalienable rights; and that, among these are, life, liberty, and the pursuit of happiness;" and yet, you hold securely, in a bondage which, according to your own Thomas Jefferson, "is worse than ages of that which your fathers rose in rebellion to oppose," a seventh part of the inhabitants of your country.

Fellow-citizens! I will not enlarge further on your national inconsistencies. The existence of slavery in this country brands your republicanism as a sham, your humanity as a base pretence, and your Christianity as a lie. It destroys your moral power abroad; it corrupts your politicians at home. It saps the foundation of religion; it makes your name a hissing, and a bye-word to a mocking earth. It is the antagonistic force in your government, the only thing that seriously disturbs and endangers your Union. It fetters your progress; it is the enemy of improvement, the deadly foe of education; it fosters pride; it breeds insolence; it promotes vice; it shelters crime; it is a curse to the earth that supports it; and yet, you cling to it, as if it were the sheet anchor of all your hopes. Oh! be warned! be warned! a horrible reptile is coiled up in your nation's bosom; the venomous creature is nursing at the tender breast of your youthful republic; for the love of God, tear away, and fling from you the hideous monster, and let the weight of twenty millions crush and destroy it forever!

But it is answered in reply to all this, that precisely what I have now denounced is, in fact, guaranteed and sanctioned by the Constitution of the United States; that the right to hold and to hunt slaves is a part of that Constitution framed by the illustrious Fathers of this Republic.

Then, I dare to affirm, notwithstanding all I have said before, your fathers stooped, basely stooped

> To palter with us in a double sense:
> And keep the word of promise to the ear,
> But break it to the heart.

And instead of being the honest men I have before declared them to be, they were the veriest imposters that ever practiced on mankind. This is the inevitable conclusion, and from it there is no escape. But I differ from those who charge this baseness on the framers of the Constitution of the United States. It is a slander upon their memory, at least, so I believe. There is not time now to argue the constitutional question at length—nor have I the ability to discuss it as it ought to be discussed. The subject has been handled with masterly power by Lysander Spooner, Esq., by William Goodell, by Samuel E. Sewall, Esq., and last, though not least, by Gerritt Smith, Esq. These gentlemen have, as I think, fully and clearly vindicated the Constitution from any design to support slavery for an hour.

Fellow-citizens! there is no matter in respect to which, the people of the North have allowed themselves to be so ruinously imposed upon, as that of the pro-slavery character of the Constitution. In that instrument I hold there is neither warrant, license, nor sanction of the hateful thing; but, interpreted as it ought to be interpreted, the Constitution is a GLORIOUS LIBERTY DOCUMENT. Read its preamble, consider its purposes. Is slavery among them? Is it at the gateway? or is it in the temple? It is neither. While I do not intend to argue this question on the present occasion, let me ask, if it be not somewhat singular that, if the Constitution were intended to be, by its framers and adopters, a slave-holding instrument, why neither slavery, slaveholding, nor slave can anywhere be found in it. What would be thought of an instrument, drawn up, legally drawn up, for the purpose of entitling the city of Rochester to a track of land, in which no mention of land was made? Now, there are certain rules of interpretation, for the proper understanding of all legal instruments. These rules are well established. They are plain, common-sense rules, such as you and I, and all of us, can understand and apply, without having passed years in the study of law. I scout the idea that the question of the constitutionality or unconstitutionality of slavery is not a question for the people. I hold that every American citizen has a right to form an opinion of the constitution, and to propagate that opinion, and to use all honorable means to make his opinion the prevailing one. Without this right, the liberty of an American citizen would be as insecure as that of a Frenchman. Ex-Vice-President Dallas tells us that the Constitution is an object to which no American mind can be too attentive, and no American heart too devoted. He further says, the Constitution, in its words, is plain and intelligible, and is meant for the home-bred, unsophisticated understandings of our fellow-citizens. Senator Berrien tell us that the Constitution is the fundamental law, that which controls all others. The charter of our liberties, which every citizen has a personal interest in understanding thoroughly. The testimony of Senator Breese, Lewis Cass, and many others that might be named, who are everywhere esteemed as sound lawyers, so regard the constitution. I take it, therefore, that it is not presumption in a private citizen to form an opinion of that instrument.

Now, take the Constitution according to its plain reading, and I defy the presentation of a single pro-slavery clause in it. On the other hand it will be found to contain principles and purposes, entirely hostile to the existence of slavery.

I have detained my audience entirely too long already. At some future period I will gladly avail myself of an opportunity to give this subject a full and fair discussion.

Allow me to say, in conclusion, notwithstanding the dark picture I have this day presented of the state of the nation, I do not despair of this country. There are forces in operation, which must inevitably work the downfall of slavery. "The arm of the Lord is not shortened," and the doom of slavery is certain. I, therefore, leave off where I began, with hope. While drawing encouragement from the Declaration of Independence, the great principles it contains, and the genius of American Institutions, my spirit is also cheered by the obvious tendencies of the age. Nations do not now stand in the same relation to each other that they did ages ago. No nation can now shut itself up from the surrounding world, and trot round in the same old path of its fathers without interference. The time was when such could be done. Long established customs of hurtful character could formerly fence themselves in, and do their evil work with social impunity. Knowledge was then confined and enjoyed by the privileged few, and the multitude walked on in mental darkness. But a change has now come over the affairs of mankind. Walled cities and empires have become unfashionable. The arm of commerce has borne away the gates of the strong city. Intelligence is penetrating the darkest corners of the globe. It makes its pathway over and under the sea, as well as on the earth. Wind, steam, and lightning are its chartered agents. Oceans no longer divide, but link nations together. From Boston to London is now a holiday excursion. Space is comparatively annihilated. Thoughts expressed on one side of the Atlantic, are distinctly heard on the other. The far off and almost fabulous Pacific rolls in grandeur at our feet. The Celestial Empire, the mystery of ages, is being solved. The fiat of the Almighty, "Let there be Light," has not yet spent its force. No abuse, no outrage whether in taste, sport or avarice, can now hide itself from the all-pervading light. The iron shoe, and crippled foot of China must be seen, in contrast with nature. Africa must rise and put on her yet unwoven garment. "Ethiopia shall stretch out her hand unto God." In the fervent aspirations of William Lloyd Garrison, I say, and let every heart join in saying it:

God speed the year of jubilee
The wide world o'er
When from their galling chains set free, Th' oppress'd shall vilely bend the knee,
And wear the yoke of tyranny
Like brutes no more.
That year will come, and freedom's reign, To man his plundered fights again
Restore.
God speed the day when human blood Shall cease to flow!
In every clime be understood,
The claims of human brotherhood, And each return for evil, good,
Not blow for blow;
That day will come all feuds to end. And change into a faithful friend Each foe.
God speed the hour, the glorious hour, When none on earth
Shall exercise a lordly power,
Nor in a tyrant's presence cower;
But all to manhood's stature tower, By equal birth!
That hour will come, to each, to all, And from his prison-house, the thrall Go forth.
Until that year, day, hour, arrive,
With head, and heart, and hand I'll strive, To break the rod, and rend the gyve,
The spoiler of his prey deprive —
So witness Heaven!
And never from my chosen post, Whate'er the peril or the cost,
Be driven.

Chapter 20

Gettysburg Address

Abraham Lincoln

The address was delivered on November 19, 1863, at the dedication of the cemetery at Gettysburg, Pennsylvania.

———◦◦◦———

Fourscore and seven years ago our fathers brought forth, on this continent, a new nation, conceived in liberty, and dedicated to the proposition that all men are created equal. Now we are engaged in a great civil war, testing whether that nation, or any nation so conceived, and so dedicated, can long endure. We are met on a great battle-field of that war. We have come to dedicate a portion of that field, as a final resting-place for those who here gave their lives, that that nation might live. It is altogether fitting and proper that we should do this. But, in a larger sense, we cannot dedicate, we cannot consecrate—we cannot hallow—this ground. The brave men, living and dead, who struggled here, have consecrated it far above our poor power to add or detract. The world will little note, nor long remember what we say here, but it can never forget what they did here. It is for us the living, rather, to be dedicated here to the unfinished work which they who fought here have thus far so nobly advanced. It is rather for us to be here dedicated to the great task remaining before us—that from these honored dead we take increased devotion to that cause for which they here gave the last full measure of devotion—that we here highly resolve that these dead shall not have died in vain—that this nation, under God, shall have a new birth of freedom, and that government of the people, by the people, for the people, shall not perish from the earth.

Chapter 21

Second Inaugural Address

Abraham Lincoln

The address was delivered on March 4, 1865. The following month the American Civil War ended, and Lincoln was assassinated.

Fellow-Countrymen:

At this second appearing to take the oath of the Presidential office there is less occasion for an extended address than there was at the first. Then a statement somewhat in detail of a course to be pursued seemed fitting and proper. Now, at the expiration of four years, during which public declarations have been constantly called forth on every point and phase of the great contest which still absorbs the attention and engrosses the energies of the nation, little that is new could be presented. The progress of our arms, upon which all else chiefly depends, is as well known to the public as to myself, and it is, I trust, reasonably satisfactory and encouraging to all. With high hope for the future, no prediction in regard to it is ventured.

On the occasion corresponding to this four years ago all thoughts were anxiously directed to an impending civil war. All dreaded it, all sought to avert it. While the inaugural address was being delivered from this place, devoted altogether to saving the Union without war, insurgent agents were in the city seeking to *destroy* it without war—seeking to dissolve the Union and divide effects by negotiation. Both parties deprecated war, but one of them would *make* war rather than let the nation survive, and the other would *accept* war rather than let it perish, and the war came.

One-eighth of the whole population were colored slaves, not distributed generally over the Union, but localized in the southern part of it. These slaves constituted a peculiar and powerful interest. All knew that this interest was somehow the cause of the war. To strengthen, perpetuate, and extend this interest was the object for which the insurgents would rend the Union even by war, while the Government claimed no right to do more than to restrict the territorial enlargement of it. Neither party expected for the war the magnitude or the duration which it has already attained. Neither anticipated that the *cause* of the conflict might cease with or even before the conflict itself should cease. Each looked for an easier triumph, and a result less fundamental and astounding. Both read the same Bible and pray to the same God, and each invokes His aid against the other. It may seem strange that any men should dare to ask a just God's assistance in wringing their bread from the sweat of other men's faces, but let us judge not, that we be not judged. The prayers of both could not be answered. That of neither has been answered fully. The Almighty has His own purposes. "Woe unto the world because of offenses; for it must needs be that offenses come, but woe to that man by whom the offense cometh." If we shall suppose that American slavery is one of those offenses which, in the providence of God, must needs come, but which, having continued through His appointed time, He now wills to remove, and that He gives to both North and South this terrible war as the woe due to those by whom the offense came, shall we discern therein any departure from those divine attributes which the believers in a living God always ascribe to Him? Fondly do we hope, fervently do we pray, that this mighty scourge of war may speedily pass away. Yet, if God wills that it continue until all the wealth piled by the bondsman's two hundred and fifty years of unrequited toil shall be sunk, and until every drop of blood drawn with the lash shall be paid by another drawn with the sword, as was said three thousand years ago, so still it must be said "the judgments of the Lord are true and righteous altogether."

With malice toward none, with charity for all, with firmness in the right as God gives us to see the right, let us strive on to finish the work we are in, to bind up the nation's wounds, to care for him who shall have borne the battle and for his widow and his orphan, to do all which may achieve and cherish a just and lasting peace among ourselves and with all nations.

Chapter 22

On Liberty

John Stuart Mill

Bring to your mind an opinion so outrageous that it would be repudiated by any sensible person. Now suppose that stating this opinion openly would be an affront to the vast majority of listeners. Under such circumstances, why shouldn't the representatives of the people be empowered to pass a law banning the public expression of this foolishness, thus ensuring that no one is offended by it or tempted to repeat it? If an opinion is wrongheaded and repugnant, why does it merit protection? The most celebrated and eloquent reply is provided in John Stuart Mill's classic work, *On Liberty.* What is most surprising about Mill's presentation is that he defends an individual's free speech by appealing not to the majority's kindheartedness but to its welfare. As he puts it, "He who knows only his own side of the case knows little of that." He maintains that those who have not heard and carefully considered the arguments against their position will soon hold their views as dead dogma, shorn of significance.

———>———

CHAPTER I

Introductory

The object of this essay is to assert one very simple principle, as entitled to govern absolutely the dealings of society with the individual in the way of compulsion and control, whether the means used be physical force in the form of legal penalties or the moral coercion of public opinion. That principle is that the sole end for which mankind are warranted, individually or collectively, in interfering with the liberty of action of any of their number is self-protection. That the only purpose for which power can be rightfully exercised over any member of a civilized community, against his will, is to prevent harm to others. His own good, either physical or moral, is not a sufficient warrant. He cannot rightfully be compelled to do or forbear because it will be better for him to do so, because it will make him happier, because, in the opinions of others, to do so would be wise or even right. These are good reasons for remonstrating with him, or reasoning with him, or persuading him, or entreating him, but not for compelling him or visiting him with any evil in case he do otherwise. To justify that, the conduct from which it is desired to deter him must be calculated to produce evil to someone else. The only part of the conduct of anyone for which he is amenable to society is that which concerns others. In the part which merely concerns himself, his independence is, of right, absolute. Over himself, over his own body and mind, the individual is sovereign. . . .

This, then, is the appropriate region of human liberty. It comprises, first, the inward domain of consciousness, demanding liberty of conscience in the most comprehensive sense, liberty of thought and feeling, absolute freedom of opinion and sentiment on all subjects, practical or speculative, scientific, moral, or theological. The liberty of expressing and publishing opinions may seem to fall under a different principle, since it belongs to that part of the conduct of an individual which concerns other people, but, being almost of as much importance as the liberty of thought itself and resting in great part on the same reasons, is practically inseparable from it. Secondly, the principle requires liberty of tastes and pursuits, of framing the plan of our life to suit our own character, of doing as we like, subject to such consequences as may follow, without impediment from our fellow creatures, so long as what we do does not harm them, even though they should think our conduct foolish, perverse, or wrong. Thirdly, from this liberty of each individual follows the liberty, within the same limits, of combination among individuals; freedom to unite for any purpose not involving harm to others: the persons combining being supposed to be of full age and not forced or deceived.

No society in which these liberties are not, on the whole, respected is free, whatever maybe its form of government; and none is completely free in which they do not exist absolute and unqualified. The only freedom which deserves the name is that of pursuing our own good in our own way, so long as we do not attempt to deprive others of theirs or impede their efforts to obtain it. Each is the proper guardian of his own health, whether bodily *or* mental and spiritual. Mankind are greater gainers by suffering each other to live as seems good to themselves than by compelling each to live as seems good to the rest. . . .

It will be convenient for the argument if, instead of at once entering upon the general thesis, we confine ourselves in the first instance to a single branch of it on which the principle here stated is, if not fully, yet to a certain point, recognized by the current opinions. This one branch is the Liberty of Thought, from which it is impossible to separate the cognate liberty of speaking and of writing. Although these liberties, to some considerable amount, form part of the political morality of all countries which profess religious toleration and free institutions, the grounds, both philosophical and practical, on which they rest are perhaps not so familiar to the general mind, nor so thoroughly appreciated by many, even of the leaders of opinion, as might have been expected. . . .

CHAPTER II

Of the Liberty of Thought and Discussion

The time, it is to be hoped, is gone by when any defense would be necessary of the "liberty of the press" as one of the securities against corrupt or tyrannical government. No argument, we may suppose, can now be needed against permitting a legislature or an executive, not identified in interest with the people, to prescribe opinions to them and determine what doctrines or what arguments they shall be allowed to hear. . . . Let us suppose, therefore, that the government is entirely at one with the people, and never thinks of exerting any power of coercion unless in agreement with what it conceives to be their voice. But I deny the right of the people to exercise such coercion, either by themselves or by their government. The power itself is illegitimate. The best government has no more title to it than the worst. It is as noxious, or more noxious, when exerted in accordance with public opinion than when in opposition to it. If all mankind minus one were of one opinion, and only one person were of the contrary opinion, mankind would be no more justified in silencing that one person than he, if he had the power, would be justified in silencing mankind. Were an opinion a personal possession of no value except to the owner, if to be obstructed in the enjoyment of it were simply a private injury, it would make some difference whether the injury was inflicted only on a few persons or on many. But the peculiar evil of silencing the expression of an opinion is that it is robbing the human race, posterity as well as the existing generation—those who dissent from the opinion, still more than those who hold it. If the opinion is right, they are deprived of the opportunity of exchanging error for truth; if wrong, they lose, what is almost as great a benefit, the clearer perception and livelier impression of truth produced by its collision with error.

It is necessary to consider separately these two hypotheses, each of which has a distinct branch of the argument corresponding to it. We can never be sure that the opinion we are endeavoring to stifle is a false opinion; and if we were sure, stifling it would be an evil still.

First, the opinion which it is attempted to suppress by authority may possibly be true. Those who desire to suppress it, of course, deny its truth; but they are not infallible. They have no authority to decide the question for all mankind and exclude every other person from the means of judging. To refuse a hearing to an opinion because they are sure that it is false is to assume that *their* certainty is the same thing as *absolute* certainty. All silencing of discussion is an assumption of infallibility. Its condemnation may be allowed to rest on this common argument, not the worse for being common.

Unfortunately for the good sense of mankind, the fact of their fallibility is far from carrying the weight in their practical judgment which is always allowed to it in theory; for while everyone well knows himself to be fallible, few think it necessary to take any precautions against their own fallibility, or admit the supposition that any opinion of which they feel very certain may be one of the examples of the error to which they acknowledge themselves to be liable. Absolute princes, or others who are accustomed to unlimited deference, usually feel this complete confidence in their own opinions on nearly all subjects. People more happily situated, who sometimes hear their opinions disputed and are not wholly unused to be set right when they are wrong, place the same unbounded reliance only on such of their opinions as are shared by all who surround them, or to whom they habitually defer; for in proportion to a man's want of confidence in his own solitary judgment does he usually repose, with implicit trust, on the infallibility of "the world" in general. And the world, to each individual, means the part of it with which he comes in contact his party, his sect, his church, his class of society; the man may be called, by comparison, almost liberal and large-minded to whom it means anything so comprehensive as his own country or his own age. Nor is his faith in this collective authority at all shaken by his being aware that other ages, countries, sects, churches, classes, and parties have thought, and even now think, the exact reverse. He devolves upon his own world the responsibility of being in the right against the dissentient worlds of other people; and it never troubles him that mere accident has decided which of these numerous worlds is the object of his reliance, and that the same causes which make him a churchman in London would have made him a Buddhist or a Confucian in Peking. Yet it is as evident in itself, as any amount of argument can make it, that ages are no more infallible than individuals—every age having held many opinions which subsequent ages have deemed not only false but absurd; and it is as certain that many opinions, now general, will be rejected by future ages, as it is that many, once general, are rejected by the present.

The objection likely to be made to this argument would probably take some such form as the following. There is no greater assumption of infallibility in forbidding the propagation of error than in any other thing which is done by public authority on its own judgment and responsibility. Judgment is given to men that they may use it. Because it may be used erroneously, are men to be told that they ought not to use it at all? To prohibit what they think pernicious is not claiming exemption from error, but fulfilling the duty incumbent on them, although fallible, of acting on their conscientious conviction. If we were never to act on our opinions, because those opinions may be wrong, we should leave all our interests uncared for, and all our duties unperformed. An objection which applies to all conduct can be no valid objection to any conduct in particular. It is the duty of governments, and of individuals, to form the truest opinions they can; to form them carefully, and never impose them upon others unless they are quite sure of being right. But when they are sure (such reasoners may say), it is not conscientiousness but cowardice to shrink from acting on their opinions and allow doctrines which they honestly think dangerous to the welfare of mankind, either in this life or in another, to be scattered abroad without restraint, because other people, in less enlightened times, have persecuted opinions now believed to be true. Let us take care, it may be said, not to make the same mistake; but governments and nations have made mistakes in other things which are not denied to be fit subjects for the exercise of authority: they have laid on bad taxes, made unjust wars. Ought we therefore to lay on no taxes and, under whatever provocation, make no wars? Men and governments must act to the best of their ability. There is no such thing as absolute certainty, but there is assurance sufficient for the purposes of human life. We may, and must, assume our opinion to be true for the guidance of our own conduct; and it is assuming no more when we forbid bad men to pervert society by the propagation of opinions which we regard as false and pernicious.

I answer, that it is assuming very much more. There is the greatest difference between presuming an opinion to be true because, with every opportunity for contesting it, it has not been refuted, and assuming its truth for the purpose of not permitting its refutation. Complete liberty of contradicting and disproving our opinion is the very condition which justifies us in assuming its truth for purposes of action; and on no other terms can a being with human faculties have any rational assurance of being right.

When we consider either the history of opinion or the ordinary conduct of human life, to what is it to be ascribed that the one and the other are no worse than they are? Not certainly to the inherent force of the human understanding, for on any matter not self-evident there are ninety-nine persons totally incapable of judging of it for one who is capable; and the capacity of the hundredth person is only comparative, for the majority of the eminent men of every past generation held many opinions now known to be erroneous, and did or approved numerous things which no one will now justify. Why is it, then, that there is on the whole a preponderance among mankind of rational opinions and rational conduct? If there really is this preponderance—which there must be unless human affairs are, and have always been, in an almost desperate state—it is owing to a quality of the human mind, the source of everything respectable in man either as an intellectual or as a moral being, namely, that his errors are corrigible. He is capable of rectifying his mistakes by discussion and experience. Not by experience alone. There must be discussion to show how experience is to be interpreted. Wrong opinions and practices gradually yield to fact and argument; but facts and arguments, to produce any effect on the mind, must be brought before it. Very few facts are able to tell their own story, without comments to bring out their meaning. The whole strength and value, then, of human judgment depending on the one property, that it can be set right when it is wrong, reliance can be placed on it only when the means of setting it right are kept constantly at hand. In the case of any person whose judgment is really deserving of confidence, how has it become so? Because he has kept his mind open to criticism of his opinions and conduct. Because it has been his practice to listen to all that could be said against him; to profit by as much of it as was just, and to expound to himself, and upon occasion to others, the fallacy of what was fallacious. Because he has felt that the only way in which a human being can make some approach to knowing the whole of a subject is by hearing what can be said about it by persons of every variety of opinion, and studying all modes in which it can be looked at by every character of mind. No wise man ever acquired his wisdom in any mode but this; nor is it in the nature of human intellect to become wise in any other manner. The steady habit of correcting and completing his own opinion by collating it with those of others, so far from causing doubt and hesitation in carrying it into practice, is the only stable foundation for a just reliance on it; for, being cognizant of all that can, at least obviously, be said against him, and having taken up his position against all gainsayers—knowing that he has sought for objections and difficulties instead of avoiding them, and has shut out no light which can be thrown upon the subject from any quarter—he has a right to think his judgment better than that of any person, or any multitude, who have not gone through a similar process. . . .

In order more fully to illustrate the mischief of denying a hearing to opinions because we, in our own judgment, have condemned them, it will be desirable to fix down the discussion to a concrete case; and I choose, by preference, the cases which are least favorable to me—in which the argument against freedom of opinion, both on the score of truth and on that of utility, is considered the strongest. Let the opinions impugned be the belief in a God and in a future state, or any of the commonly received doctrines of morality. To fight the battle on such ground gives a great advantage to an unfair antagonist, since he will be sure to say (and many who have no desire to be unfair will say it internally), Are these the doctrines which you do not deem sufficiently certain to be taken under the protection of law? Is the belief in a God one of the opinions to feel sure of which you hold to be assuming infallibility? But I must be permitted to observe that it is not the feeling sure of a doctrine (be it what it may) which I call an assumption of infallibility. It is the undertaking to decide that question *for others,* without allowing them to hear what can be said on the contrary side. And I denounce and reprobate this pretension not the less if put forth on the side of my most solemn convictions. However positive anyone's persuasion may be, not only of the falsity but of the pernicious consequences—not only of the pernicious consequences, but (to adopt expressions which I altogether condemn) the immorality and impiety of an opinion—yet if, in pursuance of that private judgment, though backed by the public judgment of his country or his contemporaries, he prevents the opinion from being heard in its defense, he assumes infallibility. And so far from the assumption being less objectionable or less dangerous because the opinion is called immoral or impious, this is the case of all others in which it is most fatal. These are exactly the occasions on which the men of one generation commit those dreadful mistakes which excite the astonishment and horror of posterity. It is among such that we find the instances memorable in history, when the arm of the law has been employed to root out the best men and the noblest doctrines; with deplorable success as to the men, though some of the doctrines have survived to be (as if in mockery) invoked in defense of similar conduct toward those who dissent from *them,* or from their received interpretation.

Mankind can hardly be too often reminded that there was once a man called Socrates, between whom and the legal authorities and public opinion of his time there took place a memorable collision. Born in an age and country abounding in individual greatness, this man has been handed down to us by those who best knew both him and the age as the most virtuous man in it. . . . This acknowledged master of all the eminent thinkers who have since lived—whose fame, still growing after more than two thousand years, all but outweighs the whole remainder of the names which make his native city illustrious—was put to death by his countrymen, after a judicial conviction, for impiety and immorality. Impiety, in denying the gods recognized by the State; indeed, his accuser asserted . . . that he believed in no gods at all. Immorality, in being, by his doctrines and instructions, a "corruptor of youth." Of these charges the tribunal, there is every ground for believing, honestly found him guilty, and condemned the man who probably of all then born had deserved best of mankind to be put to death as a criminal.

To pass from this to the only other instance of judicial iniquity, the mention of which, after the condemnation of Socrates, would not be an anticlimax: the event which took place on Calvary rather more than eighteen hundred years ago. The man who left on the memory of those who witnessed his life and conversation such an impression of his moral grandeur that eighteen subsequent centuries have done homage to him as the Almighty in person, was ignominiously put to death, as what? As a blasphemer. Men did not merely mistake their benefactor, they mistook him for the exact contrary of what he was and treated him as that prodigy of impiety which they themselves are now held to be for their treatment of him. The feelings with which mankind now regard these lamentable transactions, especially the later of the two, render them extremely unjust in their judgment of the unhappy actors. . . . Orthodox Christians who are tempted to think that those who stoned to death the first martyrs must have been worse men than they themselves are ought to remember that one of those persecutors was Saint Paul. . . .

Let us now pass to the second division of the argument, and dismissing the supposition that any of the received opinions may be false, let us assume them to be true and examine into the worth of the manner in which they are likely to be held when their truth is not freely and openly canvassed. However unwillingly a person who has a strong opinion may admit the possibility that his opinion may be false, he ought to be moved by the consideration that, however true it may be, if it is not fully, frequently, and fearlessly discussed, it will be held as a dead dogma, not a living truth.

There is a class of persons (happily not quite so numerous as formerly) who think it enough if a person assents undoubtingly to what they think true, though he has no knowledge whatever of the grounds of the opinion and could not make a tenable defense of it against the most superficial objections. Such persons, if they can once get their creed taught from authority, naturally think that no good, and some harm, comes of its being allowed to be questioned. Where their influence prevails, they make it nearly impossible for the received opinion to be rejected wisely and considerately, though it may still be rejected rashly and ignorantly; for to shut out discussion entirely is seldom possible, and when it once gets in, beliefs not grounded on conviction are apt to give way before the slightest semblance of an argument. Waiving, however, this possibility—assuming that the true opinion abides in the mind, but abides as a prejudice, a belief independent of, and proof against, argument—this is not the way in which truth ought to be held by a rational being. This is not knowing the truth. Truth, thus held, is but one superstition the more, accidentally clinging to the words which enunciate a truth.

If the intellect and judgment of mankind ought to be cultivated, a thing which Protestants at least do not deny, on what can these faculties be more appropriately exercised by anyone than on the things which concern him so much that it is considered necessary for him to hold opinions on them? If the cultivation of the understanding consists in one thing more than in another, it is surely in learning the grounds of one's own opinions. Whatever people believe, on subjects on which it is of the first importance to believe rightly, they ought to be able to defend against at least the common objections. But, someone may say, "Let them be *taught* the grounds of their opinions. It does not follow that opinions must be merely parroted because they are never heard controverted. Persons who learn geometry do not simply commit the theorems to memory, but understand and learn likewise the demonstrations; and it would be absurd to say that they remain ignorant of the grounds of geometrical truths because they never hear anyone deny and attempt to disprove them." Undoubtedly: and such teaching suffices on a subject like mathematics, where there is nothing at all to be said on the wrong side of the question. The peculiarity of the evidence of mathematical truths is that all the argument is on one side. There are no objections, and no answers to objections. But on every subject on which difference of opinion is possible, the truth depends on a balance to be struck between two sets of conflicting reasons. Even in natural philosophy, there is always some other explanation possible of the same facts; some geocentric theory instead of heliocentric, some phlogiston instead of oxygen; and it has to be shown why that other theory cannot be the true one; and until this is shown, and until we know how it is shown, we do not understand the grounds of our opinion. But when we turn to subjects infinitely more complicated, to morals, religion, politics, social relations, and the business of life, three-fourths of the arguments for every disputed opinion consist in dispelling the appearances which favor some opinion different from it. The greatest orator, save one, of antiquity, has left it on record that he always studied his adversary's case with as great, if not still greater, intensity than even his own. What Cicero practiced as the means of forensic success requires to be imitated by all who study any subject in order to arrive at the truth. He who knows only his own side of the case knows little of that. His reasons may be good, and no one may have been able to refute them. But if he is equally unable to refute the reasons on the opposite side, if he does not so much as know what they are, he has no ground for preferring either opinion. The rational position for him would be suspension of judgment, and unless he contents himself with that, he is either led by authority or adopts, like the generality of the world, the side to which he feels most inclination. Nor is it enough that he should hear the arguments of adversaries from his own teachers, presented as they state them, and accompanied by what they offer as refutations. That is not the way to do justice to the arguments or bring them into real contact with his own mind. He must be able to hear them from persons who actually believe them, who defend them in earnest and do their very utmost for them. He must know them in their most plausible and persuasive form; he must feel the whole force of the difficulty which the true view of the subject has to encounter and dispose of, else he will never really possess himself of the portion of truth which meets and removes that difficulty. Ninety-nine in a hundred of what are called educated men are in this condition, even of those who can argue fluently for their opinions. Their conclusion may be true, but it might be false for anything they know; they have never thrown themselves into the mental position of those who think differently from them, and considered what such persons may have to say; and, consequently, they do not, in any proper sense of the word, know the doctrine which they themselves profess. . . .

We have now recognized the necessity to the mental well-being of mankind (on which all their other well-being depends) of freedom of opinion, and freedom of the expression of opinion, on four distinct grounds, which we will now briefly recapitulate:

First, if any opinion is compelled to silence, that opinion may, for aught we can certainly know, be true. To deny this is to assume our own infallibility.

Secondly, though the silenced opinion be an error, it may, and very commonly does, contain a portion of truth; and since the general or prevailing opinion on any subject is rarely or never the whole truth, it is only by the collision of adverse opinions that the remainder of the truth has any chance of being supplied.

Thirdly, even if the received opinion be not only true, but the whole truth; unless it is suffered to be, and actually is, vigorously and earnestly contested, it will, by most of those who receive it, be held in the manner of a prejudice, with little comprehension or feeling of its rational grounds. And not only this, but, fourthly, the meaning of the doctrine itself will be in danger of being lost or enfeebled, and deprived of its vital effect on the character and conduct: the dogma becoming a mere formal profession, inefficacious for good, but cumbering the ground and preventing the growth of any real and heartfelt conviction from reason or personal experience.

CHAPTER III

Of Individuality, as one of the Elements of Well-being

Such being the reasons which make it imperative that human beings should be free to form opinions, and to express their opinions without reserve; and such the baneful consequences to the intellectual, and through that to the moral nature of man, unless this liberty is either conceded, or asserted in spite of prohibition; let us next examine whether the same reasons do not require that men should be free to act upon their opinions—to carry these out in their lives, without hindrance, either physical or moral, from their fellow-men, so long as it is at their own risk and peril. This last proviso is of course indispensable. No one pretends that actions should be as free as opinions. On the contrary, even opinions lose their immunity, when the circumstances in which they are expressed are such as to constitute their expression a positive instigation to some mischievous act. An opinion that corn-dealers are starvers of the poor, or that private property is robbery, ought to be unmolested when simply circulated through the press, but may justly incur punishment when delivered orally to an excited mob assembled before the house of a corn-dealer, or when handed about among the same mob in the form of a placard. Acts of whatever kind, which, without justifiable cause, do harm to others, may be, and in the more important cases absolutely require to be, controlled by the unfavorable sentiments, and, when needful, by the active interference of mankind. The liberty of the individual must be thus far limited; he must not make himself a nuisance to other people. But if he refrains from molesting others in what concerns them, and merely acts according to his own inclination and judgment in things which concern himself, the same reasons which show that opinion should be free, prove also that he should be allowed, without molestation, to carry his opinions into practice at his own cost. That mankind are not infallible; that their truths, for the most part, are only half-truths; that unity of opinion, unless resulting from the fullest and freest comparison of opposite opinions, is not desirable, and diversity not an evil, but a good, until mankind are much more capable than at present of recognizing all sides of the truth, are principles applicable to men's modes of action, not less than to their opinions. As it is useful that while mankind are imperfect there should be different opinions, so is it that there should be different experiments of living; that free scope should be given to varieties of character, short of injury to others; and that the worth of different modes of life should be proved practically, when any one thinks fit to try them. It is desirable, in short, that in things which do not primarily concern others, individuality should assert itself. Where, not the person's own character, but the traditions of customs of other people are the rule of conduct, there is wanting one of the principal ingredients of human happiness, and quite the chief ingredient of individual and social progress.

Chapter 23

Considerations on Representative Government

John Stuart Mill

While John Stuart Mill pursued a career in the East India Company, he published widely in philosophy, political theory, and economics. He argues that the ideal form of government is representative. The problem with despotic monarchy is that even if the ruler were all-good and all-knowing, the people would become passive. Their intellect, sentiments, and affections would diminish to the point of nonexistence. By contrast, when capable of participating in government, the people are invigorated. Trying to stand up for one's rights and interests not only brings about better policies but also makes better people.

⚊⚋⚊

CHAPTER III

That the ideally best Form of Government is Representative Government

It has long (perhaps throughout the entire duration of British freedom) been a common form of speech, that if a good despot could be insured, despotic monarchy would be the best form of government. I look upon this as a radical and most pernicious misconception of what good government is, which, until it can be got rid of, will fatally vitiate all our speculations on government.

The supposition is, that absolute power, in the hands of an eminent individual, would insure a virtuous and intelligent performance of all the duties of government. Good laws would be established and enforced, bad laws would be reformed; the best men would be placed in all situations of trust; justice would be as well administered, the public burdens would be as light and as judiciously imposed, every branch of administration would be as purely and as intelligently conducted as the circumstances of the country and its degree of intellectual and moral cultivation would admit. I am willing, for the sake of the argument, to concede all this, but I must point out how great the concession is, how much more is needed to produce even an approximation to these results than is conveyed in the simple expression, a good despot. Their realization would in fact imply, not merely a good monarch, but an all-seeing one. He must be at all times informed correctly, in considerable detail, of the conduct and working of every branch of administration, in every district of the country, and must be able, in the twenty-four hours per day, which are all that is granted to a king as to the humblest laborer, to give an effective share of attention and superintendence to all parts of this vast field; or he must at least be capable of discerning and choosing out, from among the mass of his subjects, not only a large abundance of honest and able men, fit to conduct every branch of public administration under supervision and control, but also the small number of men of eminent virtues and talents who can be trusted not only to do without that supervision, but to exercise it themselves over others. So extraordinary are the faculties and energies required for performing this task in any supportable manner, that the good despot whom we are supposing can hardly be imagined as consenting to undertake it unless as a refuge from intolerable evils, and a transitional preparation for something beyond. But the argument can do without even this immense item in the account. Suppose the difficulty vanquished. What should we then have? One man of superhuman mental activity managing the entire affairs of a mentally passive people. Their passivity is implied in the very idea of absolute power. The nation as a whole, and every individual composing it, are without any potential voice in their own destiny. They exercise no will in respect to their collective interests. All is decided for them by a will not their own, which it is legally a crime for them to disobey. What sort of human beings can be formed under such a regimen? What development can either their thinking or their active faculties attain under it? On matters of pure theory they might perhaps be allowed to speculate, so long as their speculations either did not approach politics, or had not the remotest connection with its practice. On practical affairs they could at most be only suffered to suggest; and even under the most moderate of despots, none but persons of already admitted or reputed superiority could hope that their suggestions would be known to, much less regarded by, those who had the management of affairs. A person must have a very unusual taste for intellectual exercise in and for itself who will put himself to the trouble of thought when it is to have no outward effect, or qualify himself for functions which he has no chance of being allowed to exercise. The only sufficient incitement to mental exertion, in any but a few minds in a generation, is the prospect of some practical use to be made of its results. It does not follow that the nation will be wholly destitute of intellectual power. The common business of life, which must necessarily be performed by each individual or family for themselves, will call forth some amount of intelligence and practical ability, within a certain narrow range of ideas. There may be a select class of *savants* who cultivate science with a view to its physical uses or for the pleasure of the pursuit. There will be a bureaucracy, and persons in training for the bureaucracy, who will be taught at least some empirical maxims of government and public administration. There may be, and often has been, a systematic organization of the best mental power in the country in some special direction (commonly military) to promote the grandeur of the despot. But the public at large remain without information and without interest on all greater matters of practice; or, if they have any knowledge of them, it is but a *dilettante* knowledge, like that which people have of the mechanical arts who have never handled a tool. Nor is it only in their intelligence that they suffer. Their moral capacities are equally stunted. Wherever the sphere of action of human beings is artificially circumscribed, their sentiments are narrowed and dwarfed in the same proportion. The food of feeling is action; even domestic affection lives upon voluntary good offices. Let a person have nothing to do for his country, and he will not care for it. . . .

A good despotism means a government in which, so far as depends on the despot, there is no positive oppression by officers of state, but in which all the collective interests of the people are managed for them, all the thinking that has relation to collective interests done for them, and in which their minds are formed by, and consenting to, this abdication of their own energies. Leaving things to the government, like leaving them to Providence, is synonymous with caring nothing about them, and accepting their results, when disagreeable, as visitations of Nature. With the exception, therefore, of a few studious men who take an intellectual interest in speculation for its own sake, the intelligence and sentiments of the whole people are given up to the material interests, and when these are provided for, to the amusement and ornamentation of private life. But to say this is to say, if the whole testimony of history is worth any thing, that the era of national decline has arrived; that is, if the nation had ever attained any thing to decline from. . . .

Such are not merely the natural tendencies, bur the inherent necessities of despotic government; from which there is no outlet, unless in so far as the despotism consents not to be despotism; in so far as the supposed good despot abstains from exercising his power, and, though holding it in reserve, allows the general business of government to go on as if the people really governed themselves. However little probable it may be, we may imagine a despot observing many of the rules and restraints of constitutional government. He might allow such freedom of the press and of discussion as would enable a public opinion to form and express itself on national affairs. He might suffer local interests to be managed, without the interference of authority, by the people themselves. He might even surround himself with a council or councils of government, freely chosen by the whole or some portion of the nation, retaining in his own hands the power of taxation, and the supreme legislative as well as executive authority. Were he to act thus, and so far abdicate as a despot, he would do away with a considerable part of the evils characteristic of despotism. Political activity and capacity for public affairs would no longer be prevented from growing up in the body of the nation, and a public opinion would form itself, not the mere echo of the government. But such improvement would be the beginning of new difficulties. This public opinion, independent of the monarch's dictation, must be either with him or against him; if not the one, it will be the other. All governments must displease many persons, and these having now regular organs, and being able to express their sentiments, opinions adverse to the measures of government would often be expressed. What is the monarch to do when these unfavorable opinions happen to be in the majority? Is he to alter his course? Is he to defer to the nation? If so, he is no longer a despot, but a constitutional king; an organ or first minister of the people, distinguished only by being irremovable. If not, he must either put down opposition by his despotic power, or there will arise a permanent antagonism between the people and one man, which can have but one possible ending. . . . The monarch would have to succumb, and conform to the conditions of constitutional royalty, or give place to some one who would. The despotism, being thus chiefly nominal, would possess few of the advantages supposed to belong to absolute monarchy, while it would realize in a very imperfect degree those of a free government, since, however great an amount of liberty the citizens might practically enjoy, they could never forget that they held it on sufferance, and by a concession which, under the existing constitution of the state might at any moment be resumed; that they were legally slaves, though of a prudent or indulgent master.

It is not much to be wondered at if impatient or disappointed reformers, groaning under the impediments opposed to the most salutary public improvements by the ignorance, the indifference, the untractableness, the perverse obstinacy of a people, and the corrupt combinations of selfish private interests, armed with the powerful weapons afforded by free institutions, should at times sigh for a strong hand to bear down all these obstacles, and compel a recalcitrant people to be better governed. But (setting aside the fact that for one despot who now and then reforms an abuse, there are ninety-nine who do nothing but create them) those who look in any such direction for the realization of their hopes leave out of the idea of good government its principal element, the improvement of the people themselves. One of the benefits of freedom is that under it the ruler can not pass by the people's minds, and amend their affairs for them without amending *them*. If it were possible for the people to be well governed in spite of themselves, their good government would last no longer than the freedom of a people usually lasts who have been liberated by foreign arms without their own cooperation. It is true, a despot may educate the people, and to do so really would be the best apology for his despotism. But any education which aims at making human beings other than machines, in the long run makes them claim to have the control of their own actions. . . .

I am far from condemning, in cases of extreme exigency, the assumption of absolute power in the form of a temporary dictatorship. Free nations have, in times of old, conferred such power by their own choice, as a necessary medicine for diseases of the body politic which could not be got rid of by less violent means. But its acceptance, even for a time strictly limited, can only be excused, if . . . the dictator employs the whole power he assumes in removing the obstacles which debar the nation from the enjoyment of freedom. A good despotism is an altogether false ideal, which practically (except as a means to some temporary purpose) becomes the most senseless and dangerous of chimeras. Evil for evil, a good despotism, in a country at all advanced in civilization, is more noxious than a bad one, for it is far more relaxing and enervating to the thoughts, feelings, and energies of the people. . . .

There is no difficulty in showing that the ideally best form of government is that in which the sovereignty, or supreme controlling power in the last resort, is vested in the entire aggregate of the community, every citizen not only having a voice in the exercise of that ultimate sovereignty, but being, at least occasionally, called on to take an actual part in the government by the personal discharge of some public function, local or general. . . .

Its superiority in reference to present well-being rests upon two principles, of as universal fairs. The first is, that the rights and interests of every or any person are only secure from being disregarded when the person interested is himself able, and habitually disposed to stand up for them. The second is, that the general prosperity attains a greater height, and is more widely diffused, in proportion to the amount and variety of the personal energies enlisted in promoting it. . . .

We need not suppose that when power resides in an exclusive class, that class will knowingly and deliberately sacrifice the other classes to themselves: it suffices that, in the absence of its natural defenders, the interest of the excluded is always in danger of being overlooked; and, when looked at, is seen with very different eyes from those of the persons whom it directly concerns. In this country, for example, what are called the working-classes may be considered as excluded from all direct participation in the government. I do not believe that the classes who do participate in it have in general any intention of sacrificing the working classes to themselves. They once had that intention; witness the persevering attempts so long made to keep down wages by law. But in the present day, their ordinary disposition is the very opposite: they willingly make considerable sacrifices, especially of their pecuniary interest, for the benefit of the working classes, and err rather by too lavish and indiscriminating beneficence; nor do I believe that any rulers in history have been actuated by a more sincere desire to do their duty towards the poorer portion of their countrymen. Yet does Parliament, or almost any of the members composing it, ever for an instant look at any question with the eyes of a working man? When a subject arises in which the laborers as such have an interest, is it regarded from any point of view but that of the employers of labor? I do not say that the working men's view of these questions is in general nearer to the truth than the other, but it is sometimes quite as near; and in any case it ought to be respectfully listened to, instead of being, as it is, not merely turned away from, but ignored. . . .

It is an adherent condition of human affairs that no intention, however sincere, of protecting the interests of others can make it safe or salutary to tie up their own hands. Still more obviously true is it that by their own hands only can any positive and durable improvement of their circumstances in life be worked out. Through the joint influence of these two principles, all free communities have both been more exempt from social injustice and crime, and have attained more brilliant prosperity than any others, or than they themselves after they lost their freedom. . . .

It must be acknowledged that the benefits of freedom, so far as they have hitherto been enjoyed, were obtained by the extension of its privileges to a part only of the community; and that a government in which they are extended impartially to all is a desideratum still unrealized. But, though every approach to this has an independent value, and in many cases more than an approach could not, in the existing state of general improvement, be made, the participation of all in these benefits is the ideally perfect conception of free government. In proportion as any, no matter who, are excluded from it, the interests of the excluded are left without the guaranty accorded to the rest, and they themselves have less scope and encouragement than they might otherwise have to that exertion of their energies for the good of themselves and of the community, to which the general prosperity is always proportioned.

Thus stands the case as regards present well-being—the good management of the affairs of the existing generation. If we now pass to the influence of the form of government upon character, we shall find the superiority of popular government over every other to be, if possible, still more decided and indisputable.

This question really depends upon a still more fundamental one, viz., which of two common types of character, for the general good of humanity, it is most desirable should predominate—the active or the passive type; that which struggles against evils, or that which endures them; that which bends to circumstances, or that which endeavours to make circumstances bend to itself.

The commonplaces of moralists and the general sympathies of mankind are in favor of the passive type. Energetic characters may be admired, but the acquiescent and submissive are those which most men personally prefer. The passiveness of our neighbors increases our sense of security, and plays into the hands of our wilfulness. Passive characters, if we do not happen to need their activity, seem an obstruction the less in our own path. A contented character is not a dangerous rival. Yet nothing is more certain than that improvement in human affairs is wholly the work of the uncontented characters; and, moreover, that it is much easier for an active mind to acquire the virtues of patience, than for a passive one to assume those of energy.

Of the three varieties of mental excellence, intellectual, practical, and moral, there never could be any doubt in regard to the first two, which side had the advantage. All intellectual superiority is the fruit of active effort. Enterprise, the desire to keep moving, to be trying and accomplishing new things for our own benefit or that of others, is the parent even of speculative, and much more of practical, talent. The intellectual culture compatible with the other type is of that feeble and vague description which belongs to a mind that stops at amusement or at simple contemplation. The test of real and vigorous thinking, the thinking which ascertains truths instead of dreaming dreams, is successful application to practice. . . . With respect to practical improvement, the case is still more evident. The character which improves human life is that which struggles with natural powers and tendencies, not that which gives way to them. The self-benefiting qualities are all on the side of the active and energetic character, and the habits and conduct which promote the advantage of each individual member of the community must be at least a part of those which conduce most in the end to the advancement of the community as a whole. . . .

But on the point of moral preferability, there seems at first sight to be room for doubt. . . . Contentment is always counted among the moral virtues. But it is a complete error to suppose that contentment is necessarily or naturally attendant on passivity of character, and useless it is, the moral consequences are mischievous. Where there exists a desire for advantages not possessed, the mind which does not potentially possess them by means of its own energies is apt to look with hatred and malice on those who do. The person bestirring himself with hopeful prospects to improve his circumstances is the one who feels good-will towards others engaged in, or who have succeeded in the same pursuit. And where the majority are so engaged, those who do not attain the object have had the tone given to their feelings by the general habit of the country, and ascribe their failure to want of effort or opportunity, or to their personal ill luck. But those who, while desiring what others possess, put no energy into striving for it, are either incessantly grumbling that fortune does not do for them what they do not attempt to do for themselves, or overflowing with envy and ill-will towards those who possess what they would like to have. . . .

The contented man, or the contented family, who have no ambition to make any one else happier, to promote the good of their country or their neighborhood, or to improve themselves in moral excellence, excite in us neither admiration nor approval. . . .

Now there can be no kind of doubt that the passive type of character is favored by the government of one or a few, and the active self-helping type by that of the many. Irresponsible rulers need the quiescence of the ruled more than they need any activity but that which they can compel. Submissiveness to the prescriptions of men as necessities of nature is the lesson inculcated by all governments upon those who are wholly without participation in them. The will of superiors, and the law as the will of superiors, must be passively yielded to. But no men are mere instruments or materials in the hands of their rulers who have will, or spirit, or a spring of internal activity in the rest of their proceedings, and any manifestation of these qualities, instead of receiving encouragement from despots, has to get itself forgiven by them. Even when irresponsible rulers are not sufficiently conscious of danger from the mental activity of their subjects to be desirous of repressing it, the position itself is a repression. Endeavour is even more effectually restrained by the certainty of its impotence than by any positive discouragement. Between subjection to the will of others and the virtues of self-help and self-government there is a natural incompatibility. This is more or less complete according as the bondage is strained or relaxed. Rulers differ very much in the length to which they carry the control of the free agency of their subjects, or the supersession of it by managing their business for them. But the difference is in degree, not in principle; and the best despots often go the greatest lengths in chaining up the free agency of their subjects. A bad despot, when his own personal indulgences have been provided for, may sometimes be willing to let the people alone; but a good despot insists on doing them good by making them do their own business in a better way than they themselves know of. . . .

Very different is the state of the human faculties where a human being feels himself under no other external restraint than the necessities of nature, or mandates of society which he has his share in imposing, and which it is open to him, if he thinks them wrong, publicly to dissent from, and exert himself actively to get altered. No doubt, under a government partially popular, this freedom may be exercised even by those who are not partakers in the full privileges of citizenship; but it is a great additional stimulus to any one's self-help and self-reliance when he starts from even ground, and has not to feel that his success depends on the impression he can make upon the sentiments and dispositions of a body of whom he is not one. It is a great discouragement to an individual, and a still greater one to a class, to be left out of the constitution; to be reduced to plead from outside the door to the arbiters of their destiny, not taken into consultation within. The maximum of the invigorating effect of freedom upon the character is only obtained when the person acted on either is, or is looking forward to becoming, a citizen as frilly privileged as any other. What is still more important than even this matter of feeling is the practical discipline which the character obtains from the occasional demand made upon the citizens to exercise, for a time and in their turn, some social function. It is not sufficiently considered how little there is in most men's ordinary life to give any largeness either to their conceptions or to their sentiments. Their work is a routine; not a labor of love, but of self-interest in the most elementary form, the satisfaction of daily wants; neither the thing done, nor the process of doing it, introduces the mind to thoughts or feelings extending beyond individuals; if instructive books are within their reach, there is no stimulus to read them; and, in most cases, the individual has no access to any person of cultivation much superior to his own. Giving him something to do for the public supplies, in a measure, all these deficiencies. . . . He is called upon, while so engaged, to weigh interests not his own; to be guided, in case of conflicting claims, by another rule than his private partialities; to apply, at every turn, principles and maxims which have for their reason of existence the general good; and he usually finds associated with him in the same work minds more familiarized than his own with these ideas and operations, whose study it will be to supply reasons to his understanding, and stimulation to his feeling for the general interest. He is made to feel himself one of the public, and whatever is their interest to be his interest. Where this school of public spirit does not exist, scarcely any sense is entertained that private persons, in no eminent social situation, owe any duties to society except to obey the laws and submit to the government. There is no unselfish sentiment of identification with the public. Every thought or feeling, either of interest or of duty, is absorbed in the individual and in the family. The man never thinks of any collective interest, of any objects to be pursued jointly with others, but only in competition with them, and in some measure at their expense. A neighbor, not being an ally or an associate, since he is never engaged in any common undertaking for joint benefit, is therefore only a rival. Thus even private morality suffers, while public is actually extinct. Were this the universal and only possible state of things, the utmost aspirations of the lawgiver or the moralist could only stretch to make the bulk of the community a flock of sheep innocently nibbling the grass side by side.

From these accumulated considerations, it is evident that the only government which can fully satisfy all the exigencies of the social state is one in which the whole people participate; that any participation, even in the smallest public function, is useful; that the participation should every where be as great as the general degree of improvement of the community will allow; and that nothing less can be ultimately desirable than the admission of all to a share in the sovereign power of the state. But since all can not, in a community exceeding a single small town, participate personally in any but some very minor portions of the public business, it follows that the ideal type of a perfect government must be representative.

CHAPTER VIII

Of the Extension of the Suffrage

. . . It is a personal injustice to withhold from any one, unless for the prevention of greater evils, the ordinary privilege of having his voice reckoned in the disposal of affairs in which he has the same interest as other people. If he is compelled to pay, if he may be compelled to fight, if he is required implicitly to obey, he should be legally entitled to be told what for; to have his consent asked, and his opinion counted at its worth, though not at more than its worth. There ought to be no pariahs in a full-grown and civilised nation; no persons disqualified, except through their own default. Every one is degraded, whether aware of it or not, when other people, without consulting him, take upon themselves unlimited power to regulate his destiny. And even in a much more improved state than the human mind has ever yet reached, it is not in nature that they who are thus disposed of should meet with as fair play as those who have a voice. Rulers and ruling classes are under a necessity of considering the interests and wishes of those who have the suffrage; but of those who are excluded, it is in their option whether they will do so or not, and, however honestly disposed, they are in general too fully occupied with things which they must attend to, to have much room in their thoughts for anything which they can with impunity disregard. No arrangement of the suffrage, therefore, can be permanently satisfactory in which any person or class is peremptorily excluded; in which the electoral privilege is not open to all persons of full age who desire to obtain it.

There are, however, certain exclusions, required by positive reasons, which do not conflict with this principle, and which, though an evil in themselves, are only to be got rid of by the cessation of the state of things which requires them. I regard it as wholly inadmissible that any person should participate in the suffrage without being able to read, write, and, I will add, perform the common operations of arithmetic. Justice demands, even when the suffrage does not depend on it, that the means of attaining these elementary acquirements should be within the reach of every person, either gratuitously, or at an expense not exceeding what the poorest who earn their own living can afford. If this were really the case, people would no more think of giving the suffrage to a man who could not read, than of giving it to a child who could not speak; and it would not be society that would exclude him, but his own laziness. When society has not performed its duty, by rendering this amount of instruction accessible to all, there is some hardship in the case, but it is a hardship that ought to be borne. If society has neglected to discharge two solemn obligations, the more important and more fundamental of the two must be fulfilled first: universal teaching must precede universal enfranchisement. No one but those in whom an *a priori* theory has silenced common sense will maintain that power over others, over the whole community, should be imparted to people who have not acquired the commonest and most essential requisites for taking care of themselves; for pursuing intelligently their own interests, and those of the persons most nearly allied to them. This argument, doubtless, might be pressed further, and made to prove much more. It would be eminently desirable that other things besides reading, writing, and arithmetic could be made necessary to the suffrage; that some knowledge of the conformation of the earth, its natural and political divisions, the elements of general history, and of the history and institutions of their own country, could be required from all electors. But these kinds of knowledge, however indispensable to an intelligent use of the suffrage, are not, in this country, nor probably anywhere save in the Northern United States, accessible to the whole people; nor does there exist any trustworthy machinery for ascertaining whether they have been acquired or not. The attempt, at present, would lead to partiality, chicanery, and every kind of fraud. It is better that the suffrage should be conferred indiscriminately, or even withheld indiscriminately, than that it should be given to one and withheld from another at the discretion of a public officer. In regard, however, to reading, writing, and calculating, there need be no difficulty. It would be easy to require from every one who presented himself for registry that he should, in the presence of the registrar, copy a sentence from an English book, and perform a sum in the rule of three;

and to secure, by fixed rules and complete publicity, the honest application of so very simple a test. This condition, therefore, should in all cases accompany universal suffrage; and it would, after a few years, exclude none but those who cared so little for the privilege, that their vote, if given, would not in general be an indication of any real political opinion. . . .

Yet in this state of things, the great majority of voters, in most countries, and emphatically in this, would be manual labourers; and the twofold danger, that of too low a standard of political intelligence, and that of class legislation, would still exist in a very perilous degree. It remains to be seen whether any means exist by which these evils can be obviated.

They are capable of being obviated, if men sincerely wish it; not by any artificial contrivance, but by carrying out the natural order of human life, which recommends itself to every one in things in which he has no interest or traditional opinion running counter to it. In all human affairs, every person directly interested, and not under positive tutelage, has an admitted claim to a voice, and when his exercise of it is not inconsistent with the safety of the whole, cannot justly be excluded from it. But though every one ought to have a voice—that every one should have an equal voice is a totally different proposition. When two persons who have a joint interest in any business differ in opinion, does justice require that both opinions should be held of exactly equal value? If, with equal virtue, one is superior to the other in knowledge and intelligence—or if, with equal intelligence, one excels the other in virtue—the opinion, the judgment, of the higher moral or intellectual being is worth more than that of the inferior: and if the institutions of the country virtually assert that they are of the same value, they assert a thing which is not. One of the two, as the wiser or better man, has a claim to superior weight: the difficulty is in ascertaining which of the two it is; a thing impossible as between individuals, but, taking men in bodies and in numbers, it can be done with a certain approach to accuracy. There would be no pretence for applying this doctrine to any case which could with reason be considered as one of individual and private right. In an affair which concerns only one of two persons, that one is entitled to follow his own opinion, however much wiser the other may be than himself. But we are speaking of things which equally concern them both; where, if the more ignorant does not yield his share of the matter to the guidance of the wiser man, the wiser man must resign his to that of the more ignorant. Which of these modes of getting over the difficulty is most for the interest of both, and most conformable to the general fitness of things? If it be deemed unjust that either should have to give way, which injustice is greatest? that the better judgment should give way to the worse, or the worse to the better?

Now, national affairs are exactly such a joint concern, with the difference, that no one needs ever be called upon for a complete sacrifice of his own opinion. It can always be taken into the calculation, and counted at a certain figure, a higher figure being assigned to the suffrages of those whose opinion is entitled to greater weight. There is not, in this arrangement, anything necessarily invidious to those to whom it assigns the lower degrees of influence. Entire exclusion from a voice in the common concerns is one thing: the concession to others of a more potential voice, on the ground of greater capacity for the management of the joint interests, is another. The two things are not merely different, they are incommensurable. Every one has a right to feel insulted by being made a nobody, and stamped as of no account at all. No one but a fool, and only a fool of a peculiar description, feels offended by the acknowledgment that there are others whose opinion, and even whose wish, is entitled to a greater amount of consideration than his. To have no voice in what are partly his own concerns is a thing which nobody willingly submits to; but when what is partly his concern is also partly another's, and he feels the other to understand the subject better than himself, that the other's opinion should be counted for more than his own accords with his expectations, and with the course of things which in all other affairs of life he is accustomed to acquiesce in. It is only necessary that this superior influence should be assigned on grounds which he can comprehend, and of which he is able to perceive the justice.

. . . The only thing which can justify reckoning one person's opinion as equivalent to more than one is individual mental superiority; and what is wanted is some approximate means of ascertaining that. If there existed such a thing as a really national education or a trustworthy system of general examination, education might be tested directly. In the absence of these, the nature of a person's occupation is some test. An employer of labour is on the average more intelligent than a labourer; for he must labour with his head, and not solely with his hands. A foreman is generally more intelligent than an ordinary labourer, and a labourer in the skilled trades than in the unskilled. A banker, merchant, or manufacturer is likely to be more intelligent than a tradesman, because he has larger and more complicated interests to manage.

In all these cases it is not the having merely undertaken the superior function, but the successful performance of it, that tests the qualifications; for which reason, as well as to prevent persons from engaging nominally in an occupation for the sake of the vote, it would be proper to require that the occupation should have been persevered in for some length of time (say three years). Subject to some such condition, two or more votes might be allowed to every person who exercises any of these superior functions. The liberal professions, when really and not nominally practised, imply, of course, a still higher degree of instruction; and wherever a sufficient examination, or any serious conditions of education, are required before entering on a profession, its members could be admitted at once to a plurality of votes. The same rule might be applied to graduates of universities; and even to those who bring satisfactory certificates of having passed through the course of study required by any school at which the higher branches of knowledge are taught, under proper securities that the teaching is real, and not a mere pretence. . . . All these suggestions are open to much discussion in the detail, and to objections which it is of no use to anticipate. The time is not come for giving to such plans a practical shape, nor should I wish to be bound by the particular proposals which I have made. But it is to me evident, that in this direction lies the true ideal of representative government; and that to work towards it, by the best practical contrivances which can be found, is the path of real political improvement.

If it be asked to what length the principle admits of being carried, or how many votes might be accorded to an individual on the ground of superior qualifications, I answer, that this is not in itself very material, provided the distinctions and gradations are not made arbitrarily, but are such as can be understood and accepted by the general conscience and understanding. . . . The plurality of votes must on no account be carried so far that those who are privileged by it, or the class (if any) to which they mainly belong, shall outweigh by means of it all the rest of the community. The distinction in favour of education, right in itself, is further and strongly recommended by its preserving the educated from the class legislation of the uneducated; but it must stop short of enabling them to practise class legislation on their own account. Let me add, that I consider it an absolutely necessary part of the plurality scheme that it be open to the poorest individual in the community to claim its privileges, if he can prove that, in spite of all difficulties and obstacles, he is, in point of intelligence, entitled to them. There ought to be voluntary examinations at which any person whatever might present himself, might prove that he came up to the standard of knowledge and ability laid down as sufficient, and be admitted, in consequence, to the plurality of votes. A privilege which is not refused to any one who can show that he has realised the conditions on which in theory and principle it is dependent would not necessarily be repugnant to any one's sentiment of justice: but it would certainly be so, if, while conferred on general presumptions not always infallible, it were denied to direct proof.

Chapter 24

The Solitude of Self

Elizabeth Cady Stanton

Elizabeth Cady Stanton (1815–1902), a leader of the women's rights movement, delivered this address in 1892 before the Judiciary Committee of the U.S. House of Representatives and then before the Committee on Woman Suffrage of the U.S. Senate. She argues that women must be given equal opportunities for education because each person is ultimately alone and responsible for her own life. The solitude of one's existence means that there is no one but oneself to aid in living. Depriving one of an education is not just cruel but takes away a basic right. As Stanton puts it, "No matter how much women prefer to lean, to be protected and supported, nor how much men desire to have them do so, they must make the voyage of life alone, and for safety in an emergency they must know something of the laws of navigation."

Mr. Chairman and Gentlemen of the Committee:

We have been speaking before Committees of the Judiciary for the last twenty years, and we have gone over all the arguments in favor of the sixteenth amendment which are familiar to all you gentlemen; therefore, it will not be necessary that I should repeat them again.

The point I wish plainly to bring before you on this occasion is the individuality of each human soul—our Protestant idea, the right of individual conscience and judgment—our republican idea, individual citizenship. In discussing the right of woman, we are to consider, first, what belongs to her as an individual, in a world of her own, the arbiter of her own destiny, an imaginary Robinson Crusoe with her woman Friday on a solitary island. Her rights under such circumstances are to use all her faculties for her own safety and happiness.

Secondly, if we consider her as a citizen, as a member of a great nation, she must have the same rights as all other members, according to the fundamental principles of our government.

Thirdly, viewed as a woman, an equal factor in civilization, her rights and duties are still the same—individual happiness and development.

Fourthly, it is only the incidental relations of life, such as mother, wife, sister, daughter, which may involve some special duties and training. In the usual discussion in regard to woman's sphere, such men as Herbert Spencer, Frederic Harrison, and Grant Allen uniformly subordinate her rights and duties as an individual, as a citizen, as a woman, to the necessities of these incidental relations, some of which a large class of women may never assume. In discussing the sphere of man we do not decide his rights as an individual, as a citizen, as a man, by his duties as a father, a husband, a brother, or a son, relations some of which he may never fill. Moreover, he would be better fitted for these very relations, and whatever special work he might choose to do to earn his bread, by the complete development of all his faculties as an individual.

Just so with woman. The education that will fit her to discharge the duties in the largest sphere of human usefulness, will best fit her for whatever special work she may be compelled to do.

The isolation of every human soul and the necessity of self-dependence must give each individual the right to choose his own surroundings.

The strongest reason for giving woman all the opportunities for higher education, for the full development of her faculties, her forces of mind and body; for giving her the most enlarged freedom of thought and action; a complete emancipation from all forms of bondage, of custom, dependence, superstition; from all the crippling influences of fear; is the solitude and personal responsibility of her own individual life. The strongest reason why we ask for woman a voice in the government under which she lives; in the religion she is asked to believe; equality in social life, where she is the chief factor; a place in the trades and professions, where she may earn her bread, is because of her birthright to self-sovereignty; because, as an individual, she must rely on herself. No matter how much women prefer to lean, to be protected and supported, nor how much men desire to have them do so, they must make the voyage of life alone, and for safety in an emergency they must know something of the laws of navigation. To guide our own craft, we must be captain, pilot, engineer; with chart and compass to stand at the wheel; to watch the wind and waves and know when to take in the sail, and to read the signs in the firmament over all. It matters not whether the solitary voyager is man or woman.

Nature having endowed them equally, leaves them to their own skill and judgment in the hour of danger, and, if not equal to the occasion, alike they perish.

To appreciate the importance of fitting every human soul for independent action, think for a moment of the immeasurable solitude of self. We come into the world alone, unlike all who have gone before us; we leave it alone under circumstances peculiar to ourselves. No mortal ever has been, no mortal ever will be like the soul just launched on the sea of life. There can never again be just such environments as make up the infancy, youth and manhood of this one. Nature never repeats herself, and the possibilities of one human soul will never be found in another. No one has ever found two blades of ribbon grass alike, and no one will ever find two human beings alike. Seeing, then, what must be the infinite diversity in human character, we can in a measure appreciate the loss to a nation when any large class of the people is uneducated and unrepresented in the government. We ask for the complete development of every individual, first, for his own benefit and happiness. In fitting out an army we give each soldier his own knapsack, arms, powder, his blanket, cup, knife, fork and spoon. We provide alike for all their individual necessities, then each man bears his own burden.

Again we ask complete individual development for the general good; for the consensus of the competent on the whole round of human interest; on all questions of national life, and here each man must bear his share of the general burden. It is sad to see how soon friendless children are left to bear their own burdens before they can analyze their feelings; before they can even tell their joys and sorrows, they are thrown on their own resources. The great lesson that nature seems to teach us at all ages is self-dependence, self-protection, self-support. What a touching instance of a child's solitude; of that hunger of heart for love and recognition, in the case of a little girl who helped to dress a Christmas tree for the children of the family in which she served. On finding there was no present for herself she slipped away in the darkness and spent the night in an open field sitting on a stone, and when found in the morning was weeping as if her heart would break. No mortal will ever know the thought that passed through the mind of the friendless child in the long hours of that cold night, with only the silent stars to keep her company. The mention of her case in the daily papers moved many generous hearts to send her presents, but in the hours of her keenest sufferings she was thrown wholly on herself for consolation.

In youth our most bitter disappointments, our brightest hopes and ambitions are known only to ourselves; even our friendship and love we never fully share with another; there is something of every passion in every situation we conceal. Even so in our triumphs and our defeats.

The successful candidate for Presidency and his opponent each have a solitude peculiarly his own, and good form forbids either to speak of his pleasure or regret. The solitude of the king on his throne and the prisoner in his cell differs in characters and degree, but it is solitude nevertheless.

We ask no sympathy from others in the anxiety and agony of a broken friendship or shattered love. When death sunders our nearest ties, alone we sit in the shadows of our affliction. Alike mid the greatest triumphs and darkest tragedies of life we walk alone. On the divine heights of human attainments, eulogized and worshipped as a hero or a saint, we stand alone. In ignorance, poverty, and vice, as a pauper or criminal, alone we starve or steal; alone we suffer the sneers and rebuffs of our fellows; alone we are hunted and hounded through dark courts and alleys, in by-ways and highways; alone we stand in the judgment seats; alone in the prison cell we lament our crimes and misfortunes; alone we expiate them on the gallows. In hours like these we realize the awful solitude of individual life, its pains, its penalties, its responsibilities; hours in which the youngest and most helpless are thrown on their own resources for guidance and consolation. Seeing then that life must ever be a march and a battle, that each soldier must be equipped for his own protection, it is the height of cruelty to rob the individual of a single natural right.

To throw obstacles in the way of a complete education, is like putting out the eyes; to deny the rights of property, like cutting off the hands. To deny political equality is to rob the ostracized of all self-respect; of credit in the market place; of recompense in the world of work; of a voice among those who make and administer the law; a choice in the jury before whom they are tried, and in the judge who decides their punishment. Shakespeare's play of Titus and Andronicus [*sic*] contains a terrible satire on woman's position in the nineteenth century—"Rude men" (the play tells us) "seize the king's daughter, cut out her tongue, cut off her hands, and then bade her go call for water and wash her hands." What a picture of woman's position. Robbed of her natural rights, handicapped by law and custom at every turn, yet compelled to fight her own battles, and in the emergencies of life to fall back on herself for protection.

The girl of sixteen, thrown on the world to support herself, to make her own place in society, to resist the temptations that surround her and maintain a spotless integrity, must do all this by native force or superior education. She does not acquire this power by being trained to trust others and distrust herself. If she wearies of the struggle, finding it hard work to swim upstream, and allows herself to drift with the current, she will find plenty of company, but not one to share her misery in the hour of her deepest humiliation. If she tries to retrieve her position, to conceal the past, her life is hedged about with fears lest willing hands should tear the veil from what she fain would hide. Young and friendless, she knows the bitter solitude of self.

How the little courtesies of life on the surface of society, deemed so important from man towards woman, fade into utter insignificance in view of the deeper tragedies in which she must play her part alone, where no human aid is possible.

The young wife and mother, at the head of some establishment with a kind husband to shield her from the adverse winds of life, with wealth, fortune, and position, has a certain harbor of safety, secure against the ordinary ills of life. But to manage a household, have a desirable influence in society, keep her friends and the affections of her husband, train her children and servants well, she must have a rare common sense, wisdom, diplomacy, and a knowledge of human nature. To do all this she needs the cardinal virtues and the strong points of character that the most successful statesman possesses.

An uneducated woman, trained to dependence, with no resources in herself must make a failure of any position in life. But society says women do not need a knowledge of the world; the liberal training that experience in public life must give, all the advantages of collegiate education; but when for the lack of all this, the woman's happiness is wrecked, alone she bears her humiliation; and the solitude of the weak and the ignorant is indeed pitiful. In the wild chase for the prizes of life they are ground to powder.

In age, when the pleasures of youth are passed, children grown up, married and gone, the hurry and bustle of life in a measure over, when the hands are weary of active service, when the old armchair and the fireside are the chosen resorts, then men and women alike must fall back on their own resources. If they cannot find companionship in books, if they have no interest in the vital questions of the hour, no interest in watching the consummation of reforms, with which they might have been identified, they soon pass into their dotage. The more fully the faculties of the mind are developed and kept in use, the longer the period of vigor and active interest in all around us continues. If from a lifelong participation in public affairs a woman feels responsible for the laws regulating our system of education, the discipline of our jails and prisons, the sanitary conditions of our private homes, public buildings, and thoroughfares, an interest in commerce, finance, our foreign relations, in any or all of these questions, her solitude will at least be respectable, and she will not be driven to gossip or scandal for entertainment.

The chief reason for opening to every soul the doors to the whole round of human duties and pleasures is the individual development thus attained, the resources thus provided under all circumstances to mitigate the solitude that at times must come to everyone. I once asked Prince Krapotkin, the Russian nihilist, how he endured his long years in prison, deprived of books, pen, ink, and paper. "Ah," he said, "I thought out many questions on which I had a deep interest. In the pursuit of an idea I took no note of time. When tired of solving knotty problems I recited all the beautiful passages in prose or verse I had ever learned. I became acquainted with my self and my own resources. I had a world of my own, a vast empire, that no Russian jailor or Czar could invade." Such is the value of liberal thought and broad culture when shut from all human companionship, bringing comfort and sunshine within even the four walls of a prison cell.

As women ofttimes share a similar fate, should they not have all the consolation that the most liberal education can give? Their suffering in the prisons of St. Petersburg; in the long, weary marches to Siberia, and in the mines, working side by side with men, surely call for all the self-support that the most exalted sentiments of heroism can give. When suddenly roused at midnight, with the startling cry of "fire! fire!" to find the house over their heads in flames, do women wait for men to point the way to safety? And are the men, equally bewildered and half suffocated with smoke, in a position to more than save themselves?

At such times the most timid women have shown a courage and heroism in saving their husbands and children that has surprised everybody. Inasmuch, then, as woman shares equally the joys and sorrows of time and eternity, is it not the height of presumption in man to propose to represent her at the ballot box and the throne of grace, do her voting in the state, her praying in the church, and to assume the position of priest at the family altar.

Nothing strengthens the judgment and quickens the conscience like individual responsibility. Nothing adds such dignity to character as the recognition of one's self-sovereignty; the right to an equal place, everywhere conceded; a place earned by personal merit, not an artificial attainment by inheritance, wealth, family, and position. Seeing, then that the responsibilities of life rest equally on man and woman, that their destiny is the same, they need the same preparation for time and eternity. The talk of sheltering woman from the fierce storms of life is the sheerest mockery, for they beat on her from every point of the compass, just as they do on man, and with more fatal results, for he has been trained to protect himself, to resist, to conquer. Such are the facts in human experience, the responsibilities of individual sovereignty. Rich and poor, intelligent and ignorant, wise and foolish, virtuous and vicious, man and woman, it is ever the same, each soul must depend wholly on itself.

Whatever the theories may be of woman's dependence on man, in the supreme moments of her life he can not bear her burdens. Alone she goes to the gates of death to give life to every man that is born into the world. No one can share her fears, no one can mitigate her pangs; and if her sorrow is greater than she can bear, alone she passes beyond the gates into the vast unknown.

From the mountain tops of Judea, long ago, a heavenly voice bade His disciples, "Bear ye one another's burdens," but humanity has not yet risen to that point of self-sacrifice, and if ever so willing, how few the burdens are that one soul can bear for another. In the highways of Palestine; in prayer and fasting on the solitary mountain top; in the Garden of Gethsemane; before the judgment seat of Pilate; betrayed by one of His trusted disciples at His last supper; in His agonies on the cross, even Jesus of Nazareth, in these last sad days on earth, felt the awful solitude of self. Deserted by man, in agony he cries. "My God! My God! Why hast Thou forsaken me." And so it ever must be in the conflicting scenes of life, in the long weary march, each one walks alone. We may have many friends, love, kindness, sympathy and charity to smooth our pathway in everyday life, but in the tragedies and triumphs of human experience each mortal stands alone.

But when all artificial trammels are removed, and women are recognized as individuals, responsible for their own environments, thoroughly educated for all positions in life they may be called to fill; with all the resources in themselves that liberal thought and broad culture can give; guided by their own conscience and judgment; trained to self-protection by a healthy development of the muscular system and skill in the use of weapons of defense, and stimulated to self-support by a knowledge of the business world and the pleasure that pecuniary independence must ever give; when women are trained in this way they will, in a measure, be fitted for those years of solitude that come to all, whether prepared or otherwise. As in our extremity we must depend on ourselves, the dictates of wisdom point to complete individual development.

In talking of education how shallow the argument that each class must be educated for the special work it proposes to do, and all those faculties not needed in this special walk must lie dormant and utterly wither for want of use, when perhaps, these will be the very faculties needed in life's greatest emergencies. Some say, "Where is the use of drilling girls in the languages, the sciences, in law, medicine, theology?"

As wives, mothers, housekeepers, cooks, they need a different curriculum from boys who are to fill all positions. The chief cooks in our great hotels and ocean steamers are men. In large cities men run the bakeries; they make our bread, cake and pies. They manage the laundries; they are now considered our best milliners and dressmakers. Because some men fill these departments of usefulness, shall we regulate the curriculum in Harvard and Yale to their present necessities? If not, why this talk in our best colleges of a curriculum for girls who are crowding into the trades and professions; teachers in all our public schools rapidly filling many lucrative and honorable positions in life? They are showing, too, their calmness and courage in the most trying hours of human experience.

You have probably all read in the daily papers of the terrible storm in the Bay of Biscay when a tidal wave made such havoc on the shore, wrecking vessels, unroofing houses and carrying destruction everywhere. Among other buildings the woman's prison was demolished. Those who escaped saw men struggling to reach the shore. They promptly by clasping hands made a chain of themselves and pushed out into the sea, again and again, at the risk of their lives until they had brought six men to shore, carried them to a shelter, and did all in their power for their comfort and protection.

What special school of training could have prepared these women for this sublime moment of their lives? In times like this humanity rises above all college curriculum and recognizes Nature as the greatest of all teachers in the hour of danger and death. Women are already the equals of men in the whole of realm of thought, in art, science, literature, and government. With telescopic vision they explore the starry firmament, and bring back the history of the planetary world. With chart and compass they pilot ships across the mighty deep, and with skillful finger send electric messages around the globe. In galleries of art the beauties of nature and the virtues of humanity are immortalized by them on their canvas and by their inspired touch dull blocks of marble are transformed into angles of light.

In music they speak again the language of Mendelssohn, Beethoven, Chopin, Schumann, and are worthy interpreters of their great thoughts. The poetry and novels of the century are theirs, and they have touched the keynote of reform in religion, politics, and social life. They fill the editor's and professor's chair, and plead at the bar of justice, walk the wards of the hospital, and speak from the pulpit and the platform; such is the type of womanhood that an enlightened public sentiment welcomes today, and such the triumph of the facts of life over the false theories of the past.

Is it, then, consistent to hold the developed woman of this day within the narrow political limits as the dame with the spinning wheel and knitting needle occupied in the past? No! No! Machinery has taken the labors of woman as well as man on its tireless shoulders; the loom and the spinning wheel are but dreams of the past; the pen, the brush, the easel, the chisel, have taken their places, while the hopes and ambitions of women are essentially changed.

We see reason sufficient in the outer conditions of human beings for individual liberty and development, but when we consider the self-dependence of every human soul we see the need of courage, judgment, and the exercise of every faculty of mind and body, strengthened and developed by use, in woman as well as man.

Whatever may be said of man's protecting power in ordinary conditions, mid all the terrible disasters by land and sea, in the supreme moments of danger, alone, woman must ever meet the horrors of the situation; the Angel of Death even makes no royal pathway for her. Man's love and sympathy enter only into the sunshine of our lives. In that solemn solitude of self, that links us with the immeasurable and the eternal, each soul lives alone forever. A recent writer says:

I remember once, in crossing the Atlantic, to have gone upon the deck of the ship in midnight, when a dense black cloud enveloped the sky, and the great dep was roaring madly under the lashes of demoniac winds. My feelings was not of danger or fear (which is a base surrender of the immortal soul), but of utter desolation and loneliness; a little speck of life shut in by a tremendous darkness. Again I remember to have climbed on the slopes of the Swiss Alps, up beyond the point where vegetation ceases, and the stunted conifers no longer struggle against the unfeeling blasts. Around me lay a huge confusion of rocks, out of which the gigantic ice peaks shot into the measureless blue of the heavens, and again my only feeling was the awful solitude.

And yet, there is a solitude, which each and every one of us has always carried with him, more inaccessible than the ice-cold mountains, more profound than the midnight sea; the solitude of self. Our inner being, which we call ourself, no eye nor touch of man or angel has ever pierced. It is more hidden than the caves of the gnome; the sacred adytum of the oracle; the hidden chamber of eleusinian mystery, for to it only omniscience is permitted to enter.

Such is individual life. Who, I ask you, can take, dare take, on himself the rights, the duties, the responsibilities of another human soul?

Chapter 25

Of the Ruling of Men

W. E. B. Du Bois

William Edward Burghardt Du Bois (1868–1963) was an activist, journalist, novelist, and philosopher. He argues for an inclusive form of deliberative democracy, for democracies have the lofty goal of benefiting the whole population, of realizing justice for all human beings. But this end is regularly thwarted by ignorance, exacerbated by the exclusion of women and minorities. As Du Bois writes, "[O]nly the sufferer knows his suffering and no state can be strong which excludes from its expressed wisdom the knowledge possessed by mothers, wives, and daughters. . . . The same arguments apply to other excluded groups." An inclusive democracy is the best form of government because it is the wisest.

The ruling of men is the effort to direct the individual actions of many persons toward some end. This end theoretically should be the greatest good of all, but no human group has ever reached this ideal because of ignorance and selfishness. The simplest object would be rule for the Pleasure of One, namely the Ruler; or of the Few—his favorites; or of many—the Rich, the Privileged, the Powerful. Democratic movements inside groups and nations are always taking place and they are the efforts to increase the number of beneficiaries of the ruling. In 18th century Europe, the effort became so broad and sweeping that an attempt was made at universal expression and the philosophy of the movement said that if All ruled they would rule for All and thus Universal Good was sought through Universal Suffrage.

The unrealized difficulty of this program lay in the widespread ignorance. The mass of men, even of the more intelligent men, not only knew little about each other but less about the action of men in groups and the technique of industry in general. They could only apply universal suffrage, therefore, to the things they knew or knew partially: they knew personal and menial service, individual craftsmanship, agriculture and barter, taxes or the taking of private property for public ends and the rent of land. With these matters then they attempted to deal. Under the cry of "Freedom" they greatly relaxed the grip of selfish interests by restricting menial service, securing the right of property in handiwork and regulating public taxes; distributing land ownership and freeing trade and barter.

While they were doing this against stubborn resistance, a whole new organization of work suddenly appeared. The suddenness of this "Industrial Revolution" of the 19th century was partly fortuitous—in the case of Watt's teakettle—partly a natural development, as in the matter of spinning, but largely the determination of powerful and intelligent individuals to secure the benefits of privileged persons, as in the case of foreign slave trade.

The result was on the one hand a vast and unexampled development of industry. Life and civilization in the late 19th and early 20th century were Industry in its whole conception, language, and accomplishment: the object of life was to make goods. Now before this giant aspect of things, the new democracy stood aghast and impotent. It could not rule because it did not understand: an invincible kingdom of trade, business, and commerce ruled the world, and before its threshold stood the Freedom of 18th century philosophy warding the way. Some of the very ones who were freed from the tyranny of the Middle Age became the tyrants of the industrial age.

There came a reaction. Men sneered at "democracy" and politics, and brought forth Fate and Philanthropy to rule the world—Fate which gave divine right to rule to the Captains of Industry and their created Millionaires; Philanthropy which organized vast schemes of relief to stop at least the flow of blood in the vaster wounds which industry was making.

It was at this time that the lowest laborers, who worked hardest, got least and suffered most, began to mutter and rebel, and among these were the American Negroes. Lions have no historians, and therefore lion hunts are thrilling and satisfactory human reading. Negroes had no bards, and therefore it has been widely told how American philanthropy freed the slave. In truth the Negro revolted by armed rebellion, by sullen refusal to work, by poison and murder, by running away to the North and Canada, by giving point and powerful example to the agitation of the abolitionists and by furnishing 200,000 soldiers and many times as many civilian helpers in the Civil War. This war was not a war for Negro freedom, but a duel between two industrial systems, one of which was bound to fail because it was an anachronism, and the other bound to succeed because of the Industrial Revolution.

When now the Negro was freed the Philanthropists sought to apply to his situation the Philosophy of Democracy handed down from the 18th century.

There was a chance here to try democratic rule in a new way, that is, against the new industrial oppression with a mass of workers who were not yet in its control. With plenty of land widely distributed, staple products like cotton, rice, and sugar cane, and a thorough system of education, there was a unique chance to realize a new modern democracy in industry in the southern United States which would point the way to the world. This, too, if done by black folk, would have tended to a new unity of human beings and an obliteration of human hatreds festering along the color line.

Efforts were begun. The 14th and 15th amendments gave the right to vote to white and black laborers, and they immediately established a public school system and began to attack the land question. The United States government was seriously considering the distribution of land and capital —"40 acres and a mule"—and the price of cotton opened an easy way to economic independence. Co-operative movements began on a large scale.

But alas! Not only were the former slave-owners solidly arrayed against this experiment, but the owners of the industrial North saw disaster in any such beginnings of industrial democracy. The opposition based its objections on the color line, and Reconstruction became in history a great movement for the self-assertion of the white race against the impudent ambition of degraded blacks, instead of, in truth, the rise of a mass of black and white laborers.

The result was the disfranchisement of the blacks of the South and a world-wide attempt to restrict democratic development to white races and to distract them with race hatred against the darker races. This program, however, although it undoubtedly helped raise the scale of white labor, in much greater proportion put wealth and power in the hands of the great European Captains of Industry and made modern industrial imperialism possible.

This led to renewed efforts on the part of white European workers to understand and apply their political power to its reform through democratic control.

Whether known as Communism or Socialism or what not, these efforts are neither new nor strange nor terrible, but world-old and seeking an absolutely justifiable human ideal—the only ideal that can be sought: the direction of individual action in industry so as to secure the greatest good of all. Marxism was one method of accomplishing this, and its panacea was the doing away with private property in machines and materials. Two mighty attacks were made on this proposal. One was an attack on the fundamental democratic foundation: modern European white industry does not even theoretically seek the good of all, but simply of all Europeans. This attack was virtually unanswered—indeed some Socialists openly excluded Negroes and Asiatics

from their scheme. From this it was easy to drift into that form of syndical-
ism which asks socialism for the skilled laborer only and leaves the common
laborer in his bonds.

This throws us back on fundamentals. It compels us again to examine the
roots of democracy.

Who may be excluded from a share in the ruling of men? Time and time
again the world has answered:

The Ignorant

The Inexperienced

The Guarded

The Unwilling

That is, we have assumed that only the intelligent should vote, or those
who know how to rule men, or those who are not under benevolent guardianship, or those who ardently desire the right.

These restrictions are not arguments for the wide distribution of the ballot—they are rather reasons for restriction addressed to the self-interest of the
present real rulers. We say easily, for instance, "The ignorant ought not to
vote." We would say, "No civilized state should have citizens too ignorant to
participate in government," and this statement is but a step to the fact: that no
state is civilized which has citizens too ignorant to help rule it. Or, in other
words, education is not a prerequisite to political control—political control is
the cause of popular education.

Again, to make experience a qualification for the franchise is absurd: it
would stop the spread of democracy and make political power hereditary, a
prerequisite of a class, caste, race, or sex. It has of course been soberly argued
that only white folk or Englishmen, or men, are really capable of exercising
sovereign power in a modern state. The statement proves too much: only yesterday it was Englishmen of high descent, or men of "blood," or sovereigns
"by divine right" who could rule. Today the civilized world is being ruled by
the descendants of persons who a century ago were pronounced incapable of
ever developing a self-ruling people. In every modern state there must come to
the polls every generation, and indeed every year, men who are inexperienced
in the solutions of the political problems that confront them and who must experiment in methods of ruling men. Thus and thus only will civilization grow.

Again, what is this theory of benevolent guardianship for women, for the
masses, for Negroes—for "lesser breeds without the law"? It is simply the
old cry of privilege, the old assumption that there are those in the world who
know better what is best for others than those others know themselves, and
who can be trusted to do this best.

In fact no one knows himself but that self's own soul. The vast and wonderful knowledge of this marvelous universe is locked in the bosoms of its

individual souls. To tap this mighty reservoir of experience, knowledge, beauty, love, and deed we must appeal not to the few, not to some souls, but to all. The narrower the appeal, the poorer the culture; the wider the appeal the more magnificent are the possibilities. Infinite is human nature. We make it finite by choking back the mass of men, by attempting to speak for others, to interpret and act for them, and we end by acting for ourselves and using the world as our private property. If this were all, it were crime enough—but it is not all: by our ignorance we make the creation of the greater world impossible; we beat back a world built of the playing of dogs and laughter of children, the song of Black Folk and worship of Yellow, the love of women and strength of men, and try to express by a group of doddering ancients the Will of the World.

There are people who insist upon regarding the franchise, not as a necessity, for the many, but as a privilege for the few. They say of persons and classes: "They do not need the ballot." This is often said of women. It is argued that everything which women with the ballot might do for themselves can be done for them; that they have influence and friends "at court," and that their enfranchisement would simply double the number of ballots. So, too, we are told that American Negroes can have done for them by other voters all that they could possibly do for themselves with the ballot and much more because the white voters are more intelligent.

Further than this, it is argued that many of the disfranchised people recognize these facts. "Women do not want the ballot" has been a very effective counter war-cry, so much so that many men have taken refuge in the declaration: "When they want to vote, why, then—" So, too, we are continually told that the "best" Negroes stay out of politics.

Such arguments show so curious a misapprehension of the foundation of the argument for democracy that the argument must be continually restated and emphasized. We must remember that if the theory of democracy is correct, the right to vote is not merely a privilege, not simply a method of meeting the needs of a particular group, and least of all a matter of recognized want or desire. Democracy is a method of realizing the broadest measure of justice to all human beings. The world has, in the past, attempted various methods of attaining this end, most of which can be summed up in three categories:

The method of the benevolent tyrant.

The method of the select few.

The method of the excluded groups.

The method of intrusting the government of a people to a strong ruler has great advantages when the ruler combines strength with ability, unselfish devotion to the public good, and knowledge of what that good calls for. Such a combination is, however, rare and the selection of the right ruler is very difficult. To leave the selection to force is to put a premium on physical strength, chance, and intrigue; to make the selection a matter of birth simply transfers the real power from sovereign to minister. Inevitably the choice of rulers must fall on electors.

Then comes the problem, who shall elect. The earlier answer was: a select few, such as the wise, the best born, the able. Many people assume that it was corruption that made such aristocracies fail. By no means. The best and most effective aristocracy, like the best monarchy, suffered from lack of knowledge. The rulers did not know or understand the needs of the people and they could not find out, for in the last analysis only the man himself, however humble, knows his own condition. He may not know how to remedy it, he may not realize just what is the matter; but he knows when something hurts and he alone knows how that hurt feels. Or if sunk below feeling or comprehension or complaint, he does not even know that he is hurt, God help his country, for it not only lacks knowledge, but has destroyed the sources of knowledge.

So soon as a nation discovers that it holds in the heads and hearts of its individual citizens the vast mine of knowledge, out of which it may build a just government, then more and more it calls those citizens to select their rulers and to judge the justice of their acts.

Even here, however, the temptation is to ask only for the wisdom of citizens of a certain grade or those of recognized worth. Continually some classes are tacitly or expressly excluded. Thus women have been excluded from modern democracy because of the persistent theory of female subjection and because it was argued that their husbands or other male folks would look to their interests. Now, manifestly, most husbands, fathers, and brothers will, so far as they know how or as they realize women's needs, look after them. But remember the foundation of the argument, —that in the last analysis only the sufferer knows his sufferings and that no state can be strong which excludes from its expressed wisdom the knowledge possessed by mothers, wives, and daughters. We have but to view the unsatisfactory relations of the sexes the world over and the problem of children to realize how desperately we need this excluded wisdom.

The same arguments apply to other excluded groups: if a race, like the Negro race, is excluded, then so far as that race is a part of the economic and social organization of the land, the feeling and the experience of that race are absolutely necessary to the realization of the broadest justice for all citizens. Or if the "submerged tenth" be excluded, then again, there is lost from the world an experience of untold value, and they must be raised rapidly to a place where they can speak for themselves. In the same way and for the same reason children must be educated, insanity prevented, and only those put under the guardianship of others who can in no way be trained to speak for themselves.

The real argument for democracy is, then, that in the people we have the source of that endless life and unbounded wisdom which the rulers of men must have. A given people today may not be intelligent, but through a democratic government that recognizes, not only the worth of the individual to himself, but the worth of his feelings and experiences to all, they can educate, not only the individual unit, but generation after generation, until they accumulate vast stores of wisdom. Democracy alone is the method of showing the whole experience of the race for the benefit of the future and if democracy tries to exclude women or Negroes or the poor or any class because of innate characteristics which do not interfere with intelligence, then that democracy cripples itself and belies its name.

From this point of view we can easily see the weakness and strength of current criticism of extension of the ballot. It is the business of a modern government to see to it, first, that the number of ignorant within its bounds is reduced to the very smallest number. Again, it is the duty of every such government to extend as quickly as possible the number of persons of mature age who can vote. Such possible voters must be regarded, not as sharers of a limited treasure, but as sources of new national wisdom and strength.

The addition of the new wisdom, the new points of view, and the new interests must, of course, be from time to time bewildering and confusing. Today those who have a voice in the body politic have expressed their wishes and sufferings. The result has been a smaller or greater balancing of their conflicting interests. The appearance of new interests and complaints means disarrangement and confusion to the older equilibrium. It is, of course, the inevitable preliminary step to that larger equilibrium in which the interests of no human soul will be neglected. These interests will not, surely, be all fully realized, but they will be recognized and given as full weight as the conflicting interests will allow. The problem of government thereafter would be to reduce the necessary conflict of human interests to the minimum.

From such a point of view one easily sees the strength of the demand for the ballot on the part of certain disfranchised classes. When women ask for the ballot, they are asking, not for a privilege, but for a necessity. You may not see the necessity, you may easily argue that women do not need to vote. Indeed, the women themselves in considerable numbers may agree with you. Nevertheless, women do need the ballot. They need it to right the balance of a world sadly awry because of its brutal neglect of the rights of women and children. With the best will and knowledge, no man can know women's wants as well as women themselves. To disfranchise women is deliberately to turn from knowledge and grope in ignorance.

So, too, with American Negroes: the South continually insists that a benevolent guardianship of whites over blacks is the ideal thing. They assume
that white people not only know better what Negroes need than Negroes
themselves, but that they are anxious to supply these needs. As a result they
grope in ignorance and helplessness. They cannot "understand" the Negro;
they cannot protect him from cheating and lynching; and, in general, instead
of loving guardianship we see anarchy and exploitation. If the Negro could
speak for himself in the South instead of being spoken for, if he could defend
himself instead of having to depend on the chance sympathy of white citizens,
how much healthier a growth of democracy the South would have.

So, too, with the darker races of the world. No federation of the world, no
true inter-nation—can exclude the black and brown and yellow races from its
counsels. They must equally and according to number act and be heard at the
world's council,

It is not, for a moment, to be assumed that enfranchising women will
not cost something. It will for many years confuse our politics. It may even
change the present status of family life. It will admit to the ballot thousands of
inexperienced persons, unable to vote intelligently. Above all, it will interfere
with some of the present prerogatives of men and probably for some time to
come annoy them considerably.

So, too, Negro enfranchisement meant reconstruction, with its theft and
bribery and incompetency as well as its public schools and enlightened, social
legislation. It would mean today that black men in the South would have to
be treated with consideration, have their wishes respected and their manhood
rights recognized. Every white Southerner, who wants peons beneath him,
who believes in hereditary menials and a privileged aristocracy, or who hates
certain races because of their characteristics, would resent this.

Notwithstanding this, if America is ever to become a government built on
the broadest justice to every citizen, then every citizen must be enfranchised.
There may be temporary exclusions, until the ignorant and their children are
taught, or to avoid too sudden an influx of inexperienced voters. But such
exclusions can be but temporary if justice is to prevail.

The principle of basing all government on the consent of the governed is
undenied and undeniable. Moreover, the method of modern democracy has
placed within reach of the modern state larger reserves of efficiency, ability,
and even genius than the ancient or mediaeval state dreamed of. That this
great work of the past can be carried further among all races and nations no
one can reasonably doubt.

Great as are our human differences and capabilities there is not the slightest scientific reason for assuming that a given human being of any race or
sex cannot reach normal, human development if he is granted a reasonable

chance. This is, of course, denied. It is denied so volubly and so frequently and with such positive conviction that the majority of unthinking people seem to assume that most human beings are not human and have no right to human treatment or human opportunity. All this goes to prove that human beings are, and must be, woefully ignorant of each other. It always startles us to find folks thinking like ourselves. We do not really associate with each other, we associate with our ideas of each other, and few people have either the ability or courage to question their own ideas. None have more persistently and dogmatically insisted upon the inherent inferiority of women than the men with whom they come in closest contact. It is the husbands, brothers, and sons of women whom it has been most difficult to induce to consider women seriously or to acknowledge that women have rights which men are bound to respect. So, too, it is those people who live in closest contact with black folk who have most unhesitatingly asserted the utter impossibility of living beside Negroes who are not industrial or political slaves or social pariahs. All this proves that none are so blind as those nearest the thing seen, while, on the other hand, the history of the world is the history of the discovery of the common humanity of human beings among steadily-increasing circles of men.

If the foundations of democracy are thus seen to be sound, how are we going to make democracy effective where it now fails to function—particularly in industry? The Marxists assert that industrial democracy will automatically follow public ownership of machines and materials. Their opponents object that nationalization of machines and materials would not suffice because the mass of people do not understand the industrial process. They do not know:

What to do

How to do it

Who could do it best

or

How to apportion the resulting goods.

There can be no doubt but that monopoly of machines and materials is a chief source of the power of industrial tyrants over the common worker and that monopoly today is due as much to chance and cheating as to thrift and intelligence. So far as it is due to chance and cheating, the argument for public ownership of capital is incontrovertible even though it involves some interference with long vested rights and inheritance. This is being widely recognized in the whole civilized world. But how about the accumulation of goods due to thrift and intelligence—would democracy in industry interfere here to such an extent as to discourage enterprise and make impossible the intelligent direction of the mighty and intricate industrial process of modern times?

The knowledge of what to do in industry and how to do it in order to attain the resulting goods rests in the hands and brains of the workers and managers, and the judges of the result are the public. Consequently it is not so much a question as to whether the world will admit democratic control here as how can such control be long avoided when the people once understand the fundamentals of industry. How can civilization persist in letting one person or a group of persons, by secret inherent power, determine what goods shall be made—whether bread or champagne, overcoats or silk socks? Can so vast a power be kept from the people?

But it may be opportunely asked: has our experience in electing public officials led us to think that we could run railways, cotton mills, and department stores by popular vote? The answer is clear: no, it has not, and the reason has been lack of interest in politics and the tyranny of the Majority. Politics have not touched the matters of daily life which are nearest the interests of the people—namely, work and wages; or if they have, they have touched it obscurely and indirectly. When voting touches the vital, everyday interests of all, nominations and elections will call for more intelligent activity. Consider too the vast unused and misused power of public rewards to obtain ability and genius for the service of the state. If millionaires can buy science and art, cannot the Democratic state outbid them not only with money but with the vast ideal of the common weal?

There still remains, however, the problem of the Majority.

What is the cause of the undoubted reaction and alarm that the citizens of democracy continually feel? It is, I am sure, the failure to feel the full significance of the change of rule from a privileged minority to that of an omnipotent majority, and the assumption that mere majority rule is the last word of government; that majorities have no responsibilities, that they rule by the grace of God. Granted that government should be based on the consent of the governed, does the consent of a majority at any particular time adequately express the consent of all? Has the minority, even though a small and unpopular and unfashionable minority, no right to respectful consideration?

I remember that excellent little high school text book, "Nordhoff's Politics," where I first read of government, saying this sentence at the beginning of its most important chapter: "The first duty of a minority is to become a majority." This is a statement which has its underlying truth, but it also has its dangerous falsehood; viz., any minority which cannot become a majority is not worthy of any consideration. But suppose that the out-voted minority is necessarily always a minority? Women, for instance, can seldom expect to be a majority; artists must always be the few; ability is always rare, and black folk in this land are but a tenth. Yet to tyrannize over such minorities, to browbeat and insult them, to call that government a democracy which makes majority votes an excuse for crushing ideas and individuality and self-development, is manifestly a peculiarly dangerous perversion of the real democratic ideal. It is right here, in its method and not in its object, that democracy in America and elsewhere has so often failed. We have attempted to enthrone any chance majority and make it rule by divine right. We have kicked and cursed minorities as upstarts and usurpers when their sole offense lay in not having ideas or hair like ours. Efficiency, ability, and genius found often no abiding place in such a soil as this. Small wonder that revolt has come and high-handed methods are rife, of pretending that policies which we favor or persons that we like have the anointment of a purely imaginary majority vote.

Are the methods of such a revolt wise, howsoever great the provocation and evil may be? If the absolute monarchy of majorities is galling and inefficient, is it any more inefficient than the absolute monarchy of individuals or privileged classes have been found to be in the past? Is the appeal from a numerous-minded despot to a smaller, privileged group or to one man likely to remedy matters permanently? Shall we step backward a thousand years because our present problem is baffling?

Surely not and surely, too, the remedy for absolutism lies in calling these same minorities to council. As the king-in-council succeeded the king by the grace of God, so in future democracies the toleration and encouragement of minorities and the willingness to consider as "men" the crankiest, humblest and poorest and blackest peoples, must be the real key to the consent of the governed. Peoples and governments will not in the future assume that because they have the brute power to enforce momentarily dominant ideas, it is best to do so without thoughtful conference with the ideas of smaller groups and individuals. Proportionate representation in physical and spiritual form must come.

That this method is virtually coming in vogue we can see by the minority groups of modern legislatures. Instead of the artificial attempts to divide all possible ideas and plans between two great parties, modern legislatures in advanced nations tend to develop smaller and smaller minority groups, while government is carried on by temporary coalitions. For a time we inveighed against this and sought to consider it a perversion of the only possible method of practical democracy. Today we are gradually coming to realize that government by temporary coalition of small and diverse groups may easily become the most efficient method of expressing the will of man and of setting the human soul free. The only hindrance to the faster development of this government by allied minorities is the fear of external war which is used again and again to melt these living, human, thinking groups into inhuman, thoughtless, and murdering machines.

The persons, then, who come forward in the dawn of the 20th century to help in the ruling of men must come with the firm conviction that no nation, race, or sex, has a monopoly of ability or ideas; that no human group is so small as to deserve to be ignored as a part, and as an integral and respected part, of the mass of men; that, above all, no group of twelve million black folk, even though they are at the physical mercy of a hundred million white majority, can be deprived of a voice in their government and of the right to self-development without a blow at the very foundations of all democracy and all human uplift; that the very criticism aimed today at universal suffrage is in reality a demand for power on the part of consciously efficient minorities, —but these minorities face a fatal blunder when they assume that less democracy will give them and their kind greater efficiency. However desperate the temptation, no modern nation can shut the gates of opportunity in the face of its women, its peasants, its laborers, or its socially damned. How astounded the future world-citizen will be to know that as late as 1918 great and civilized nations were making desperate endeavor to confine the development of ability and individuality to one sex,—that is, to one-half of the nation; and he will probably learn that similar effort to confine humanity to one race lasted a hundred years longer.

The doctrine of the divine right of majorities leads to almost humorous insistence on a dead level of mediocrity. It demands that all people be alike or that they be ostracized. At the same time its greatest accusation against rebels is this same desire to be alike: the suffragette is accused of wanting to be a man, the socialist is accused of envy of the rich, and the black man is accused of wanting to be white. That any one of these should simply want to be himself is to the average worshiper of the majority inconceivable, and yet of all worlds, may the good Lord deliver us from a world where everybody looks like his neighbor and thinks like his neighbor and is like his neighbor.

The world has long since awakened to a realization of the evil which a privileged few may exercise over the majority of a nation. So vividly has this truth been brought home to us that we have lightly assumed that a privileged and enfranchised majority cannot equally harm a nation. Insane, wicked, and wasteful as the tyranny of the few over the many may be, it is not more dangerous than the tyranny of the many over the few. Brutal physical revolution can, and usually does, end the tyranny of the few. But the spiritual losses from suppressed minorities may be vast and fatal and yet all unknown and unrealized because idea and dream and ability are paralyzed by brute force.

If, now, we have a democracy with no excluded groups, with all men and women enfranchised, what is such a democracy to do? How will it function? What will be its field of work?

The paradox which faces the civilized world today is that democratic control is everywhere limited in its control of human interests. Mankind is engaged in planting, forestry, and mining, preparing food and shelter, making clothes and machines, transporting goods and folk, disseminating news, distributing products, doing public and private personal service, teaching, advancing science, and creating art.

In this intricate whirl of activities, the theory of government has been hitherto to lay down only very general rules of conduct, marking the limits of extreme anti-social acts, like fraud, theft, and murder.

The theory was that within these bounds was Freedom—the Liberty to think and do and move as one wished. The real realm of freedom was found in experience to be much narrower than this in one direction and much broader in another. In matters of Truth and Faith and Beauty, the Ancient Law was inexcusably strait and modern law unforgivably stupid. It is here that the future and mighty fight for Freedom must and will be made. Here in the heavens and on the mountaintops, the air of Freedom is wide, almost limitless, for here, in the highest stretches, individual freedom harms no man, and, therefore, no man has the right to limit it.

On the other hand, in the valleys of the hard, unyielding laws of matter and the social necessities of time production, and human intercourse, the limits on our freedom are stern and unbending if we would exist and thrive. This does not say that everything here is governed by incontrovertible "natural" law which needs no human decision as to raw materials, machinery, prices, wages, news-dissemination, education of children, etc.; but it does mean that decisions here must be limited by brute facts and based on science and human wants.

Today the scientific and ethical boundaries of our industrial activities are not in the hands of scientists, teachers, and thinkers; nor is the intervening opportunity for decision left in the control of the public whose welfare such decisions guide. On the contrary, the control of industry is largely in the hands of a powerful few, who decide for their own good and regardless of the good of others. The making of the rules of Industry, then, is not in the hands of All, but in the hands of the Few. The Few who govern industry envisage, not the wants of mankind, but their own wants. They work quietly, often secretly, opposing Law, on the one hand, as interfering with the "freedom of industry"; opposing, on the other hand, free discussion and open determination of the rules of work and wealth and wages, on the ground that harsh natural law brooks no interference by Democracy.

These things today, then, are not matters of free discussion and determination. They are strictly controlled. Who controls them? Who makes these inner, but powerful, rules? Few people know. Others assert and believe these rules are "natural"—a part of our inescapable physical environment. Some of them doubtless are; but most of them are just as clearly the dictates of self-interest laid down by the powerful private persons who today control industry. Just here it is that modern men demand that Democracy supplant skilfully concealed, but all too evident, Monarchy.

In industry, monarchy and the aristocracy rule, and there are those who, calling themselves democratic, believe that democracy can never enter here. Industry, they maintain, is a matter of technical knowledge and ability, and, therefore, is the eternal heritage of the few. They point to the failure of attempts at democratic control in industry, just as we used to point to Spanish-American governments, and they expose, not simply the failures of Russian Soviets,—they fly to arms to prevent that greatest experiment in industrial democracy which the world has yet seen. These are the ones who say: We must control labor or civilization will fail; we must control white labor in Europe and America; above all, we must control yellow labor in Asia and black labor in Africa and the South, else we shall have no tea, or rubber, or cotton. And yet,—and yet is it so easy to give up the dream of democracy? Must industry rule men or may men rule even industry? And unless men rule industry, can they ever hope really to make laws or educate children or create beauty?

That the problem of the democratization of industry is tremendous, let no man deny. We must spread that sympathy and intelligence which tolerates the widest individual freedom despite the necessary public control; we must learn to select for public office ability rather than mere affability. We must stand ready to defer to knowledge and science and judge by result rather than by method; and finally we must face the fact that the final distribution of goods—the question of wages and income is an ethical and not a mere mechanical problem and calls for grave public human judgment and not secrecy and closed doors. All this means time and development. It comes not complete by instant revolution of a day, nor yet by the deferred evolution of a thousand year—it comes daily, bit by bit and step by step, as men and women learn and grow and as children are trained in Truth.

These steps are in many cases clear: the careful, steady increase of public democratic ownership of industry, beginning with the simplest type of public utilities and monopolies, and extending gradually as we learn the way; the use of taxation to limit inheritance and to take the unearned increment for public use beginning (but not ending) with a "single tax" on monopolized land values; the training of the public in business technique by co-operation in buying and selling, and in industrial technique by the shop committee and manufacturing guild.

But beyond all this must come the Spirit—the Will to Human Brotherhood of all Colors, Races, and Creeds; the Wanting of the Wants of All. Perhaps the finest contribution of current Socialism to the world is neither its light nor its dogma, but the idea back of its one mighty word—Comrade!

Chapter 26

Democracy

John Dewey

John Dewey (1859–1952) was a leading American philosopher in the first half of the twentieth century. This talk, delivered in 1937 to a meeting of educational administrators, outlines his account of democracy. He argues that democracy is not merely a mode of government; it is a way of life. Democracy, so understood, is a commitment to the idea that each person is to have an equal opportunity to contribute to the society, and that all are to be afforded freedom to develop their individual capacities and opinions. These democratic convictions are not to be restricted to official government activities but are to pervade all aspects of life, from family and business to church and social clubs.

John Dewey, *The Collected Works of John Dewey, Later Works*, vol. 11, ed. Jo Ann Boydston (Carbondale: Southern Illinois University Press, 2008).

[D]emocracy is much broader than a special political form, a method of conducting government, of making laws and carrying on governmental administration by means of popular suffrage and elected officers. It is that of course. But it is something broader and deeper than that.

The political and governmental phase of democracy is a means, the best means so far found, for realizing ends that lie in the wide domain of human relationships and the development of human personality. It is, as we often say, though perhaps without appreciating all that is involved in the saying, a way of life, social and individual. The key-note of democracy as a way of life may be expressed, it seems to me, as the necessity for the participation of every mature human being in formation of the values that regulate the living of men together—which is necessary from the standpoint of both the general social welfare and the full development of human beings as individuals.

Universal suffrage, recurring elections, responsibility of those who are in political power to the voters, and the other factors of democratic government are means that have been found expedient for realizing democracy as the truly human way of living. They are not a final end and a final value. They are to be judged on the basis of their contribution to an end. It is a form of idolatry to erect means into the end which they serve. Democratic political forms are simply the best means that human wit has devised up to a special time in history. But they rest back upon the idea that no man or limited set of men is wise enough or good enough to rule others without their consent; the positive meaning of this statement is that all those who are affected by social institutions must have a share in producing and managing them. The two facts that each one is influenced in what he does and enjoys and in what he becomes by the institutions under which he lives, and that therefore he shall have, in a democracy, a voice in shaping them, are the passive and active sides of the same fact.

The development of political democracy came about through substitution of the method of mutual consultation and voluntary agreement for the method of subordination of the many to the few enforced from above. Social arrangements which involve fixed subordination are maintained by coercion. The coercion need not be physical. There have existed, for short periods, benevolent despotisms. But coercion of some sort there has been; perhaps economic, certainly psychological and moral. The very fact of exclusion from participation is a subtle form of suppression. It gives individuals no opportunity to reflect and decide upon what is good for them. Others who are supposed to be wiser and who in any case have more power decide the question for them and also decide the methods and means by which subjects may arrive at the enjoyment of what is good for them. This form of coercion and suppression is more subtle and more effective than is overt intimidation and restraint. When it is habitual and embodied in social institutions, it seems the normal and natural state of affairs. The mass usually become unaware that they have a claim to a development of their own powers. Their experience is so restricted that they are not conscious of restriction. It is part of the democratic conception that they as individuals are not the only sufferers, but that the whole social body is deprived of the potential resources that should be at its service. The individuals of the submerged mass may not be very wise. But there is one thing they are wiser about than anybody else can be, and that is where the shoe pinches, the troubles they suffer from.

The foundation of democracy is faith in the capacities of human nature; faith in human intelligence, and in the power of pooled and cooperative experience. It is not belief that these things are complete but that if given a show they will grow and be able to generate progressively the knowledge and wisdom needed to guide collective action. Every autocratic and authoritarian scheme of social action rests on a belief that the needed intelligence is confined to a superior few who because of inherent natural gifts are endowed with the ability and the right to control the conduct of others; laying down principles and rules and directing the ways in which they are carried out. It would be foolish to deny that much can be said for this point of view. It is that which controlled human relations in social groups for much the greater part of human history. The democratic faith has emerged very, very recently in the history of mankind. Even where democracies now exist, men's minds and feelings are still permeated with ideas about leadership imposed from above, ideas that developed in the long early history of mankind. After democratic political institutions were nominally established, beliefs and ways of looking at life and of acting that originated when men and women were externally controlled and subjected to arbitrary power, persisted in the family, the church, business and the school, and experience shows that as long as they persist there, political democracy is not secure.

Belief in equality is an element of the democratic credo. It is not, however, belief in equality of natural endowments. Those who proclaimed the idea of equality did not suppose they were enunciating a psychological doctrine, but a legal and political one. All individuals are entitled to equality of treatment by law and in its administration. Each one is affected equally in quality if not in quantity by the institutions under which he lives and has an equal right to express his judgment, although the weight of his judgment may not be equal in amount when it enters into the pooled result to that of others. In short, each one is equally an individual and entitled to equal opportunity of development of his own capacities, be they large or small in range. Moreover, each has needs of his own, as significant to him as those of others are to them. The very fact of natural and psychological inequality is all the more reason for establishment by law of equality of opportunity, since otherwise the former becomes a means of oppression of the less gifted.

While what we call intelligence be distributed in unequal amounts, it is the democratic faith that it is sufficiently general so that each individual has something to contribute whose value can be assessed only as it enters into the final pooled intelligence constituted by the contributions of all. Every authoritarian scheme, on the contrary assumes that its value may be assessed by some *prior* principle, if not of family and birth or race and color or possession of material wealth, then by the position and rank a person occupies in the existing social scheme. The democratic faith in equality is the faith that each individual shall have the chance and opportunity to contribute whatever he is capable of contributing, and that the value of his contribution be decided by its place and function in the organized total of similar contributions—not on the basis of prior status of any kind whatever.

I have emphasized in what precedes the importance of the effective release of intelligence in connection with personal experience in the democratic way of living. I have done so purposely because democracy is so often and so naturally associated in our minds with freedom of *action*, forgetting the importance of freed intelligence which is necessary to direct and to warrant freedom of action. Unless freedom of individual action has intelligence and informed conviction back of it, its manifestation is almost sure to result in confusion and disorder. The democratic idea of freedom is not the right of each individual to do as he pleases, even if it be qualified by adding "provided he does not interfere with the same freedom on the part of others." While the idea is not always, not often enough, expressed in words, the basic freedom is that of freedom of mind and of whatever degree of freedom of action and experience is necessary to produce freedom of intelligence. The modes of freedom guaranteed in the Bill of Rights are all of this nature: Freedom of belief and conscience, of expression of opinion, of assembly for discussion and conference, of the press as an organ of communication. They are guaranteed because without them individuals are not free to develop and society is deprived of what they might contribute. . . .

There is some kind of government, of control, wherever affairs that concern a number of persons who act together are engaged in. It is a superficial view that holds government is located in Washington and Albany. There is government in the family, in business, in the church, in every social group. There are regulations, due to custom if not to enactment, that settle how individuals in a group act in connection with one another.

It is a disputed question of theory and practice just how far a democratic political government should go in control of the conditions of action within special groups. At the present time, for example, there are those who think the federal and state governments leave too much freedom of independent action to industrial and financial groups and there are others who think the Government is going altogether too far at the present time. I do not need to discuss this phase of the problem much less to try to settle it. But it must be pointed out that if the methods of regulation and administration in vogue in the conduct of secondary social groups are non-democratic, whether directly or indirectly or both, there is bound to be an unfavorable reaction back into the habits of feeling, thought and action of citizenship in the broadest sense of that word. The way in which any organized social interest is controlled necessarily plays an important part in forming the dispositions and tastes, the attitudes, interests, purposes and desires, of those engaged in carrying on the activities of the group. For illustration, I do not need to do more than point to the moral, emotional, and intellectual effect upon both employers and laborers of the existing industrial system. Just what the effects specifically are is a matter about which we know very little. But I suppose that every one who reflects upon the subject admits that it is impossible that the ways in which activities are carried on for the greater part of the waking hours of the day; and the way in which the shares of individuals are involved in the management of affairs in such a matter as gaining a livelihood and attaining material and social security, can only be a highly important factor in shaping personal dispositions; in short, forming character and intelligence.

In the broad and final sense all institutions are educational in the sense that they operate to form the attitudes, dispositions, abilities, and disabilities that constitute a concrete personality. The principle applies with special force to the school. For it is the main business of the family and the school to influence directly the formation and growth of attitudes and dispositions, emotional, intellectual and moral. Whether this educative process is carried on in a predominantly democratic or non-democratic way becomes therefore a question of transcendent importance not only for education itself but for its final effect upon all the interests and activities of a society that is committed to the democratic way of life.

. . . [T]here are certain corollaries which clarify the meaning of the issue. Absence of participation tends to produce lack of interest and concern on the part of those shut out. The result is a corresponding lack of effective responsibility. Automatically and unconsciously, if not consciously, the feeling develops, "this is none of our affair; it is the business of those at the top; let that particular set of Georges do what needs to be done." The countries in which autocratic government prevails are just those in which there is least public spirit and the greatest indifference to matters of general as distinct from personal concern. . . . Where there is little power, there is correspondingly little sense of positive responsibility—It is enough to do what one is told to do sufficiently well to escape flagrant unfavorable notice. About larger matters a spirit of passivity is engendered.

. . . [I]t still is also true that incapacity to assume the responsibilities involved in having a voice in shaping policies is bred and increased by conditions in which that responsibility is denied. I suppose there has never been an autocrat, big or little, who did not justify his conduct on the ground of the unfitness of his subjects to take part in government. . . . But, as was said earlier, habitual exclusion has the effect of reducing a sense of responsibility for what is done and its consequences. What the argument for democracy implies is that the best way to produce initiative and constructive power is to exercise it. Power, as well as interest, comes by use and practice. . . .

The fundamental beliefs and practices of democracy are now challenged as they never have been before. In some nations they are more than challenged. They are ruthlessly and systematically destroyed. Everywhere there are waves of criticism and doubt as to whether democracy can meet pressing problems of order and security. The causes for the destruction of political democracy in countries where it was nominally established are complex. But of one thing I think we may be sure. Wherever it has fallen it was too exclusively political in nature. It had not become part of the bone and blood of the people in daily conduct of its life. Democratic forms were limited to Parliament, elections, and combats between parties. What is happening proves conclusively, I think, that unless democratic habits of thought and action are part of the fiber of a people, political democracy is insecure. It cannot stand in isolation. It must be buttressed by the presence of democratic methods in all social relationships. The relations that exist in educational institutions are second only in importance in this respect to those which exist in industry and business, perhaps not even to them. . . .

I can think of nothing so important in this country at present as a rethinking of the whole problem of democracy and its implications. Neither the rethinking nor the action it should produce can be brought into being in a day or year. The democratic idea itself demands that the thinking and activity proceed cooperatively.

Chapter 27

The Idea of Public Reason Revisited

John Rawls

John Rawls (1921–2002) was Professor of Philosophy at Harvard University. He argues that democracies, due to their free institutions, will be characterized by a plurality of reasonably held comprehensive moral, religious, and philosophical doctrines. Such reasonable pluralism gives rise to a serious problem: How can state coercion be justified to citizens who deeply, but reasonably, disagree? Rawls's solution appeals to the idea of public reason. The justification for a given coercive policy should at some point be given in terms of reasons that all citizens can see by their own lights. Only democracies that enjoy the overlapping consensus afforded by public reason can sustain fair terms of cooperation and foster relationships of mutual respect.

John Rawls, "The Idea of Public Reason Revisited," *University of Chicago Law Review* 64, no. 3 (1997): 765–807.

⸺◈◈◈⸺

INTRODUCTION

The idea of public reason, as I understand it, belongs to a conception of a well ordered constitutional democratic society. The form and content of this reason—the way it is understood by citizens and how it interprets their political relationship—is part of the idea of democracy itself. This is because a basic feature of democracy is the fact of reasonable pluralism—the fact that a plurality of conflicting reasonable comprehensive doctrines,[1] religious, philosophical, and moral, is the normal result of its culture of free institutions. Citizens realize that they cannot reach agreement or even approach mutual understanding on the basis of their irreconcilable comprehensive doctrines. In view of this, they need to consider what kinds of reasons they may reasonably give one another when fundamental political questions are at stake. I propose that in public reason comprehensive doctrines of truth or right be replaced by an idea of the politically reasonable addressed to citizens as citizens.

Central to the idea of public reason is that it neither criticizes nor attacks any comprehensive doctrine, religious or nonreligious, except insofar as that doctrine is incompatible with the essentials of public reason and a democratic polity. The basic requirement is that a reasonable doctrine accepts a constitutional democratic regime and its companion idea of legitimate law. While democratic societies will differ in the specific doctrines that are influential and active within them—as they differ in the western democracies of Europe and the United States, Israel, and India—finding a suitable idea of public reason is a concern that faces them all.

§1: THE IDEA OF PUBLIC REASON

1. The idea of public reason specifies at the deepest level the basic moral and political values that are to determine a constitutional democratic government's relation to its citizens and their relation to one another. In short, it concerns how the political relation is to be understood. Those who reject constitutional democracy with its criterion of reciprocity will of course reject the very idea of public reason. For them the political relation may be that of friend or foe, to those of a particular religious or secular community or those who are not; or it may be a relentless struggle to win the world for the whole truth. Political liberalism does not engage those who think this way. The zeal to embody the whole truth in politics is incompatible with an idea of public reason that belongs with democratic citizenship.

The idea of public reason has a definite structure, and if one or more of its aspects are ignored it can seem implausible, as it does when applied to the background culture. It has five different aspects: (1) the fundamental political questions to which it applies; (2) the persons to whom it applies (government officials and candidates for public office); (3) its content as given by a family of reasonable political conceptions of justice; (4) the application of these conceptions in discussions of coercive norms to be enacted in the form of legitimate law for a democratic people; and (5) citizens' checking that the principles derived from their conceptions of justice satisfy the criterion of reciprocity.

Moreover, such reason is public in three ways: as the reason of free and equal citizens, it is the reason of the public; its subject is the public good concerning questions of fundamental political justice, which questions are of two kinds, constitutional essentials and matters of basic justice; and its nature and content are public, being expressed in public reasoning by a family of reason able conceptions of political justice reasonably thought to satisfy the criterion of reciprocity.

It is imperative to realize that the idea of public reason does not apply to all political discussions of fundamental questions, but only to discussions of those questions in what I refer to as the public political forum. This forum may be divided into three parts: the discourse of judges in their decisions, and especially of the judges of a supreme court; the discourse of government officials, especially chief executives and legislators; and finally, the discourse of candidates for public office and their campaign managers, especially in their public oratory, party platforms, and political statements. We need this three-part division because, as I note later, the idea of public reason does not apply in the same way in these three cases and elsewhere. In discussing what I call the wide view of public political culture, we shall see that the idea of public reason applies more strictly to judges than to others, but that the requirements of public justification for that reason are always the same.

Distinct and separate from this three-part public political forum is what I call the background culture.[2] This is the culture of civil society. In a democracy, this culture is not, of course, guided by any one central idea or principle, whether political or religious. Its many and diverse agencies and associations with their internal life reside within a framework of law that ensures the familiar liberties of thought and speech, and the right of free association. The idea of public reason does not apply to the background culture with its many forms of nonpublic reason nor to media of any kind. Sometimes those who appear to reject the idea of public reason actually mean to assert the need for full and open discussion in the background culture. With this political liberalism fully agrees.

Finally, distinct from the idea of public reason, as set out by the five features above, is the *ideal* of public reason. This ideal is realized, or satisfied, whenever judges, legislators, chief executives, and other government officials, as well as candidates for public office, act from and follow the idea of public reason and explain to other citizens their reasons for supporting fundamental political positions in terms of the political conception of justice they regard as the most reasonable. In this way they fulfill what I shall call their duty of civility to one another and to other citizens. Hence, whether judges, legislators, and chief executives act from and follow public reason is continually shown in their speech and conduct on a daily basis.

How though is the ideal of public reason realized by citizens who are not government officials? In a representative government citizens vote for representatives—chief executives, legislators, and the like—and not for particular laws (except at a state or local level when they may vote directly on referenda questions, which are rarely fundamental questions). To answer this question, we say that ideally citizens are to think of themselves as if they were legislators and ask themselves what statutes, supported by what reasons satisfying the criterion of reciprocity, they would think it most reasonable to enact. When firm and widespread, the disposition of citizens to view themselves as ideal legislators, and to repudiate government officials and candidates for public office who violate public reason, is one of the political and social roots of democracy, and is vital to its enduring strength and vigor. Thus citizens fulfill their duty of civility and support the idea of public reason by doing what they can to hold government officials to it. This duty, like other political rights and duties, is an intrinsically moral duty. I emphasize that it is not a legal duty, for in that case it would be incompatible with freedom of speech.

2. I now turn to a discussion of what I have labeled the third, fourth, and fifth aspects of public reason. The idea of public reason arises from a conception of democratic citizenship in a constitutional democracy. This fundamental political relation of citizenship has two special features: first, it is a relation of citizens within the basic structure of society, a structure we enter only by birth and exit only by death; and second, it is a relation of free and equal citizens who exercise ultimate political power as a collective body. These two features immediately give rise to the question of how, when constitutional essentials and matters of basic justice are at stake, citizens so related can be bound to honor the structure of their constitutional democratic regime and abide by the statutes and laws enacted under it. The fact of reasonable pluralism raises this question all the more sharply, since it means that the differences between citizens arising from their comprehensive doctrines, religious and nonreligious, may be irreconcilable. By what ideals and principles, then, are citizens who share equally in ultimate political power to exercise that power so that each can reasonably justify his or her political decisions to everyone?

To answer this question we say: Citizens are reasonable when, viewing one another as free and equal in a system of social cooperation over generations, they are prepared to offer one another fair terms of cooperation according to what they consider the most reasonable conception of political justice; and when they agree to act on those terms, even at the cost of their own interests in particular situations, provided that other citizens also accept those terms. The criterion of reciprocity requires that when those terms are proposed as the most reasonable terms of fair cooperation, those proposing them must also think it at least reasonable for others to accept them, as free and equal citizens, and not as dominated or manipulated, or under the pressure of an inferior political or social position. Citizens will of course differ as to which conceptions of political justice they think the most reasonable, but they will agree that all are reasonable, even if barely so.

Thus when, on a constitutional essential or matter of basic justice, all appropriate government officials act from and follow public reason, and when all reasonable citizens think of themselves ideally as if they were legislators following public reason, the legal enactment expressing the opinion of the majority is legitimate law. It may not be thought the most reasonable, or the most appropriate, by each, but it is politically (morally) binding on him or her as a citizen and is to be accepted as such. Each thinks that all have spoken and voted at least reasonably, and therefore all have followed public reason and honored their duty of civility.

Hence the idea of political legitimacy based on the criterion of reciprocity says: Our exercise of political power is proper only when we sincerely believe that the reasons we would offer for our political actions—were we to state them as government officials—are sufficient, and we also reasonably think that other citizens might also reasonably accept those reasons. This criterion applies on two levels: one is to the constitutional structure itself, the other is to particular statutes and laws enacted in accordance with that structure. To be reasonable, political conceptions must justify only constitutions that satisfy this principle.

To make more explicit the role of the criterion of reciprocity as expressed in public reason, note that its role is to specify the nature of the political relation in a constitutional democratic regime as one of civic friendship. For this criterion, when government officers act from it in their public reasoning and other citizens support it, shapes the form of their fundamental institutions. For example—I cite an easy case—if we argue that the religious liberty of some citizens is to be denied, we must give them reasons they can not only understand—as Servetus could understand why Calvin wanted to burn him at the stake—but reasons we might reasonably expect that they, as free and equal citizens, might reasonably also accept. The criterion of reciprocity is normally violated whenever basic liberties are denied. For what rea sons can both satisfy the criterion of reciprocity and justify denying to some persons religious liberty, holding others as slaves, imposing a property qualification on the right to vote, or denying the right of suffrage to women?

Since the idea of public reason specifies at the deepest level the basic political values and specifies how the political relation is to be understood, those who believe that fundamental political questions should be decided by what they regard as the best reasons according to their own idea of the whole truth—including their religious or secular comprehensive doctrine—and not by reasons that might be shared by all citizens as free and equal, will of course reject the idea of public reason. Political liberalism views this insistence on the whole truth in politics as incompatible with democratic citizenship and the idea of legitimate law.

3. Democracy has a long history, from its beginning in classical Greece down to the present day, and there are many different ideas of democracy. Here I am concerned only with a well ordered constitutional democracy—a term I used at the outset—understood also as a deliberative democracy. The definitive idea for deliberative democracy is the idea of deliberation itself. When citizens deliberate, they exchange views and debate their supporting reasons concerning public political questions. They suppose that their political opinions may be revised by discussion with other citizens; and therefore these opinions are not simply a fixed outcome of their existing private or nonpolitical interests. It is at this point that public reason is crucial, for it characterizes such citizens' reasoning concerning constitutional essentials and matters of basic justice. While I cannot fully discuss the nature of deliberative democracy here, I note a few key points to indicate the wider place and role of public reason.

There are three essential elements of deliberative democracy. One is an idea of public reason,[3] although not all such ideas are the same. A second is a framework of constitutional democratic institutions that specifies the setting for deliberative legislative bodies. The third is the knowledge and desire on the part of citizens generally to follow public reason and to realize its ideal in their political conduct. Immediate implications of these essentials are the public financing of elections, and the providing for public occasions of orderly and serious discussion of fundamental questions and issues of public policy. Public deliberation must be made possible, recognized as a basic feature of democracy, and set free from the curse of money. Otherwise politics is dominated by corporate and other organized interests who through large contributions to campaigns distort if not preclude public discussion and deliberation.

Deliberative democracy also recognizes that without widespread education in the basic aspects of constitutional democratic government for all citizens, and without a public informed about pressing problems, crucial political and social decisions simply cannot be made. Even should farsighted political leaders wish to make sound changes and reforms, they cannot convince a misinformed and cynical public to accept and follow them. . . .

§2: THE CONTENT OF PUBLIC REASON

1. A citizen engages in public reason, then, when he or she deliberates within a framework of what he or she sincerely regards as the most reasonable political conception of justice, a conception that expresses political values that others, as free and equal citizens might also reasonably be expected reason-

ably to endorse. Each of us must have principles and guidelines to which we appeal in such a way that this criterion is satisfied. I have proposed that one way to identify those political principles and guidelines is to show that they would be agreed to in . . . the original position.[4] Others will think that different ways to identify these principles are more reasonable. Thus, the content of public reason is given by a family of political conceptions of justice, and not by a single one. There are many liberalisms and related views, and therefore many forms of public reason specified by a family of reasonable political conceptions. Of these, justice as fairness, whatever its merits, is but one. The limiting feature of these forms is the criterion of reciprocity, viewed as applied between free and equal citizens, themselves seen as reasonable and rational. Three main features characterize these conceptions:

First, a list of certain basic rights, liberties, and opportunities (such as those familiar from constitutional regimes);

Second, an assignment of special priority to those rights, liberties, and opportunities, especially with respect to the claims of the general good and perfectionist values; and

Third, measures ensuring for all citizens adequate all purpose means to make effective use of their freedoms.

Each of these liberalisms endorses the underlying ideas of citizens as free and equal persons and of society as a fair system of cooperation over time. Yet since these ideas can be interpreted in various ways, we get different formulations of the principles of justice and different contents of public reason. Political conceptions differ also in how they order, or balance, political principles and values even when they specify the same ones. I assume also that these liberalisms contain substantive principles of justice, and hence cover more than procedural justice. They are required to specify the religious liberties and freedoms of artistic expression of equal citizens, as well as substantive ideas of fairness involving fair opportunity and ensuring adequate all-purpose means, and much else.

Political liberalism, then, does not try to fix public reason once and for all in the form of one favored political conception of justice. That would not be a sensible approach. . . . Even if relatively few conceptions come to dominate over time, and one conception even appears to have a special central place, the forms of permissible public reason are always several. Moreover, new variations may be proposed from time to time and older ones may cease to be represented. It is important that this be so; otherwise the claims of groups or interests arising from social change might be repressed and fail to gain their appropriate political voice.

2. We must distinguish public reason from what is sometimes referred to as secular reason and secular values. These are not the same as public reason. For I define secular reason as reasoning in terms of comprehensive nonreligious doctrines. Such doctrines and values are much too broad to serve the purposes of public reason. Political values are not moral doctrines, however available or accessible these may be to our reason and commonsense reflection. Moral doctrines are on a level with religion and first philosophy. By contrast, liberal political principles and values, although intrinsically moral values, are specified by liberal political conceptions of justice and fall under the category of the political. These political conceptions have three features:

First, their principles apply to basic political and social institutions (the basic structure of society);

Second, they can be presented independently from comprehensive doctrines of any kind (although they may, of course, be supported by a reasonable overlapping consensus of such doctrines); and

Finally, they can be worked out from fundamental ideas seen as implicit in the public political culture of a constitutional regime, such as the conceptions of citizens as free and equal persons, and of society as a fair system of cooperation.

Thus, the content of public reason is given by the principles and values of the family of liberal political conceptions of justice meeting these conditions. To engage in public reason is to appeal to one of these political conceptions—to their ideals and principles, standards and values—when debating fundamental political questions. This requirement still allows us to introduce into political discussion at any time our comprehensive doctrine, religious or nonreligious, provided that, in due course, we give properly public reasons to support the principles and policies our comprehensive doctrine is said to support. I refer to this requirement as *the proviso*, and consider it in detail below.

A feature of public reasoning, then, is that it proceeds entirely within a political conception of justice. Examples of political values include those mentioned in the preamble to the United States Constitution: a more perfect union, justice, domestic tranquility, the common defense, the general welfare, and the blessings of liberty for ourselves and our posterity. These include under them other values: so, for example, under justice we also have equal basic liberties, equality of opportunity, ideals concerning the distribution of income and taxation, and much else.

The political values of public reason are distinct from other values in that they are realized in and characterize political institutions. This does not mean that analogous values cannot characterize other social forms. The values of effectiveness and efficiency may characterize the social organization of teams and clubs, as well as the political institutions of the basic structure of society. But a value is properly political only when the social form is itself political: when it is realized, say, in parts of the basic structure and its political and social institutions. It follows that many political conceptions are nonliberal, including those of aristocracy and corporate oligarchy, and of autocracy and dictatorship. All of these fall within the category of the political. We, however, are concerned only with those political conceptions that are reasonable for a constitutional democratic regime, and as the preceding paragraphs make clear, these are the ideals and principles expressed by reasonable liberal political conceptions.

3. Another essential feature of public reason is that its political conceptions should be complete. This means that each conception should express principles, standards, and ideals, along with guidelines of inquiry, such that the values specified by it can be suitably ordered or otherwise united so that those values alone give a reasonable answer to all, or to nearly all, questions involving constitutional essentials and matters of basic justice. Here the ordering of values is made in the fight of their structure and features within the political conception itself, and not primarily from how they occur within citizens' comprehensive doctrines. Political values are not to be ordered by viewing them separately and detached from one another or from any definite context. They are not puppets manipulated from behind the scenes by comprehensive doctrines. The ordering is not distorted by those doctrines provided that public reason sees the ordering as reasonable. And public reason can indeed see an ordering of political values as reasonable (or unreasonable), since institutional structures are open to view and mistakes and gaps within the political ordering will become exposed. Thus, we may be confident that the ordering of political values is not distorted by particular reasonable comprehensive doctrines. (I emphasize that the only criterion of distortion is that the ordering of political values be itself unreasonable.)

The significance of completeness lies in the fact that unless a political conception is complete, it is not an adequate framework of thought in the fight of which the discussion of fundamental political questions can be carried out.[5] What we cannot do in public reason is to proceed directly from our comprehensive doctrine, or a part thereof, to one or several political principles and values, and the particular institutions they support. Instead, we are required first to work to the basic ideas of a complete political conception and from there to elaborate its principles and ideals, and to use the arguments they provide. Otherwise public reason allows arguments that are too immediate and fragmentary.

4. I now note several examples of political principles and values to illustrate the more specific content of public reason, and particularly the various

ways in which the criterion of reciprocity is both applicable and subject to violation.

(a) As a first example, consider the value of autonomy. It may take two forms: one is political autonomy, the legal independence and assured integrity of citizens and their sharing equally with others in the exercise of political power; the other is purely moral and characterizes a certain way of life and reflection, critically examining our deepest ends and ideals, as in Mill's ideal of individuality. Whatever we may think of autonomy as a purely moral value, it fails to satisfy, given reasonable pluralism, the constraint of reciprocity, as many citizens, for example, those holding certain religious doctrines, may reject it. Thus moral autonomy is not a political value, whereas political autonomy is.

(b) As a second example, consider the familiar story of the Good Samaritan. Are the values appealed to properly political values and not simply religious or philosophical values? While the wide view of public political culture allows us, in making a proposal, to introduce the Gospel story, public reason requires us to justify our proposal in terms of proper political values.

(c) As a third example, consider appeals to desert in discussing the fair distribution of income: people are wont to say that ideally distribution should be in accordance with desert. What sense of desert do they have in mind? Do they mean that persons in various offices should have the requisite qualifications—judges must be qualified to judge—and all should have a fair opportunity to qualify themselves for favored positions? That is indeed a political value. But distribution in accordance with moral desert, where this means the moral worth of character, all things considered, and including comprehensive doctrines, is not. It is not a feasible political and social aim.

(d) Finally, consider the state's interest in the family and human life. How should the political value invoked be specified correctly? Traditionally it has been specified very broadly. But in a democratic regime the government's legitimate interest is that public law and policy should support and regulate, in an ordered way, the institutions needed to reproduce political society over time. These include the family (in a form that is just), arrangements for rearing and educating children, and institutions of public health generally. This ordered support and regulation rests on political principles and values, since political society is regarded as existing in perpetuity and so as maintaining itself and its institutions and culture over generations. Given this interest, the government would appear to have no interest in the particular form of family life, or of relations among the sexes, except insofar as that form or those relations in some way affect the orderly reproduction of society over time. Thus, appeals to monogamy as such, or against same-sex marriages, as within the government's legitimate interest in the family, would reflect religious or comprehensive moral doctrines. Accordingly, that interest would appear improperly specified. Of course, there may be other political values in the fight of which such a specification would pass muster: for example, if monogamy were necessary for the equality of women, or same-sex marriages destructive to the raising and educating of children. . . .

§4: THE WIDE VIEW OF PUBLIC POLITICAL CULTURE

1. Now we consider what I call the wide view of public political culture and discuss two aspects of it. The first is that reason able comprehensive doctrines, religious or nonreligious, may be introduced in public political discussion at any time, provided that in due course proper political reasons—and not reasons given solely by comprehensive doctrines—are presented that are sufficient to support whatever the comprehensive doctrines introduced are said to support. This injunction to present proper political reasons I refer to as *the proviso*, and it specifies public political culture as distinct from the background culture. The second aspect I consider is that there may be positive reasons for introducing comprehensive doctrines into public political discussion. I take up these two aspects in turn. . . .

2. Citizens' mutual knowledge of one another's religious and nonreligious doctrines expressed in the wide view of public political culture recognizes that the roots of democratic citizens' allegiance to their political conceptions he in their respective comprehensive doctrines, both religious and nonreligious. In this way citizens' allegiance to the democratic ideal of public reason is strengthened for the right reasons. We may think of the reason able comprehensive doctrines that support society's reasonable political conceptions as those conceptions' vital social basis, giving them enduring strength and vigor. When these doctrines accept the proviso and only then come into political debate, the commitment to constitutional democracy is publicly manifested.[6] Made aware of this commitment, government officials and citizens are more willing to honor the duty of civility, and their following the ideal of public reason helps foster the kind of society that ideal exemplifies. These benefits of the mutual knowledge of citizens' recognizing one another's reasonable comprehensive doctrines bring out a positive ground for introducing such doc trines, which is not merely a defensive ground, as if their intrusion into public discussion were inevitable in any case.

3. Public reasoning aims for public justification. We appeal to political conceptions of justice, and to ascertainable evidence and facts open to public view, in order to reach conclusions about what we think are the most reasonable political institutions and policies. Public justification is not simply

valid reasoning, but argument addressed to others: it proceeds correctly from premises we accept and think others could reasonably accept to conclusions we think they could also reasonably accept. This meets the duty of civility, since in due course the proviso is satisfied.

There are two other forms of discourse that may also be mentioned, though neither expresses a form of public reasoning. One is declaration: here we each declare our own comprehensive doctrine, religious or nonreligious. This we do not expect others to share. Rather, each of us shows how, from our own doctrines, we can and do endorse a reasonable public political conception of justice with its principles and ideals. The aim of doing this is to declare to others who affirm different comprehensive doctrines that we also each endorse a reasonable political conception belonging to the family of reasonable such conceptions. On the wide view, citizens of faith who cite the Gospel parable of the Good Samaritan do not stop there, but go on to give a public justification for this parable's conclusions in terms of political values. In this way citizens who hold different doctrines are reassured, and this strengthens the ties of civic friendship.

The second form is conjecture, defined thus: we argue from what we believe, or conjecture, are other people's basic doctrines, religious or secular, and try to show them that, despite what they might think, they can still endorse a reasonable political conception that can provide a basis for public reasons. The ideal of public reason is thereby strengthened. However, it is important that conjecture be sincere and not manipulative. We must openly explain our intentions and state that we do not assert the premises from which we argue, but that we proceed as we do to clear up what we take to be a misunderstanding on others' part, and perhaps equally on ours. . . .

§7: CONCLUSION

1. Throughout, I have been concerned with a torturing question in the contemporary world, namely: Can democracy and comprehensive doctrines, religious or nonreligious, be compatible? And if so, how? At the moment a number of conflicts between religion and democracy raise this question. To answer it political liberalism makes the distinction between a self-standing political conception of justice and a comprehensive doctrine. A religious doctrine resting on the authority of the Church or the Bible is not, of course, a liberal comprehensive doctrine: its leading religious and moral values are not those, say, of Kant or Mill. Nevertheless, it may endorse a constitutional democratic society and recognize its public reason. Here it is basic that public reason is a political idea and belongs to the category of the political. Its content is given by the family of (liberal) political conceptions of justice sat-

isfying the criterion of reciprocity. It does not trespass upon religious beliefs and injunctions insofar as these are consistent with the essential constitutional liberties, including the freedom of religion and liberty of conscience. There is, or need be, no war between religion and democracy. In this respect political liberalism is sharply different from and rejects Enlightenment Liberalism, which historically attacked orthodox Christianity.

The conflicts between democracy and reasonable religious doctrines and among reasonable religious doctrines themselves are greatly mitigated and contained within the bounds of reason able principles of justice in a constitutional democratic society. This mitigation is due to the idea of toleration, and I have distinguished between two such ideas. One is purely political, being expressed in terms of the rights and duties protecting religious liberty in accordance with a reasonable political conception of justice. The other is not purely political but expressed from within a religious or a nonreligious doctrine. However, a reason able judgment of the political conception must still be confirmed as true, or right, by a reasonable comprehensive doctrine. I assume, then, that a reasonable comprehensive doctrine accepts some form of the political argument for toleration. Of course, citizens may think that the grounding reasons for toleration and for the other elements of a constitutional democratic society are not political but rather are to be found in their religious or nonreligious doctrines. And these reasons, they may well say, are the true or the right reasons; and they may see the political reasons as superficial, the grounding ones as deep. Yet there is no conflict here, but simply concordant judgments made within political conceptions of justice on the one hand, and within comprehensive doctrines on the other.

There are limits, however, to reconciliation by public reason. Three main kinds of conflicts set citizens at odds: those deriving from irreconcilable comprehensive doctrines; those deriving from differences in status, class position, or occupation, or from differences in ethnicity, gender, or race; and finally, those deriving from the burdens of judgment.[7] Political liberalism concerns primarily the first kind of conflict. It holds that even though our comprehensive doctrines are irreconcilable and cannot be compromised, nevertheless citizens who affirm reasonable doctrines may share reasons of another kind, namely, public reasons given in terms of political conceptions of justice. I also believe that such a society can resolve the second kind of conflict, which deals with conflicts between citizens' fundamental interests—political, economic, and social. For once we accept reasonable principles of justice and recognize them to be reasonable (even if not the most reasonable), and know, or reasonably believe, that our political and social institutions satisfy them, the second kind of conflict need not arise, or arise so forcefully. Political liberalism does not explicitly consider these conflicts but leaves them to be considered by justice as fairness, or by some other reasonable conception of political justice. Finally, conflicts arising from the burdens of judgment always exist and limit the extent of possible agreement.

2. Reasonable comprehensive doctrines do not reject the essentials of a constitutional democratic polity. Moreover, reason able persons are characterized in two ways: First, they stand ready to offer fair terms of social cooperation between equals, and they abide by these terms if others do also, even should it be to their advantage not to; second, reasonable persons recognize and accept the consequences of the burdens of judgment, which leads to the idea of reasonable toleration in a democratic society. Finally we come to the idea of legitimate law, which reasonable citizens understand to apply to the general structure of political authority. They know that in political life unanimity can rarely if ever be expected, so a reasonable democratic constitution must include majority or other plurality voting procedures in order to reach decisions.

The idea of the politically reasonable is sufficient unto itself for the purposes of public reason when basic political questions are at stake. Of course, fundamentalist religious doctrines and autocratic and dictatorial rulers will reject the ideas of public reason and deliberative democracy. They will say that democracy leads to a culture contrary to their religion, or denies the values that only autocratic or dictatorial rule can secure. They assert that the religiously true, or the philosophically true, overrides the politically reasonable. We simply say that such a doctrine is politically unreasonable. Within political liberalism nothing more need be said.

I noted in the beginning the fact that every actual society, however dominant and controlling its reasonable citizens may be, will normally contain numerous unreasonable doctrines that are not compatible with a democratic society—either certain religious doctrines, such as fundamentalist religions, or certain non religious (secular) doctrines, such as those of autocracy and dictatorship, of which our century offers hideous examples. How far unreasonable doctrines may be active and are to be tolerated in a constitutional democratic regime does not present a new and different question, despite the fact that in this account of public reason we have focused on the idea of the reasonable and the role of reasonable citizens. There is not one account of toleration for reasonable doctrines and another for unreasonable ones. Both cases are settled by the appropriate political principles of justice and the conduct those principles permit. Unreasonable doctrines are a threat to democratic institutions, since it is impossible for them to abide by a constitutional regime except as a *modus vivendi*. Their existence sets a limit to the aim of fully realizing a reasonable democratic society with its ideal of public reason and the idea of legitimate law. This fact is not a defect or failure of the idea of public reason, but rather it indicates that there are limits to what public reason can accomplish. It does not diminish the great value and importance of attempting to realize that ideal to the fullest extent possible.

II

CONTEMPORARY ISSUES

A

JUSTIFICATION

Chapter 28

Democracy Is Not Intrinsically Just

Richard J. Arneson

Richard J. Arneson is the Valtz Family Chair in Philosophy at the University of California, San Diego. He argues that the justice of political arrangements is determined by their consequences. An arrangement is just insofar as it grants authority to those who exercise political power in ways that promote the common good. Accordingly, democracy, like any other political arrangement, is not in itself just. Rather, the justice of democracy, if it is indeed just, depends on whether it brings about the best consequences.

Richard J. Arneson, "Democracy Is Not Intrinsically Just," in *Justice and Democracy: Essays for Brian Barry*, edited by Keith Dowding, Robert E. Goodin, and Carole Pateman (Cambridge: Cambridge University Press, 2004), 40–58.

In Bertolt Brecht's glorious Communist propaganda play *The Caucasian Chalk Circle*, a character who is a mouthpiece for the author declares that "things belong to people who are good for them."[1] In other words, you are entitled to ownership of some item only if your exercise of ownership promotes the common good. This should be understood to be a maximizing doctrine. If one person's ownership of land prevents another person from using the land more productively, the first is wasting resources. At this point in the play what is at issue is rights to use land, but later the same point is applied to politics. The wily judge Azdak displays Solomonic wisdom and demonstrates that it is a grave misfortune for the country that his political rule is coming to an end. Political power rightfully belongs to those people who are good for it.

I am an egalitarian liberal and a democrat, not a communist, but I accept the principle of political legitimacy that Brecht espouses. Systems of governance should be assessed by their consequences; any individual has a moral right to exercise political power just to the extent that the granting of this right is productive of best consequences overall. No one has an ascriptive right to a share of political power. Assigning political power to an hereditary aristocracy on the ground that the nobles deserve power by birth is wrong, but so too it is wrong to hold that each member of a modern society just by being born has a right to an equal say in political power and influence, to equal rights of political citizenship and democratic political institutions. The choice between autocracy and democracy should be decided according to the standard of best results. Which political system best promotes the common good over the long run? Many types of evidence support the conclusion that constitutional democracies produce morally best results on the whole and over the long run, but this judgement is contingent, somewhat uncertain, and should be held tentatively rather than dogmatically. In some possible worlds, probably some past states of the actual world, and possibly in some future actual scenarios, autocracy wins by the best results test and should be installed. Democracy is extrinsically not intrinsically just.

Many contemporary political philosophers addressing the issue of the justification of democracy reject the purely instrumental approach this chapter defends. The alternative view is that democracy is a uniquely fair process for reaching political decisions. Democratic political procedures may be valued for their tendency to produce morally superior laws and policies than would tend to emerge from other procedures, and democracy may also be valued for other good effects that it generates. But even if the results overall of having a non-democratic political regime would be better than the results of having democracy, given that democracy itself qua fair procedure is a substantial intrinsic component of justice, it might well be that opting for democracy would still be morally preferred all things considered.

Formulating the issue as a dispute between those who assert and those who deny that democracy is intrinsically just can be misleading. The former do not hold that a democratic system of government is unconditionally morally valuable in virtue of its non-relational properties. Most would say democracy is conditionally valuable. It is valuable only given mass literacy and the presence of other cultural background conditions, according to its advocates. The idea rather is that democracy is not merely instrumentally valuable but also qualifies as a worthwhile moral goal and also that democracy is one of the requirements of justice, so that other things being equal, the more democratic the society, the more just it is. . . .

My position is that democracy, when it is just, is so entirely in virtue of the tendency of democratic institutions and practices to produce outcomes that are just according to standards that are conceptually independent of the standards that define the democratic ideal. Democracy, in other words, should be regarded as a tool or instrument that is to be valued not for its own sake but entirely for what results from having it. I take it to be obvious that we have a lot of knowledge about the substance of justice—that slavery is unjust, for example, or that it is unjust if some people avoidably face horrible life prospects through no fault or choice of their own. Moreover, our grounds for holding these beliefs are independent of any convoluted account one might give to the effect that these positions would win a majority rule vote under procedurally ideal conditions.

My focus in this chapter is on the moderate and seemingly reasonable position that political institutions and constitutions should be assessed both according to the extent to which they promote substantively just outcomes and according to the extent that they conform to standards of intrinsic fairness for political procedures. This chapter argues against moderation.[2] I also target a view that lies between the moderate and radical positions as just described. This view holds that even if, as a matter of moral metaphysics, there are truths about substantive justice, they are epistemically unavailable when what is at issue is the justification of democracy, because the need for politics stems from the fact that deep and intractable disagreement about what justice requires persists in modern times even among reasonable people.[3]

The purely instrumental approach to democracy can sound more extreme than it needs to be. The instrumentalist holds that democracy is to be assessed by the consequences of its adoption and operation compared with alternatives. Some might hear this as implying that "we" now have infallible knowledge of the correct moral standards, the principles of justice. This is not so. The instrumentalist as I conceive her is a realist about morality but can and should be a fallibilist about our present moral knowledge. There is moral truth, but our current epistemic access to it is uncertain, shaky. Hence one crucial standard for judging a society's institutions and practices is the extent to which they are efficiently arranged to increase the likelihood that as time goes on our epistemic access to moral truth will improve. All of this is perfectly compatible with pure instrumentalism. Analogy: we are searching for genuine treasure, and our practices should be assessed instrumentally, by the degree to which they enable us to gain treasure. Our current maps guiding us to treasure are flawed, and our current ideas about what "treasure" is are somewhat crude, and we have reason to believe there are better maps to be located and better conceptions of "treasure" to be elaborated. So our practices should be judged by the degree to which they enable us to attain genuine treasure, and the extent to which our practices improve our understanding of the nature of treasure and help us locate better maps is an important aspect of their instrumental efficacy.

THE IDEA OF DEMOCRACY

The question whether or not it is intrinsically just that society be governed democratically cannot be addressed without some specification of the idea of democracy. As is well known, the idea is complex. In a society governed democratically, elections determine what laws will be enforced and who will occupy posts that involve political rule. In these elections, all adult members of society have a vote, and all votes are weighed equally. All adult members are eligible to run for political office in these elections, or can become eligible by some non-onerous process such as establishing residency in a particular state or federal division. Majority rule determines the outcome of elections. Political freedoms, including freedom of association and freedom of speech, are protected in the society, so the group or faction that currently holds power cannot rig election results by banning or restricting the expression of opposing views.

A democratic society may operate in indirect rather than direct fashion. That is, rather than its being the case that all citizens together vote on proposed laws, citizens might vote for the members of a representative assembly, whose members enact laws. But indirectness does lessen the degree to which a society qualifies as democratic. This becomes clear if one imagines indirectness iterated many times—voters vote for an assembly that votes for an assembly that votes for another assembly that votes for a political group that votes for laws and votes in officials to administer them. Indirectness diminishes the democratic character of a regime because it lessens the extent to which the present will of a majority of voters controls political outcomes. The contrast between direct and indirect democracy is connected to another, between immediate and mediate accountability of elected rulers to majority rule of citizen voters. In a political system that allows for immediate recall of officials by citizen initiative, the accountability is more immediate, other things being equal, than it would be if recall by this means were not permitted. If some part of the law-making power is exercised by a judicial branch of government, top members of which are appointed by some process that is more rather than less indirect, the political process is to that extent less democratic. If political officials in any branch of government, legislative, executive, or judicial, may not be removed from office once they are validly appointed, this factor also lessens the extent to which the society qualifies as democratic.

Another dimension on which a political system can register as more or less democratic concerns the scope of the authority of the majority will of the citizen voters. If there is a substantial set of restrictions, for example, a list of individual or group rights, which are constitutionally specified as the supreme law of the land, and which may not validly be altered or extinguished by majority will vote, the greater the extent of these limits on majority rule, the lesser the extent to which the political system qualifies as democratic. A provision here is that there are some individual rights that are themselves conceptually required by democracy itself, and the insulation of these rights from majority will control does not render a society less democratic.

Finally, a political system qualifies as more democratic insofar as all citizens have equal opportunity for political influence. This norm admits of various construals. Let us say that citizens have equal opportunity for political influence when all citizens with the same ambition to influence politics and the same political talents will have equal prospects of influencing political outcomes. The idea is roughly that if such factors as one's wealth or family connections affect the impact one could have on the political process if one worked to achieve an impact, then opportunities are unequal and the society to that extent less democratic. If only ambition and political talent, which includes administrative and entrepreneurial skill and the ability to persuade others and build coalitions, affect the chances that one could influence the outcomes of the political process if one tried, then opportunities in the relevant sense are equal and the society to that extent more democratic.

The statement of equal opportunity given above takes individuals as they are, with the political talents they happen to possess at a particular time, as setting the standard of equal opportunity. One might view this statement as inadequate in view of the following sort of example. Society might give access to the opportunities for training and developing political talent only to a restricted social group. If some individuals lack the opportunity to become politically talented, then one might hold equal opportunity does not prevail even though the equally ambitious and talented enjoy equal opportunities. One might then . . . hold that citizens have equal opportunity for political influence only when all citizens with the same native potential for political talent and the same ambition to develop and exercise it have equal prospects for affecting the outcomes of the political process. This version of equal opportunity for political influence might seem better as a theoretical formulation than the one stated in the previous paragraph, but in practical terms it has the defect that it may be hard in many situations to tell whether it is being fulfilled, given that the idea of potential for political talent is a vague notion.

Democracy is, then, a complex ideal. The judgement as to how democratic the political process of a given society is combines several dimensions of assessment, each of which varies by degree.

AGAINST THE RIGHT TO A DEMOCRATIC SAY

Consider the proposition that each member of society has a basic moral right to an equal say in the political process that determines the laws that the government enforces and also which people shall be political rulers or top public officials. One has an equal say when one could, if one chose, have the same chance of influencing the outcomes of the political process as any other member of society with equal political skills and equal willingness to devote one's resources to participation in politics. Saying the right to an equal say is a basic moral right includes denying that one has the right merely derivatively, on instrumental grounds. Call this right the "right to a democratic say."

The right to a democratic say so understood is a right to political power—a right to set coercive rules that significantly limit how other people will live their lives. With this right secured, one has power over the lives of other people—a small bit of power, to be sure, but power nonetheless. My position is that there is no such basic moral right, because one does not have a basic moral right to exercise significant power over the lives of other people, to direct how they shall live their lives. Rights to power over the lives of others always involve an element of stewardship. If one has such a moral right, this will be so only because one's having the right is more conducive to the flourishing of all affected parties than any feasible alternative.

Parents standardly have extensive power to control the lives of their children who have not yet attained adult age. My position is that there is no basic moral right to have such power. The system of parental control is justified just in case it is maximally conducive to the flourishing of those affected. In just the same way, no one has a basic moral right to be the chief warden of a prison or the director of an insane asylum.

This position has attracted the objection that any substantive moral right involves power over the lives of other people. If you have full private property in some object, you have the right to determine what shall be done with it and to forbid other people from interacting with it. Since all rights involve power to direct the lives of others to some degree, nothing yet has been said to single out the right to a democratic say as specially problematic and not an appropriate candidate for inclusion in the class of basic moral rights.

In response: everything is like everything else, I suppose, in some way or to some degree. Still, a rough line can be drawn between rights that confer on the right-holder the power to direct how another shall live and rights that do not confer such power. Consider the moral right not to be "bashed"—severely injured by unprovoked non-consensual violent physical attack. If this right is enforced, the right-holder has power over the lives of others to an extent, since she can give or withhold consent to attack and thus determine by fiat whether any other person may attack. But a right that constrains other people from engaging in a certain type of conduct toward the right-holder differs from a right to set rules that might specify what others shall do across a broad range of important types of conduct. I concede this is a difference in degree but when the difference in degree is large the difference is large and in my view morally significant.[4]

A second response is that perhaps we should acknowledge that many ordinary rights, such as rights to private ownership, do often involve significant power over others. These rights, then, on my view are not appropriate candidates for the status of basic moral right. Consider the owner of a factory, the sole employer in a region, who is also the owner of a company town. Here, private ownership definitely gives the right-holder significant power over others. Perhaps, strictly speaking, only rights to capabilities (real freedom to achieve important human functionings) or rights to opportunities to genuine well-being or the like should count as appropriate candidates for the status of basic moral rights. Even if, in particular circumstances, one's right to capability is secured by control over resources that give one power over others, what one is strictly morally entitled to on an approach that takes capabilities to be basic will never be the power over others but the freedom to achieve and enjoy in the ways central to human flourishing, where these core freedoms could always in principle be secured in some alternative way without the control and the power.

These two responses have some force, but to the advocate of the right to a democratic say they might seem close to question-begging. After all, what rules it out that the freedom to participate on equal terms with others in collective decision-making is a core human capability, on a par with the capabilities to attain knowledge, friendship and love, and achievement? Saying no one has a basic moral right to power over others invites the counter-assertion that the examples of parental rights and democratic rights show that people do indeed have such moral rights. To make further progress we need to investigate the positive arguments for the right to a democratic say. The case for instrumentalism would be strengthened if the search turns up empty pockets. The rest of this chapter follows this roundabout strategy.

WHAT FREE AND EQUAL RATIONAL PERSONS CAN ACCEPT

We are looking for the strongest and most plausible arguments for the right to a democratic say, regarded as tantamount to the claim that democracy is an intrinsic component of justice. My search strategy is to elaborate simple considerations, raise objections, then attempt to refine the argument to see if it becomes more compelling.

Start with the idea that each person is owed equal concern and respect. Each person's interests should be given equal consideration in the design of political institutions. But any system that violates the right to a democratic say, assigning or allowing some people greater rights to participate than others, manifestly violates the basic right to equal concern and respect. This argument might be put in a contractualist formulation: free and equal rational persons would not agree to principles that give some greater basic political rights than others. Any such principle would be reasonably rejectable.

The instrumentalist will maintain that principles of equal concern and respect are best satisfied by choice of political arrangements that maximize the fulfilment of basic human rights (other than the disputed right to an equal democratic say). We show concern and respect for people by showing concern and respect for the fulfilment of their rights. It would be question-begging to say in reply that one can only show equal concern and respect by showing respect for all basic moral rights including the right to a democratic say. This argument is supposed to establish, not presuppose, the existence of such a right.

Much the same applies to the contractualist formulation. The instrumentalist need not reject the contractualist idea that what is morally required is what free and equal rational persons would agree to as morally required. But if the choices of ideal moral reasoners determine what is moral, it should be noted that these ideal reasoners are choosing principles for a world in which human agents are not perfectly rational. There is nothing *prima facie* puzzling in the thought of ideal reasoners choosing moral principles that require that some actual persons, less than fully rational, be denied equal rights to political power if that is necessary to produce morally best results.

Persons are not equally free and equal in ways that matter for the question, whether democracy or autocracy is morally superior as a form of governance for people under modern conditions. People vary significantly in the degree to which they are motivated to discover what is just and conform to its requirements. They vary significantly in their capacity to figure out what the requirements of justice are, either in general or in particular circumstances. They vary significantly in their capacity to figure out what ways of life and conceptions of the good are choiceworthy. They also differ significantly in the extent to which they are motivated to exercise whatever practical reasoning abilities they have in order to bring it about that they end up affirming more rather than less reasonable conceptions of what is valuable and worthy of human pursuit. Moreover, all of these significant inequalities bear directly on the issue, who should have political power. These differences in competence render it the case that it could be that under some types of circumstances some autocratic constitution of society would predictably and reliably bring about morally superior outcomes to the outcomes that any feasible form of democracy would reach. In such circumstances (which may not be the actual circumstances of our world), autocracy would be the morally superior form of governance. Given all of this, persons who are free and equal in the threshold sense specified above may reasonably accept an undemocratic political constitution for their governance.

Recall that the question at issue is not whether autocracy is morally required all things considered, but rather whether autocracies (non-democratic political arrangements) are intrinsically unjust, other things being equal.[5]

MUST COMPETENCE TESTS
BE OBJECTIONABLY CONTROVERSIAL?

Perhaps we can make headway toward understanding the claimed intrinsic justice of democracy by noting that substantive claims regarding the shape and content of people's basic moral rights are controversial in modern diverse democracies. Reasonable members of society do not converge to agreement. Nor is there a long-term tendency toward agreement.

In the face of such disagreement, any assertion that this particular group of persons is more competent than others at determining what rights people have and designing laws and policies to implement rights is bound to be intractably controversial. Why this particular group and not some other? Any proposal of a set of qualifications that determines who is more competent and should rule will run up against the objection that it is morally arbitrary to favour this particular proposal over many alternatives that might have been advanced. The claim that the specially competent should rule thus conceals a naked preference for some conceptions of justice and against others with just as much rational backing.

David Estlund urges a similar argument against what he calls the doctrine of Epistocracy—rule by competent knowers. Estlund asserts that "no knower will be so knowable as to be known by all reasonable persons."[6] Disagreeing about justice, reasonable people will also disagree about proposed criteria of competence and about who is more qualified than others to rule. He combines this assertion with a contractualist premise and concludes that political rule by a knowledgeable elite could never be morally legitimate. The contractualist premise is that it is wrong to act in ways that affect people except on the basis of principles they could not reasonably reject. The conclusion is that any version of Epistocracy is reasonably rejectable, hence morally illegitimate.

This line of thought collapses when one asks what counts as a "reasonable" person. If a reasonable person makes no cognitive errors and deliberates with perfect rationality, then reasonable people will agree in selecting the conceptions of justice and rights that are best or tied for best. There are other conceptions of justice that attract the allegiance of less than fully reasonable persons, but these can be set aside. The notion of competence that figures in the idea of a competent political agent can then be calibrated in terms of the best conceptions of justice. This notion of competence will not be controversial among reasonable people. So if a "reasonable person" is identified with the idea of a maximally reasonable person, a notion of competence can be non-arbitrarily selected.

Suppose instead that we use the idea of a satisficing threshold to identify the "reasonable person." A "reasonable person" is reasonable enough. The lower the satisficing threshold level is set, the more plausible becomes Estlund's conjecture that "no knower [or knowledge standard] will be so knowable as to be known by all reasonable persons." The question then arises, why set the threshold at any particular less than maximal point? Estlund's set of reasonable persons might be unable to agree on a competence standard for political rule because some of them are adding two plus two and getting five or making some comparable subtler mistake of reasoning. Given that the political rulers will be charged with the task of designing and administering laws and policies that will maximize fulfilment of human rights, it is incorrect to accept any satisficing standard (unless in context the maximizing strategy calls for satisficing). Only the best is good enough.

One might attempt to defend a satisficing standard for identifying the 'reasonable person' by appeal to a requirement of respect. If a person has sufficient rational agency capacity to be able to recognize and formulate reasons and debate about principles, then it is wrongfully disrespectful to act toward him in ways that dismiss or slight this rational agency capacity, as though he were a mere tool to be manipulated for the common good. The requirement that the principles on the basis of which we interact with people, including the principles that determine the proper mode of political governance for our society, should be able to elicit their assent at least if they qualify as reasonable, expresses a fundamental norm of respect for persons.

The reply is that appropriate respect for an agent's rational agency capacity is shown by recognizing it for what it is. It shows no wrongful disrespect to me to notice that I am imperfectly rational and to take efficient steps to prevent my proclivity to mistakes from wrongfully harming others or for that matter myself. This is true in face-to-face personal interaction and it is just as true in a context where what is at issue is identifying institutional procedures and norms for collective decision-making. Respect for rational agency should not be interpreted as requiring us to pretend that anyone has more capacity than she has or to pretend that variation in capacity does not matter when it does. Respect for rational agency in persons requires treating them according to the moral principles that fully rational persons would choose, the principles best supported by moral reasons. Supposing there is a divergence between the principles that threshold reasonable people would unanimously accept and the principles that ideally reasonable people would accept, I submit that the latter not the former are the norms, acting on which manifests respect for persons (beings with rational agency capacity). The point I am trying to make in this paragraph was stated clearly by Mill long ago: "Every one has a right to feel insulted by being made a nobody, and stamped as of no account at all. No one but a fool, and only a fool of a peculiar description, feels offended by the acknowledgement that there are others whose opinion, and even whose wish, is entitled to a greater amount of consideration than his."[7]

In passing I observe that those who deny that standards of political competence that in some circumstances might justify non-democratic forms of governance can be non-arbitrarily and rationally identified seem to have no trouble with the idea that minimal competence standards can be non-arbitrarily formulated. But if we say correctly that insane and feeble-minded persons lack rational agency capacity and are in virtue of these facts rightly deemed incompetent in certain contexts for certain purposes, we are pointing to traits that vary by degree above whatever threshold level is singled out as "good enough."

Of course, nothing guarantees that fully reasonable persons will be able to select a single uniquely best conception of justice, which can serve as the reference point for defining a non-arbitrary standard of political competence. Suppose ten conceptions are tied for best, given the best moral theorizing and reasons assessment that is presently ideally available. In that case, it would not be unreasonable to implement a political system geared to achieving any of the ten. From the possibility of reasonable disagreement one gets a loose disjunctive standard of moral acceptability, not an argument for the unique fairness of democracy. Note that the fact that several conceptions of justice are equally acceptable for all we can know is fully compatible with there being a plethora of popular and decisively unreasonable views concerning the requirements of justice, any of which might command a majority vote in a democracy.

In the face of disagreement about what justice requires, one might flatly deny that the opinion of any member of society can be dismissed as unreasonable. In that case one is abandoning the moderate position about justice and democracy that is my main target in this chapter and is instead dismissing the possibility that a standard of justice can be available to provide an independent standard for assessing the political outcomes produced by the democratic process. The moderate, as I imagine her, agrees that we can have knowledge about justice but insists that democracy is an intrinsically just and fair procedure independently of its tendency to produce good results. Perhaps moderation, when pressed, slides toward radicalism.

Some readers will suspect that my position involves an illicit sleight of hand. What we observe is the members of society disagreeing about justice. From their different standpoints they will affirm opposed standards of political competence. Even if one grants that metaphysically there are right answers to questions about the substance of justice, one cannot in this context invoke these right answers to justify some elite form of political rule, because our agreed circumstances preclude any claim that any of us has epistemic access to the truth about justice. If we disagree, then we disagree. Jeremy Waldron expresses the sense that the instrumentalist is playing an illogical trick when he writes that "any theory that makes authority depend on the goodness of political outcomes is self-defeating, for it is precisely because people disagree about the goodness of outcomes that they need to set up and recognize an authority." Or again: "rights-instrumentalism seems to face the difficulty that it presupposes our possession of the truth about rights in designing an authoritative procedure whose point is to settle that very issue."[8]

These are sensible concerns.[9] There are sensible ways to address them. Consider a simple example with epistemic uncertainty. A violent altercation is underway in the street. Many people observe some of it. It is not certain who has done what to whom, with what justification or lack of justification. Among onlookers, some have a better vantage point to see what is happening, some make better use of the observational data they get, and some have a better, some a worse grip on the moral principles of self-defence, provocation and proportionality that determine who of those involved in the altercation have right on their side. There is no consensus among reasonable spectators as to what is taking place or what should be done. Any proposal as to what intervention is justified meets with reasonable suspicion from some person's standpoint. Still, none of this excludes the possibility that you in fact perceive correctly what has happened and judge correctly what ought to be done and are rationally confident that your opinions on these matters are correct. If you happen to have the power to implement this correct assessment, you should do so, despite the fact that your assessment will not attract the unanimous assent of those affected. As Anscombe observes, "Just as an individual will constantly think himself in the right, whatever he does, and yet there is still such a thing as being in the right, so nations will constantly think themselves to be in the right—and yet there is still such a thing as their being in the right."[10] Paraphrasing this to highlight its relevance to our topic, we should say that just as people think they are acting justly, whether they are or not, yet there is such a thing as acting justly, so also people will think their preferred standards of competence and criteria for eligibility for political office are correct, yet there is such a thing as there being correct standards of political competence and correct inferences from these standards to judgements as to what form of political governance in given actual circumstances is just.

The resourceful Waldron has another arrow in his quiver.[11] He argues that to suppose that an individual possesses moral rights is already to suppose that the individual has the competence to exercise them. A being that lacks rational agency capacity is not the sort of being who can be regarded as a right-bearer. Hence, there is tension and perhaps incoherence in arguing that to achieve the overall fulfilment of the rights of all members of society we must deny some the right to participate as equals in the political governance process on grounds that they are incompetent. If they are incompetent, how can they be right-bearers at all?

The tension Waldron sees eases when we look more closely. Competence is not all-or-nothing. An individual might be fully competent for many tasks but less competent at some. I may have rational agency capacity that a snake or even a gorilla lacks, and so be a candidate for ascription of moral rights that they could not sensibly be thought to possess, yet lack political competence at the level needed to contribute in a positive way to the determination of what laws and policies should be passed in order best to protect human rights. Also, the ground for ascribing some rights to people need not include strong claims about their competence to exercise the rights. I may believe that each individual has the right to live her own life as she chooses within wide moral limits. I may believe that each person has this right of autonomy without for a moment doubting that some persons have marginal or problematic competence to make good life plans and execute them. . . . The particular nature of the putative right to a democratic say is such that competence requirements apply with special force to it.

PUBLICITY

Some theorists who claim that democratic governance is intrinsically just point to the requirement of publicity. It is not enough that justice is done, it should be manifest that justice is done. Moreover, this requirement that justice be visible at least to a reasonable and careful observer is itself a further requirement of justice.

In a narrow sense, a society satisfies publicity when all members of society can check for themselves that the practices and institutions of the society as they actually function fully satisfy the norms and rules to which it is committed.[12] In a broader sense, publicity requires in addition that all members of society if they engage in reflective deliberation can see that the rules and norms to which the society is committed are themselves morally justifiable.

This asserted requirement of publicity is parlayed into an argument for the intrinsic justice of democracy. The idea is that in a world rife with reasonable disagreement about morality and the good, it can be difficult to discern whether or not a government's policies conform closely to elementary requirements of justice. Consider the fundamental norm that each person should be treated with equal consideration and respect. All persons are of fundamentally equal worth; no one's life is inherently worth more than anyone else's.

The fact that a society is autocratic thereby fuels a suspicion that some people's lives are being counted as more valuable than other people's. A society that is substantively democratic, that brings it about that all its citizens enjoy equal opportunity to influence political outcomes, goes further toward manifesting a commitment to the principle of equal consideration. The society with democratic governance, other things being equal, satisfies publicity to a greater degree than it would if it were undemocratic, and since publicity is a component of justice, this democratic society simply in virtue of being democratic is more just.

In reply: neither the wide nor the narrow ideal of publicity qualifies as an element in the set of basic moral rights definitive of justice. That it is manifest that the rules a society claims to enforce are actually fully implemented likely tends to elicit people's allegiance and in this way contribute to the long-run stability of the system. If the rules manifestly conform to principles that almost all citizens accept, this tendency is likely reinforced. If these speculative hunches are empirically corroborated, publicity promotes justice and should be valued in this purely instrumental way.

None of this provides any support at all for the quite different claim that there is a basic moral right to publicity, that publicity is intrinsically just. Consider cases in which the aim of achieving publicity and the aim of achieving justice (aside from publicity) conflict. Let us say we must choose between a policy that over the long run secretly prevents more murders or an alternative policy that prevents fewer murders but does so in a way that satisfies publicity. Once we get the issue clearly in focus, and set aside the here irrelevant likely instrumental benefits of publicity (that it possibly might prevent more murders overall in the long run), I submit that publicity should have no weight at all in conflict with other justice values.

I deny that publicity is an intrinsic component of justice. But I also deny that autocracy inherently is incompatible with publicity. If instrumental or best-results justifications of democracy in a particular setting do not succeed, and autocracy would in that setting produce morally superior results—let's say, more just results—then autocracy can satisfy publicity.

In the argument from publicity to the claim that democracy is intrinsically just, the fact that society is democratic evidently conveys a message to members of society. Democratic governance procedures are used to signal the commitment of society to the principle of equal consideration. But messages can be communicated in various ways. Why suppose that the only effective way to convey a commitment to justice is through instituting and maintaining democracy?

If autocracy is chosen on the ground that it leads to morally superior results, and this surmise is correct, then over time autocracy will produce justice, or at least more justice than would be obtainable under any other type of political regime. What could manifest a commitment to doing justice more obviously and credibly than actually doing justice over time? We are not talking here about private acts performed in people's bedrooms, we are talking about the public policies pursued by a government and the changes over time in its institutions, social norms and practices.

The claim is made that in a diverse society whose members fan out to embrace a wide array of conflicting views of morality and value, there will inevitably be a degree of uncertainty and a lack of precision in people's estimation about the extent to which their government over time brings about basic social justice. So publicity cannot be satisfied merely by aiming at morally better policies. More is needed. The symbolism of democracy—everyone counts for one, nobody for more than one—has an important role to play in securing that it is manifest that justice is done, or approximated to a good enough degree.

If the fact that the government over the long haul enacts policies that bring it about that social justice requirements are fulfilled across the society does not suffice to satisfy publicity, because people of diverse standpoints disagree about justice, I do not see why the fact that the society is democratically run must succeed in conveying the message to all that the society is committed to justice. Some may see democracy as catering to the lowest common denominator of public opinion.

The thought might be that the very existence of an autocratic system, a clique of persons who wield power and are not accountable to those over whom power is wielded, must fuel suspicion. But an autocracy need not select the members of the ruling group by a hidden process. The process by which membership in the ruling group is set may be open for public inspection, and conform to the norm of careers open to talents or a stronger meritocratic principle such as the norm of equality of fair opportunity.

For concreteness, imagine an egalitarian social justice party that overthrows a clearly unjust regime and institutes autocratic rule. Any adult member of society is eligible to apply for party membership, and the criteria for membership are a matter of public record. Applications are assessed on their merits, and those deemed most qualified are admitted to the ruling group. Moreover, education and other forms of societal assistance to child-rearing practices are set so that any individuals with the same ambition to participate in political rule by joining the ruling party and the same native (potential for) political talent have identical prospects of success in gaining party admission. In other words, the political process satisfies norms of formal equality of opportunity and also substantive equality of opportunity. Here, then, is a further response to the demand for publicity. The imagined autocratic society makes manifest its commitment to social justice, especially to the fundamental norm that all are entitled to equal consideration and respect, by bringing it about that its policies and practices achieve justice and also by regulating access to membership in the group that exercises political power according to meritocratic norms. So if publicity were itself an intrinsic component of justice, this would not tend to show that democracy is intrinsically just, because some versions of autocracy can satisfy publicity.

Fans of publicity and democracy have a riposte to the argument made to this point. The idea is that the meritocratic ideal that political rule should be exercised by the competent, not by all citizens, unravels and reveals itself as inherently unfair as we try to specify it. There are no neutral criteria of competence. The criteria of political competence will inevitably be calibrated in terms of some controversial moral ideal, which the ruling autocrats label "justice." But this gambit takes us back to the claim—already discussed and rejected in this chapter—that standards of political competence invoked to support some type of non-democratic regime must be morally arbitrary and capricious.

CONCLUSION

This chapter has searched without any success for sound arguments for the claim that there is a non-instrumental moral right to a democratic say. This is good news for the purely instrumental approach that I favour. The victory for instrumentalism is nonetheless incomplete pending a full account of human rights that enables us to see why the justifications for the fundamental human rights do not include a justification of a fundamental intrinsic right to a democratic say. This is a story for another day.

Chapter 29

Democracy: Instrumental vs. Non-Instrumental Value

Elizabeth Anderson

Elizabeth Anderson is the Arthur F. Thurnau Professor and John Dewey Distinguished University Professor of Philosophy and Women's Studies at the University of Michigan. She conceives of democracy as operating on three levels. It is a membership organization, where citizens have equal standing to make claims. It is a way of life, where citizens participate in a culture of respect. And it is a mode of governance, where institutions ensure that the claims of citizens are given due consideration. So understood, democratic arrangements are not only instrumentally but also non-instrumentally valuable. For engaging in collective self-governing, through relationships of reciprocal concern, is desirable for its own sake.

Elizabeth Anderson, "Democracy: Instrumental Vs. Non-Instrumental Value," *Contemporary Debates in Political Philosophy*, eds. Thomas Christiano and John Christman (Oxford: Wiley-Blackwell, 2009): 213–28.

What is democracy? Does it have only instrumental value? One common picture of democracy identifies it with certain governing practices, and claims that it has only instrumental value. On this view, the purpose of government, like that of the market, is to satisfy individual preferences. Individual preferences are assumed to be formed exogenously to democratic processes. Democratic mechanisms of accountability are instituted to ensure that government tries to satisfy these preferences. The main such mechanism is voting, a device for choosing public officials and policies by aggregating individual preferences into a collective decision. Voting is the primary way in which citizens participate in democracy. Its value, like the value of other democratic governing practices, is plainly instrumental.

In this essay, I shall not deny that voting has instrumental value. If voting were not a means to reaching collective decisions responsive to the desires of the electorate, or if it led to results that systematically undermined the interests of the electorate, it would be worthless. But it does not follow that voting has *only* instrumental value. In our consumer culture, we take it for granted that shopping is an activity many people enjoy, beyond its instrumental value in enabling people to acquire goods they desire. Even if a computer could be perfectly programmed with a consumer's tastes so that it automatically ordered online exactly what the consumer prefers, many consumers would prefer to personally survey their options and choose for themselves. For these consumers, shopping has non-instrumental as well as instrumental value. *Yet its non-instrumental value is conditional on its instrumental value.* Although some people can content themselves with pure window-shopping for goods beyond their reach, most would stay home if shopping malls contained only goods that they could not acquire by shopping.

I shall argue the same about democratic participation. It would make no sense if it didn't achieve the ends for which it is instituted. Yet in virtue of its instrumental value, it acquires a non-instrumental value too—if not, for many citizens, as an activity people *enjoy*, then as something they rightly value as a constitutive part of a way of life that they value non-instrumentally. Even if a dictatorship could give them what they wanted . . . democratic citizens would prefer to govern themselves.

I shall also argue that the democratic way of life can be justified as a matter of justice. Each member of a state is entitled to have equal standing to make claims on others regarding the protection of their interests, and to participate in decisions concerning the shared background conditions of their interactions and the adoption of collective goals. The democratic way of life realizes the universal and equal standing of the members of society, and is therefore justified as morally right.

To appreciate these non-instrumental values of democracy, we need to alter our understanding of democracy. I join a tradition of democratic thinking advanced by John Stuart Mill and John Dewey. Both held that democracy is more than a set of governing practices. It is a culture or way of life of a community defined by equality of membership, reciprocal cooperation, and mutual respect and sympathy and located in civic society. On Mill's view, democratic participation is a way of life that unites two higher pleasures—sympathy and autonomy. On Dewey's view, it is the exercise of practical intelligence in discovering and implementing collective solutions to shared problems, which is the basic function of community life. On both of their views, voting is just one mode of democratic self-expression among many others that constitute a democratic way of life.

I'll also be arguing for a change in the way we think about instrumental vs. non-instrumental justification. Here, I join John Dewey, who offered a trenchant critique of traditional ways of understanding noninstrumental or "intrinsic" values. As my shopping example illustrates, "intrinsic" values cannot always be identified prior to and independently of instrumental values. Among reflective persons, judgments of intrinsic and instrumental value interact bi-directionally. This contrasts with the standard philosophical view, according to which we fix on the intrinsic values first, and then identify the instrumental values as whatever brings about the intrinsic values.

DEMOCRACY AS A WAY OF LIFE

I shall begin by broadening our conception of democracy. Democracy can be understood on three levels: as a membership organization, a mode of government, and a culture. As a membership organization, democracy involves universal and equal citizenship of all the permanent members of a society who live under the jurisdiction of a state. As a mode of government, democracy is government by discussion among equals. As a culture, democracy consists in the freewheeling cooperative interaction of citizens from all walks of life on terms of equality in civil society. These three levels work together. In particular, democracy as a mode of government cannot be fully achieved apart from a democratic culture. At the same time, the point of a democratic culture is not simply to make democratic government work; rather, democratic government is a manifestation of democratic culture; its point is to serve the democratic community, to realize its promise of universal and equal standing.

Consider first democracy as a membership organization. A constitutive principle of democracy is that all who are permanently subject to the laws of a government should be entitled a say in its operations, either directly, in participatory democracy, or indirectly, through the election of representatives. This entails that all the permanent members of a society should be entitled to the status of *citizens*, not subjects, with rights to vote upon reaching adulthood, and all of the other rights—to permanent residence, freedom of speech, to petition government, run for political office, sit on juries, etc.—that are required for having a say.

Exceptions to the general rule of universal citizenship may be tolerable at the margins, with respect to small numbers of legal permanent residents who may work in a country without acquiring citizenship. But even here, a democratic society's interest in universal citizenship is substantial. The democratic ideal supports the major push that occurred in the 1990s to move permanent U.S. residents to citizenship, and the relaxation of standards for foreign permanent guest workers to gain citizenship in several European countries. What democracy cannot allow for long without compromising itself is a large permanent population of metics, of people designated as outsiders, subject to laws although they have no rights to participate in shaping them.

This is intolerable because democracy as a membership organization requires equality as well as inclusion. Pressure toward universal inclusion follows from the demands of equality. Equality is understood here as a relation among persons, whereby each adult actively recognizes everyone else's equal authority to make claims concerning the rules under which all shall live and cooperate, and this recognition is common knowledge among all. As the standard democratic slogan goes, everyone counts for one and no one for more than one. This is not merely a voting aggregation rule ("one man, one vote") but a more general principle for organizing social interaction in a democratic society.

Consider next democracy as a mode of government. We are accustomed to thinking of democracy as a set of governing institutions, involving such things as a universal franchise, periodic elections, representative public officials accountable to the people, decisions by majority vote, transparent government, a free press, and the rule of law. What is the point of this set of governing institutions? Democratic theory is split between two broad views: majority rule (aggregation of given preferences), and deliberative democracy. Following the second view, Walter Bagehot famously defined democracy as "government by discussion."[1] It contrasts both with government by custom and government by the decree of a ruling class. I would add to Bagehot's definition that democracy is government by discussion *among equals*. In a democracy, there is but one class of citizens; no citizen is second-class, and no permanent member of society is excluded from access to citizenship.

Deliberative democrats have several reasons for resisting the "majority rule" formula for democracy. First, within a conception of democracy as majority rule, individual rights tend to be construed as constraints on democracy rather than constitutive features of it. "Majority rule" suggests that the majority is entitled to get whatever it wants. If the majority prefers to silence, marginalize, or subordinate various minority groups, majority rule supports this outcome. Against this, many have decried the "tyranny of the majority" as a threat to individual rights. On this construal, individual rights impose *constraints* on democracy.

From the standpoint of deliberative democracy, this way of counterposing individual rights to democratic forms is deeply confused. Many individual rights are *constitutive* of democracy. Democracy requires that citizens from different walks of life *talk* to one another about matters of common interest, to determine what issues warrant collective action, what kinds of action might make sense, and who is most trusted to hold political office. This entails that numerous rights, including the rights to vote, and freedom of speech, association, and movement, are part of the structural features of democracy rather than constraints upon it. The same point applies to various rights that help secure the equality of citizens, such as rights against establishment of religion, the prohibition of religious tests for holding public office, and the prohibition of racial segregation in public institutions and civil society. It applies as well to the U.S. Constitutional limitation on criminal charges of treason to making war against one's country or aiding its enemies—a limitation designed to secure room for the "loyal opposition" of minorities who are out of power. A majority that silences or segregates minorities, limits their rights to participate because they have the "wrong" religion, or threatens dissenters with treason charges, is tyrannically *un*democratic.

A second reason deliberative democrats reject "majority rule" as a definition of democracy is that the latter takes individual preferences as unqualified inputs into collective decisions. But not every preference is entitled to collective satisfaction, even if it is held by a majority of citizens. As we have seen, some preferences, such as to stamp minority groups with badges of inferiority, or to mark them as outsiders, are ruled out by the requirements of democracy itself. More generally, democratic discussion is a critical way for the public to come to an understanding of what its aims are as a public—to decide *which* concerns are properly matters of public interest, entitled to lay a claim on collective resources and cooperation to secure their fulfillment. Democratic dialogue does not take preferences as given, but transforms them, not just in the sense of changing individuals' minds about what each wants, but of changing *our* mind of what *we* want when we act collectively as citizens.

A third reason deliberative democrats reject "majority rule" as a definition of democracy is that it fails to make central a role for intelligence and learning in democratic decision-making. If democracy is just giving the majority what it wants, why not just let the public decide issues directly by popular referendum? Deliberative democrats reply that to make intelligent decisions and learn from their mistakes, decision-makers must be able to think and deliberate *together*. This requires that legislative bodies be relatively small, investigate issues jointly, and reason together on the basis of common knowledge. They must have feedback mechanisms, tied to mechanisms for accountability, that inform them of the consequences of their decisions and provide them with the means and incentives to revise their decisions in light of knowledge of their effects. While the representative vs. direct democracy distinction is orthogonal to the deliberative vs. preference aggregation distinction, deliberative democrats, because they stress the centrality of deliberation to democratic processes, have an edge in explaining why representative institutions are preferable.

Deliberative democrats have sometimes been thought to go too far in assuming that the aim of democracy is to construct and promote a common good, which is the object of overwhelming consensus. If that were consistently possible, then we would hardly need voting rules such as the majority rule at all. Decision-making could proceed by consensus. Those who are experienced with decision-making by consensus understand its weaknesses. Often, decisions must be made before a true consensus has been reached. The need to make a decision puts overwhelming pressure on dissenters to conform. That process isn't democratic. It is essential to the democratic process to leave room for legitimate dissent.

Because democratic decisions must often be made in the absence of consensus, and must preserve room for legitimate dissent, voting is a necessary moment in the extended process of democratic decision-making. But even when dissenters lose, their role is not thereby cancelled. Deliberative democrats who follow Dewey stress the provisional and experimental character of voting.[2] Voting does not make a final decision, but rather represents the citizens' or the state's legitimate decision of what to try next until something better comes along. Citizens' collective deliberation and feedback on public decision-making is continuous and does not stop just because a law has been enacted. The rise of the regulatory state has entailed that administrative agencies issue thousands of rules pursuant to general laws. Critical to the democratic process is participatory citizen feedback on proposed regulations prior to their enactment. This is a form of citizen input into regulatory deliberation. Once a regulation is adopted, citizens provide feedback to one another and to public officeholders on the effects of the regulation as they see it. This provides further deliberative input into the regulatory process, sometimes leading to revision or withdrawal of regulations. If the effects of policies are bad enough as judged by affected citizens, they will demand reform and elect those whom they view as better able to make them.

On the view of democracy I propose, voting and deliberation represent alternating moments in a continuous process of provisional decision-making, the aim of which is simultaneously to learn about what works and to decide upon criteria of what counts as working from the perspective of citizens acting and thinking collectively. Decisions are provisional and continuously subject to revision in light of feedback from citizens about their consequences. Feedback gets its bite through mechanisms of accountability, including not just periodic elections but public protest, petitions to representatives, citizen participation in regulatory deliberation, and participation in public opinion polling, among many other mechanisms, not least scrutiny of public problems, policies, and officeholders by a skeptical press. Citizens communicate not just with their representatives and other public officeholders, but with one another, so that they may come to an understanding of what they demand *as a public*, and not just as isolated individuals.

None of this would work if democracy were nothing more than a set of governing institutions. Dewey urged us to "to get rid of the habit of thinking of democracy as something institutional and external and to acquire the habit of treating it as a way of personal life," for only so could genuine democracy be realized.[3] Democratic institutions amount to little unless citizens enact, in their day-to-day interactions, a spirit of tolerant discussion and cooperation. This leads to the third aspect of democracy, which is cultural. As a culture or way of life, democracy consists in "free gatherings of neighbors on the street corner to discuss back and forth what is read in uncensored news of the day," and "personal day-by-day working together with others." It

> is the belief that even when needs and ends or consequences are different for each individual, the habit of amicable cooperation – which may include, as in sport, rivalry and competition – is itself a priceless addition to life. To take as far as possible every conflict which arises – and they are bound to arise – out of the atmosphere and medium of force, of violence as a means of settlement into that of discussion and of intelligence is to treat those who disagree – even profoundly – with us as those from whom we may learn, and in so far, as friends.[4]

As the citizens of ex-communist countries of Eastern Europe are aware, democracy requires not just the installation of democratic governing institutions but the flourishing of civil society. Civil society, the locus of democratic culture, is a sphere of life intermediate between the private sphere of family and friends, and the sphere of the state. It consists in the domains where citizens freely interact and cooperate, spontaneously in public streets and parks, and in more organized fashion in firms and non-profit associations of all kinds. These are the primary locations where citizens from different walks of life communicate with each other, in ways that shape their sense of what their proper goals are *as a public*. This is where citizens' preferences are transformed through discussion and become matters of public and even shared interest, not simply isolated private preferences. This is where matters of private concern can *become* matters of public concern, when citizens pool information about their problems and discover that some problems they thought were personal are shared by others in the same predicament, and caused by factors subject to collective control.

The construction of a democratic culture in civil society requires several elements. One—foremost in the minds of those who seek to construct civil society in Eastern Europe—is to promote the spontaneous self-organization of citizens into numerous associations not directed by the state. Most of these associations, including private firms, clubs, and fraternal associations, do not have direct political aims. Yet they contribute to a democratic culture by providing experience in citizen self-organization and self-governance on a small scale, settings in which informal discussions contribute to the formation of public opinion, and sites of feedback on government decisions.

My own work on democracy stresses another requirement of a democratic culture: associations where citizens from different walks of life can learn to interact and cooperate on terms of equality.[5] This requires that the dominant associations of civil society, notably the workplace, be *integrated* along whatever social divisions—racial, ethnic, religious, sexual—mark significant systematic inequalities among citizens. Successful integration requires not just contact, but willing and active cooperation. In such cooperative associations, citizens learn to treat one another as equals: as eligible for inclusion in collective projects, entitled to an equal voice, whose concerns merit equal attention and response.

THE VALUES OF A DEMOCRATIC WAY OF LIFE

What good is leading a democratic way of life—living in a democratic culture, based on universal and equal membership of all permanent residents of a state, constituted in part by political participation? Here I want to stress the plurality of goods realized in living up to democratic ideals, postponing consideration of whether these goods are "intrinsic" or "instrumental." First, democracy embodies relations of mutual respect and equality, which are required as a matter of right. Second, democracy helps avoid some of the evils of undemocratic ways of life. It helps secure individuals against abuse, neglect, subordination, and pariah status. It also protects against the corruption of character of those who occupy privileged positions in society. Third, democratic ways of life realize the shared goods of sympathy and autonomy. Fourth, democracy is a mode of collective learning.

My list of the goods of a democratic way of life focuses on goods *specific* to or *inherent in* that way of life. This approach contrasts with another way one might argue for democracy: one could first lay out the goods that any government is supposed to provide for its people, and then argue that democracy is best able to secure them. Any minimally decent government needs to provide basic external and internal security for its members; to lay out common rules of interaction and cooperation; and to either directly supply or secure the conditions for other institutions to supply public goods such as the infrastructure of transportation and communication, and public health measures. If we start off with a fixed list of such goods, as in theories of the minimal state, it could be argued that democracy is not necessary to secure them. . . .

Turning to the first item on my list, the core value of democracy is equality of social relations. By equality I do not mean that everyone enjoys equal esteem or reputation, or equally good jobs or income, nor that everyone is equal in virtue or merit. Democratic equality rather denotes a kind of standing in civil society to make claims on others, that they respect one's rights, pay due regard to one's interests, and include one as a full participant in civil society, including those that inform democratic governance. Democracy regards each citizen as "a self-originating source of claims."[6] They make claims in their own right, not merely as functionaries in a social order designed for other ends, such as the greater glory of God or the state. Everyone *counts*, and everyone counts *equally*.

This is a claim of right. Call the "good" that which properly *appeals* to us or attracts us; and the "right" that which may be *exacted* from us, as an authoritative demand.[7] I claim as a matter of right that everyone subject to a common set of coercive rules and policies is entitled to equal consideration in their construction. I shall not offer an elaborate argument for this claim. Instead, I point to the experience in which it is rooted: namely, the experience of being called to account by another whose interests we are neglecting or would otherwise neglect. This experience is a deep, constitutive part of growing up in society. Granting its purported authority with respect to some persons, there is no case for denying it to anyone. The failure of all arguments of the form "the purported authority of claims originating from people of type x is invalid" where x refers to any of the supposed grounds of antidemocratic subordination (race, ethnicity, class, caste, sex, religion, ignoble birth, etc.), vindicates the democratic standard of right.

The experience of the authority of another's claims is the feeling known as respect. We express this feeling in action by heeding other's claims—taking them seriously in deliberation, weighing them equally with the symmetrical claims we make on others. Democracy is a way of life whereby we collectively heed our mutual claims on one another in constructing rules and goals for those parts of our lives that we live in common with our fellow citizens. It thereby embodies relations of mutual respect, which are required as a matter of right. This is the first distinctive value of democracy.

Having distinguished the right from the good, we may wonder whether a democratic way of life is also *good*, or whether it is merely something exacted from us reluctantly. What is the good of democratic equality? Consider what life is like for those in undemocratic societies, who are deemed not to count at all, or only as subordinates or functionaries. Nonpersons, pariahs, untouchables, and outlaws enjoy no protection against the cruelty and abuse of others. Subordinates suffer under the humiliating contempt of superiors. Mere functionaries are thrown away when no longer useful. These evils are avoided by effective standing as an equal. Thus, John Stuart Mill argued that even if women were properly subordinate to their husbands, they would still need political rights to ensure against men's abuse of their domestic authority. "Men, as well as women . . . need political rights . . . in order that they may not be misgoverned."[8]

Mill also argued that the character of those who enjoy superior rank in undemocratic societies is corrupted by their power over others. Where lords are free to exploit their tenants, slaveowners to whip their slaves, husbands to rape their wives, Hindus to riot against Muslims, those on top become cruel, despotic, and depraved. Even milder forms of inequality, institutionalized through norms that exclude and silence those of lower rank, propagate ignorance and negligence on the part of the powerful. Democratic equality protects the advantaged from the vices of arrogance, malice, and stupidity.

A democratic way of life is not merely good for each member of society, considered individually. It is also a *shared* good, realized by all of us together. Call a good "shared" by the members of a group if a condition of its goodness is that it be good, and commonly known to be good, for everyone else in the group. Equality of social relations, as realized in a democratic community, is a shared good. Democratic citizens feel this whenever they decry the subordination or exclusion of their fellow citizens. It is felt as an assault not just on their fellow citizens, but on them—even if they are, through that subordination, granted a superior status. To be placed high through the degradation of fellow citizens—as whites were placed high through the subordination of blacks in the U.S.—is, from a democratic point of view, to be deprived of the good of equal standing, and hence to be in an important sense degraded. As John Stuart Mill claimed,

> There ought to be no pariahs in a full-grown and civilized nation. . . . Everyone is degraded, whether aware of it or not, when other people, without consulting him, take upon themselves unlimited power to regulate his destiny.[9]

True democrats despise titles of nobility and badges of higher-caste status that may be offered to or imposed on them as not simply unjust but degrading, in depriving them of the equal standing they need to live in democratic community with their fellow citizens. To be held high is to be excluded from camaraderie and candid relations with others. To be a democrat is to locate one's sense of dignity in equal social relations with others, and one's good in living in a community of mutual respect and sympathy with them.

The democratic way of life in a community of equals has characteristic forms of activity: meeting together and talking freely about common problems, forging collective plans to solve these problems, observing what life in accordance with these plans is like and revising the plans accordingly, all with equal regard to the interests of all members of the community. These activities exercise three powers: sympathy, autonomy, and intelligence.

Sympathy or solidarity—what Mill called the "feeling of unity with others"—is expressed in a person's never conceiving of himself "otherwise than as a member of a body" whose governing principle is that of a "society between equals," which "can only exist on the understanding that the interests of all are to be regarded equally" and "consulted."[10] Mill thought such mutually sympathetic societies of equals existed in many forms, including marriage and workers' cooperatives. But its broadest form is democratic government.

To insist on the importance of sympathy among citizens is not to deny that partisan rivalry and competition among interest groups is part and parcel of democratic life. Recalling Dewey's remarks above, democratic sympathy requires recognition of rivals as loyal opponents from whom one may learn. (Partisan rivals are often loath to publicly admit this, even while "stealing issues" from one another.) It also requires that one cast one's justifications for public policies in terms of the public interest, and not just in terms of narrow partisan or factional interests. Finally, it requires a search for mutually acceptable cooperative solutions to problems, instead of conquest and repression.

Autonomy in democratic participation is expressed in citizens' setting shared principles, goals, and representatives for themselves. What counts as a legitimate matter of public interest is not given to citizens. It is something they decide for themselves, through discussion, voting, and petitioning. The process of coming to a shared understanding of problems of public interest and determination to solve these problems collectively (either directly, or through representatives) was what Dewey called the public coming to recognize itself as a public.[11] For members of a community to recognize themselves as constituting a public is for them to become a collective agent in determining their own affairs—for citizens to act together to determine the collective conditions and goals of their cooperative life. This is to exercise autonomy collectively.

Finally, democratic activity is an exercise of intelligence, in the sense of learning better ways to live our collective lives. Citizens from all walks of life learn from one another in sympathetic discussion about their problems and prospective solutions to them. More heads are generally better than fewer, in that they bring to bear a wider diversity of experiences and knowledge to the identification and solution of collective problems, and ensure that everyone's interests are voiced. Citizens also learn from discussing problems with the solutions they have already implemented.

Here I endorse an "epistemic" conception of democracy without claiming that the outcome of voting constitutively determines the right answer. The true epistemic virtues of democracy are not found in the static outcomes of voting but rather in the dynamic processes of discussion and feedback to government on policies already implemented. Dewey saw democracy as the collective implementation of experimental intelligence in determining how to live.[12] Voting does not decide what answer is right. It rather selects a preferred hypothesis to be tried—that these officeholders will lead the country in a better direction, that these policies will solve our problems. These hypotheses are then tested by living in accordance with them, seeing what happens, and pooling information about disparate citizens' favorable and unfavorable responses to them. The feedback mechanisms of democratic participation—voting, petitioning, discussion in public media—deliver judgments that either support the current leadership or demand change in what the public hypothesizes is a better direction. By these means, citizens roughly steer the ship of state, but not toward a destination determined outside of the democratic way of life itself. Rather, we figure out on the way what paths seem more promising, much as hikers exploring new territories without a map take the trails that interest them at the time.

INTRINSIC AND INSTRUMENTAL VALUES OF DEMOCRACY

Does my list of the values of democracy show it to be only instrumentally valuable? On a standard instrumentalist model, we first establish intrinsically valuable states of affairs to be attained, where the value of these states is independent of the processes that bring them about, and then justify actions and institutions as causally efficacious in bringing about these independently identified states. Some aspects of my account of the value of democracy appear to fit this model. Thus, I argued that democracy helps avoid the oppression and neglect of those who would otherwise lack a voice in governance, and corruption of the character of those who would otherwise have arbitrary power over those without voice.

Notice, however, that in characterizing democracy as a mode of collective autonomy, I reject the idea that we can comprehensively identify, independent of democratic processes, the proper goals that democracy should seek. There are *some* such goals, such as security and social order. But these can be attained by a libertarian minimal state. The goals of a democratic state range more widely, but not, in a liberal state, over anything whatever. (Recall the liberal state's abstention from religious impositions.) Rather, democracy is a mode of collective governance whereby citizens work out together what goals they shall share. This is specifically to *reject* the idea that democracy is a generic preference satisfaction mechanism. In democracies, some outcomes, even if *individually* preferred by a majority, enjoy no public standing.

Suppose we adopted an expanded instrumentalist model, according to which some of the intrinsically valuable states of affairs include causal processes, and not just outcomes. On such an expanded view, some worlds can be better than others because their end states were achieved in a particular way. To justify democracy on the expanded model is to claim not just that democratic processes bring about better states than nondemocratic processes, but that the world is a better place for containing acts that instantiate democratic processes. I do not think this model captures the value of democratic processes, however. We do not vote in order to have more acts of voting in the world. The world is not better for containing more such acts than fewer.

On the instrumentalist model, whether standard or expanded, states of affairs are assumed to have "intrinsic" value, and everything else is *extrinsically* valuable as an instrument to bringing about the intrinsically valuable states of affairs. Here, "intrinsic" value denotes the point at which justification comes to an end. This is the point where we have identified something that is valuable, independent of the value of anything else. Value is essentially normative for action and feeling: it prescribes an "ought" to agents to bring about and/or care about what is valuable. So, to say that something is intrinsically valuable means we have reason to bring about and/or care about it, independently of any reason we may have to care about anything else. . . .

The proper point of politics is to serve *people*. The proper form of political justification, then, recognizes that states of affairs are to be pursued *for the sake of people, in recognition of the authority of people to set their own ends*. This entails that the states of affairs properly sought in politics do *not* figure in political justification as intrinsic values. They are only extrinsically valuable. We properly care about states of affairs in the political realm, only because we care about people. People, not states of the world, are what has intrinsic value in politics. Instrumentalist models of political justification neglect this point. Thus, even when my list of the values of democracy appears to be instrumentalist, it is not, because the outcomes democratic processes are supposed to bring about are themselves not intrinsically valuable, but good only for the sake of people, who are the original sources of value.

The proper form of political justification starts from the premise that people are intrinsically valuable, in the sense that they are self-originating sources of claims, and have equal authority to make claims. Recall my three-level account of democracy: as a membership organization, a form of culture or way of life, and a mode of governance. Each of these three levels is founded on recognition of the value of people as equal and self-originating sources of claims. As a membership organization, democracy recognizes the universal and equal standing of all permanent residents within the territorial jurisdiction of the state to make claims as citizens. As a culture or way of life, the locus of which is civil society, democracy realizes this equality in habits of mutual consultation and cooperation that express respect and sympathy for all fellow citizens. As a mode of governance, institutions and practices such as "one person, one vote," recognition of a loyal opposition, a free press, protests and petitions, aim to realize equal consideration of citizens' claims and thereby establish citizens as equals in relation to each other. Hence, my justification of democracy as grounded in considerations of right or justice, tracks the proper form of political justification.

I hasten to distance myself from a particular way of understanding political justification that might look similar to what I have proposed. On that model, political justification is an *a priori* affair, a matter of principle rather than pragmatism. This follows from the supposition that, in rejecting an instrumentalist justification of democracy, one commits oneself to *a priori* arguments that abstract from consideration of the consequences of democratic practices.

I ally myself with John Dewey in rejecting the premises behind this model. There *is* a deep principle of equal moral standing underlying the justification of democracy. However, like all moral claims, this one is not derived from pure *a priori* argument, but rooted in our *experiences* of the authority of others to make claims on us, which are rooted in our experiences of respect for them. (That these experiences are veridical—i.e., ought to be heeded—and that their proper ground is not based on arbitrary characteristics such as ancestry, requires critical reflection on these experiences as well as on the consequences of heeding them.)

Furthermore, the supposedly sharp distinction between principled and pragmatic justification is itself questionable. I agree with Dewey and Mill that practical principles are subject to empirical testing through experiments in living. We test our principles by living in accordance with them, and seeing whether doing so solves the problems we were trying to solve, and delivers other consequences that we find acceptable. There is no *a priori* deduction of the value of periodic elections, transparent government, a free press, and so forth. If these processes led to social disorder and misery, as conservative critics of democracy supposed, they would be bad. Nor can we simply examine the concept of equal standing of citizens so as to logically deduce what concrete social norms of democratic interaction in civil society actually realize this elusive ideal. Rather, such insights can only be won through the hard work of testing rival democratic conceptions in practice and seeing how they work. This requires systematic reform not just of external institutional rules, as of voting, but of our habits and affects. A century and a half after abolishing slavery, Americans are still mired in disdain and antipathy for the descendants of slaves, and many of us are still searching for a shared way out.

To insist on the importance of evaluating practical principles in light of their consequences is *not* to revert to "merely" instrumentalist justification. Recall: consequences are not good in themselves; their value depends on the value of people, for the sake of which we seek them. Moreover, for purposes of political justification, that the consequences are autonomously willed by citizens as a collective goal is not an accidental feature of most goals of a democratic state, but critical to legitimating the use of state coercion to bring them about. Hence, the justification of political goals does not rest outside of democratic processes. Which goals are legitimately pursued by the state is itself determined within democratic processes, and justified in part because those processes embody a form of collective autonomy.

I have been focusing on a large object of evaluation: democracy as a membership organization and as a way of life, including a mode of governance. I have argued that the justification for democracy, so understood, is not merely instrumental, but is based on a conception of persons as self-originating sources of claims, as worthy of respect and sympathy. Justification takes the consequences of democratic organization and practices into account. But those consequences are not intrinsically valuable. They are rather justified in terms of democratic processes, which express the autonomy and equal standing of citizens.

Most debates over the value of democracy have focused more narrowly on democratic processes or activities in a narrow sense: those activities of citizens that directly impact governance, such as voting, participating in town meetings, and petitioning representatives. Perhaps *these* are only "instrumentally" justified, in the sense that their value is limited to their production of independently justified states of affairs? Again, not if "independently justified" means justified independently of the democratic character of the processes that bring them about.

Suppose we narrow our target of evaluation further, by setting aside considerations of justice and legitimacy, and just look at the good or appealing value of democratic activities. Should we say then that their goodness is wholly dependent on the value (appeal) of their consequences? Since I reject the idea that political practices can be justified apart from consideration of their consequences, I do agree that the value of democratic practices does depend on their consequences. If democratic elections regularly resulted in policies catastrophic to the electors—and worse than what alternative systems of governance would deliver—they would not be justified.

But this is not enough to show that their goodness is *wholly* derivative of the goodness of their consequences. The proper test of the noninstrumental goodness of an activity is not whether we'd still prefer to do it, even if it didn't result in desirable consequences. It is rather whether we'd still prefer to engage in it, even if the same consequences could be brought about by other (passive) means.

I alluded to this test in the introduction to this paper, when I discussed the value of shopping. Even if a computer perfectly predicted all of one's wants, shopped on one's behalf, and arranged for the goods to be delivered to one's home without any intervention on one's own part, one may still prefer to shop oneself. The activity itself is valued: imagining oneself wearing various clothes and jewelry, actually trying on the props, is an enjoyable form of adult play, as well as an expression of autonomy in forming one's preferences.

I follow Mill and Dewey in holding that participating in democratic ways of life, including democratic governance, satisfies the same test of non-instrumental appealing value. Even if a dictator delivered the same consequences as the people would want, were they to choose democratically, citizens would still prefer to achieve those consequences through democratic activities.

Why should this be so? Recall that democratic activities express sympathy for fellow citizens, exercise our collective autonomy, and manifest a form of collective learning. Mill argued that sympathetic and autonomous activities, as expressions of higher faculties, are higher pleasures: those experienced with them would not give them up even for any amount of lower pleasures (those that gratify the motives we share with animals).[13] Even if a dictator could arrange our affairs to our liking, we would still prefer to be autonomous—to manage our collective affairs for ourselves, according to our own collective judgment. And even if a dictator could deliver happiness to all, we'd still prefer to do this ourselves, as a way of expressing mutual sympathy and respect for our fellow citizens.

Dewey made the same case for the value of learning. Activity is not valuable just for the states of the world it achieves. The value of life is in the active living of it, not some goal external to activity.[14] Learning is integral to human living. We are always learning about what is good by confronting problems, testing solutions, seeing what works, incorporating discoveries about what works into our practices. We are constantly remaking our practices in light of reflection on living in accordance with them. This does not describe a mere phase of life, but the whole of practical intelligence in action. Learning is not just for the sake of knowing; those who take this attitude are forever postponing gratification in the learning process, until it is "complete." But learning is never complete, because circumstance are always changing, requiring the continuous modification of our practices. To desire to skip ahead to the "final results" is to desire to skip human life itself. Democracy as a way of life is the collective exercise of practical intelligence or learning, applied to the problems of living together as equals. It makes no more sense to skip ahead to "the end" than it does to exit the life of a democratic community itself.

Dewey argued that the sharp contrast between "instrumental" and "intrinsic" valuation, as applied to activities and states of the world, is false.[15] They represent transitory and alternating moments in an ongoing process of living, not fixed points of justification and evaluative dependence. What is immediately valued at one moment is reassessed in light of its consequences, which may either reinforce or undermine the original immediate valuation. Valuations of the consequences themselves may change, once we understand what it takes to achieve them. What is valued as a means at one moment is valued in itself at another. The same point applies to the values of a democratic way of life, of which participation in governance is a constitutive part. Once we see democracy as a way of life of a community of equals, and not just as a mode of governance, it is hard to conclude otherwise. The good of a way of community life is in the active living of it with others, not in some state of the world external to it.

B

DELIBERATION

Chapter 30

Toward a Deliberative Model of Democratic Legitimacy

Seyla Benhabib

Seyla Benhabib is Eugene Mayer Professor of Political Science and Philosophy at Yale University. She maintains that in order for political decisions to be legitimate they must be the outcome of collective deliberation that is conducted rationally among free and equal citizens. But what does it take for deliberation to be rational? Benhabib argues for the following answer: All citizens have the same chances to speak, to question, to interrogate in open debate; all citizens have the right to adjust the topics of conversation; and all citizens have the right to question the rules of the discourse procedure. This model of deliberation ensures not only that the relevant information is made available but also that the discourse itself is subject to critique and revision.

Seyla Benhabib, "Toward a Deliberative Model of Democratic Legitimacy," in *Democracy and Difference: Contesting the Boundaries of the Political*, ed. Seyla Benhabib (Princeton, NJ: Princeton University Press, 1996), 67–83.

DEMOCRATIC LEGITIMACY AND PUBLIC GOODS

The present essay is concerned with one good among others which democratic societies must attain: the good of legitimacy. I am concerned to examine the philosophical foundations of democratic legitimacy. I will argue that legitimacy in complex democratic societies must be thought to result from the free and unconstrained public deliberation of all about matters of common concern. Thus a public sphere of deliberation about matters of mutual concern is essential to the legitimacy of democratic institutions.

Democracy, in my view, is best understood as a model for organizing the collective and public exercise of power in the major institutions of a society on the basis of the principle that decisions affecting the well-being of a collectivity can be viewed as the outcome of a procedure of free and reasoned deliberation among individuals considered as moral and political equals. Certainly any definition of essentially contested concepts like democracy, freedom, and justice is never a mere definition; the definition itself already articulates the normative theory that justifies the term. Such is the case with the preceding definition. My understanding of democracy privileges a deliberative model over other kinds of normative considerations. This is not to imply that economic welfare, institutional efficiency, and cultural stability would not be relevant in judging the adequacy of a normative definition of democracy. Economic welfare claims and collective identity needs must also be satisfied for democracies to function over time. However, the normative basis of democracy as a form of organizing our collective life is neither the fulfillment of economic welfare nor the realization of a stable sense of collective identity. For just as the attainment of certain levels of economic welfare may be compatible with authoritarian political rule, so too antidemocratic regimes may be more successful in assuring a sense of collective identity than democratic ones.

My goal in the first half of this article will be to examine the relationship between the normative presuppositions of democratic deliberation and the idealized content of practical rationality. . . .

A DELIBERATIVE MODEL OF DEMOCRACY

According to the deliberative model of democracy, it is a necessary condition for attaining legitimacy and rationality with regard to collective decision making processes in a polity, that the institutions of this polity are so arranged that what is considered in the common interest of all results from processes of collective deliberation conducted rationally and fairly among free and equal individuals. The more collective decision-making processes approximate this model the more increases the presumption of their legitimacy and rationality. Why?

The basis of legitimacy in democratic institutions is to be traced back to the presumption that the instances which claim obligatory power for themselves do so because their decisions represent an impartial standpoint said to be equally in the interests of all. This presumption can be fulfilled only if such decisions are in principle open to appropriate public processes of deliberation by free and equal citizens.

The discourse model of ethics formulates the most general principles and moral intuitions behind the validity claims of a deliberative model of democracy. The basic idea behind this model is that only those norms (i.e., general rules of action and institutional arrangements) can be said to be valid (i.e., morally binding), which would be agreed to by all those affected by their consequences, if such agreement were reached as a consequence of a process of deliberation that had the following features: 1) participation in such deliberation is governed by the norms of equality and symmetry; all have the same chances to initiate speech acts, to question, to interrogate, and to open debate; 2) all have the right to question the assigned topics of conversation; and 3) all have the right to initiate reflexive arguments about the very rules of the discourse procedure and the way in which they are applied or carried out. There are no prima facie rules limiting the agenda of the conversation, or the identity of the participants, as long as each excluded person or group can justifiably show that they are relevantly affected by the proposed norm under question. In certain circumstances this would mean that citizens of a democratic community would have to enter into a practical discourse with noncitizens who may be residing in their countries, at their borders, or in neighboring communities if there are matters that affect them all. Ecology and environmental issues in general are a perfect example of such instances when the boundaries of discourses keep expanding because the consequences of our actions expand and affect increasingly more people.

The procedural specifics of those special argumentation situations called "practical discourses" are not automatically transferable to a macroinstitutional level, nor is it necessary that they should be so transferable. A theory of democracy, as opposed to a general moral theory, would have to be concerned with the question of institutional specifications and practical feasibility. Nonetheless, the procedural constraints of the discourse model can act as test cases for critically evaluating the criteria of membership and the rules for agenda setting, and for the structuring of public discussions within and among institutions. . . .

According to the deliberative model, procedures of deliberation generate legitimacy as well as assure some degree of practical rationality. But what are the claims to practical rationality of such deliberative democratic processes? Deliberative processes are essential to the rationality of collective decision-making processes for three reasons. First . . . deliberative processes are also processes that impart information. New information is imparted because 1) no single individual can anticipate and foresee all the variety of perspectives through which matters of ethics and politics would be perceived by different individuals; and 2) no single individual can possess all the information deemed relevant to a certain decision affecting all. Deliberation is a procedure for being informed.

Furthermore, much political theory under the influence of economic models of reasoning in particular proceeds from a methodological fiction: this is the methodological fiction of an individual with an ordered set of coherent preferences. This fiction does not have much relevance in the political world. On complex social and political issues, more often than not, individuals may have views and wishes but no ordered set of preferences, since the latter would imply that they would be enlightened not only about the preferences but about the consequences and relative merits of each of their preferred choices in advance. It is actually the deliberative process itself that is likely to produce such an outcome by leading the individual to further critical reflection on his already held views and opinions; it is incoherent to assume that individuals can start a process of public deliberation with a level of conceptual clarity about their choices and preferences that can actually result only from a successful process of deliberation. Likewise, the formation of coherent preferences cannot precede deliberation; it can only succeed it. Very often individuals' wishes as well as views and opinions conflict with one another. In the course of deliberation and the exchange of views with others, individuals become more aware of such conflicts and feel compelled to undertake a coherent ordering.

More significantly, the very procedure of articulating a view in public imposes a certain reflexivity on individual preferences and opinions. When presenting their point of view and position to others, individuals must support them by articulating good reasons in a public context to their co-deliberators. This process of *articulating good reasons in public* forces the individual to think of what would count as a good reason for all others involved. One is thus forced to think from the standpoint of all involved for whose agreement one is "wooing." Nobody can convince others in public of her point of view without being able to state why what appears good, plausible, just, and expedient to her can also be considered so from the standpoint of all involved. Reasoning from the standpoint of all involved not only forces a certain coherence upon one's own views but also forces one to adopt a standpoint that Hannah Arendt, following Kant, had called the "enlarged mentality."

A deliberative model of democracy suggests a necessary but not sufficient condition of practical rationality, because, as with any procedure, it can be misinterpreted, misapplied, and abused. Procedures can neither dictate outcomes nor define the quality of the reasons advanced in argumentation nor control the quality of the reasoning and rules of logic and inference used by participants. Procedural models of rationality are underdetermined. Nonetheless, the discourse model makes some provisions against its own misuses and abuses in that the reflexivity condition built into the model allows abuses and misapplications at the first level to be challenged at a second, metalevel of discourse. Likewise, the equal chance of all affected to initiate such discourse of deliberation suggests that no outcome is prima facie fixed but can be revised and subjected to reexamination. Such would be the normative justification of majority rule as a decision procedure following from this model: in many instances the majority rule is a fair and rational decision procedure, not because legitimacy resides in numbers but because if a majority of people are convinced at one point on the basis of reasons formulated as closely as possible as a result of a process of discursive deliberation that conclusion A is the right thing to do, then this conclusion can remain valid until challenged by good reasons by some other group. It is not the sheer numbers that support the rationality of the conclusion, but the presumption that if a large number of people see certain matters a certain way as a result of following certain kinds of rational procedures of deliberation and decision-making, then such a conclusion has a presumptive claim to being rational until shown to be otherwise. The simple practice of having a ruling and an opposition party in democracies in fact incorporates this principle: we accept the will of the majority at the end of an electoral process that has been fairly and correctly carried out, but even when we accept the legitimacy of the process we may have grave doubts about the rationality of the outcome. The practice of there being a parliamentary opposition says that the grounds on which the majority party claims to govern can be examined, challenged, tested, criticized, and rearticulated. Parliamentary procedures of opposition, debate, questioning, and even impeachment proceedings, and investigatory commissions incorporate this rule of deliberative rationality that majoritarian decisions are temporarily agreed-upon conclusions, the claim to rationality and validity of which can be publicly reexamined.

This deliberative model of democracy is proceduralist in that it emphasizes first and foremost certain institutional procedures and practices for attaining decisions on matters that would be binding on all. Three additional points are worthy of note with respect to such a conception of democracy: first, I proceed from the assumption of value pluralism. Disagreement about the highest goods of human existence and the proper conduct of a morally righteous life are a fundamental feature of our modern value-universe since the end of natural law cosmologies in the sixteenth and seventeenth centuries, and the eventual separation of church and state. The challenge to democratic rationality is to arrive at acceptable formulations of the common good despite this inevitable value-pluralism. We cannot resolve conflicts among value systems and visions of the good by reestablishing a strong unified moral and religious code without forsaking fundamental liberties. Agreements in societies living with value-pluralism are to be sought for not at the level of substantive beliefs but at that of procedures, processes, and practices for attaining and revising beliefs. Proceduralism is a rational answer to persisting value conflicts at the substantive level.

Second, the deliberative model of democracy proceeds not only from a conflict of values but also from a conflict of interests in social life. Social life necessitates both conflict of interests and cooperation. Democratic procedures have to convince, even under conditions when one's interests as an individual or as a group are negatively affected, that the conditions of mutual cooperation are still legitimate. Procedures can be regarded as methods for articulating, sifting through, and weighing conflicting interests. The more conflicts of interests there are the more it is important to have procedural solutions of conflict adjudication through which parties whose interests are negatively affected can find recourse to other methods of the articulation and representation of their grievances. Proceduralist models of democracy allow the articulation of conflicts of interests under conditions of social cooperation mutually acceptable to all.

Finally, any proceduralist and deliberative model of democracy is prima facie open to the argument that no modern society can organize its affairs along the fiction of a mass assembly carrying out its deliberations in public and collectively. Here more than an issue of size is at stake. The argument that there may be an invisible limit to the size of a deliberative body that, when crossed, affects the nature of the reasoning process is undoubtedly true. Nonetheless the reason why a deliberative and proceduralist model of democracy does not need to operate with the fiction of a general deliberative assembly is that the procedural specifications of this model privilege a *plurality of modes of association* in which all affected can have the right to articulate their point of view. These can range from political parties, to citizens' initiatives, to social movements, to voluntary associations, to consciousness-raising groups, and the like. It is *through the interlocking net of these multiple forms of associations, networks, and organizations that an anonymous "public conversation" results. It is central to the model of deliberative democracy that it privileges such a public sphere of mutually interlocking and overlapping networks and associations of deliberation, contestation, and argumentation.* The fiction of a general deliberative assembly in which the united people expressed their will belongs to the early history of democratic theory; today our guiding model has to be that of a medium of loosely associated, multiple foci of opinion formation and dissemination which affect one another in free and spontaneous processes of communication.

Such a strong model of deliberative democracy is subject to three different kinds of criticism: first, liberal theorists will express concern that such a strong model would lead to the corrosion of individual liberties and may in fact destabilize the rule of law. . . . Second, feminist theorists are skeptical about this model, because they see it as privileging a certain mode of discourse at the cost of silencing others: this is the rationalist, male, univocal, hegemonic discourse of a transparent polity that disregards the emotions, polyvocity, multiplicity, and differences in the articulation of the voice of the public; third, institutional-ists and realists consider this discourse model to be hopelessly naive, maybe even dangerous, in its seemingly plebiscitary and anti-institutional implications. I would briefly like to consider these objections. . . .

BASIC RIGHTS AND DELIBERATIVE DEMOCRACY

Deliberative democracy models often seem subject to the argument that they do not protect individuals' basic rights and liberties sufficiently. This objection is rooted in two assumptions: first, insofar as deliberative models appear to make a high degree of consensus or unanimity on public issues a value, it is fair to suspect that such unanimity could only be attained at the cost of silencing dissent and curtailing minority viewpoints. Second, what protection does a deliberative model allow against the tyranny of democratic majorities from imposing its choices and norms upon the minority? . . .

Precisely because I share with the liberal tradition the assumption that moral respect for the autonomous personality is a fundamental norm of morality and democracy, the deliberative model of democracy presupposes a discourse theory of ethics to supply it with the most general moral principles upon which rights claims would be based. Insofar as a discourse theory of ethics considers participants to be equal and free beings, equally entitled to take part in those discourse which determine the norms that are to affect their lives, it proceeds from a view of persons as beings entitled to certain "moral rights." I have named this moral right the entitlement to universal moral respect. . . . I further maintain that within a discourse theory each individual has the same symmetrical rights to various speech acts, to initiate new topics, to ask for reflection about the presuppositions of the conversations, and so on. I call this the principle of egalitarian reciprocity. In my view the norms of universal moral respect and egalitarian reciprocity are moral rights in that they are entitlements that accrue to individuals insofar as we view them as moral persons.

The step that would lead from a recognition of these two moral rights to the formulation of a principle of basic rights and liberties is certainly not very wide. Basically it would involve a hypothetical answer to the question. If it is plausible for individuals to view one another as beings entitled to universal moral respect and egalitarian reciprocity, which most general principles of basic rights and liberties would such individuals also be likely to accept as determining the conditions of their collective existence? . . .

What is distinctive about the discourse model is that although it presupposes that participants must recognize one another's entitlement to moral respect and reciprocity in some sense, the determination of the precise content and extent of these principles would be a consequence of discourses themselves.[1] Insofar as the precise meaning and entailment of the norms of universal moral respect and egalitarian reciprocity would be subject to discursive validation, we can speak here of a procedure of "recursive validation."[2] The methodological procedure of recursive validation rules out the two consequences most feared by liberals vis-à-vis the model of deliberative democracy—namely, too strong a formulation of the conditions of consent, and the tyranny of the majority. The norms of universal moral respect and egalitarian reciprocity allow minorities and dissenters both the right to withhold their assent and the right to challenge the rules as well as the agenda of public debate. For what distinguishes discourses from compromises and other agreements reached under conditions of coercion is that only the *freely given assent of all concerned* can count as a condition of having reached agreement in the discourse situation.

DELIBERATIVE DEMOCRACY AND CONSTITUTIONALISM

Upon reflection, we can see that institutionally as well, complex constitutional democracies, and particularly those in which a *public sphere* of opinion formation and deliberation has been developed, engage in such recursive validation continually. Basic human civil and political rights, . . . as embodied in the constitution of most democratic governments, are never really "off the agenda" of public discussion and debate. They are simply constitutive and regulative institutional norms of debate in democratic societies that cannot be transformed and abrogated by simple majority decisions. The language of keeping these rights off the agenda mischaracterizes the nature of democratic debate in our kinds of societies: although we cannot change these rights without extremely elaborate political and juridical procedures, we are always disputing their meaning, their extent, and their jurisdiction. Democratic debate is like a ball game where there is no umpire to interpret the rules of the game and their application definitively. Rather, in the game of democracy the rules of the game no less than their interpretation and even the position of the umpire are essentially contestable. Contestation means neither the complete abrogation of these rules nor silence about them. When basic rights and liberties are violated the game of democracy is suspended and becomes either martial rule, civil war, or dictatorship; when democratic politics is in full session, the debate about the meaning of these rights, what they do or do not entitle us to, their scope and enforcement, is what politics is all about. One cannot challenge the specific interpretation of basic rights and liberties in a democracy without taking these absolutely seriously.

The deliberative theory of democracy transcends the traditional opposition of majoritarian politics vs. liberal guarantees of basic rights and liberties to the extent that the normative conditions of discourses, like basic rights and liberties, are to be viewed as rules of the game that can be contested within the game but only insofar as one first accepts to abide by them and play the game at all. . . . Crucial to the deliberative model of democracy is the idea of a "public sphere" of opinion-formation, debate, deliberation, and contestation among citizens, groups, movements, and organizations in a polity. When this concept of a public sphere is introduced as the concrete embodiment of discursive democracy in practice, it also becomes possible to think of the issue of conversational constraints in a more nuanced way. While the deliberative model of democracy shares with liberalism a concern for the protection of the rights to autonomy of equal citizens, the conceptual method of discursive validation and the institutional reality of a differentiated public sphere of deliberation and contestation provide plausible beginning points for a mediation of the stark opposition between liberalism and deliberative democracy. . . .

FEMINIST SUSPICIONS
TOWARD DELIBERATIVE DEMOCRACY

While liberals criticize the model of deliberative democracy for possibly overextending itself and corroding the sphere of individual privacy, feminist theorists criticize this model for not extending itself broadly enough to be truly inclusive. In an illuminating article entitled "Impartiality and the Civic Public," Iris Young, for example, has argued:

> The distinction between public and private as it appears in modern political theory expresses a will for homogeneity that necessitates the exclusion of many persons and groups, particularly women and radicalized groups culturally identified with the body, wildness and rationality. In conformity with the modern idea of normative reason, the idea of the public in modern political theory and practice designates a sphere of human existence in which citizens express their rationality and universality, abstracted from their particular situations and need, and opposed to feeling. . . . Examination of the exclusionary and homogeneous ideal in modern political theory, however, shows that we cannot envision such renewal of public life as a recovery of Enlightenment ideals. Instead, we need to transform the distinction between public and private that does not correlate with an opposition between reason and affectivity and desire, or universal and particular.[3]

Iris Young's cogent and penetrating feminist critique of the ideal of the impartial public applies to the model of deliberative democracy suggested in the preceding only in certain respects. Certainly, the model of a general deliberative assembly that governed our conceptions of the public sphere well into the twentieth century was historically, socially, and culturally a space for male bodies. I mean this not only in the sense that only men were active citizens, entitled to hold office and appear in public, but also in the sense that the institutional iconography of early democratic theory privileged the male mode of self-representation.

Yet here we must distinguish between the *institutional* and the *conceptual* critiques. There is a certain ambivalence in the feminist critique of such models of the public sphere and deliberative democracy. On the one hand, the critique appears to take democratic institutions at their principled best and to criticize their biased and restrictive implementations in practice; on the other hand, the feminist critique appears to aim at a rejection of the ideals of free public reason and impartiality altogether. . . . A normative theory of deliberative democracy requires a strong concept of the public sphere as its institutional correlate. The public sphere replaces the model of the general deliberative assembly found in early democratic theory. In this context, it is important for feminist theorists to specify the level of their conceptual objection, and to differentiate among institutional and normative presuppositions.

Iris Young does not reject the ideal of a public sphere, only its Enlightenment variety. She proposes to replace the ideal of the "civil public" with that of a heterogeneous public. In her recent work she has advocated a number of institutional measures that would guarantee and solidify group representation in such a public sphere.[4] Yet wanting to retain the public sphere and according it a place in democratic theory is not compatible with the more radical critique of the ideal of impartial reason that Young also develops in some of her essays.

. . . Iris Young distinguishes between "deliberative" and "communicative" democracy on the grounds that most theories of deliberative democracy offer too narrow a conception of the democratic process because they continue to privilege an ideal of "a common good in which [the discussion participants] are all supposed to leave behind their particular experience and interests."

By contrast, Young advocates a theory of communicative democracy according to which individuals would attend to one another's differences in class, gender, race, religion, and so on. Each social position has a partial perspective on the public that it does not abandon; but through the communicative process participants transcend and transform their initial situated knowledges. Instead of critical argumentation, such processes of communicative confrontation privilege modalities of communication like "greeting, rhetoric, and storytelling."

I think this distinction between deliberative and communicative democracy is more apparent than real. To sustain her critique of the ideals of impartiality and objectivity, which she associates with the deliberative model, Young must be able to distinguish the kind of transformation and transcendence of partial perspectives that occurs in communicative democracy from the mutual agreement to be reached in processes of deliberative democracy. Yet how can we distinguish between the emergence of common opinion among members of one group, if we do not apply to such processes of communication or deliberation some standards of fairness and impartiality in order to judge the manner in which opinions were allowed to be brought forth, groups were given chances to express their points of view, and the like? The model of communicative democracy, far from dispensing with the need for standards of impartiality and fairness, requires them to make sense of its own formulations. Without some such standards, Young could not differentiate the genuine transformation of partial and situated perspectives from mere agreements of convenience or apparent unanimity reached under conditions of duress.

With respect to modes of communication like "greeting, rhetoric, and storytelling," I would say that each of these modes may have their place within the *informally structured process of everyday communication among individuals who share a cultural and historical life world*. However, it is neither necessary for the democratic theorist to try to formalize and institutionalize these aspects of communicative everyday competence, nor is it plausible—and this is the more important objection—to build an opposition between them and critical argumentation. Greeting, storytelling, and rhetoric, although they may be aspects of informal communication in our everyday life, cannot become the public language of institutions and legislatures in a democracy for the following reason: to attain legitimacy, democratic institutions require the articulation of the bases of their actions and policies in discursive language that appeals to commonly shared and accepted public reasons. In constitutional democracies such public reasons take the form of general statements consonant with the rule of law. The rule of law has a certain rhetorical structure of its own: it is general, applies to all members of a specified reference group on the basis of legitimate reasons. Young's attempt to transform the language of the rule of law into a more partial, affective, and situated mode of communication would have the consequence of inducing arbitrariness, for who can tell how far the power of a greeting can reach? It would further create capriciousness—what about those who simply cannot understand my story? It would limit rather than enhance social justice because rhetoric moves people and achieves results without having to render an account of the bases upon which it induces people to engage in certain courses of action rather than others. In short, some moral ideal of impartiality is a regulative principle that should govern not only our deliberations in public but also the articulation of reasons by public institutions. What is considered impartial has to be "in the best interests of all equally." Without such a normative principle, neither the ideal of the rule of law can be sustained nor deliberative reasoning toward a common good occur. Some Enlightenment ideals are part of any conception of democratic legitimacy and the public sphere. The point therefore is not a rejection of the Enlightenment in toto but a critical renegotiation of its legacy. . . .

INSTITUTIONALIST DISTRUST
OF DELIBERATIVE DEMOCRACY

The criticism most frequently leveled against normative models of democracy is that of utopian irrelevance. "This may sound good in theory, but it is irrelevant to practice!" "Complex, modern societies," the objection continues, "with their highly differentiated cultural, economic, social and artistic spheres of life, can never be and will never be organized along the lines suggested by a model of deliberative ddemocracy." . . .

The deliberative model of democracy does not represent a counterfactual thought experiment. As I suggested at the beginning, I understand such a theory to be elucidating the already implicit principles and logic of existing democratic practices. Among the practices that such a theory of democracy can elucidate are the significance of deliberative bodies in democracies, the rationale of parliamentary opposition, the need for a free and independent media and sphere of public opinion, and the rationale for employing majority rule as a decision procedure. For this reason, the deliberative theory of democracy is not a theory in search of practice; rather it is a theory that claims to elucidate some aspects of the logic of existing democratic practices better than others. Theorists of social complexity should really reframe the question: the question is not whether discursive democracy can become the practice of complex societies but whether complex societies are still capable of democratic rule. . . .

My goal in this essay has been to outline a deliberative model of democracy that incorporates features of practical rationality. Central to practical rationality is the possibility of free public deliberation about matters of mutual concern to all. The discourse model of ethics and politics suggests a procedure for such free public deliberation among all concerned. Such processes of public deliberation have a claim to rationality because they increase and make available necessary information, because they allow the expression of arguments in the light of which opinions and beliefs need to be revised, and because they lead to the formation of conclusions that can be challenged publicly for good reasons. Furthermore, such procedures allow self-referential critique of their own uses and abuses. The chief institutional correlate of such a model of deliberative democracy is a multiple, anonymous, heterogeneous network of many publics and public conversations. In other domains of social life as well, the model of deliberative democracy based on the centrality of public deliberation can inspire the proliferation of many institutional designs.

Chapter 31

The Epistemic Dimension
of Democratic Authority

David Estlund

David Estlund is the Lombardo Family Professor of Philosophy at Brown University. He argues that the authority of democracy stems from its being a procedure that is both fair and likely to yield better over worse decisions. Consider, by way of analogy, the decisions made by juries in criminal trials. If we thought the force of such verdicts were due entirely from their being the product of a fair procedure, we could use a coin toss to determine the guilt of the accused. If we thought the force of such verdicts were due entirely from their getting it right, we should each use our own judgment and carry out private punishment. Neither the fairness nor correctness alone accounts for the force of a jury's decision. Rather, a jury's verdict has authority when it is the product of a procedure that is both fair and tends to find those who committed crimes guilty and those who didn't commit crimes not guilty. The same thought holds, Estlund maintains, for democratic decisions.

David Estlund, "The Epistemic Dimension of Democratic Authority," *The Modern Schoolman* 74, no. 4 (1997): 259–76.

Assume that for many choices faced by a political community, some alternatives are better than others by standards that are in some way objective. (For example, suppose that progressive income tax rates are more just than a flat rate, even after considering effects on efficiency.) If so, it must count in favor of a social decision procedure that it tends to produce the better decision. On the other hand, there is wide disagreement about what justice requires, and no citizen is required to defer to the expertise or authority of any other. Thus, normative democratic theory has largely proceeded on the assumption that the most that can be said for a legitimate democratic decision is that it was produced by a procedure that treats voters equally in certain ways. The merits of democratic decisions are held to be in their past.

One sort of theory treats every voter's views as equally valid from a political point of view and promises only the procedural value of equal power over the outcome. A distinct approach urges that citizens' existing views should be subjected to the rational criticism of other citizens prior to voting. In both cases, the legitimacy of the decision is typically held to lie in facts about the procedure and not the quality of the outcome by procedure-independent or epistemic standards.

This contrast between procedural and epistemic virtues ought to be questioned. Certainly, there are strong arguments that some form of proceduralism must be preferable to any theory in which correctness is necessary and sufficient for a decision's legitimacy. Democratic accounts of legitimacy seek to explain the legitimacy of the general run of laws (though not necessarily all of them) under favorable conditions. However, even under good conditions many laws are bound to be incorrect, inferior, or unjust by the appropriate objective standard. If the choice is between proceduralism and such correctness theories of legitimacy, proceduralism is vastly more plausible. Correctness theories, however, are not the only form available for approaches to democratic legitimacy that emphasize the epistemic value of the democratic process—its tendency to produce outcomes that are correct by independent standards. Epistemic criteria are compatible, at least in principle, with proceduralism. Thus, rather than supposing that the legitimacy of an outcome depends on its correctness, I shall suggest that it derives, partly, from the epistemic value, even though it is imperfect, of the procedure that produced it. Democratic legitimacy requires that the procedure is procedurally fair and can be held, in terms acceptable to all reasonable citizens, to be epistemically the best among those that are better than random.

After preliminaries, then, two classes of nonepistemic proceduralist accounts will be scrutinized. I will criticize several variants and relatives of Fair Proceduralism and Deliberative Proceduralism in support of a subsequent sketch of Epistemic Proceduralism.

Why suppose that there is any kind of legitimacy for a political decision other than whether it meets some independent standard such as justice? Why not say that it is legitimate if correct, and otherwise not? Call this denial of proceduralism a *correctness theory* of legitimacy.

One thing to notice about a correctness theory of legitimacy is that in a diverse community there is bound to be little agreement on whether a decision is legitimate, since there will be little agreement about whether it meets the independent standard of, say, justice. If the decision is made by majority rule, and voters address the question whether the proposal would be independently correct, then at least a majority will accept its correctness. However, nearly half of the voters might deny its correctness, and on a correctness theory they would in turn deny the legitimacy of the decision—deny that it warrants state action or places them under any obligation to comply.

This potential instability makes it tempting to seek a proceduralist standard of legitimacy that might become widely accepted, so that the legitimacy of a decision could be accepted even by many of those who believe it is incorrect. It is important, though, to ask whether there is anything more to this impulse than the temptation to capitulate to the threat of the brute force that could be unleashed by large numbers of dissident citizens. Without something more, the correctness theory of legitimacy would be undaunted; those dissidents, for all we have said, might be simply in the wrong—renouncing their genuine political obligations.

So leave aside the brute fact of controversy and the potential for instability. Rather, the morally deeper concern is that much of the controversy is among conscientious citizens, rather than merely unreasonable troublemakers. We are far less timid about insisting on, and even enforcing, decisions whose legitimacy is rejected only on unreasonable grounds. Consider someone who rejects the legitimacy of our laws because he insists on being king; or someone who rejects the legitimacy of any laws that are not directly endorsed by the pope. I believe we would not, or at least should not, see any significant moral objection to the correctness theory in the fact that such people might be numerous. We ought to be led by such reflections as these to a general criterion of legitimacy that holds that the legitimacy of laws is not adequately established unless it can be defended on grounds it would be unreasonable to object to. Legitimacy requires the possibility of reasons that are not objectionable to any reasonable citizens. This criterion is liberal in its respect for conscientious disagreement, and I will call it the *liberal criterion of legitimacy.* . . . The aim here is not to defend this particular criterion of legitimacy, but to use it as a well worked out and demanding liberal constraint on political justification. I accept that some such demanding version of liberalism is appropriate, and note that this is the greatest obstacle to an epistemic theory of democratic legitimacy. I hope to show that, at least in this form, it is not insuperable.

BEYOND FAIRNESS AND DELIBERATION

A critical taxonomy will allow the argument for Epistemic Proceduralism to develop in an orderly way.

Fair Proceduralism

Fair Proceduralism is the view that what makes democratic decisions legitimate is that they were produced by the fair procedure of majority rule. A problem for this approach is that, while democratic procedures may indeed be fair, the epitome of fairness among people who have different preferences over two alternatives is to flip a coin. Nothing could be fairer. Insofar as we think this is an inappropriate way to decide some question, we are going beyond fairness. Of course, if there is some good to be distributed, we would not think a fair distribution to be one that gives it all to the winner of a coin toss or a drawing of straws. This reflects our attention to procedure-independent moral standards applying to this choice. Since we think some of the alternative distributions are significantly more appropriate than others, we are not satisfied that mere procedural fairness is an appropriate way to make the decision. A fair procedure would be a fair way to make the decision. But if making the decision in a fair way (as in a coin flip) is insufficiently likely to produce the fair or just or morally required outcome, it may not be good enough.

I assume that making political decisions by randomly selecting from the alternatives, as in a coin flip, would not provide any strong moral reason to obey or any strong warrant for coercive enforcement. I conclude from this that the procedural fairness of democratic procedures does not lend them much moral legitimacy.

A second problem is that in this pure, spare form, Fair Proceduralism allows nothing to favor one citizen's claims or interests over another's—not even good reasons. It entails that no one should be favored by any reasons there might be for treating his or her claims as especially important. . . . Fair Proceduralism is insensitive to reasons. This does not, of course, mean that it simply favors brute power over reason or morality. The partisan of brute power has no interest in equalizing individuals' power over outcomes, nor in giving any reasons for his recommended arrangements. Fair Proceduralism aims to place severe constraints on the use of power; indeed, the problem is that the constraints are too strong, since effective rational argument in favor of certain outcomes is, in this context, a form of power which Fair Proceduralism is led implausibly to equalize.

It is not clear that any theorists, even those who claim to appeal only to procedural fairness, have advanced this implausible pure form of Fair Proceduralism.[1] It is widely acknowledged that the legitimating force of democratic procedures depends on conceiving them as, at least partly, procedures of rational interpersonal deliberation. "Deliberative democracy," then, is not generally in dispute. What divides democratic theorists is, rather, whether democratic deliberation improves the outcomes by independent standards (its epistemic value), or at least whether this is any part of the account of democratic authority. Two nonepistemic versions say "no," and two epistemic versions say "yes." Begin with the naysayers.

Fair Deliberative Proceduralism

Consider Fair Deliberative Proceduralism: it makes no claims about the epistemic value of democratic deliberation, but it insists that citizens ought to have an equal or at least fair chance to enter their arguments and reasons into the discussion prior to voting. The impartiality is among individuals' convictions or arguments rather than among their preferences or interests. Reasons, as the voters see them, are explicitly entered into the process, but no particular independent standard need be appealed to in this theory. The result is held to be legitimate without regard to any tendency to be correct by independent standards; its legitimacy lies in the procedure's impartiality among individuals' convictions and arguments.[2]

This account interprets the inputs somewhat differently, but also conceives of the entire process more dynamically. Inputs are not merely to be tallied; they are first to be considered and accommodated by other participants, and, likewise, revised in view of the arguments of others. To allow this there must be indefinitely many rounds of entering inputs into the deliberative process, though of course it eventually ends in a vote.

Why does deliberation help? Perhaps the idea is that voters' convictions will be more genuinely their own after open rational deliberation. This would make it simply a more refined version of Fair Proceduralism. Fair Deliberative Proceduralism, however, cannot really explain why deliberation is important. If the outcome is to be selected from individuals' views, it can perhaps be seen as enhancing fairness if their views are well considered and stable under collective deliberation. If the goal is fairness, though, why select the outcome from individuals' views? It is true that if the outcome is not selected in this way it might be something no one would have voted for. But that does not count against the fairness of doing so. It is just as fair to choose randomly from the available alternatives.

If we add to fairness the aim of satisfying at least some citizens, we will want the outcome to be one that some would have voted for. There is still no reason, however, to let an alternative's chance of being chosen vary with the amount of support it has among the citizens. It would be perfectly fair to take the outcome randomly from the set of alternatives that at least some voters support after deliberation. Call this method a *Post-Deliberative Coin Flip*. This is importantly different from randomly choosing a citizen to decide (which I'll call *Queen for a Day*; see below on this method). That would favor the more popular alternatives. The idea here is rather to let all alternatives with any support have an equal chance of being chosen. In one respect this can look even more fair: no one's view is disadvantaged by the fact that few others support it.

The objection is not that these views are undemocratic in allowing coin flips; I leave that question aside. Rather, their allowing coin flips highlights their indifference to the epistemic value of the procedure. Post-deliberative voting probably has considerable epistemic value, but Fair Deliberative Proceduralism must be indifferent between it and a coin flip. The legitimacy of the coin flip is all the legitimacy Fair Deliberative Proceduralism can find in democratic social choice. But it is too epistemically blunt to have much legitimacy, at least if there are better alternatives.

Rational Deliberative Proceduralism

Some authors seem to advocate a view that is like Fair Deliberative Proceduralism except that the procedure's value is primarily in recognizing good reasons rather than in providing fair access (though fair or equal access would be a natural corollary).[3] We might thus distinguish Fair Deliberative Proceduralism (FD) from Rational Deliberative Proceduralism (RD). This latter view would not claim that the procedure produces outcomes that (tend to) approximate some standard (of, say, justice or the common good) that is independent of actual procedures, and does so by recognizing better reasons and giving them greater influence over the outcome (e.g., by way of voters being rationally persuaded). That would be an epistemic view. Instead, RD insists that the only thing to be said for the outcomes is that they were produced by a reason-recognizing procedure; no further claim has to be made about whether the outcomes tend to meet any independent standard of correctness. The outcomes are rational only in a procedural sense, not in any more substantive sense. This claim would be analogous to Fair Proceduralism's claim that outcomes are fair in a procedural but not a substantive sense.

This procedural sense of rational outcomes is not available to the advocate of this reason-recognizing procedure, however. If the procedure is held to recognize the better reasons, those reasons are being counted as better by procedure-independent standards. Then to say that the outcome reflects the better reasons can only mean that the outcome meets or tends to meet that same procedure-independent standard. By contrast, in the case of Fair Proceduralism, the procedure is never held to recognize the more fair individual inputs. If that were the basis of its claim to fairness, then it too would be an epistemic view. The space held out for a nonepistemic Rational Deliberative Proceduralism has disappeared. Deliberative democracy, as a theory of legitimacy, then, is either an inadequate refinement of Fair Proceduralism, or it is led to base its recommendation of democratic procedures partly on their performance by procedure-independent standards.

This is a good place to recall what is meant here by "procedure-independent standards." This does not mean that the standards are independent of any possible or conceivable procedure, but only that they are independent (logically) of the actual procedure that gave rise to the outcome in question. Fair Proceduralism's standard of fairness is defined in terms of the actual procedures producing the decision to be called fair, and so Fair Proceduralism admits no procedure-independent standard in this sense.

Consider, in light of this point, a view that says that democratic outcomes are legitimate where they (tend to) match what would have been decided in a certain hypothetical procedure. . . . Joshua Cohen writes, "outcomes are democratically legitimate if and only if they would be the object of an agreement arrived at through a free and reasoned consideration of alternatives by equals."[4] This may seem not to require recognizably democratic institutions at all, but he also says, "The ideal deliberative procedure provides a model for institutions, a model that they should mirror, so far as possible."[5] The combination of these two claims implies that actual procedures that mirror the ideal procedure will tend to produce the same results as the ideal, though not necessarily always. This would be an epistemic view as defined here, since the ideal procedure is logically independent of the actual procedures. For this reason, I interpret Cohen as developing one kind of epistemic theory. This implication is in some conflict, however, with his claim that "what is good is fixed by deliberation, not prior to it."[6] That may be misleading, since on his view, it is fixed by ideal, not actual, deliberation, and actual deliberation is held to this logically prior and independent standard. Within the class of epistemic theories there will be a number of important distinctions, such as dial between standards defined in terms of hypothetical procedures and those defined in other ways. Those are not the distinctions at issue here, for all such views invoke procedure independent standards in one important respect: the standards are logically independent of the actual procedures.[7]

Without any space for the view that democratic outcomes are procedurally, even if not substantively, rational, deliberative conceptions of democracy are forced to ground democratic legitimacy either in the infertile soil of an impartial proceduralism, or in a rich but combustible appeal to the epistemic value of democratic procedures.

TWO EPISTEMIC THEORIES: THREE CHALLENGES

Turning then to epistemic theories of democratic legitimacy, there is a fork in the road. The challenges for epistemic theories are helpful in choosing between them: the problem of *deference . . .* and the problem of *invidious comparisons*. Epistemic Proceduralism, I will argue, can meet these challenges better than non-proceduralist epistemic approaches, which I am calling correctness theories of democratic legitimacy. The latter sort of theory holds that political decisions are legitimate only if they are correct by appropriate procedure-independent standards, and adds the claim that proper democratic procedures are sufficiently accurate to render the general run of laws and policies legitimate under favorable conditions. . . . Having pushed things in an epistemic direction, I now want to prevent things from getting out of hand. Existing epistemic conceptions of democracy are, in a certain sense, too epistemic.

Deference

It is important to appreciate the reasons many have had for resisting epistemic accounts of political authority. Some seem to have thought that if there existed epistemic standards then it would follow that some know better, and that the knowers should rule. . . . In order to reject what we might call epistocracy," or rule of the knowers, some think it is necessary to deny that there are any procedure-independent epistemic standards for democratic decisions. An adequate answer to this worry, I believe, is to argue that sovereignty is not distributed according to moral expertise unless that expertise would be beyond the reasonable objections of individual citizens. But reasonable citizens should (or, at the very least, may) refuse to surrender their moral judgment on important matters to anyone. Then, unless all reasonable citizens actually agreed with the decisions of some agreed moral/political guru, no one could legitimately rule on the basis of wisdom. So there might be political truth, and even knowers of various degrees, without any moral basis for epistocracy.

The moral challenge for any epistemic conception of political authority, then, is to let truth be the guide without illegitimately privileging the opinions of any putative experts. Experts should not be privileged because citizens cannot be expected or assumed (much less encouraged or forced) to surrender their moral judgment, at least on important matters—to say, "that still doesn't seem right to me, but I shall judge it to be right because I expect this person or that thing to indicate reliably what is right." . . .

Suppose there were no good reason to challenge the overwhelming likelihood that the procedure's outcome is correct. . . . Since correctness theories treat outcomes as legitimate because they are correct, the reason, given to the minority voter, for obedience is the correctness of the outcome, something the minority voter is on record as denying. So correctness theories go on to say to the minority voter that it is overwhelmingly probable that the outcome is correct. . . . Correctness theories need this claim for two reasons: first, to supply legitimacy in the vast majority of cases; second, to give the minority voter in any given case reason to change her opinion to match that of the outcome of a majority vote and so to accept its legitimacy. Correctness theories, then, apparently rely on the following premise:

> **Probability Supports Moral Judgment:** One who accepts that all things considered the correctness of a given moral judgment is extremely probable has good reason to accept the moral judgment.

Epistemic Proceduralism does not rely on any such assumption since it does not rest the minority voter's acceptance of an outcome's legitimacy on the outcome's correctness. This is an advantage for Epistemic Proceduralism, since the claim that probability supports moral judgment is deeply problematic. It may be false; at least it is not something all reasonable citizens can be expected to accept, as the following thought experiment suggests.

Suppose there is a deck of 1,000 cards, and each has written on it a moral statement about which you have no strong opinion either way. Suppose further that you accept on some evidence that exactly 999 of these contain true statements, and 1 is false. Now you cut the deck and the card says, "Physician-assisted suicide is sometimes morally permissible" (or some other moral statement about which you are otherwise uncertain). It is not clear that you have been given very good reason to accept that physician-assisted suicide is sometimes permissible. Of course, you might doubt the reliability of the deck of cards (or the "expert"), but suppose you do not. There is nothing inconsistent in holding that "While there is almost no chance that this is incorrect, still, that doesn't make physician-assisted suicide seem permissible to me, and so I do not accept that it is. The expert is almost certainly correct, and yet I am not prepared to share in the expert's judgment." This attitude may make sense for moral judgments even though it apparently does not for factual judgments.

Correctness theories assume that probabilistic considerations support moral judgment in expecting the minority to come around to the majority judgment on the basis of the procedure's reliability. Epistemic Proceduralism has the advantage of avoiding this commitment. There is no expectation that the minority voter will conform her opinion to that of the majority, since the reason given to the minority voter for obedience does not depend on the correctness of the outcome in question.[8] . . .

Invidious Comparisons

Just as moral experts will be too controversial, even if they exist, to figure in any justification of authoritarian political arrangements, any particular set of criteria for determining whether the average voter is better than random . . . will be just as controversial. If the qualifications of an alleged moral expert will always be subject to reasonable disagreement, then so will any list of qualifications itself. So, even if (as I doubt) we might sometimes have . . . good reason to surrender our moral judgment to the majority outcome when we disagree with it, there will always be reasonable grounds for others to deny this by rejecting the criteria of moral competence that we have used. It would violate the liberal criterion of legitimacy, then, to employ any such claims in political justification. This is a third challenge faced by epistemic approaches to democracy; call it the problem of *Invidious Comparisons*.

I propose to answer this objection indirectly. I shall sketch an account of social and structural circumstances that might suffice for the weaker kind of epistemic value required by Epistemic Proceduralism. Of course, a social/ structural account might be employed in support of a correctness theory's strong epistemic claims as well, and if successful it could meet the challenge of avoiding invidious comparisons. I assume, however, that showing a procedure to have higher epistemic value requires more appeal to the epistemic capacities of the participating individuals. If so, a social/structural basis for the procedure's epistemic value has a better chance of supplying the moderate epistemic value required by Epistemic Proceduralism than the strong epistemic value required by correctness theories. There is no intention of showing that these considerations suffice for moderate epistemic value, nor of showing that they could not suffice for strong epistemic value. The point is only that the need, stemming from the problem of invidious comparisons, to stay with a social/structural account favors the more moderate needs of Epistemic Proceduralism. I propose the following conditions as examples drawn from familiar ideas:

1. Every adult in the society is permitted to participate.
2. Participants sincerely address questions of justice, not of interest group advantage, and it is common knowledge that this is so.
3. Participants accept and address a shared conception of justice, and this is common knowledge.
4. Participants evaluate arguments fairly, irrespective of the identity of the person, or the size of the group offering the argument.
5. Each participant's views are easily available to the others (at least via some other proponent of the views, and at least those views that would have any chance of gaining adherents).
6. Participants represent a personal, educational, and cultural variety of life experiences.

7. Participants' needs for health and safety are sufficiently well met that it is possible for them to devote some time and energy to public political deliberations, and in general all are literate.

No individual experts are involved in the way they are in the case of epistocracy, but the epistemic needs of Epistemic Proceduralism cannot be met without the voters having a certain decent level of competence. The thing to avoid is using any considerations that would also imply specific conclusions about which individuals are likely to be morally wiser than others. First, there are the situational assumptions, that all are allowed to participate, all are sincere, all address a shared conception of justice, and so on. Then we must add a claim about the usual power of interpersonal deliberative procedures under such conditions. This, too, leaves aside any claims about which kind of person is morally wisest. In this way, the account avoids what appears to be the main threat of reasonable disagreement.

QUEEN FOR A DAY

Having laid out the epistemic needs of Epistemic Proceduralism, the question arises whether certain non-voting procedures might also meet all the criteria. If so, is this a defect in Epistemic Proceduralism? The challenge I have in mind is . . . called Queen for a Day: Suppose a voter is picked at random to make each decision. So long as most voters are better than random this is bound to perform better than a random selection from alternatives, even after deliberation.

Justifying this procedure on the basis of its better performance already goes beyond procedural fairness. But, assuming it is still fair, it poses a possible challenge to the case I am presenting for Epistemic Proceduralism. Queen for a Day meets several criteria urged here for accounts of democratic legitimacy. First, it is procedurally fair. Second, it can be held to perform better than a random selection from the alternatives in a way that is acceptable to all reasonable citizens. But is it the best among the procedures that meet these conditions? The case for voting comes down, then, to whether it performs better than Queen for a Day (or any other fair procedure).

Good performance should take into account more than just how likely it is to get the correct answer, but also *how far* it is likely to deviate from the best outcome. The existence of a small number of evil voters is literally no threat to a majoritarian procedure's performance, but they would occasionally, or at least with some chance, be Queen for a Day. This counts against that method. On the other hand, a small number of esoteric moral experts is no benefit to a majoritarian procedure, but they will have some chance of being Queen for a Day. These two considerations appear to balance out. . . .

Should we be disturbed that Epistemic Proceduralism does not have a more decisive way to reject Queen for a Day? Can it really come down to the difficult question of whether majority rule voting performs better? Is Epistemic Proceduralism otherwise indifferent between democratic and undemocratic modes of social choice? This objection would need to defend its assumption that Queen for a Day is undemocratic. If it were stipulated that a social choice procedure is not democratic unless it involves voting, then of course Queen for a Day is not democratic. But then the question becomes why this should matter morally? Unless it fails to treat voters equally in some morally important way, or leaves them all entirely out of social choice, we should regard it as democratic whether or not it involves voting. . . .

Would Queen for a Day deprive citizens of power they would have if there were voting? What power does a voter have? It is not the power to choose outcomes, so that is not lost under Queen for a Day. Each voter faces a choice only between ways of voting. The outcome is largely out of the voter's control, since it depends on how others choose to vote. Does a voter influence the decision in a way the uncrowned citizens do not in Queen for a Day? A voter, by voting, has no influence on the decision unless she is decisive, which almost no one ever is. Each voter has an equal initial chance of being decisive, but a vote's influence on the social choice stops there. Queen for a Day offers citizens an equal chance of being decisive too. Moreover, it can add the guarantee that there will always be a decisive citizen; in voting usually no voter is decisive.

In voting, there is a margin of victory, and every vote influences that. That is not, strictly, part of the outcome of the vote, in that it does not affect the social choice. Still, margin of victory can be very important. Again, though, there is no fundamental difference between voting and Queen for a Day. In both cases, the social choice can be made without paying any attention to any further facts about the number of supporters for each alternative. If such further information is important, it can be gotten under either system. In Queen for a Day, citizens could become eligible to be chosen as monarch for a certain issue by disclosing in advance the decision they would make, with the decision to take effect only if it is drawn by lot. Then all other advance declarations could be counted and publicized for whatever value this has.

One begins to see how much like voting Queen for a Day is, or could be. I know of no strong moral argument against it as compared with ordinary voting. Insofar as it is distasteful, bear in mind that none of the approaches to democratic legitimacy canvassed in this essay has any reason to reject it. It is fair, and it can take place after individual views are shaped by public deliberation. Only Epistemic Proceduralism has even a potential reason to reject it: First, it must at least be better than a random selection from alternatives (the other approaches don't require this); second, it might not be as epistemically valuable as another fair procedure, such as voting. But if it is epistemically better than voting, Epistemic Proceduralism would not be embarrassed to recommend it as the appropriate procedure for democratic social choice. In offering an account of democratic legitimacy in terms of other values it is impossible to avoid the implication that other methods that meet the other values at least as well would be at least as legitimate. The question is whether this conclusion is so implausible as to defeat the general account. Without knowing whether Queen for a Day does meet the proposed conditions as well as voting, it appears in any case that this would not be a morally unacceptable conclusion.

WHY OBEY BAD LAWS?

What moral reason is there to obey the decisions of the majority, when they meet the criteria of Epistemic Proceduralism, even if they are incorrect? I know of no moral principle, widely accepted, from which this obligation can be derived. It finds support, however, in the limitations of the idea of procedural fairness. Procedural fairness is a way of being impartial among individuals' competing interests, even while producing a command or direc-tive that suits the interests of some and not of others. Procedural fairness is designed for the case where the only standards of evaluation are first, each individual's interests, and second, the moral principle of impartial treatment. It is not well suited to cases where there is a procedure independent standard of moral correctness that applies to the decision that must be made.

Begin, then, with a case where it is granted that each individual is under an obligation to abide by the outcome of a fair procedure. The question "What should we do?" is treated as answered by aggregating what each of us wants to do in some impartial way. But now suppose it is known that the choice we make will be morally better or worse, and we do not all agree on which choices are morally better. First, it would be odd to use a procedure that operated solely on our individual interests, ignoring our moral judgments. I assume that there would be little obligation to obey the outcome of such a procedure despite its procedural fairness. Second, it still seems an insufficient ground of obligation merely to use a procedure that chose the alternative in accord with the moral judgments of a majority for reasons of fairness. There is no point in attending to moral judgments rather than interests if they are simply to be counted up on the model of procedural fairness. Why should this produce any stronger sort of obligation than the straight procedurally fair aggregation of interests? The reason for moving to the moral judgments could only be to apply intelligence to the moral issue at hand.

I propose, as the counterpart of the idea of procedural fairness in cases where there is an independent moral standard for the outcome, the idea of Epistemic Proceduralism: procedural impartiality among individuals' opinions, but with a tendency to be correct; the impartial application of intelligence to the cognitive moral question at hand.

Why does one have any obligation to obey such a procedure when one firmly believes it is mistaken? The question is produced by supposing that the epistemic dimension is meant to make the procedure's outcome also the individual's best guess as to the answer, as if the goal of the procedure were epistemic reasons.[9] But that is not the role of the epistemic dimension in Epistemic Proceduralism. That would be roughly like supposing the role of majority rule in Fair Proceduralism is to make the outcome conducive to one's own interests. Thus, one would ask, why obey a fair procedure when it doesn't accord with one's own best interests? I am taking as a starting assumption that the fairness of the procedure is a fully adequate reason to obey in simple nonepistemic cases. The problem is to stay as close to this model as possible, while making adjustments to fit the case where there is a procedure-independent moral standard for the outcome. In neither case will the reason to obey be based on any substantive feature of the outcome—both are pure proceduralist accounts of the reason or obligation to obey.

Mere procedural fairness is a very weak reason to obey when I believe the outcome is morally mistaken. It may seem, then, that my own moral judgment about the outcome is supreme in my own deliberations. That is not, however, the only reason for thinking procedural fairness is insufficient in such cases. A different reason is that procedural fairness is not equipped to address cognitive issues—it is not a cognitive process. This can be remedied without making my own moral judgment supreme, if fair proceduralism can be adapted to cognitive purposes. This is what is accomplished by a process that is impartial among individual opinions, yet has some tendency to be correct. It is suited to the cognitive task and is impartial among participants. Thus, there is a moral reason to abide by its decisions quite apart from their substantive merits, just as there is reason to abide by a procedure that fairly adjudicates among competing interests quite apart from whether it serves one's interests. Epistemic Proceduralism is proposed as a conservative adaptation of the idea of procedural fairness to cases of morally evaluable outcomes. It is conservative in requiring no more epistemic value than necessary (just-better-than-randomness so long as it is the best available)—while still fitting the cognitive nature of the cases.[10]

The case for a moral reason to obey Epistemic Proceduralist outcomes is, as I have said, not derived from any more basic moral principles. Still, it can be made compelling in other ways, and I have just attempted one. A second supporting stratagem is to suggest a metaphor that triggers roughly the right inferences and associations. It is instructive, I believe, to see Epistemic Proceduralism as an account of the public view of justice and its authority.

THE PUBLIC VIEW

The idea of a public view fits Epistemic Proceduralism in a number of ways. For one thing, it signals the application of cognitive intelligence to the moral question collectively faced. Another connection is the explanation this metaphor yields of the obligation to abide by the public view even when one believes (and even correctly believes) that it is mistaken. One's own belief is one's personal view, and it conflicts with one's view as member of the public, or as citizen. . . . Just as each agent has a duty to do what he believes to be right, the agency of the public—and each person qua public citizen—has a duty to do what seems right from the public point of view. The public, like any agent, has a duty to do what it believes to be right, even when it happens to be mistaken.[11] There is such a duly only if the agent's judgment meets some epistemic criteria; for example, a person with utterly distorted moral judgment may get no moral credit for being conscientious. This qualification is reflected in Epistemic Proceduralism's account of the public view by the requirement that the procedure be better than random.[12] In these ways, Epistemic Proceduralism's outcomes produce obligations to obey in much the way that they would if they were conceived as the public view of justice, by analogy to an individual's view of what is right.

It may be suspected that Epistemic Proceduralism relies on this being more than a metaphor, and actually posits a collective social entity with intentional states of its own. Many would object to this (though I leave aside the question whether it should be thought to be objectionable). To test this suspicion, consider whether Fair (NB: not Epistemic) Proceduralism would have to be seen as positing a spooky subject, the public, if it turned out to be useful to speak of its outcomes as constituting the public interest. This might be useful because it is indeed constructed out of interests, even though no individual's or group's particular interest is privileged by the procedure. So it is interest-like, and yet there is no ordinary subject who owns it. Clearly the usefulness of treating it as the interest of the public has no metaphysical implications. The usefulness of treating Epistemic Proceduralism's outcomes as the public view of justice is no less metaphysically innocent. No opinion is taken here even on the intermediate question whether these outcomes constitute a collective opinion about justice, where this idea might be analyzed without collectivist metaphysical commitments. Epistemic Proceduralism's democratic outcomes are view-like in certain respects, and the right inferences are produced by this heuristic device only if the subject of the view is imagined to be an entity called the public rather than any single citizen or subset of citizens. The public point of view is no more committed to an additional collective subject than is the traditional idea of the moral point of view.

Even without controversial metaphysical implications, the very idea of an obligation to do what is thought just from the public point of view even where this conflicts with what seems just from one's personal point of view may seem objectionable. Plainly I cannot be morally required (or even permitted) to do what it is morally wrong to do, but I might yet be morally required to abide by laws that are unjust.[13] Granted there are limits to the degree of injustice that can coexist with a moral obligation to comply. Still, within limits, the injustice of a directive is not generally thought to settle the question of whether one must obey it. If classrooms are assigned to professors in what I believe to be an unjust way—say, by seniority rather than by instructional needs—this is not immediately grounds for disobedience. So the fact that Epistemic Proceduralism would require citizens often to obey laws and policies they believe not to be just does not mean that it calls for some abdication of moral responsibility.

It may seem that Epistemic Proceduralism goes back on its critique of deference, since in the end it requires citizens to defer to the public point of view. But it doesn't; it requires obedience, not any surrender of moral judgment. There is no intention here of showing that political authority is possible without requirements to obey.

C

VOTING

Chapter 32

Polluting the Polls:
When Citizens Should Not Vote

Jason Brennan

Jason Brennan is Robert J. and Elizabeth Flanagan Family Professor of Strategy, Economics, Ethics, and Public Policy at the McDonough School of Business and Professor of Philosophy at Georgetown University. He argues that under certain circumstances citizens should not vote. In particular, citizens ought not vote when doing so will promote bad governance while minimally benefiting themselves. He maintains that citizens are permitted to put themselves in a position where they would vote badly by pursuing their own non-political projects rather than obtaining the information needed to vote well.

Jason Brennan, "Polluting the Polls: When Citizens Should Not Vote," *Australasian Journal of Philosophy* 87, no. 4 (2009): 535–49.

I. INTRODUCTION

The typical citizen of a Western democracy has a political right to vote, founded on justice. By "political right," I mean a right that ought to be legally protected. Yet the right to vote does not imply the rightness of voting. For instance, I have the political right of free association to participate in neo-Nazi rallies. A society that failed to allow me to do this would be to that extent unjust. No one should coerce me to prevent me from participating. Still, my participation would be morally wrong. I also have the political right of free speech to write pamphlets advocating slavery, but it would be morally wrong for me to do so. This paper discusses some conditions under which voting might be morally wrong. I argue that one has a moral obligation not to vote badly, even though one has the political right to do so.

An outline of my argument is:

1. One has an obligation not to engage in collectively harmful activities when refraining from such activities does not impose significant personal costs.
2. Voting badly is to engage in a collectively harmful activity, while abstaining imposes low personal costs.
3. Therefore, one should not vote badly.

Below I will make the argument in a more complete manner and consider various objections.

My goal in this paper is to argue for the position that one ought not to vote badly. I will assume for the sake of argument that there is no general duty to vote well. In a later section, I will explain why the reasons underlying the duty to refrain from voting badly are not also reasons to vote well. . . .

Irresponsible individual voters ought to abstain rather than vote badly. This thesis may seem anti-democratic. Yet it is really a claim about voter responsibility and how voters can fail to meet this responsibility. On my view, voters are not obligated to vote, but if they do vote, they owe it to others and themselves to be adequately rational, unbiased, just, and informed about their political beliefs. Similarly, most of us think we are not obligated to become parents, but if we are to be parents, we ought to be responsible, good parents. We are not obligated to become surgeons, but if we do become surgeons, we ought to be responsible, good surgeons. We are not obligated to drive, but if we do drive, we ought to be responsible drivers. The same goes for voting. My view contrasts with those that think 1) we have no obligations regarding voting, 2) we are obligated to vote, but any or nearly any vote is acceptable, 3) we must vote well, and 4) (the comparatively rare view that) we ought not to vote.

II. WHAT IS BAD VOTING?

As a first pass, we could characterize bad voting as occurring when citizens vote for harmful or unjust policies or for candidates likely to enact harmful or unjust policies. However, this seems too strong of a characterization. One might vote for what is in fact a harmful policy but be justified in doing so. For instance, imagine that the past two hundred years of work by thousands of independent political scientists, each of whom exhibits all the characteristic epistemic virtues, points towards a particular policy's being good. The policy might still end up being harmful, though everyone was justified in thinking it would not be. We shouldn't characterize people who vote on the basis of strong evidence as having voted badly.

So, as a second pass, let us say that bad voting occurs when a citizen votes without sufficient reason for harmful or unjust policies or for candidates that are likely to enact harmful or unjust policies. Note that this characterization of bad voting does not make it tautologous that one should not vote badly. Even if one accepts this characterization, one might hold that there is no duty to refrain from bad voting so defined.

Note that this characterization allows that one might sometimes be justified in voting for the lesser of two (or more) evils. Putting Mussolini in power is harmful, but not as harmful as putting Hitler in power. We can construct scenarios under which voting for the equivalent of Mussolini is the better alternative as compared to abstaining from voting or voting for the equivalent of Hitler. Note that this characterization also allows that one might be justified in voting for a policy or candidate whose probable degree of harmfulness is unknown, provided this helps prevent a known-to-be dangerous policy or candidate from winning. So, if I had to choose between Stalin and a random unknown person, I could be justified in voting for the unknown person as opposed to abstaining or voting for Stalin. This characterization also allows that a good voter can sometimes vote for otherwise unknown candidates because of party affiliation, provided the voter really has sufficient reason to believe that most members of that party do not promote bad policies.

The "without sufficient reason" clause is important because one might vote for a harmful policy but not be negligent in doing so. I have compared voters to surgeons: not everyone has to be a surgeon or a voter, but if a person is a surgeon or a voter, she should be a good one. Surgeons make mistakes. Some mistakes are excusable. We don't typically blame clinicians when they misdiagnose an unknown, extremely rare disease that has all the symptoms of a common disease. We don't hold it against a surgeon today that she isn't using better techniques that won't be invented until the next century. Since she has performed properly by a reasonable standard of care appropriate to the current level of knowledge, she is not culpable. On the other hand, some mistakes result from negligence, from falling below a reasonable standard of care.

In medicine and other professions, standards of care are usually defined as what a normal, prudent practitioner would do in similar circumstances. However, note that quality of care from a surgeon 1,000 years ago was so low that one might reasonably claim that all surgeons at that time were culpable for doing surgery. Accordingly, this definition of a standard of care in medicine presupposes that average levels of competence are generally high. Thus, we shouldn't use this definition of standard of care for voting—it might be that normal, prudent voters have been voting badly.

Instead, voters can be said to have voted well, despite having voted for what turned out to be bad policies, provided they have a sufficient moral or epistemic justification for their votes. Otherwise, they vote badly when they vote without sufficient reason for harmful policies or candidates that are likely to enact harmful policies. . . .

In some elections, it will be difficult even for highly educated experts to judge the expected consequences of electing one candidate over another. Judging candidates' comparative merits is often, but not always, difficult even for experts. Provided that the evidence shows that each candidate is likely to be on the whole good rather than harmful, then well-informed, adequately rational, just voters can be said to vote well regardless of which candidate they select. The claim that voters ought not to vote badly does not imply the stronger claim that they must vote only for the most optimal candidate.

The most common forms of bad voting are voting 1) from immoral beliefs, 2) from ignorance, or 3) from epistemic irrationality and bias. This is not to give a new formula for bad voting. Sometimes, as per the characterization of bad voting above, voting on the basis of 1–3 won't count as bad voting.

For an instance of 1: Suppose Alex believes that blacks are inferior and should be treated as second-class citizens. This is an immoral belief. If Alex votes for policies because he wishes to see blacks treated as inferiors, he votes badly.

As an instance of 2: Suppose Bob is completely ignorant about a series of propositions on a ballot. While he desires to promote the common good, he has no idea which policy would in fact promote the common good. In this case, if he votes either way, he votes badly.

As an instance of 3: Candice might vote with the goal of increasing the nation's material prosperity. However, she might have formed her beliefs about what stimulates economic growth via an unreliable, biased process. She might find a candidate espousing a regressive neo-mercantilist (i.e., imperialist, protectionist) platform emotionally appealing, and vote for that candidate despite the evidence showing that the candidate's platform is inimical to the goal of creating prosperity. In this case, Candice has false means-ends beliefs on the basis of irrational belief formation processes. If she votes on these beliefs, she votes badly.

III. THE DUTY TO REFRAIN FROM COLLECTIVE HARMS

I will argue that one has the duty not to vote badly because this violates a more general duty not to engage in collectively harmful activities. A collectively harmful activity is an activity that is harmful when many people engage in it, though it might not be harmful (or is negligibly harmful) when only a few individuals engage in it. My argument relies on the empirical premise that politicians generally attempt to give people what they ask for. I will not examine this point at length in this paper.

The duty to refrain from voting badly is not generally grounded in the harmfulness of individual votes. In most elections, individual bad votes are unlikely to have significant expected disutility. Suppose electing candidate P over candidate Q will cost the economy 33 billion dollars next year, and this comparative loss will not be offset by any other value P provides. At the time of the election, P commands an anticipated proportional majority of 50.5% of the voters (i.e., there is a 50.5% chance a random voter will vote for P), and there is a turn-out of 122,293,332 voters (the number of voters in the 2004 U.S. presidential election). In this case, if I also vote for P, the objectively worse candidate, my individual vote has an expected disutility of a mere 4.77×10^{-2650}, thousands of orders of magnitude below a penny.

Bad voting is collectively, not individually, harmful. The harm is not caused by individual voters, but by voters together. (In this respect, voting is unlike surgery or driving.) When I refrain from voting badly, this does not fix the problem. Still, it is plausible that I am obligated to refrain from collectively harmful activities, even when my contribution has negligible expected cost, provided I do not incur significant personal costs from my restraint. I will argue that this is the reason I ought not to vote badly.

What does morality require of us in a collective action problem, especially in cases where we are acting in collectively harmful ways? Suppose the problem can be solved only if everyone or the vast majority of people acts differently. Morality does not require me, as an individual, to solve the problem. It can't require me to solve the problem, in part, because I can't solve it. If, e.g., I am in a prisoner's dilemma or a tragic commons, restraining myself from contributing to the problem fails to solve the problem. Rather, my restraint exposes me to exploitation as a sucker and can exacerbate the problem.

In some cases, I might be able to solve the problem through extraordinary personal effort. Suppose I live in a small village where everyone except me litters. If I spend ninety hours a week picking up litter, the town will be clean. Here I can solve the problem as an individual, but it is implausible to think morality requires me to do so. It's too much of a burden, and it's unfair that I have to clean up after everyone else.

It's more plausible that morality requires something weaker. When there is a collective action problem, I don't have to solve the problem, but I should not be part of the problem, provided I can avoid being part of the problem at a low personal cost. In classic prisoner's dilemmas, I can't avoid being part of the problem. My attempt to avoid causing the problem opens me up to exploitation. Also, in cases of tragic commons, I often cannot avoid being part of the problem without incurring a high personal cost. If the only way I can feed my children is to join in exploiting a common resource others are already turning to dust, arguably I am permitted to do so.

Bad voting is a collective action problem. But it is not generally like a prisoner's dilemma or a tragic commons. In the prisoner's dilemma or tragic commons, it's individually rational for me to engage in collectively harmful behavior. A fortiori, it's often downright necessary for me to engage in the behavior. If I don't contribute to the problem, I suffer a personal disaster. But bad voting is not like that. Refraining from bad voting has little personal cost. That's not to say it has no cost. Voting makes people feel good about themselves or makes them feel like they've done their duty as citizens, even if they have no such duty.

Why does morality require me not to be part of the problem, at least in cases where there is little personal cost in not being part of the problem? The principle that one should not engage in collectively harmful activities (when the cost of restraint is low) needn't be grounded in any particular moral theory. It is a freestanding idea that coheres with a variety of plausible background theories. For example, . . . a Kantian might argue that engaging in collectively harmful behavior is not universalizable. Imagine a maxim of the form, "I shall feel free to engage in collectively harmful behavior when there is little personal benefit doing so." If everyone followed this maxim, it would be harmful to almost everyone. The maxim would thus fail the "contradiction in the will" test, because no rational agent would will that everyone behave according to that maxim. Or a eudaimonist might claim the type of person who contributes to certain kinds of collective harms is vicious. And so on.

For illustrative purposes, I will discuss at greater length how a duty to avoid engaging in collective harms could be grounded in plausible views about fairness. Consider that the problem of bad voting is analogous in many respects to the problem of air pollution. Rita Manning asks:

> Why then does it sound odd to suggest that each driver is morally obligated to control air pollution? Presumably because air pollution is not caused by any one driver and cannot be ended by the single actions of any one driver. If I were the owner of the only car in America, I could drive to my heart's content and not cause any air pollution.[1]

(Manning recognizes that one will cause some pollution, but she means that this pollution will be negligible.) Of course, polluting and bad voting are not completely analogous. (The surgery and driving analogies are not perfect either.) If I am the only small-scale polluter, my pollution makes no significant difference. However, if I am the only voter, my vote makes all the difference. Still, when I am one of many bad voters or many polluters, my individual contribution is negligible, but I am nonetheless part of the problem. Yet, if I stop voting badly or polluting, the problem does not go away.

Individual drivers are part of the group causing the problem. Individual obligations derive from finding fair ways to solve the problem. Suppose pollution would be at acceptable levels if cut in half. One way to achieve this is could be to require half the population not to drive, while the other half may continue to drive at their current levels with their current highly polluting cars. One is assigned driver/non-driver status by lottery. This solution is unfair because it burdens some but not all who cause the problem. The default moral position is that everyone causing the problem should bear at least some of the burden of correcting it. More controversially, one might claim either that people should bear this burden equally, or in proportion to how much they contribute to the problem, at least in the absence of countervailing conditions.

Fairness is one way to bridge the gap between collectively harmful behavior and individual action. We should pollute less because pollution harms us all, but I should pollute less because, all things equal, it is unfair for me to benefit from polluting as I please while others suffer the burden of polluting less. Ceteris paribus, we should share the burdens of not polluting. The duty not to vote badly could follow this pattern. We bad voters should not vote because it is harmful to everyone, but I, the individual bad voter, should not vote because it is unfair that I benefit from polluting democracy as I please while others suffer the burden of polluting democracy less. Ceteris paribus, we should share the burdens of not polluting the polls.

If restraining oneself from voting caused significant personal harm, then individuals might be permitted to vote badly. In fact, such restraint does have costs. Individual bad voters receive various psychological payoffs from voting—it makes them feel good about themselves for a short time. If they were prohibited (by morality) from voting, they lose this payoff. However, elections decided by bad voters mean that citizens have to live with racist and sexist laws, unnecessary wars, lower economic opportunities, lower levels of welfare, etc. The type of harm or loss of pleasure suffered by the bad voter from abstention seems relatively trivial compared to the type of harm suffered by the citizen who bears the burden of bad policy. The bad voter's pleasure in voting is not sufficient to counterbalance a potential duty to refrain from polluting the polls. By voting, bad voters consume psychological goods at our collective expense.

In parallel, an individual might drive a gas-guzzling Hummer to promote his self-image, getting real pleasure from this activity. I do not take his pleasure to be sufficient to counterbalance the harms imposed on all by smog and global warming. This is not to say that one must never drive, or even that one may not pollute in the pursuit of pleasure. We all have reason to favor principles that allow us to lead happy lives. Rather, it is to say that at some point, the pursuit of individual pleasure is outweighed by the need to preserve the healthy environment that makes pleasurable lives possible.

There are also collective costs from bad voters staying home. Widespread voting helps produce more social cohesion. It's at least empirically possible that when bad voters vote, this tends to make them care about voting more, and this may inspire them to reform and become better voters. I think these opportunity costs are likely to be outweighed by the benefits of reducing bad voting, but it's hard to say without something like an empirical study of the indirect positive effects of bad voting. Another complaint is that it's hard to take democracy seriously when most voters abstain from voting. I agree, but in response, it's also hard to take democracy seriously when a large percentage of bad voters vote. Regardless, democracy performs better, even with low voter participation, than its competitors (oligarchy, etc.) do. So, at worst, low voter participation means we are not able to take democracy as seriously as some people would like to, but this doesn't mean we must replace democracy with something else.

IV. DOING ONE'S PART IN MODERN DEMOCRACY

Citizens of modern democracies are not obligated to vote, but if they do vote, they are obligated not to vote badly. They should abstain rather than impose bad governance on everyone.

Since I describe good governance as a public good (like roads or police protection), one might object that instead of there being a duty not to vote badly (a duty that can be performed by abstaining), there is instead a duty for all to vote well. If good governance is valuable, shouldn't people do their part to help produce it, rather than simply refraining from producing bad governance? I agree that we have an obligation not to free ride on the provision of good governance, so doesn't that commit me to holding that everyone ought to vote well? While I don't intend to refute all possible arguments that there is a duty to vote well, I will explain here why the reasons I've articulated not to vote badly are not also sufficient reasons to vote well.

Consider how difficult it is to have justified beliefs, e.g., about good economic policy. As anyone who has taught basic economics knows, overcoming basic economic fallacies takes significant effort. Most people find it painful to contemplate how their (emotionally-charged ideological) beliefs could be false. Our biases make economics counterintuitive. Thus, understanding basic economics is difficult. Consider what else is needed to form good policy preferences. One might need some political philosophy to assist one in developing a well-grounded conception of justice. Even if we agree that government ought to provide for the equal welfare of citizens, it is an empirical, social scientific question what type of institutional response best achieves that goal. What strategies actually can be expected to succeed is an empirical question and cannot be determined by looking at the intentions or values of people advocating different policies. One will need some knowledge of statistics, political science, sociology, international relations, and the other social sciences to grasp the expected effectiveness of various policies. While political science, economics, and philosophy are all worthwhile endeavors, studying them to develop even a basic level of comprehension requires serious investment.

This investment has major opportunity costs. Time is scarce. Time spent overcoming economic bias is not spent learning the violin, becoming a medical doctor, playing football, or watching grass grow. There are myriad worthwhile life goals, which, owing to time scarcity, are incompatible with becoming a level-headed amateur social scientist.

One might say that people should vote well so that they can contribute to social welfare. However, besides voting, debating, rallying, supporting causes, writing to senators, writing letters to editors, and so on, there are countless other ways of contributing to society and the common good. One contributes one's share of the social surplus just by working at a productive job that provides goods and services others want. One makes the world a better place to live in by participating in culture and counterculture. One makes the world safer by fighting in just wars.

Though good governance is a public good, it doesn't follow that every member of society that benefits from that good must directly contribute to it. Instead, even if people have debts to pay to society for the goods they receive, there are many ways of paying those debts. Some people will pay by providing good governance, others by providing good culture, and others by providing good economic opportunity. One reason to favor this model of paying debts—where the debts can be paid with multiple currencies—is that it's more compatible with the pluralism liberals want to protect.

To live in a well-functioning liberal democracy is a great gift and something citizens should be thankful for. Yet one reason liberal democracy is such a great gift is that it does not require us to be political animals. It makes space for many ways of life, including avowedly non-political lives. In parallel, we might say that a good feature of well-functioning markets is that they make people rich enough to afford to engage in non-market activities and even in some cases to avoid the market altogether. A good liberal democracy would make people safe enough in their status as free and equal citizens that they could freely choose to avoid politics.

Liberal democracy is an important public good. We should all do our part to maintain it. One way a person can do his part is by bowing out. A bad vote cancels a good vote. If a good vote is a gift to society, avoiding a bad vote is also a kind of gift. . . .

If the survival of a well-functioning democracy depended on more people voting well, this might impose a duty to do so. For example, though John Rawls rejected civic humanism (which claims that active political participation is part of a fully human life), he claimed that justice as fairness is compatible with classical republicanism. Classic republicanism holds that we ought to participate in politics, not because it is constitutive of the good life, but because it is a necessary instrument to maintaining a constitutional regime. However, Rawls stressed, and I agree, that the extent and type of participation needed from citizens on classical republican grounds is largely an empirical question. It seems that reasonably just constitutional democracies survive despite less than full participation and despite serious shortcomings in citizens' civic virtue. Given the extent of bad voting and its effects on policy, some of these democracies might function better with even less participation than is now seen. What contemporary democracies need most to preserve equality and liberty is not full, informed participation, but an electorate that retains a constitutional culture and remains vigilant enough that it will rise against any leader that tries to abuse their liberties. . . .

VI. VOTING FOR CHARACTER, NOT POLICIES

One objection to my position is that voters tend to vote for character, not for policies. They might be quite good at judging the character of candidates, even if they are bad at judging the efficacy of different proposed policies for achieving different ends. If so, the objection goes, then most voters do not act wrongly when they vote.

First, this paper does not take a position regarding how well or badly actual voters vote. Taking such a position would require significant surveying of voting behavior and why voters choose the policies they do. My goal is to establish a normative conclusion—one should not vote badly—not to show how frequently people violate this norm. Even if we fortuitously lived in a world where everyone voted well, it would still be true that people should not vote badly. Even if it turned out that people were good judges of character, voted as such, and that voting for virtuous candidates meant good policies would be enacted, it would still be true that people should not vote badly. Thankfully, this would just mean that citizens act well.

However, character-based voting might actually be the most common form of bad voting, because (to a significant degree) voting for character is voting for the wrong reasons. Politicians tend to take votes as mandates even when they shouldn't. They tend to try to enact the policies they favor. Except at the extremes, character is not a reliable guide to political leadership. A virtuous politician with a powerful sense of justice might still be deeply misguided and committed to all sorts of counterproductive, harmful policies. Having the right values is not sufficient for making good policy, because it requires social scientific knowledge to know whether any given set of policies is likely to achieve those values. Just as an incompetent surgeon can be still be a virtuous person, so an incompetent politician can be a virtuous person. If there is good evidence that a politician is likely to enact harmful policies, one should not vote for her (without sufficient reason) even if she is a good person. Voting on the moral virtue of a candidate counts as good voting only when the candidate's moral virtue is evidence that she will not enact harmful policies.

The objection might be recast in terms of political skill rather than moral virtue. Politicians extol their years of experience and ability to work across party lines in generating outcomes. Still, even if voters are good judges of such political skills and vote accordingly, it's possible that such skill means bad policies will be enacted. Senator P might be excellent at getting bills passed, but perhaps all of the bills have been harmful. Just as voting on moral character is not obviously a reliable way of generating good policy outcomes, neither is voting on this kind of political skill.

Perhaps, though, voters are good at judging which candidates are likely to produce good policy, even if the voters don't themselves know what the good policies are. One might think that just as the average person can pick a good surgeon or plumber without much knowledge of medicine or plumbing, so she can pick a good candidate without knowing economics. To some extent this is true—voters rarely vote in completely disastrous candidates. However, there are more resources for a non-expert to judge surgeons or plumbers than political candidates. When a surgeon or plumber makes a mistake, the mistake is often obvious to the clients. Not so with politicians. It's hard to determine what harms they've caused. Bad surgeons are easily sued; bad politicians are not. Medical and plumbing standards are more uniform. That a surgeon went to Harvard Medical School is a count in his favor. It's less obvious that a candidate's having gone to Yale as an undergraduate shows he will enact good policy.

VIII. CONCLUSION

I see myself as a defender of democracy. I wish to keep the voting process free of pollution, and what defender of democracy wishes to see her favored system polluted? Many democrats are concerned both with democratic procedures and democratic outcomes. Not just any outcome produced by democratic procedure is acceptable, nor is every outcome aligning with democratic values acceptable regardless of what procedure produced it. Universal voting by bad voters might make procedures more democratic than massive abstention by people who would vote badly. Yet, this does not mean the outcome of this procedure will be align better with democratic values, and thus does not mean that opposing universal voting is inherently undemocratic.

When people call for universal or extended participation, we have to ask what would be the point of the institution of universal participation. If we are passionate lovers of democracy, we might celebrate what universal participation would symbolize. Yet, in the real world, we have to ask how institutions would function. Institutions are not people. They are not ends in themselves. They are not paintings, either, to be judged by their beauty, by what they symbolize, or who made them. Institutions are more like hammers—they are judged by how well they work. Good institutions get us good results; bad institutions get us bad results.

Chapter 33

Being a Good
Samaritan Requires You to Vote

Julia Maskivker

Julia Maskivker is associate professor of political science at Rollins College. She maintains that citizens are morally obligated to vote well. She argues that Samaritan duties—obligations to intervene to help when it is not unduly costly—are widely recognized in commonsense morality. Voting well is not unduly costly and often improves societal welfare. Hence, voting well falls squarely within a class of duties widely recognized in commonsense morality.

Julia Maskivker, "Being a Good Samaritan Requires You to Vote," *Political Studies* 66, no. 2 (2018): 409–24.

Do citizens have a moral duty to vote, or is the franchise just a right they are free to exercise or to abstain from, at will? The prevalent position in voting ethics—which I refer to as the "minimalist position"—is that citizens should be free to choose whether or not to exercise their right to vote. The minimalist theorist argues that citizens only have a moral duty not to vote carelessly. They are free to vote thoughtfully but they are not morally required to do so.[1] The minimalist position on voting ethics emphasizes the idea that voting is only one way among many in which we can contribute to society, but it is no more special than others. In short, there is nothing morally special about voting that should render it morally obligatory.

This article is a contribution to this debate. It situates itself in opposition to the minimalist account and develops an argument supporting a moral duty to vote. This duty also calls us to acquire enough information so as to make a voting choice that is better than random.[2] To my knowledge, no direct response to the (powerful) minimalist argument against the duty to vote has been provided so far. Discussions about the effectiveness of compulsory voting, for example, abound in the political theory literature, and some of these discussions perfunctorily touch on the minimalist argument against the duty to vote. However, hardly any democratic theory work that I know of concentrates on the rather grueling effort of justifying a moral duty to vote, whether or not such duty is legally enforceable. I intend to fill this gap and leave the question of whether enforcement is justifiable and useful for another occasion.

This article proposes that citizens are bound by a moral duty of Samaritan justice to aid society via the ballot. In other words, being a good Samaritan requires us to vote with care, that is, with sufficient information and knowledge, for the sake of society. Samaritan duties of aid bind us when an intervention would not be unduly costly—not when it would be totally costless. I argue that voting with care is a cost that society can reasonably expect citizens to assume given what elections have the potential to achieve, namely, the installment of acceptably just governments and the ousting of deficient or unresponsive ones.[3] This article proposes that failing to vote with minimal information can be compared to failing to provide relatively noncostly assistance to those sufficiently imperiled. This may strike some as an incorrect analogy, but the impression is ultimately mistaken. The most likely image evoked by the notion of the good Samaritan is the one-time calamitous situation such as the child drowning in the pond that could be easily saved by a passerby wearing new shoes. One may wonder in what ways society and democracy are imminently imperiled, and whether viewing the vote as a Samaritan obligation is adequate. I think the analogy is sufficiently valid: We should not judge emergencies as such because they happen one time; rather, we should judge them as such because they are threatening enough. The widely accepted understanding of an emergency is something that needs to be addressed immediately, not that it is nonhabitual or unusual.

For example, it makes sense to think of dire poverty as an emergency because it causes people to die from starvation. However, if poverty did not kill but kept the hungry at a continual point of steep suffering, would we consider it less normatively apt to justify help? We would be hard-pressed to think so. Bad governance is a question of degree, for sure, but the worse it is and the longer it lasts, the more it can produce results that are gravely harmful and permanent. Just as poverty may call for ready action, the results of bad governance may also call for action despite not being the worst they could possibly be, all the time. Bad governance may mean that children are denied opportunities for healthy growth and a good-enough education. It can also mean that the elderly will be denied opportunities to end their lives with dignity and in financial security. Bad governance can further translate into citizens losing (partially or wholly) benefits (such as accessible health care, to name just one), which many may find necessary to keep on living or to maintain a minimally decent standard of living. Bad governance can also ensue in wrong-headed and expensive wars that cost human lives and deplete valuable resources. These harms can be quite serious for present and future generations even if in some societies they are less acute than in others. In other words, the results of bad governance can contravene basic interests that all rational individuals can be thought to want to further such as an interest in good health, in a minimally good quality of life, in income security, and in peace, among others.

I believe that we must not feel regret for devoting most of our time and energy to personal projects and relationships, but we should recognize that, sometimes, a Samaritan duty of assistance will call us to act. There are many pressing social problems that could be alleviated with better, fair-minded, morally responsible governance. Under the assumption that the machinery of elections works transparently, voting to elect minimally decent governments in episodic elections is one reasonably easy way to contribute to relieving society from the evils of injustice and incompetence, although by no means the only one or the most effective under all possible circumstances (i.e., if injustice is so rampant that rebellion is the only alternative, or if elections are a mere façade to disguise a de facto authoritarian regime, for example, voting as a collective act turns futile, dangerous, and possibly nonobligatory, ethically).

Section "Against the Minimalist Grain" develops the argument of political Samaritanism. It proposes that even though our individual vote is unlikely to determine the result of elections—because it will get lost in a proverbial ocean of votes—we still have a duty to participate in elections since their result can be valuable from the standpoint of justice. Section "Why Is Voting Special?" addresses the objection that voting is not the only way to further the common good. I suggest that despite the fact that we can obviously contribute to aiding society in many ways besides voting, voting with care constitutes a special kind of contribution that would be morally wrong to ignore given that citizens are, normally, extra-ordinarily well situated to help, thanks to the existence of elections as enabling mechanisms of collective action.

AGAINST THE MINIMALIST GRAIN

In the last decade, political theory has witnessed the potent revival of the minimalist argument against the duty to vote. Minimalists offer the intuitive idea that voting badly—with no information and based on prejudices—is immoral because it harms society by leading to bad governance and the emergence of unfair policies.[4] Underlying the minimalist argument against the duty to vote is a more basic understanding of commonsense morality. This is the idea that our duties to others require us to refrain from hurting them (a negative duty) but not to actively help them (a positive duty). When many people vote carelessly, that can result in the selection of bad governments, which is a high price to pay for ignorance. However, nobody should be required to make an effort to vote responsibly, only to refrain from voting if unable or unwilling to do so carefully.[5]

I do not think that voting with care is beyond the call of moral duty. This is so because positive duties should not ipso facto demand much of the individual. For example, if we come across a fire on our way to work, we are not expected to jump into the flames and rescue people from the burning building. We may be expected to immediately call the fire department, though. A compelling duty of aid does not demand that we jump into a dangerous situation to perform rescue operations that put life and health at risk. Doing so would be heroic and, therefore, supererogatory. However, we may be morally required to call in for help, because doing so would not pose a reasonable risk to our well-being.

I want to press the point that voting with care—which entails voting with sufficient information of what is at stake in the election—can be analogized to a duty of easy aid. It is reasonable to believe that we are all bound by duties of aid when our intervention would be relatively easy. These duties of "Samaritan assistance" are commonplace in our moral vocabulary. For example, if you are driving by a desolate area and see a pedestrian in distress by the side of the road—say, having an epileptic attack—it makes sense to think that you are obligated to stop and call in for help. Duties of assistance are stringent if they are not unduly costly to the assisting. If you were on your way to the hospital because you think you are having a heart attack, in no way are you expected to help someone else needing assistance. But in normal circumstances, you would be. Why not think of voting as a duty of Samaritan assistance in circumstances that make your intervention expected?

If we believe that elections can help societies select good governments and expel bad ones, it follows that a duty to promote the common good entails a duty to vote with care, that is, with information and a sense of responsibility for society's well-being. Societies need to be rescued from unaccountable, corrupt, and indifferent leaders, and one obvious way to do that (although not the only way) is to put more good ones in power and ensure the bad ones are out of a job. Elections are the mechanisms that formally enable this change. Episodic voting does not have to require constant or even frequent political participation. Voting with a sense of responsibility for society at important elections does not amount to becoming a *homo politicus*, although it does require attention to issues of concern as important elections draw closer. One can spend most of one's life away from politics and still be a virtuous, happy human being. But at certain points, we ought to get involved. When? When elections afford us the opportunity to assist society by choosing governments that we expect to rule fairly—or more fairly than all the other realistic alternatives.

The duty of Samaritan aid to vote is rooted in a more general duty to support just institutions and just social arrangements. This prior duty calls us to act as good Samaritans toward society via the ballot because fair-minded governments and fair-minded ruling coalitions chosen electorally can have a significant impact on how basic institutions in society treat citizens. Many times, elected officials or their appointees will steward and administer those institutions. Thus, one could say that, in the same way as we have a basic duty of humanity to save the drowning infant when doing so would be relatively non-costly to us, all things considered, we also have a basic duty of justice to relieve society of bad governance when doing so would not be unduly difficult to us.

Some could object that voting is indeed costly. After all, voting with care consumes time and resources needed to gather information. Information-seeking efforts and the physical act of going to the polls entail time that could be used for other pursuits. In economic jargon, we could say that voting has "opportunity costs." But does not everything we do in life have an opportunity cost since we cannot be in two places at once? It is true, duties of aid are not costless. Stopping to aid the person in distress may make us late for work. But this is a morally innocuous datum. Duties of aid are binding provided the cost is not *too* high for us—not provided the cost is zero. Voting with information and a sense of responsibility for society could be seen as an acceptable cost for contributing to an important collective good such as good governance.

The claim that some actions may be seen as duties, rather than as mere freedoms, is based on a principle of "easy altruism," which most theories of ethics find uncontroversial. The principle of easy altruism derives from a general concern with impartiality as a basis for political morality in society. Impartiality as a political morality asks that I put myself in the place of another—while they put themselves in my place—to choose basic norms of co-existence we can all live by without disrespecting each other. This unbiased attitude to justifying norms of social organization can help us understand norms of moral behavior, as it requires people to aid others in need out of a concern with how they would like to be treated when in need themselves. On this reading, the principle of impartiality can naturally justify positive duties to help others—not just negative ones to refrain from hurting them. Generally, impartiality is a way of thinking about justice in abstract terms and it encapsulates the basic notion that we are all entitled to equal consideration, regardless of separating factors such as race, gender, sex, and so forth, so that we can stand an equal chance of having our shared, basic interests fulfilled. Basic interests are interests that we can reasonably attribute to most rational human beings; they include an interest in security, decent livelihood, good health, and peace, among others.

When the citizen casts a considered vote with the intention of helping the common good and promoting fair governance in her society, she is seeing her fellow citizens as deserving of equal consideration. She is discharging a duty of justice via the vote and expecting others to do the same so that the government elected can be trusted with protecting and furthering the basic interests of all, not just a few.

The principle of easy altruism is not a matter of moral choice despite its misleading name. It is, however, sensitive to the distinction between "morally expected" and "heroic" actions because commonsense morality does not demand burdensome sacrifices on the part of the individual. Like the duty to call for help, the duty to vote with care requires from us that we act—it is a positive duty—but it is not unreasonably burdensome because it is episodic and does not entail an interrupted, overwhelming commitment to politics. Neither is it unassailable. Other moral considerations (and duties) can override the duty to vote under particular circumstances. For example, our duty to care for a sick relative on election day may be stringent enough to take precedence over our duty to vote. There are many other examples of the duty to vote losing to other obligations.

It is usually clear why certain actions are morally unacceptable. For example, the duty to refrain from inflicting harm on other people, except in self-defense, is uncontroversial. This being the case, sometimes there is a moral imperative *to* act in certain ways, not just to refrain from acting. Some positive duties are stringent because *failure* to act may produce results that are morally comparable to actions produced by direct harm. Although this equivalence is not automatic, it can exist. The philosophical literature is no stranger to the argument that a *failure* to *act* can at times be as harmful as an *injurious act* properly speaking. John Stuart Mill, writes in *On Liberty* that "a person may cause evil to others not only by his actions but by his inaction, and in either case he is justly accountable to them for the injury."[6]

The idea that it is solely incompetent, uninformed voters who determine bad electoral outcomes from the perspective of justice is akin to thinking that it is only the number of car accidents your vehicle has been involved in that determines how fast it deteriorates throughout the years. In reality, your failure to have the car serviced every so often also plays a part in causing the vehicle to malfunction. Failure to act, not only acting badly or recklessly, contributes to things happening the way they do. When not enough citizens bother to get out and vote with information, the incompetent voters may get to determine an election, but one could see this result as partly enabled by the fact that the bad votes were not canceled out by the good ones, especially if the turnout was not high. What I want to say is that voting may many times be the problem, but it can also be the solution.

By omitting to vote in a considered fashion, individuals are indeed contributing to injustice, namely, the harm that results from bad voting on the part of others as well as the unjust governance that results from those bad votes. This contribution is not causally direct, however, in the same way as pushing someone down the stairs is, for example (or voting badly oneself). Omissions are not direct causal contributors to state of affairs. However, omissions can be causally implicated in the emergence and sustenance of state of affairs because when the individual acts, her actions can modify a given situation even if the individual herself did not cause that situation to come into being. For example, I can prevent someone's death if I throw him a lifesaver when he is drowning in the pool even if I played no part whatsoever in explaining how he fell into the water. In this example, my failure to act when I stumble upon the struggling swimmer is one (sufficient but not necessary) causal factor that explains the latter's death.

The concept of "causal factor" can be applied to discussions about the morality of voting. Voters may not be directly responsible for the bad policies that governments enact and implement. They may have been deceived or betrayed in their expectations of good governance, so they may not be to blame for the bad performance of governments all the time. Additionally, no individual voter can be said to be causally responsible for good or bad governance since her impact on the result of the election is likely to be negligible. Voters may encounter themselves, in a way, in a similar-enough situation as the bypasser who spots a person drowning. The bypasser has not caused the harm himself but he can assuage or prevent it. By the same token, voters have the *collective power* and the means, via elections, to avert the prolongation of injustice by removing the incompetent and corrupt from office and putting someone better in their place. Because of this collective power—and assuming that exercising it with others is not unreasonably costly for the citizen—refusing to stand by should be seen as a duty, not a choice that the citizen will not be blamed for avoiding. In the same way as we are, under general circumstances, morally expected to lend a hand to the troubled swimmer, we are also morally expected to avoid or minimize societal injustice by devoting some time to voting for the sake of good governance in society. Our individual contribution to reducing injustice may not be strictly necessary to attain the collective result of good governance. However, our contribution is surely valuable if we conceive of it as part a larger collective activity that we have objective reasons to value highly because of its potential impact on justice. Thus, the duty to vote is a Samaritan duty to contribute, however marginally, to a collective activity that will or can have a discernible (worthy) effect. It is, ultimately, a duty of *common pursuit* that calls us to join forces with others to bring about a desirable collective result from the standpoint of justice (I elaborate further on what this duty entails below).

In arguing that our actions matter even when they are not individually powerful to determine an outcome by themselves, I evoke a nondifference-making view of morality. According to that view of morality, we do not assess the moral permissibility of individual actions according to their *particular* impact on a collective result. Rather, we assess individual actions according to the nature of the collective activity *to which they contribute*. To reinforce the argument, think about the following situation. . . . Imagine a collection of people who work together toward a goal they all endorse. Additionally, suppose that no single individual contribution will make a difference to the achievement of that goal because the contribution will be too small. If what really matters to assess the worth of an individual act is whether that act changes things, then, all participants to this enterprise may act fully permissibly even if the collective goal that they support is not. For example, if the joint goal is the destruction of some community's clean environment (as part of an extermination war, let us say), then, each individual act of purposely spilling a few drops of poison onto the targeted community's river can be seen as morally permissible since its impact on the overall level of pollution will be almost nil. However, the intention to cooperate in the joint goal of environmental destruction is condemnable, and it should, therefore, play a part in evaluating the individual's action. In this case, each individual is willingly participating in the production of a goal that is morally repugnant. Sharing intentions that are connected to a larger, reproachable goal bespeaks a type of complicity that can be source of blame for the individual. The blame is a direct consequence of the larger collective project's moral character. On this view, the individual acts inherit the moral qualities of the larger enterprise of which they are parts, and this is independent of how perceptible those acts are on their own.

In the same vein, I submit that sharing intentions that are connected to a larger morally valuable goal—like bringing about just governance in society or relieving society of injustice—denotes a moral disposition that is an apt candidate for moral praise. Many acts denote moral praise because they signify a supererogatory action, that is, individuals who did them went above and beyond the call of duty. However, many other acts may also deserve praise because the individual simply did them, and the individual was expected to do them because the acts were not too costly or difficult, and they provided needed assistance. The noncostly individual act that resonates with a larger goal of relieving suffering or injustice can very well be morally obligatory under circumstances we can imagine. In the case of an individual good vote, the potential to determine an election's result is virtually zero. However, I suggest that, in the same way as contributing to a morally suspicious project is ethically troubling for the individual *even* if his contribution to the final outcome is negligible, taking part of a larger collective effort oriented toward improving justice in society should be seen as valuable *even* if the single individual's capacity to determine a result is also negligible.

The logic should be the same for both cases. If it is morally problematic to form part of a collective effort that seeks to harm others, by parity of reasoning, it should be morally praiseworthy to form part of a collective effort that seeks to reduce injustice affecting others. But there is more. If it is morally obligatory to refrain from participating in activities that purposely harm others—it is not *just* recommended—then, by the same logic, we should see that it is morally required to participate in activities that relieve injustice and suffering affecting others *provided that* doing so does not burden us unduly (in other words, the positive duty must fall within the purview of the principle of easy altruism). We ensure that other people's dignity is preserved *not only* when we refrain from violating it ourselves but also when we can, easily, do something to secure a general respect for that dignity, especially if is being patently jeopardized by others or by a particular situation (as when governmental injustices undermine people's well-being and rights). This is what impartiality as a principle of social morality mandates. It does not require us to act like heroes, seriously sacrificing ourselves for other people. But there is a long way in- between Samaritanism and Sainthood. We can summarize the latter argument somewhat more formally in the following.

We contribute to a morally valuable collective activity, X, when our individual not-unduly-costly action, Y—however powerless on its own—has the *tendency* to add to the desirable effects of the larger activity, which is only possible, thanks to the accumulation of many individual acts similar in kind to Y. The moral value and obligatoriness of individual act Y derives from the value of the collective activity X, which in turn is a function of its good effects from the perspective of justice and fair-minded governance—or another stipulated basic social good. Thus, voting is a valuable contribution to a larger collective activity—that is, the election mechanism—that we have reasons to support for its potential to favor justice and decent governance.

However, there are many collective activities that are potentially capable of helping society (e.g., rallies to beat cancer, rallies to beat AIDS, or rallies to beat domestic violence). Are we morally required to participate in all of them insofar as our participation is relatively easy and noncostly? Or are we morally free to refuse participation in a valuable collective activity if we do not voluntarily accept to participate in it and reap its benefits? What is morally special about voting that makes it morally obligatory vis-à-vis other forms of contributing to society?

WHY IS VOTING SPECIAL?

It bears clarification that my case for a Samaritan duty to aid society via the ballot is not an argument for requiring contribution to a collective scheme on the grounds that said scheme is capable of producing benefits that any rational individual should want for herself, regardless of whether the would-be contributor voluntarily accepts, or asks for, the benefits in question. It may be largely true that good and fair-minded governance is personally beneficial for most of us, but the normative force of the Samaritan obligation to vote as defended in this article springs from an altruistic consideration, not a consideration of objective self-interest: If we can help others at no unacceptably high cost to us, we should do so. . . . On my reading, the individual ought to cooperate via the ballot despite the fact that, hypothetically, good governance may not be as beneficial to him as it may be to others (i.e., because he would stand to personally lose from some of the policies enacted by a fair-minded government).

Now, the following objection arises: If there is a Samaritan duty to vote so as to help society minimize bad governance, are we also bound by a duty to participate politically in other ways, besides voting, that may influence who will govern? I want to say that street demonstrations, letters to public officials, and other nonstrictly electoral ways of influence may surely have greater impact than elections at very specific times, but voting is generally less costly than nonelectoral participation, which carries the same informational costs as voting (i.e., one ought to know why one is marching) as well as stronger requisites of physical presence that may make involvement costly in terms of time and coordination efforts. For this reason, it is easier to see voting as a duty than it is to see all nonelectoral political participation as a duty—all else equal. But the most interesting question still is: Why is one to see political participation, and voting in particular, as a moral duty at all to the detriment of one of the so many nonpolitical ways in which one can further the common good?

If we care about civic duty, there are many ways to be a good citizen other than voting. For example, we can give to charity, make art, teach, or work productively more generally. But we do not need to deny that there are indeed many ways to further the common good in order to conclude that some of those ways may still be required of us (not by the law but by our conscience). An analogy will help to clarify this point: Imagine that your good friend is using crutches, and you are both waiting for a bus to arrive. Your friend would benefit from your assistance to board the bus. The effort to help him board the bus would not be unduly strenuous for you. Your friend also happens to have a lot of credit card debt. While the bus is approaching, you hand him a check and say, "Take this money to pay your bills, but I'm not going to help you get onto the bus." Your monetary help is surely beneficial to your friend. However, in that moment, he needs you to help him board the bus.

Voting provides us with a similar choice. The quality of government significantly affects every person in society. Elections offer us a relatively easy way to improve society if we vote with minimal information and end up choosing decent governments. Other forms of contributing to the common good may be valuable and beneficial, but it is not clear that they let the individual off the hook when it comes to voting in order to contribute to the emergence of good governance.

The effect that governments have on the common good—as opposed to the effect that private individuals or organizations may have—cannot be dismissed as morally trivial. I call this the *Governmental Salience Fact* (GSF). It means that governments are massively powerful giants whose policies can influence the economy, the geopolitics, and the general welfare of society in a way that few other entities can. The GSF is an empirical datum that tells us that good and bad government profoundly affects the quality of people's lives. Because of this great impact, it is not unreasonable to think that governments are morally distinctive entities. I call the latter proposition the *Governmental Salience Principle* (GSP). The principle builds on the GSF. It tells us that *because* governments are so influential, their justice *should* be seen as a central justification for voting. In other words, governments are distinguished from other entities and institutions because it is reasonable to assume that they have more power to affect people's life prospects by way of their capacity to enact, or block, far-reaching public and social policy. Thus, if we ought to act as good Samaritans and help the common good, it seems that partaking of the mechanism that makes governments elected is essential. Even though voting is surely not the only way to affect government, it seems to me that it is the only way to choose it, and choosing a government is necessary before we can influence it. Importantly, the nature of the government we choose can make a great deal of difference as to how badly we need to make sure we actually influence people in government. If good governance is possible without extreme vigilance on the part of the electorate, because the administration elected is prima facie fair-minded, then, it appears that voting with care plays a big role in explaining this circumstance. This does not mean that vigilance is ever unnecessary, but it only means that the first, most basic step we can take to maximize the chances of good governance is to elect the right type of government—understanding this as a government whose policies and promises appear to be better than others to further the common good of society and the basic interests of its members. Governments understood as the cadre of officials in power also play an important part in enforcing rights-protecting laws that make democracies procedurally fair. Because people who occupy seats in government make decisions about how primary social goods will be made available to citizens, and they have the capacity to disrupt enforcement of laws and measures that protect rights, their actions while in office can have a vast impact on people's prospects and on the quality of democracy. The nature of the government in power, then, matters to justice. And if this is so, the specific mechanism that enables a given coalition to install itself at the center of political power has a moral significance that seems unparalleled among other mechanism of political influence or actions for the common good more generally.

It is undeniable that many ways to affect the common good exist besides voting. Insofar as we do something for the common good, we could think of the duty to vote as an imperfect one (in Kantian language). We know we have to fulfill it, but how and when is left to us to decide. However, as the example above illustrates, just because we can help in diverse ways does not mean that we are morally free to ignore certain ways in which we ought to help.

Consider another example to bring the point home: imagine that you are walking down the street and witness a petty robbery. A thief has grabbed someone's wallet and run away. The victim, a woman walking in front of you, is now left with no money and is disoriented. To make the case more dramatic, imagine that the woman is a foreign tourist and has no one to turn to in the city, where she had planned to spend the night. The Kantian logic of imperfect duty suggests that you do nothing wrong by ignoring the woman's plight because last week you helped a homeless person buy lunch. How many helpful things can one person be expected to do? But is this the right way to proceed? I would say that it does not seem to be. Doing something in this case would be easy since you are well equipped to offer aid: You happen to be right there and you have a wallet. For example, you could give the woman some change for a bus ride that will take her to her embassy.

But does this mean that you ought to help anybody who conceivably may need help? Of course not. However, you are in such a good position to help in *this* case. Sure, you can think that the two coins for the bus ride could be given to a charity organization of your choice, but how bad is it to forgo this particular chance of aiding that you happen to be so well situated to act on? I argue that it would be an impermissible bad *given* your circumstances. Let us call this the *Principle of Moral Inescapability*. It says that *given* certain confluence of factors, aiding is the right and obligatory thing to do. In the case of the stranded woman, the confluence of factors include how easy it would be for you to help, given your proximity and possession of a wallet *and* how bad it would be for the woman to have to sleep in a park that night.

In the same vein, elections entail a particular confluence of factors that render participation in them morally required, all else equal. First, they constitute a structure that situates us in a perfect position to render help easily. Assuming minimal efficiency and transparency, the machinery of elections emerges in front of you for you to vote and vanishes shortly after the choice period is over. You do not need to create this structure, but it is part and parcel of the democratic system. It exists automatically, at least from your individual perspective. Because of this, one could say that you happen to be well situated to use elections to help society. Second, given the importance of the GSF, we know that elections are not morally innocuous events. They are not because they establish and replace governments, and governments' actions affect peoples' lives in nontrivial ways. Thus, we can conclude that ignoring elections (ignoring the GSP, more concretely) carries with it costs that we should not accept simply because we prefer not to help or because we would rather help in other ways besides participating in them. It is not valid to say that I want to contribute to the common good in ways other than voting just as it is not a valid to refuse to help the stranded woman because I would rather donate the cash to Oxfam. Certainly, it would be equally easy to donate to Oxfam, which may be why one should do so regardless of whether one helps the woman. But the *Principle of Moral Inescapability* dictates that one is still required to aid the woman because she needs the help *now*, and we are *right there*, able to provide it. The principle also requires us to help because the good of sparing the woman a homeless night trumps the cost (i.e., the two coins). By the same token, society needs our help now (child poverty, anyone?) and elections exist so that we can provide such help relatively easily, and our cost being no more than the acquisition of available information. (If we would rather avoid the lines at the polling booths, we can always send the ballot by post.) To ignore this confluence of factors, I would say, is morally wrong.

At this juncture, it could be objected that I am using an incorrect analogy: My two coins will suffice to aid the woman in trouble, but my vote will most likely not make a difference to the result of elections. Duties of assistance are not good tools to argue for the obligation to participate in collective activities such as elections, the objection goes. Although intuitive, this idea is incorrect. Acting on duties toward other human beings does not always require the capacity to make a measurable difference. In elections, although a single vote will not have a discernible impact by itself, an accumulation of many certainly will. Our reason for action can be a duty of Samaritan justice even if we know that we would not achieve much acting alone. The duty to aid calls us to join forces with others, in a common pursuit, by participating in elections when we would not incur high costs by doing so. It is not far-fetched to think that we ought to commit to participating in a collective endeavor that is instrumentally valuable for justice reasons. This is a duty *not to stay in the sidelines* when we could act so that our actions, *together with those of others*, help society at no unreasonable cost to ourselves. But someone could still object that a duty of aid that needs to be carried out with others to be impactful cannot be binding on the individual since the she cannot bring about a result through her own individual contribution. How can one be bound to do something that will have no effect on the world?

Duties of Samaritan justice do not lose moral force when they need to be carried out by many, collectively, in order to have a discernible impact. To see why, consider the following situation. . . . In a subway car, an individual passenger attacks another individual passenger. A number of subway riders, unrelated to each other but sitting in the same car where the attack is taking place, witness the aggression. No individual rider by himself is assured to be able to stop the attack (and it may be too dangerous, therefore costly, to do so). However, all together will be able to subjugate the aggressor easily. If this is so, all the riders witnessing the attack have a duty to act in concert in order to protect the victim from further harm, by restraining the attacker.

Similarly, I submit that we have a duty to vote with care—acting in concert with other members of the electorate at elections—in order to prevent the harm of bad governance, regardless of the insufficient effect of our vote alone. Despite this rationale, one could fear that the smallness of one single vote may weaken the moral stringency of the duty to vote. Because one individual vote is so minuscule in its effects, it can be superfluous since the threshold needed to win the election will be met without it. Am I still required to vote if I know that a given result will easily unfold without the need for my contribution? In other words, am I still required to bother to vote with care if I know that my vote is not necessary to secure the result I favor?

The fact that each single vote in isolation will most likely be superfluous in the final vote count is hard to deny, but such mathematical truth does not detract from the moral force of a duty of aid via the vote. Everybody's vote is strictly unnecessary in a mathematical sense since it is almost certain that the threshold of votes needed to win an election will be met regardless of it. Thus, everybody would seem to have an equal claim to not fulfilling the duty to vote with care. However, this conclusion makes little sense from a neutral, broader viewpoint. It may be empirically true that my actions are superfluous in enabling a given result, but if this is true, so are everybody else's. Does it follow, then, that nobody has a duty to act? Imagine for a second the subway attack scenario described above: If only five people were necessary to stop the attacker, but there are six riders witnessing the attack, does it follow that none of them has a duty to intervene? It would hardly follow. It makes more sense to think that everybody has an equal duty to act because it is difficult to see anyone's claim to be relieved from the duty as more weighty than another's.

As advanced, an individual action that is not impactful by itself may still be morally required because it is the type of act that derives its value from a worthy, larger effort. In other words, an individual contribution that is negligible may still be morally valuable (and required) because it is the type of action that, together with many other actions of its kind, produces a valuable result. Parfit echoes this reasoning when he explains that:

> Even if an act harms no one [because it is negligible] this act may be wrong because it is one of a set of acts that *together* harm other people. Similarly, even if some act benefits no one [because it is negligible] it can be what someone ought to do, because it is one of a set of acts that *together* benefit other people.[7]

I think Parfit's logic can support a general notion of "collective Samaritanism" whereby a duty to act springs from the moral obligatoriness of cooperating in a common pursuit, whose effect will be perceptible, even though the individual contributions that make it possible will not have a perceptible impact. The fact that our contribution may be overdetermined—that is, strictly unnecessary to elicit an electoral result—does not free us from the obligation to make it, all else equal, given that all other would-be contributors have an equally strong claim to being exempted. This means that, prima facie, nobody's claim to being exempted from cooperation is more stringent than anybody else's. Thus, the logical shape of the duty of common pursuit in general would be as follows.

1. Under circumstances X, person Y finds herself in need of help.
2. Under circumstances X, you are particularly well situated to help person Y because doing so would not demand strenuous effort on your part. However, your single act of help will be insufficient to relieve the plight of Y.
3. Under circumstances X, other people around you, A, B, and C, are equally well situated to help person Y and are as equally well situated to help as you are. None of their acts of help alone are sufficient to relieve the plight of Y, but together, A, B, C, and yourself can provide Y with what she needs.

4. Under circumstances X, joining forces with A, B, and C to help person Y is not unduly costly for you. It is neither for A, B, and C.

5. The cost to A, B, C, and yourself of helping person Y is less morally significant than the harm that would accrue to Y if A, B, C, and you did nothing. In other words, your (collective and individual) cost can be offset by the avoidance of suffering that your help would cause.

6. Therefore, under circumstances X, it would be morally subpar for you to refrain from joining forces with A, B, and C to help Y. The same applies to A, B, and C, respectively.

7. This reasoning holds valid even if your individual participation is not causally necessary to effect the aid in question. Your claim to being exempted from the obligation to join others in the collective effort is no stronger than any other individual's. Thus, all have an equally stringent duty to jump in. In the case of considered voting, this means that all citizens, prima facie, have an equally stringent duty to contribute to aiding society with a considered vote.

The duty of common pursuit that underlies the obligation to vote with care entails nothing more than a call to be well disposed toward cooperating with others in the framework of a larger collective enterprise that we have reason to value because of its overall effects such as the furthering of justice, good governance, or the protection of rights. It is a prima facie duty because it is not absolute (it cannot require us to cooperate if doing so is unduly costly to us or if doing so collides with another duty or moral consideration that should have priority in particular cases). The duty of common pursuit is really a duty to see the merits of collective rationality over the merits of individual rationality narrowly understood as the pursuit of personal utility. Cooperatively disposed people understand the stringency of this duty and act accordingly when doing so is not unduly burdensome.

At this point, one may rightfully wonder whether making a small contribution to a collective project with a large (valuable) impact invariably counts as an instance of the Samaritan duty of justice to aid others. Are all cases of easy altruism also cases involving Samaritanism?

Of course not. Even though I use the term "Samaritanism" in a nontraditional way, since aiding society does not equal aiding someone at risk of dying or physical harm, I said before that strong conceptual parallels exist given the urgency of what is at stake when societies are governed unfairly. What is at stake when societies are governed unfairly or inaptly is access to primary social goods and the fulfillment of basic interests in enjoying those goods. Situations in which access to these goods are imperiled or diminished, I argued, could be compared to situations where ready aid is called for because of how indecent it would be to leave individuals without attention. Governments have the capacity to affect the flow of primary social goods, thus failing to act toward ensuring that fair-minded leaders gain access to the seats of power in the first place seems to violate considerations of Samaritanism.

It would seem to follow from this reasoning that instances of cooperation not geared toward restoring or gaining access to primary social goods are not examples of Samaritanism, however important and necessary those joint efforts may be. Unfortunately, I do not have the space here to provide a detailed, elaborate account of how to identify issues of basic justice understood as access to primary social goods. However, I think it is not controversial to say that there is consensus about the idea that most rational human beings will have an interest in having ready access to things like income security, decent health, peace as absence of violence and war, and freedom from oppression, among others. Elections can affect people's access to these goods; therefore, it is not unreasonable to think of voting as required by considerations of Samaritan justice.

CONCLUDING THOUGHTS

Nobody is morally required to be a Saint, but we are surely expected to behave like decent Samaritans toward society if we can easily do so. A careful and sufficiently informed vote in episodic elections allows us to behave in just that manner by acting with others in a common pursuit. In his *Considerations of Representative Government*, John Stuart Mill said that the vote should be conceived of as a trust because it gives the citizen power over others. The concept of a trust implies the goal of protecting the interests of another. Mill saw the ballot as a vehicle for furthering the well-being of our fellow citizens:

> [t]he voter is under an absolute moral obligation to consider the interest of the public, not his private advantage, and give his vote to the best of his judgement exactly as he would be bound to do if he were the sole voter and the election depended upon him alone.[8]

It seems reasonable to interpret Mill as saying that the franchise gives the electorate *collective* power to affect the fate of society since we know, as did he, that individual voters do not have a perceptible capacity to affect elections. Consistent with Mill's logic, I say that voting with knowledge and a sense of justice can be a truly effective way to aid society by acting in concert, even if not the only way or the best way at all times. Hannah Arendt was mistaken when she wrote that "the booth in which we deposit our ballots is unquestionably too small, for this booth has room for only one."[9] Voting is anything but solitary. We must see it as a collective endeavor if it is to mean anything at all for democracy.

D

CHALLENGES

Chapter 34

Activist Challenges to
Deliberative Democracy

Iris Marion Young

Iris Marion Young (1949–2006) was professor of political science at the University of Chicago. She argues that deliberative democracy faces two serious challenges. First, when starting premises are set by the more powerful, deliberation is not the answer but protest is called for. Second, even if the starting premises are agreed upon, they may be the product of unjust background conditions. As a result, even if deliberation ends with a consensus, this agreement will only further entrench oppressive social structures. Indeed, more insidiously, such deliberation may give injustice a veneer of legitimacy.

Iris Marion Young, "Activist Challenges to Deliberative Democracy," *Political Theory* 29, no. 5 (2001): 670–90.

Screen and song celebrate social justice movements that protested in the streets when they were convinced that existing institutions and their normal procedures only reinforced the status quo. Many rights have been won in democratic societies by means of courageous activism—the eight-hour day, votes for women, the right to sit at any lunch counter. Yet contemporary democratic theory rarely reflects on the role of demonstration and direct action. Indeed, it might be thought that one of the major strains of contemporary democratic theory, the theory of deliberative democracy, should be critical of typical tactics of activism such as street marches, boycotts, or sit-ins, on the grounds that there activities confront rather than engage in discussion with people the movement's members disagree with.

This essay constructs a dialogue between two "characters" with these differing approaches to political action, a deliberative democrat and an activist.

A dialogue between them is useful because their prescriptions for good citizenship clash in some respects. I aim through this exercise to bring out some of the limitations of at least some understandings of deliberatively democratic norms, especially if they are understood as guiding practices in existing democracies where structural inequalities underlie significant injustices or social harms. At the same time, I aim to foreground some of the virtues of nondeliberative political practices for democratic criticism. The "characters" of the deliberative democrat and the activist I construct as ideal types. Many political theorists and citizens doubtless sympathize with both, and the stances often shift and mix in the political world.

As I construe her character, the deliberative democrat claims that parties to political conflict ought to deliberate with one another and through reasonable argument try to come to an agreement on policy satisfactory to all. The activist is suspicious of exhortations to deliberate because he believes that in the real world of politics, where structural inequalities influence both procedures and outcomes, democratic processes that appear to conform to norms of deliberation are usually biased toward more powerful agents. The activist thus recommends that those who care about promoting greater justice should engage primarily in critical oppositional activity, rather than attempt to come to agreement with those who support or benefit from existing power structures.

In the dialogue I construct, the deliberative democrat's claims that the activist only aims to promote a partial interest does not adopt a stance of reasonableness. After answering these commonly heard charges on behalf of the activist, I consider four challenges the activist brings to the recommendation that responsible citizens should follow norms of deliberative democracy as the best form of political engagement. I find that the early challenges are easier for the deliberative democrat to answer than the latter.

The purpose of the dialectic is not to recommend one side over the other because I think that both approaches are valuable and necessary to democratic practice that aims to promote justice. Bringing the approaches into critical relation with one another in this way, however, helps sound a caution about trying to put ideals of deliberative democracy into practice in societies with structural inequalities. This dialogue also reveals tensions between the two stances that cannot be thoroughly resolved.

I. THE CHARACTERS

In the effort to give the characters an embodied feel, I have endowed each with gender pronouns, rather than repeatedly using "he or she" for each. This decision reveals a disturbing dilemma: shall they both be male, both female, or one each male and female? Deciding that one shall be male and the other female only magnifies the dilemma: which should be which? As I try each one out, I discover that my assignment evokes undesirable stereotypes wherever way it goes. If the deliberative democrat is male, then that position appears to carry added weight of rationality and calm, and the corresponding female activist seems to appear flighty and moved by passion primarily. Despite its own stereotyping dangers of making the activist appear aggressive, I have decided to cast the deliberative democrat as female and activist as male because at least this assignment more associates the female with power.

For the purposes of this essay, I understand deliberative democracy as both a normative account of the bases of democratic legitimacy and a prescription for how citizens ought to be politically engaged. The best and most appropriate way to conduct political action, to influence and make public decisions, is through public deliberation. In deliberation, parties to conflict, disagreement, and decision making propose solutions to their collective problems and offer reasons for them; they criticize one another's proposals and reasons and are open to being criticized by others. Deliberative democracy differs from some other attitudes and practices in democratic politics in that it exhorts participants to be concerned not only with their own interests but to listen to and take account of the interests of others insofar as these are compatible with justice. Practices of deliberative democracy also aim to bracket the influence of power differentials in political outcomes because agreement between deliberators should be reached on the basis of argument, rather than as a result of threat or force.

The theory of deliberative democracy thus expresses a set of normative ideals according to which actual political processes are evaluated and usually found wanting. Political decisions ought to be made by processes that bring all the potentially affected parties or their representatives into a public deliberative process. Deliberators should appeal to justice and frame the reasons for their proposals in terms they claim that others ought to accept. Doing so rules out the assertion of simple partisan interest or the attempt to compel assent by means of threats and sanctions.

As I construct the character of the deliberative democrat here, however, she not only finds in the ideals of deliberative democracy means to criticize political processes. She also advocates processes and action to implement deliberative procedures in actually existing democracy, with all its conflict, disagreement, and economic, social, and political inequality. The deliberative democrat thinks that the best way to limit political domination and the naked imposition of partisan interest and to promote greater social justice through public policy is to foster the creation of sites and processes of deliberation among diverse and disagreeing elements of the polity. She thus attributes several dispositions to the good citizen. The politically engaged citizen aiming to promote social justice seeks to criticize and debate with those with whom she disagrees or those with whom her interests initially conflict in public settings where she tries to persuade others that some policies or interests have unjust or harmful aspects or consequences. Through critical argument that is open to the point of view of others, she aims to arrive at policy conclusions freely acceptable by all involved.

Like that of the deliberative democrat, the stance of the activist offers itself as a model of citizen virtue. The activist is committed to social justice and normative value and the idea that politically responsible persons ought to take positive action to promote these. He also believes that the normal workings of the social economic and political institutions in which he dwells enact or reproduce deep wrongs—some laws or policies have unjust effects, or social and economic structures cause injustice, or nonhuman animals and things are wrongly endangered, and so on. Since the ordinary rules and practices of these institutions tend to perpetuate these wrongs, we cannot redress them within those rules. The activist opposes particular actions or policies of public or private institutions, as well as systems of policies or actions, and wants them changed. Sometimes he also demands positive policies and action to reduce injustice or harm.

Besides being motivated by a passion for justice, the activist is often also propelled by anger or frustration at what he judges is the intransigence of people in power in existing institutions, who behave with arrogance and indifference toward the injustices the activist finds they perpetuate or flatly deny them and rationalize their decisions and the institutions they serve as beneficent. Since many of his fellow citizens are ignorant of these institutional harms or accept them with indifference or resignation, the activist believes it important to express outrage at continued injustice to motivate others to act.

Typically, the activist eschews deliberation, especially deliberation with persons wielding political or economic power and official representatives of institutions he believes perpetuate injustice or harm. He finds laughable the suggestion that he and his comrades should sit down with those whom he criticizes and whose policies he opposes to work out an agreement through reasoned argument they all can accept. The powerful officials have no motive to sit down with him, and even if they did agree to deliberate, they would have the power unfairly to steer the course of the discussion. Thus, the activist takes other action that he finds more effective in conveying his criticism and furthering the objectives he believes right: picketing, leafleting, guerilla theater, large and loud street demonstrations, sit-ins, and other forms of direct action, such as boycotts. Often activists make public noise outside when deliberation is supposedly taking place on the inside. Sometimes activists invade the houses of deliberation and disrupt their business by unfurling banners, throwing stink bombs, or running and shouting through the aisles. Sometimes they are convinced that an institution produces or perpetuates such wrong that the most morally appropriate thing for them to do is to try to stop its business—by blocking entrances, for example.

Morally acceptable tactics are much disputed by activists. Should they be strictly nonviolent or not, and precisely what does being nonviolent mean? Is being annoying and insulting acceptable, or should the activist be respectful? Is it acceptable to destroy or damage property as long as one does not hurt people or animals? I do not here wish to enter these debates. For the purposes of this characterization, I will assume that the activist believes that intentional violence directed at others is neither morally nor politically acceptable but that he has the right physically to defend himself if he is physically attacked. I will assume that the activist rejects tactics of intentionally producing serious damage to property—such as bombing or burning. Less damaging forms of defacement or breakage, especially as by-products of protest actions, need not be condemned.

II. DELIBERATIVE JUDGMENT OF ACTIVISM

Theories of deliberative democracy rarely mention political activities such as those I have made typical of activism, and thus we cannot derive from them a direct account of the extent to which political virtue as understood by deliberative democrats stands opposed to political virtue as I have characterized it for the activist. Nevertheless, we do know that many responsible political participants routinely condemn activists, claiming they are irrational nihilists who bring a bad name to good causes.

From the point of view of principles of deliberative democracy, what reasons might they have? We can reconstruct two kinds of reasons, I suggest. Some who see themselves guided by norms of deliberative democracy might say that activists engage in interest group politics rather than orienting their commitment to principles all can accept. They might also say that the stance of the activist is flatly unreasonable. Here I review such possible criticisms of activism from the point of view of deliberative democracy and answer them on behalf of the activist.

As I construe her for the purposes of this encounter, the deliberative democrat judges the approach to democracy the activist takes as little different from the pressure group interest-based politics that she thinks should be transcended to achieve workable agreement and legitimate policy outcomes. An interest group approach to politics encourages people to organize groups to promote particular ends through politics and policy by pressuring or cajoling policy makers to serve those interests. By means of lobbying, buying political advertisements, contributing funds to parties and candidates, and mobilizing votes for or against candidates who hold positions on certain issues, interest groups further their goals and defeat their opponents. They feel no obligation to discuss issues with those with whom their interests conflict to come to an agreement they all can accept. They simply aim to win the most for their group and engage in power politics to do so.

To this charge, the activist responds that his stance differs from that of simple interest advocacy because he is committed to a universalist rather than partisan cause. There is a significant difference, he claims, between self-interest or group interest and an interest in redressing harm and injustice. The good citizen activist is not usually motivated by personal gain or by the gain of groups he defends at an unfair expense of others. He sacrifices his time, career advancement, and money for the sake of the causes to which he is committed. He does indeed seek to bring pressure, the power of collective action, disruption, and shame to effect change in the direction of greater justice. The power he and his comrades exert in the streets, however, is usually a mere David to the Goliath of power wielded by the state and corporate actors whose policies he opposes and aims to change. The deliberative democrat who thinks that power can be bracketed by the soft tones of the seminar room is naive.

While he is suspicious of the claim that he ought to engage in deliberation with the powerful agents he believes perpetuate injustice and harm or with those who support them, moreover, the activist does not reject discussion altogether. The promulgation and exchange of information and ideas are a major part of his political work, both within his activist organizations and more broadly among other citizens whom he aims to convince that there are serious harms and injustices that they should protest and resist. When social, economic, and political institutions produce unjust structural inequalities and other serious social and environmental harms, insists the activist, it is important for citizens to try to avoid complicity with the workings of those institutions. Activities of protest, boycott, and disruption are most appropriate for getting citizens to think seriously about what until then they may have found normal and acceptable. Activities of deliberation, on the contrary, tend more to confer legitimacy on exiting institutions and effectively silence real dissent.

The deliberative democrat might claim that the stance of the activist is unreasonable. Reasonable political engagement, on this account, consists of the willingness to listen to those whom one believes is wrong, to demand reasons from them, and to give arguments aimed at persuading them to change their views. For the most part, the activist declines so to engage persons he disagrees with. Rather than on reason, according to this deliberative democrat, the activist relies on emotional appeal, slogans, irony, and disruptive tactics to protest and make his claims.

It is common in the political life of many democracies thus to label an activist stance unreasonable and even "extremist." One can interpret such blanket labeling itself as a power ploy whose function is to rule out of bounds all claims that question something basic about existing institutions and the terms in which they put political alternatives. It is important, therefore, to consider the activist answer to the charge of being an irrational extremist: it relies on far too narrow an understanding of what is reasonable.

By "reasonable" here, I mean having a sense of a range of alternatives in belief and action and engaging in considered judgment in deciding among them. The reasonable person thus is also able and willing to justify his or her claims and actions to others. As I have constructed the stance of the activist, he is principled and reasonable in this sense. He reflects on some of the wrongs that come to people and nonhuman things and has an account of some of the social causes of those wrongs that he believes are alterable. He considers alternative means for bringing attention to those wrongs and calling on others to help redress them, and he is usually quite prepared to justify the use of specific means on specific occasions, both to his comrades and to others, such as television reporters. While his principles often lead him to protest outside of or disrupt the meetings of powerful people with whom he disagrees, one of his primary reasons for such protest is to make a wider public aware of institutional wrongs and persuade that public to join him in pressuring for change in the institutions. While not deliberative, then, in the sense of engaging in orderly reason giving, most activist political engagements aim to communicate specific ideas to a wide public. They use slogans, humor, and irony to do so because discursive arguments alone are not likely to command attention or inspire action.

In the real world of politics, some nihilistic and destructive persons demonstrate and protest from blind rage or because they get pleasure from destruction. Such a nihilistic stance describes few activists, however; activists are often more self-conscious than other political actors about having good reasons for what they do and disciplining their fellows to follow rules in their collective actions. The common rhetorical move of official powers to paint all protest action with the tar of "extremism" should be resisted by anyone committed to social justice and reasonable communication.

Now that the activist has answered the deliberative democrat's suspicion that he is not worth talking to, we can hear his criticism of deliberative recommendations for political engagement and citizen virtue. I will present these challenges in four steps, giving the deliberative democrat the opportunity to respond to each.

III. DELIBERATIVE PROCEDURES ARE EXCLUSIVE

Exhorting citizens to engage in respectful argument with others they disagree with is a fine recommendation for the ideal world that the deliberative democrat theorizes, says the activist, where everyone is included and the political equal of one another. This is not the real world of politics, however, where powerful elites representing structurally dominant social segments have significant influence over political processes and decisions.

Deliberation sometimes occurs in this real world. Officials and dignitaries meet all the time to hammer out agreements. Their meetings are usually well organized with structured procedures, and those who know the rules are often able to further their objectives through them by presenting proposals and giving reasons for them, which are considered and critically evaluated by the others, who give their own reasons. Deliberation, the activist says, is an activity of boardrooms and congressional committees and sometimes even parliaments. Elites exert their power partly through managing deliberative settings. Among themselves they engage in debate about the policies that will sustain their power and further their collective interests. Entrance into such deliberative settings is usually rather tightly controlled, and the interests of many affected by the decisions made in them often receive no voice or representation. The proceedings of these meetings, moreover, are often not open to general observation, and often they leave no public record. Observers and members of the press come only by invitation. Deliberation is primarily an activity of political elites who treat one another with cordial respect and try to work out their differences. Insofar as deliberation is exclusive in this way, and insofar as the decisions reached in such deliberative bodies support and perpetuate structural inequality or otherwise have unjust and harmful consequences, says the activist, then it is wrong to prescribe deliberation for good citizens committed to furthering social justice. Under these circumstances of structural inequality and exclusive power, good citizens should be protesting outside these meetings, calling public attention to the assumptions made in them, the control exercised, and the resulting limitations or wrongs of their outcomes. They should use the power of shame and exposure to pressure deliberators to widen their agenda and include attention to more interests. As long as the proceedings exercise exclusive power for the sake of the interests of elites and against the interests of most citizens, then politically engaged citizens who care about justice and environmental preservation are justified even in taking actions aimed at preventing or disrupting the deliberations. . . .

The advocate of deliberative democracy as a prescription for political processes and the behavior of good citizens has an easy answer to this criticism of deliberation. She agrees with many things the activist says. Insofar as the proceedings of elite meetings are exclusive and nonpublic, they are not democratic, even if they are deliberative. The norms of deliberative democracy call not only for discussion among parties who use the force of argument alone and treat each other as equals. They also require publicity, accountability, and inclusion. To be democratically legitimate, policies and actions decided on by means of deliberation ought to include representation of all affected interests and perspectives. The deliberations of such inclusively representative bodies ought to be public in every way. The people who speak and vote in such deliberative settings, finally, ought to be accountable to their fellow citizens for their opinions and decisions. The deliberative democrat will likely join the activist to protest outside exclusive and private deliberations. She exhorts the activist to join her call for deliberations whose proceedings are public, accountable, and inclusive, and she allies with the activist in regarding deliberative processes as illegitimate unless they meet these conditions. She may consider activist protest a healthy means of deepening democracy, of creating open and inclusive settings of deliberative democracy.

IV. FORMAL INCLUSION IS NOT ENOUGH

Criticism of political processes of discussion and decision making, which include only powerful insiders and take place behind closed doors, is frequent and often effective in democratic politics. In response to such criticisms, official deliberative bodies have sometimes taken steps to make their processes more public and inclusive. They open their doors to observation by press and citizens, as well as publish their proceedings and evaluations of their operations. Some legislative and other official bodies have discussed and implemented measures intended to open their seats to a wider diversity of representatives, including campaign finance regulation, electoral process reform, or even quotas in party lists for underrepresented groups. In the United States in the past thirty years, norms of inclusiveness and publicity have been taken more seriously than before. Public agencies and even some powerful private agencies hold hearings to discuss policy proposals at which members of the public are invited to testify. . . .

The deliberative democrat endorses measures such as these. She thinks the good citizen should vigorously advocate for creative ways to expand the publicity of deliberations about problems and policy proposals and make them inclusive. If they have the opportunity to participate in such consultative deliberative processes, they should do so, and if they are invited to help design them, they should accept.

The activist is more suspicious even of these deliberative processes that claim to give all affected by projected policies, or at least representatives of everyone, the opportunity to express their opinions in a deliberative process. In a society structured by deep social and economic inequalities, he believes that formally inclusive deliberative processes nevertheless enact structural biases in which more powerful and socially advantaged actors have greater access to the deliberative process and therefore are able to dominate the proceedings with their interests and perspectives.

Under conditions of structural inequality, normal processes of deliberation often in practice restrict access to agents with greater resources, knowledge, or connections to those with greater control over the forum. We are familiar with the many manifestations of this effective exclusion from deliberation. Where radio and television are major fora for further deliberation, for example, citizens either need the money or connections to get airtime. Even when a series of public hearings are announced for an issue, people who might wish to speak at them need to know about them, be able to arrange their work and child care schedule to be able attend, be able to get to them, and have enough understanding of the hearing process to participate. Each of these abilities is unevenly present among members of a society.

Some have argued that such differential access and participation characterized both of the ostensibly inclusive public deliberative processes I cited above: the Oregon Medicaid process and the deliberations about the South African constitution. In the first case, participants in the consultative process turned out to be largely white, middle-class, able-bodied people, despite the fact that the program specifically was to serve lower income people. Many citizens of South Africa understood too little about the meaning of a constitution, or their lives were too occupied by survival, for them to become involved in that deliberative process.

The activist thus argues that citizens who care about justice should continue to criticize processes of public deliberation from the outside, even when the latter have formal rules aimed at producing wide participation. To the extent that structural inequalities in the society operate effectively to restrict access to these deliberative processes, their deliberations and conclusions are not legitimate. Responsible citizens should remain at least partially outside, protesting the process, agenda, and outcome of these proceedings and demonstrating against the underlying relations of privilege and disadvantage that condition them. They should aim to speak on behalf of those de facto excluded and attempt to use tactics such as strikes, boycotts, and disruptive demonstrations to pressure these bodies to act in ways that respond to the needs and interests of those effectively excluded. If we participate in these formally inclusive processes, the activist says, we help confer undeserved legitimacy on them and fail to speak for those who remain outsiders. . . .

The deliberative democrat agrees with the activist's exposure and critique of the way that structural inequalities effectively limit access of some people to formally inclusive deliberative settings. Unlike the activist, however, she thinks that the responsible citizen should engage and argue with those who design and implement these settings to persuade them that they should devote thought and resources to activities that will make them more inclusive and representative of all the interests and perspectives potentially affected by the outcome of policy discussions. In a polity that claims to be committed to democracy, it should be possible to persuade many members of a formally inclusive deliberative public that special measures may need to be taken to facilitate voice and representation for segments of the society subject to structural disadvantages. Protesting and making demands from the outside may be an effective way to bring attention to injustices that require remedy, says the deliberative democrat, but on their own they do not propel the positive institutional change that would produce greater justice. Those who believe such change is necessary must enter deliberative proceedings with those indifferent or hostile to them in an effort to persuade a democratic public of their rightness.

The activist's first two challenges have focused on the publicity and inclusiveness of the deliberative public, rather than on the terms and content of deliberations. So far, the deliberative democrat and the activist perspectives are rather close on the issues of morally legitimate political processes, inasmuch as both criticize formal and de facto exclusions from deliberations. The difference between them may reduce to how optimistic they are about whether political agents can be persuaded that there are structural injustices, the remedy for which an inclusive deliberative public ought to agree on. Once we turn to analyze issues of the terms and content of deliberations, however, we see more divergence between the deliberative democrat and the activist.

V. CONSTRAINED ALTERNATIVES

Let us suppose that by some combination of activist agitation and deliberative persuasion, some deliberative settings emerge that approximately represent all those affected by the outcome of certain policy decisions. Given the world of structural inequality as we know it, the activist believes such a circumstance will be rare at best but is willing to entertain the possibility for the sake of this argument. The activist remains suspicious of the deliberative democrat's exhortation to engage in reasoned and critical discussion with people he disagrees with, even on the supposition that the public where he engages in such discussion really includes the diversity of interests and perspectives potentially affected by policies. That is because he perceives that existing social and economic structures have set unacceptable constraints on the terms of deliberation and its agenda.

Problems and disagreements in the real world of democratic politics appear and are addressed against the background of a given history and sedimentation of unjust structural inequality, says the activist, which helps set agenda priorities and constrains the alternatives that political actors may consider in their deliberations. When this is so, both the deliberative agenda and the institutional constraints it mirrors should themselves be subject to criticism, protest, and resistance. Going to the table to meet with representatives of those interests typically served by existing institutional relations, to discuss how to deal most justly with issues that presuppose those institutional relations, gives both those institutions and deliberative process too much legitimacy. It co-opts the energy of citizens committed to justice, leaving little time for mobilizing people to bash the institutional constraints and decision-making process from the outside. Thus, the responsible citizen ought to withdraw from implicit acceptance of structural and institutional constraints by refusing to deliberate about policies within them. Let me give some examples.

A local anti-poverty advocacy group engaged in many forms of agitation and protest in the years leading up to passage of the Personal Responsibility and Work Opportunity Reconciliation Act by the U.S. Congress in the spring of 1996. This legislation fundamentally changed the terms of welfare policy in the United States. It abolished entitlements to public assistance for the first time in sixty years, allowing states to deny benefits when funds have run out. It requires recipients of Temporary Assistance to Needy Families to work at jobs after a certain period and allows states to vary significantly in their programs. Since passage of the legislation, the anti-poverty advocacy group has organized recipients and others who care about welfare justice to protest and lobby the state house to increase welfare funding and to count serving as a welfare rights advocate in local welfare offices as a "work activity."

In its desire to do its best by welfare clients, the county welfare department proposes to establish an advisory council with significant influence over the implementation and administration of welfare programs in the county. They have been persuaded by advocates of deliberative democracy that proceedings of this council should be publicly accountable and organized so as to facilitate serious discussion and criticism of alternative proposals. They believe that democratic justice calls for making this council broadly inclusive of county citizens, and they think legitimate deliberations will be served particularly if they include recipients and their advocates on the council. So they invite the anti-poverty advocacy group to send representatives to the council and ask them to name recipient representatives from among the welfare rights organization with which they work.

After deliberating among themselves for some weeks, the welfare activists decline to join the council. The constraints that federal and state law have put on welfare policy, they assert, make it impossible to administer a humane welfare policy. Such a council will deliberate about whether it would be more just to place local welfare offices here or there but will have no power to expand the number of offices. They will decide how best to administer child care assistance, but they will have no power to decide who is eligible for that assistance or the total funds to support the program. The deliberations of a county welfare implementation council face numerous other constraints that will make its outcomes inevitably unjust, according to the activist group. All citizens of the county who agree that the policy framework is unjust have a responsibility to stay outside such deliberations and instead pressure the state legislature to expand welfare options, by, for example, staging sit-ins at the state department of social services.

The deliberative democrat finds such refusal and protest action uncooperative and counterproductive. Surely it is better to work out the most just form of implementation of legislation than to distract lawmakers and obstruct the routines of overworked case workers. The activist replies that it is wrong to cooperate with policies and processes that presume unjust institutional constraints. The problem is not that policy makers and citizen deliberations fail to make arguments but that their starting premises are unacceptable.

It seems to me that advocates of deliberative democracy who believe that deliberative processes are the best way to conduct policies even under the conditions of structural inequality that characterize democracies today have no satisfactory response to this criticism. Many advocates of deliberative procedures seem to find no problem with structures and institutional constraints that limit policy alternatives in actual democracies, advocating reflective political reasoning within them to counter irrational tendencies to reduce issues to sound bites and decisions to aggregate preferences. . . . To the extent that such constraints assume existing patterns of class inequality, residential segregation, and gender division of labor as given, the activist's claim is plausible that there is little difference among the alternatives debated, and he suggests that the responsible citizen should not consent to these assumptions but instead agitate for deeper criticism and change.

The ongoing business of legislation and policy implementation will assume existing institutions and their priorities as given unless massive concerted action works to shift priorities and goals. Most of the time, then, politics will operate under the constrained alternatives that are produced by and support structural inequalities. If the deliberative democrat tries to insert practices of deliberation into existing public policy discussions, she is forced to accept the range of alternatives that existing structural constraints allow. While two decades ago in the United States, there were few opportunities for theorists of deliberative democracy to try to influence the design and process of public discussion, today things have changed. Some public officials and private foundations have become persuaded that inclusive, reasoned extensive deliberation is good for democracy and wish to implement these ideals in the policy formation process. To the extent that such implementation must presuppose constrained alternatives that cannot question existing institutional priorities and social structures, deliberation is as likely to reinforce injustice as to undermine it.

I think that the deliberative democrat has no adequate response to this challenge other than to accept the activist's suspicion of implementing deliberative processes within institutions that seriously constrain policy alternatives in ways that, for example, make it nearly impossible for the structurally disadvantaged to propose solutions to social problems that might alter the structural positions in which they stand. Only if the theory and practice of deliberative democracy are willing to withdraw from the immediacy of the already given policy trajectory can they respond to this activist challenge. The deliberative democracy should help create inclusive deliberative settings in which basic social and economic structures can be examined; such settings for the most part must be outside of and opposed to ongoing settings of official policy discussion.

VI. HEGEMONIC DISCOURSE

The deliberative democrat responds to this activist challenge, then, by proposing to create deliberative fora removed from the immediacy of the given economic imperatives and power structures, where representatives of diverse social sectors might critically discuss those imperatives and structures, with an eye to reforming the institutional context. Even at this point, however, the activist remains suspicious of deliberative practices, for still another reason traceable to structural inequality. He worries that the majority of participants in such a reflective deliberative setting will be influenced by a common discourse that itself is a complex product of structural inequality. By a "discourse," I mean a system of stories and expert knowledge diffused through the society, which convey the widely accepted generalizations about how society operates that are theorized in these terms, as well as the social norms and cultural values to which most of the people appeal when discussing their social and political problems and proposed solutions. In a society with longstanding and multiple structural inequalities, some such discourses are . . . "hegemonic": most of the people in the society think about their social relations in these terms, whatever their location in the structural inequalities. When such discursive systems frame a deliberative process, people may come to an agreement that is nevertheless at least partly conditioned by unjust power relations and for that reason should not be considered a genuinely free consent. . . . When such hegemonic discourse operates, parties to deliberation may agree on premises, they may accept a theory of their situation and give reasons for proposals that the others accept, but yet the premises and terms of the account mask the reproduction of power and injustice.

Deliberative democrats focus on the need for agreement to give policies legitimacy, and they theorize the conditions for achieving such agreement, but the idea of false or distorted agreement seems outside the theory. In opening the possibility that some consensus is false and some communication systematically distorted by power, I am not referring to consensus arrived at by excluding some affected people or that is extorted by means of threat and coercion. The phenomenon of hegemony or systematically distorted communication is more subtle than this. It refers to how the conceptual and normative framework of the members of a society is deeply influenced by premises and terms of discourse that make it difficult to think critically about aspects of their social relations or alternative possibilities of institutionalization and action. The theory and practice of deliberative democracy have no tools for raising the possibility that deliberations may be closed and distorted in this way. It lacks a theory of, shall we call it, ideology, as well as an account of the genealogy of discourses and their manner of helping to constitute the way individuals see themselves and their social world. For most deliberative democrats, discourse seems to be more "innocent." . . .

In analyzing how actual public discussions may fall short of the normative requirements of legitimate democratic discussion, Bohman invokes a notion of distorted communication or ideology. This level of the influence of structural inequality over public discussion is the most insidious because it is the least apparent to all participants. It concerns the conceptual and imagistic frame for discussion, which often contains falsifications, biases, misunderstandings, and even contradictions that go unnoticed and uncriticized largely because they coincide with hegemonic interests or reflect existing social realities as though they are unalterable. For example, a discourse may distort communication, for example, by means of a rhetoric that presents as universal a perspective on experience or society derived from a specific social position.

Let me offer a couple of examples of hegemonic discourses that may produce false consensus. The first comes from discourses about poverty and ways of addressing poverty through policy. Despite wide and vigorous debates about the causes and cures of poverty, both in the United States and increasingly in other parts of the world, there is a significant new consensus on many terms of the debate. There seems to be wide agreement that poverty should be conceptualized as a function of the failure of individuals to develop various skills and capacities necessary for inclusion in modern labor markets. Disagreement rages about the degree to which responsibility for such failure should be laid on those individuals and their families or instead should be located in social institutions of education, social service, or economic development. That anti-poverty policy must ultimately transform individuals to fit better into the contemporary structures of wage employment, however, almost goes without saying. There is almost no other way to think about poverty policy than as a labor market policy.

International debates about greenhouse gas emissions, to take another example, contain fierce disagreement about whether and how such emissions should be reduced and how the burdens of reductions should be distributed across the globe. Should richer, more advanced industrial states be required to reduce emissions in greater proportion to less developed countries? Are markets in pollution rights useful policy tools? Should governments subsidize development of "green" technologies for industrial production and private transportation? These debates take place within terms of discussion that only marginalized environmentalists question. The discussions assume that the economies of any developed society must rely heavily on the burning of fossil fuels and that a high standard of living involves air-conditioned buildings and lots of consumer goods, including a private automobile for every household. The social imaginations of both "developed" and "less developed" countries have few ideas for alternative forms of living that would not produce large carbon emissions.

Certain activists concerned with specific areas of social life claim to identify such ideologies and hegemonic discourses. Their doing so is necessarily partial with respect to social problems and policy issues because ideology critique of this nature requires considerable thought and study, even for one set of issues. Democratic theory that emphasizes discussion as a criterion of legitimacy requires a more developed theory of the kinds and mechanisms of ideology and methods for performing critique of specific political discussion. Such ideology critique needs not only to be able to analyze specific exchanges and speech but also theorize how media contribute to naturalizing assumptions and making it difficult for participants in a discussion to speak outside of a certain set of concepts and images. Because he suspects some agreements of masking unjust power relations, the activist believes it is important to continue to challenge these discourses and the deliberative processes that rely on them, and often he must do so by nondiscursive means—pictures, song, poetic imagery, and expressions of mockery and longing performed in rowdy and even playful ways aimed not at commanding assent but disturbing complacency. One of the activist's goal is to make us wonder about what we are doing, to rupture a stream of thought, rather than to weave an argument.

I have presented the deliberative democrat and the activist as two distinct characters with different recommendations for the best forms of political engagement. Such exclusive opposition between the stances is artificial, of course. Many people and organizations move between the stances in their political lives, depending on the issues at stake, who they are interacting with or confronting, and what they see as possibilities for action and achievement. I have put the stances in dialogue with one another precisely because I think they both are important for democratic theory and practice.

I have separated the stances into two opposing characters, however, to highlight the activist stance more than most recent democratic theory has done and to cast a critical eye on some tendencies in deliberative democratic theory and practice. The activist's charges are serious, and they raise some issues not thematized in recent deliberative theory. From this dialogue, I draw two conclusions about where democratic theory should go.

First, democratic theory should keep a distance from democratic practices in existing structural circumstances. While theorists ought to learn from on-going processes of discussion and decision making, and as citizens should participate in them in whatever ways seem most just and effective, we should resist the temptation to consider that ideals of deliberative democracy are put into practice when public officials or foundations construct procedures influenced by these ideas. Democratic theory, including the theory of deliberative democracy, should understand itself primarily as a critical theory, which exposes the exclusions and constraints in supposed fair processes of actual decision making, which make the legitimacy of their conclusions suspect.

Second, we can deny that deliberative democracy recommends that citizens be willing always to engage discursively with all interests and social segments, reasonably expressing opinions and criticizing others. We can conceive the exchange of ideas and processes of communication taking place in a vibrant democracy as far more rowdy, disorderly, and decentered. . . . In this alternative conceptualization, processes of engaged and responsible democratic communication include street demonstrations and sit-ins, musical works, and cartoons, as much as parliamentary speeches and letters to the editor. Normatively emblematic democratic communication here shifts from simply a willingness to give reasons for one's claims and listen to others to a broader understanding of the generation and influence of public opinion. In this broader understanding, participants articulate reasonable appeals to justice and also expose the sources and consequences of structural inequalities in law, the hegemonic terms of discourse, and the environment of everyday practice.

Even if we follow these recommendations, however, the dissonance between the stance of the deliberative democrat and the activist does not dissolve. Individuals and organizations seeking to undermine injustice and promote justice need both to engage in discussion with others to persuade them that there are injustices that ought to be remedied and to protest and engage in direct action. The two kinds of activities cannot usually occur together, however, and for this reason one of them is liable to eclipse the other. The best democratic theory and practice will affirm them both while recognizing the tension between them.

Chapter 35

Polarization and Democratic Citizenship

Robert B. Talisse

Robert B. Talisse explores the problems that polarization poses for democracy. He distinguishes "political" from "belief" polarization. The former is the condition where political factions share no common ground. The latter, however, is a widespread phenomenon by which individuals come to adopt extreme beliefs. Talisse argues that belief polarization undermines our ability to fulfill our duties as democratic citizens.

It is often asserted that contemporary democracy is being undermined by extreme political divisions. The lamentations over political divides are frequently accompanied by related warnings about political "bubbles" and "echo chambers"; these are said to produce "intellectual closure," "groupthink," "spin," "post-truth," and forms of "derangement." All in all, these phenomena are claimed to be the marks of *polarization*, a condition where political officials and others are so deeply divided that there is no basis for compromise, coordination, or even productive communication among them. In order to thrive, a democracy needs to get things done, yet polarization paralyzes democracy. Thus the situation seems dire.

Matters seem even more urgent once it is noted that polarization extends beyond the formal apparatus of parties and officials. These days, the citizenry is polarized as well. A recent Pew study shows that U.S. citizens are more inclined than ever to regard the ideas of their political opponents as not only misguided, but as a significant threat to the wellbeing of the nation; they are also more likely to regard citizens who affiliate with an opposing party as unintelligent, dishonest, untrustworthy, lazy, and immoral.[1] Intriguingly, citizens also report a strong desire for political compromise among governing parties. Alas, there's no silver lining in that result. The Pew study also shows that in this context, U.S. citizens understand "compromise" to mean what one would otherwise call capitulation. In other words, they want compromise "on their own terms"; their yearning for compromise is actually a desire for their political opponents to simply give way.[2] Compromise in this sense involves overcoming obstructionists rather than meeting others in the middle. Arguably, this is not compromise at all. Hence citizens' longing for compromise and an easing of partisan division is itself another manifestation of polarization.

Unsurprisingly, there has emerged a genre of popular political commentary devoted to explaining the dangers of polarization. However, it is not always clear from this literature what is meant by *polarization* beyond the general intransigence among politicians. Stubbornness and consequent logjams within government are certainly frustrating, and sometimes even disconcerting. But they are also nothing new. Yet popular discussions are animated by the sense that polarization is a new, or at least newly ascendant, phenomenon. To make sense of this, we need a more precise account of what polarization is. Only then will we be able to discern why polarization is problematic and how it should be addressed.

In this essay, then, I begin by distinguishing two broad concepts of polarization: *political* polarization and *belief* polarization. After providing a detailed analysis of the latter, I will argue that belief polarization lies at the root of current political dysfunctions. In addition, the argument will show that belief polarization is best understood as initiating a social dynamic that results not only in the deadlock and distrust that characterizes political polarization, but also a mounting incapacity on the part of individuals to enact democratic citizenship. Hence it will be argued that whereas polarization presents several problems for democratic politics, the overarching difficulty is that it is politically degenerative—it erodes our democratic capacities. Accordingly, the aims of this paper are strictly diagnostic; my proposal for addressing polarization is developed elsewhere.[3]

1. TWO CONCEPTS OF POLARIZATION

To begin, two broad kinds of polarization need to be distinguished: *political polarization* and *belief polarization.*

Political polarization denotes a family of phenomena having to do with what might be called the *political distance* between political opponents and the consequent dissolution of common ground between them. There are several ways in which this distance can be conceived. For example, we can measure political polarization by looking at the distance between the *platforms* of competing political parties. Where *platform* polarization is acute, competing political parties diverge sharply on nearly every issue. Another measure of political polarization is partisan ideological uniformity, what might be aptly characterized as ideological *purity* among partisans. An especially high level of *partisan* political polarization is marked by the absence of moderates within partisan groups, and the gradual weeding out of, say, "conservative Democrats" and "liberal Republicans." A third metric looks at the *affective* distance between political opponents. *Affective* political polarization is marked by high levels within a partisan group of distrust and antagonism toward the members of opposing groups.

Although all three forms of political polarization are often found together, they are nonetheless distinct. For example, affective political polarization may obtain among persons who are not especially at odds over particular policy issues. Similarly, high levels of platform polarization are consistent with meager degrees of partisan polarization. The phenomena get complicated quickly. For our purposes, however, it suffices to note that political polarization in all of its forms has to do with the distance *between* opposing groups.

Political polarization is to be distinguished from belief polarization.[4] In contrast with political polarization, belief polarization afflicts individuals within groups. To be more specific, when individuals talk with mainly likeminded others about the matters upon which they are in agreement, each discussant tends gradually to embrace a more extreme version of his or her initial opinion. Although belief polarization often will have the effect of intensifying the ideological distance between opposing political groups, the phenomenon itself is not a measure of that distance; it instead involves a shift *internal* to likeminded groups. In short, belief polarization is that phenomenon by which interaction with likeminded others turns us into more extreme versions of ourselves.

Belief polarization presents us with a lot to unpack. But before attempting the necessary analysis, we should first examine the experimental findings documenting the phenomenon.

2. THE BASIC PHENOMENON

The first thing to note is that belief polarization has been found to be operative within groups of an impressive variety of kinds, from officially defined assemblies—juries, panels of judges, Boards of Trust, and investment groups—to informal clusters of ordinary people simply talking about views they share.[5] Furthermore, belief polarization does not discriminate between the different *kinds* of belief that group members may hold in common. Likeminded groups polarize regardless of whether they are discussing banal matters of fact such as the elevation of a given city, personal matters of taste (assessments the attractiveness of a face or comfortableness of a chair) or questions about value.[6] What's more, the phenomenon operates regardless of the explicit *point* of the group's discussion. Likeminded groups polarize when they are talking for the sake of deciding an action that the group will take (e.g., participating in a protest, rendering a verdict, placing a bet); and they polarize also when there is no specific decision to be reached and no collective action to be taken. Finally, the phenomenon has been studied throughout the world, and is found to be prevalent in likeminded groups regardless of the demographic profiles of their members; we are vulnerable to belief polarization regardless of nationality, race, gender, religion, economic status, and level of education.

Next turn to the phenomenon itself. One of the earliest experiments regarding group polarization was conducted in France in the late 1960s with a group of teenage males. They were asked to discuss both their (variously positive) views about their prime minister and their (variously negative) views about American foreign policy. The individuals emerged from the discussion with more thoroughly positive views of de Gaulle and more intensely negative views of American foreign policy than those they held prior to the conversation.[7]

In another early study, Michigan high-schoolers were sorted according to their antecedently expressed level of racial prejudice. The likeminded groups then were tasked with discussing several issues concerning race in the United States, including the question of whether racism is the cause of the socio-economic disadvantages faced by African Americans. Following the conversations with their respective groups of likeminded others, those who antecedently showed a high level of racial prejudice came to embrace more ardently the view that racism is *not* responsible for the disadvantages faced by African Americans, while those antecedently disposed toward low levels of racial prejudice grew more accepting of the view that racism is the cause of such disadvantages. Once again, discussion among likeminded people amplified the members' pre-discussion tendencies. Accordingly, the ideological distance between the two groups also expanded.[8]

A similar experiment involved adults who on the basis of an initial screening were classified into gender-mixed groups according to their views concerning the social roles of women. Once sorted into "feminist" and "chauvinist" groups, each discussed amongst themselves the merits of various statements about the role of women in society—statements like "a woman should be as free as a man to propose marriage," and "women with children should not work outside the home if they don't have to financially." The result was that members of the feminist discussion group became more profeminist, while the chauvinist group became more chauvinist—though not to a significant degree.[9]

In 2005, a collection of Coloradoans were sorted according to an initial screening test into "liberal" and "conservative" groups. Each group was then asked to discuss the following three policy issues that admitted of an obvious liberal-conservative divide: same-sex marriage, affirmative action, and international treaties to combat global warming. The pattern of belief polarization was observed. After discussion within likeminded groups, liberal participants, who were antecedently disposed to favor a global warming treaty, came to endorse more enthusiastically the proposition that the United States should enter into such a treaty. Conservatives who were initially neutral on the idea of such a treaty came to ardently oppose it after discussion with fellow conservatives. Similarly, attitudes toward same-sex civil unions and affirmative action belief-polarized following group discussion: liberal support intensified, while opposition among conservatives grew more resolute. Importantly, the shift in group members' attitudes also resulted in a greater degree of internal homogeneity. That is, after discussion, not only did the members of each group tend to shift to a view more extreme than the one he or she held prior to the discussion, attitudes within the group became more uniform. Each shifted into a more extreme version of his or her prior self *and also* became more like the others in the group.[10]

Thus far, I have described experiments demonstrating that discussion in likeminded groups produces shifts in opinion toward extremity in the direction of the individual's pre-discussion inclination. These shifts have been described mainly as intensifications of attitude or view. But, as one would expect, such shifts also affect behavior.

Consider two cases where this practical ramification of belief polarization is evident. In mock jury experiments involving punitive damage awards, when jury members are initially agreed that the harm is severe and damages should be awarded, their deliberation produces a verdict of a significantly larger award than any individual juror's initial pre-deliberation assessment. The same goes for juries whose members are initially inclined to think that the harm in question is not particularly extreme and only a low degree of punishment is in order. After deliberation, the verdict is more lenient than individual jurors' initial inclination.[11]

Another study finds that group discussion of an event that participants agree constitutes a serious violation of justice—sex discrimination committed by an elected official, for example—leads to a greater inclination among the discussants to engage in organized protest. Crucially, that's not all. Among discussants who see the violation as especially egregious, the enhanced readiness to protest is accompanied by a willingness that exceeds their pre-discussion inclination to protest in ways that are overtly militant and thus riskier.[12]

In summary, belief polarization is an uncommonly robust phenomenon. It involves a shift toward greater extremity in the opinions of individuals who interact only or mainly with others who are likeminded. As one would expect, those shifts tend to manifest in behaviors that are more extreme than those that individuals would otherwise be inclined to enact. The pervasiveness of the belief polarization phenomenon and the vastness of the documentation amplify the need for explanation of the *mechanisms* that produce it.

3. THE MECHANISM OF BELIEF POLARIZATION

We have seen that discussion among likeminded people drives discussants to shift toward extremity in the direction of their pre-discussion inclination. What explains this? Two views are found in the literature, what I will call the *informational* account and the *social comparison* account. We will see in this section that although each captures something important about belief polarization, neither is sufficient.

The *informational* account has it that the belief polarization phenomenon admits of an obvious explanation. Those engaged in discussion with likeminded others are exposed to a high concentration of affirming reasons, ideas, and "persuasive arguments."[13] Moreover, it is likely that for any particular participant, some of what is heard in the course of group discussion will be novel and innovative, considerations that he or she had not noticed before. This circumstance is accompanied by a corresponding scarcity within the group of articulations of countervailing or disconfirming considerations. Consequently, group members absorb the new information, and revise their own view in light of it. When this revision occurs amidst a general tendency among group members to underestimate the extent to which the "argument pool" from which they are drawing is skewed decidedly in favor of their position, one should expect shifts in the direction of extremity.[14] In fact, under such conditions, we often have *adequate reason* to shift.

Although information-exchange is surely part of the explanatory story of belief polarization, it cannot be the *entire* story. Consider a few findings that are inconsistent with the strictly informational account. First, belief polarization has been found to occur even when new and novel information is not presented in group discussion. In fact, it has been found to occur even in contexts where group interactions involve no exchange of information at all;

"mere exposure" to the fact that a group shares a general belief tendency has been found sufficient to produce polarization.[15] Consider additionally that in likeminded groups, members who already hold an extreme view of the matter under discussion shift to an even more extreme position more drastically and more rapidly than those who begin from a more moderate stance.[16] Finally, within likeminded groups, the presence of an extremist member does not significantly amplify polarization, despite the fact that in discussion the most extreme members talk the most and speak at greater length.[17]

The competing *social comparison* account holds that belief polarization is driven entirely by social dynamics. Specifically, the account holds that belief polarization is the result of in-group *comparisons*. Members of a likeminded group care about how they are perceived by the other members. In the course of discussion, they get a better feel for the general tendencies within the group, and, wanting to appear to others neither as a half-hearted outlier nor as an over-the-top fanatic, they update their opinions to keep them in pace with what they perceive to be the dominant tendencies. More precisely, group members revise so that their view lies notably above what they perceive to be the mean, but beneath what they regard as unacceptably radical; they seek to be perceived by the group as "basically similar" to the rest of the group and yet "desirably distinctive."[18] Now, given that group members are engaging simultaneously in this kind of recalibration, and that the most fervent group members are likely to speak more and more often in discussion, the tendency to escalating extremity is to be expected. Espousing a view that reflects what one perceives to be the non-fanatical hardline within the group is a reliable way to signal to others one's authenticity *qua* group member.

Unsurprisingly, then, belief polarization is enhanced in contexts where group identity is made salient to the discussants.[19] That is, group members shift further and more rapidly in the direction of extremity when their discussion is accompanied by an acknowledgment that members constitute a group not merely because they agree about the matter under discussion, but that they agree on that issue *because* they share some deeper social identity. What's more, likeminded groups shift less rapidly and to a lesser extent when discussion of the issue upon which they agree is conducted after the recognition that the discussants share no deeper identity or are in some significant respect unalike.[20]

The social comparison view improves upon the strictly informational account. However, it too is incomplete. It turns out that just as belief polarization can occur in the absence of the exchange of information, it can be induced in the absence of in-group comparisons, too. Indeed, the phenomenon can be activated even in the absence of anything that would count as *interaction* among the members of the likeminded group. It is not face-to-face *comparisons* that drive the phenomenon so much as the subject's own internal estimations of the dominant tendencies within his or her identity group. Neither information-exchange nor in-group comparison is strictly necessary for the effect; rather, the relevant extremity shifts occur simply in light of group-affiliated *corroboration* of one's views. That is, belief polarization can occur simply when an individual is caused to feel that a group with which she identifies widely shares a view that she espouses. She need not hear any reasons in favor of the view, nor need she be in the presence of other members of the group with whom she can compare herself. The brute impression that the relevant people affirm roughly the things that she affirms suffices for an extremity shift in belief content.[21] In short, the realization that one's belief is popular among one's identity group suffices for belief polarization.

Thus a third account of the mechanism driving belief polarization emerges, what we can call the *corroboration view*. According to this account, an extremity shift in belief content and in overall commitment to our perspective can occur simply as a result of in-group corroboration. Importantly, the corroboration can come by way of highly indirect channels. For example, being presented with data showing that liberals widely oppose genetically modified food can prompt belief polarization within liberals who already incline toward that view. Exposure to a poll showing that conservatives overwhelmingly favor a particular military action can produce an extremity shift in the belief content of a conservative already favorably disposed to that action. The details are complicated, but here's a simplistic explanation that captures what's going on. Corroboration from others with whom we identify makes us *feel* good about our shared beliefs.[22] When we feel good about what we believe, we feel *affirmed* in our social identity. In turn, when we feel affirmed in this way, we intensify our attitudes and shift to more extreme belief contents. This indicates that although belief polarization predictably occurs in discussions and other kinds of comparison-enabling interaction among likeminded people, these settings are not strictly *necessary* in order to produce the effect.

An intriguing implication follows. As the relevant kind of corroboration can be indirect, extremity shifts can be induced simply by features of the social environment that make salient to individuals that some group with which they identify tends to embrace a belief that they hold. These prompts need not be verbal, explicit, or literal; they can be merely implicit signals to group members that some belief is prevalent among them.[23] Note further that as corroboration is really a numbers game, those with the power to present the *appearance* of widespread acceptance among a particular social group of some particular view thereby have the power to induce extremity shifts among those who identify with that group. I take it that readers are familiar with various warnings about how the Internet and, in particular, social media platforms are polarization machines.[24] The corroboration view suggests a result that is even more troubling. Irrespective of the choices we make to curate our informational exposure, our surroundings—the physical and social environments that we inhabit in our day-to-day life—can prompt belief polarization.

To summarize, belief polarization is a phenomenon by which we are transformed into more extreme versions of ourselves. It is activated when we are primed to think that the beliefs that we hold on the basis of our salient *social identities* are popular among those who share that identity. In other words, when we are given the impression that our beliefs are highly corroborated among the members of a social group with which we identify, we will shift into more extreme versions of ourselves. Consequently, although likeminded discussion is a fertile *site* for belief polarization it is not necessary; the phenomenon owes less to any features of *discussion* and more to the fact that group discussion is reliably a context in which shared identity is made salient and dominant group beliefs are corroborated.

4. THE POLARIZATION DYNAMIC

Belief polarization is disconcerting in several respects. For one thing, it suggests that we are far more susceptible to a kind of peer pressure, more conformist, and more driven in our thinking by group membership than we may like. It also seems that counteracting these vulnerabilities is more difficult than we might have expected. Features of our *environment* can induce belief polarization, and they might be impossible to evade. But the trouble does not stop with our *individual* vulnerability to the phenomenon. Belief polarization has implications for interactions across identity groups. As belief polarization changes what we think, it also changes what we think of others. And this is where we find polarization's most troubling threat to democracy.

As members of a given group transform into more extreme versions of themselves, there is a corresponding shift in their views regarding those who do not share their group identity. Indeed, belief polarization is accompanied by an intensification of *negative* assessments of opposing groups, their members, and their views. So although belief polarization occurs *internally* to believers in light of their group identities, it nonetheless involves spillovers that impact social relations more generally.

We might say that belief polarization initiates a broader social and political dynamic. Corroboration from the relevant identity group renders us more extreme. But from the standpoint of that kind of shift, opposing views and countervailing considerations begin to appear to us as distorted, feeble, and unfounded. So as belief polarization takes effect, we come not only to believe firmly more extreme things in line with our social identity, we also lose sensitivity to the reasons of our opponents. Accordingly, once we are sufficiently belief polarized, those who espouse views that differ from ours will strike us as progressively more benighted, incoherent, irrational, and perhaps even unintelligible. Thus the intellectual distance separating us from others seems to expand momentously; and indeed, those who hold views that run directly contrary to our own will strike us as extremists, people devoted to obviously untenable ideas.[25] What's more, as the opposition grows more unintelligible to us, their views will also come to look to us as increasingly monolithic. Consequently, we will be prone to conclude that their ideas, arguments, and criticisms are wholly without merit and thus not worth engaging, and we might even actively avoid contact with them. Furthermore, we grow more inclined to see those who hold views that differ from ours to be in need of *diagnosis* and *treatment* rather than reasons and explanations; we thereby also come to see them as political obstacles that need to be surmounted rather than fellow citizens in need of convincing. Of course, this further ensconces us within our own group, which in turn further entrenches our group identity and enhances the belief polarization, driving us to further extremity.

This troubling dynamic will be evident to even casual observers of political discourse in contemporary democracies. Our social environments are increasingly crowded with calls to our political allegiances, which thereby make salient to us our political identities. On the basis of these prompts, we are exposed to belief polarization. And as belief polarization affects our views of others, we can discern a tight link between it and the three forms of political polarization that we set out earlier. As we become more extreme versions of ourselves, we thereby increase uniformity within our political group (partisan political polarization), intensify our distrust and animosity for those who are different, and also create progressively deeper affective rifts across partisan divides (affective political polarization); and this in turn incentivizes parties and political elites to punctuate their opposition (platform political polarization). Again, all of this occurs within a self-reinforcing and downward-spiraling dynamic: belief polarization generates political polarization, which in turn fosters further belief polarization and sets the polarization dynamic in motion. Thus we actually become more like what our most vehement political opponents say we are; and they grow more closely to fit our images of them.

5. POLARIZATION AS A THREAT TO DEMOCRACY

We now can see the problem that polarization poses for democracy. Deadlock and partisan rancor are only the tip of the iceberg. Given the account of belief polarization developed above, we see how political polarization often has belief polarization at its root. And belief polarization strikes at the most fundamental capacities that we need as democratic citizens. As I suggested at the beginning of this essay, belief polarization is democratically degenerative. By way of conclusion, I will spell this out.

Democracy is many things: a form of constitutional republic, a system of government, a decision procedure, a method for selecting officials, and so on. But underneath all of these ways of understanding democracy lies a commitment to the moral ideal of collective self-government among political equals.

The democrat's commitment to political equality does not amount to the idea that all citizens equally admirable, or equal in *every* respect. Political equality is the commitment to the idea that in *politics*, no one is another's subordinate. Put differently, among political equals, all political power is always *accountable*. The democratic thought is that where citizens have equal rights to hold government accountable, they retain their status as political equals even while being subject to laws that they may find objectionable.

Accordingly, democracy is built on the premise that disputes over how political power should be deployed will be ongoing among citizens. Yet this commitment to enduring political contestation presents a difficulty. Democracy depends on the capacity of citizens to regard *each other* as political equals, even when they disagree bitterly about things that matter most.[26] They must sustain a commitment to recognizing one another as *entitled* to an equal say in politics, even when they are vehemently opposed on political issues.

Maintaining this stance is not easy. It's plausible to think that a central element of our present political dysfunctions lies within the dissolution of our capacities to see our fellow citizens as our political equals, despite our ongoing political disagreements. Recall that the polarization dynamic leads us to regard those with whom we disagree as increasingly alien, irrational, immoral, and untrustworthy. Again, this leads us to see them as mere *obstacles* and *impediments*; and this, in turn, encourages us to regard politics as the simple exercise of power. In regarding politics in this way, we abandon a core element of the democratic ideal and thereby exacerbate democracy's dysfunctions. It has not been my aim in this essay to propose a remedy for the problems that polarization raises for democracy. However, in thinking about how to address these problems, it helps to see that belief polarization does not merely transform us into more extreme versions of ourselves; given the dynamic it sets in motion, it also turns us into people who are less capable of dealing reasonably with those who are unlike us.

Notes

CHAPTER 14

1. Superseded by section 3 of the 20th amendment.
2. Changed by section 1 of the 26th amendment.

CHAPTER 27

1. I shall use the term *doctrine* for comprehensive views of all kinds and the term *conception* for a political conception and its component parts, such as the conception of the person as citizen. The term *idea* is used as a general term and may refer to either as the context determines.

2. The background culture includes, then, the culture of churches and associations of all kinds, and institutions of learning at all levels, especially universities and professional schools, scientific and other societies. In addition, the nonpublic political culture mediates between the public political culture and the background culture. This comprises media—properly so named—of all kinds.

3. Deliberative democracy limits the reasons citizens may give in supporting their political opinions to reasons consistent with their seeing other citizens as equals.

4. See John Rawls, *Political Liberalism* (New York: Colombia University Press, 1996), lecture I, §4.

5. Note here that different political conceptions of justice will represent different interpretations of the constitutional essentials and matters of basic justice. There are also different interpretations of the same conception, since its concepts and values may be taken in different ways. There is not, then, a sharp line between where a political conception ends and its interpretation begins, nor need there be. All the same, a conception greatly limits its possible interpretations, otherwise discussion and argument could not proceed. For example, a constitution declaring the freedom

427

of religion, including the freedom to affirm no religion, along with the separation of church and state, may appear to leave open the question whether church schools may receive public funds, and if so, in what way. The difference here might be seen as how to interpret the same political conception, one interpretation allowing public funds, the other not; or alternatively, as the difference between two political conceptions. In the absence of particulars, it does not matter which we call it. The important point is that since the content of public reason is a family of political conceptions, that content admits the interpretations we may need. It is not as if we were stuck with a fixed conception, much less with one interpretation of it.

6. Political liberalism is sometimes criticized for not itself developing accounts of these social roots of democracy and setting out the formation of its religious and other supports. Yet political liberalism does recognize these social roots and stresses their importance. Obviously the political conceptions of toleration and freedom of religion would be impossible in a society in which religious freedom were not honored and cherished.

7. These burdens . . . are sources or causes of reasonable disagreement between reasonable and rational persons. They involve balancing the weight of different kinds of evidence and kinds of values, and the like, and they affect both theoretical and practical judgments.

CHAPTER 28

1. Bertolt Brecht, *The Caucasian Chalk Circle*, trans. Eric Bentley (New York: Grove Press, 1947).

2. "Moderation" as conceived here includes a wide array of possible views. At one extreme, the moderate might hold that the right to a democratic say is just a tie-breaker that favours a democratic over a non-democratic regime if the results of each would be equally good. At the other extreme, one might hold that the right to a democratic say is the right of rights in the sense that it trumps all others combined, and one should always prefer the more democratic over the less democratic regime, allowing the justice of the results of the operation of the system only to act as a tie-breaker among equally democratic regimes. Of course, there are indefinitely many intermediate views.

3. Christiano and Waldron develop versions of this position. For Christiano, the intrinsic fairness of democratic procedures follows as a uniquely uncontroversial inference from a conception of substantive justice whose other significant implications are controversial. See Thomas Christiano, *The Rule of the Many* (Boulder, CO: Westview Press, 1996), and "Knowledge and Power in the Justification of Democracy," *Australasian Journal of Philosophy* 79, no. 2 (2001): 197–215; Jeremy Waldron, *Law and Disagreement* (Oxford: Oxford University Press, 1999).

4. The claim in the text that rights vary in the extent to which they confer power over the lives of other people and that rights that involve significant power over the lives of others require a best results justification might be challenged. The challenge repeats the point that any moral right involves power over others. Consider many peo-

ple's exercise of their private ownership rights over small resource holdings. In the aggregate, these exercises of a very small degree of power might very significantly restrict other people's life options. Millions of people might exercise their rights in ways that leave some individuals with just a single employment option or access to just one person who is willing to sell them food needed to live. How does this differ from the way that many people's exercises of the franchise might aggregate to issue in coercive rules that specify how others shall live their lives? In reply: I don't deny that any moral right you might care to name might in some circumstances confer power over the lives of others. I deny this must be so. Consider a world in which small groups of voluntarily associating adults live at great distance from each other. The members of each group may have many moral rights that do not, in isolation or in the aggregate, involve significant power over the lives of others. Moreover, in the case just imagined, where many people exercise rights over small bits of property that in the aggregate significantly begin to restrict the lives of others, I would say the "intrinsic moral right" gives way and a best results standard becomes operative. Here I intend to contrast moral rights that confer lots of power over the individual's own life and moral rights that involve significant power to direct the lives of others. One might hold that moral rights that confer significant control over the direction of one's own life are justified by a principle of autonomy or personal sovereignty. Hence your right to act as you choose so long as you do not harm others in certain specified ways might be thought not to require a best results justification. Your right stems from a right of personal sovereignty, not from the fact that you are more competent to run your own life than others are to run it for you.

5. Why do not the pro-autocracy considerations adduced here suffice to establish at least a strong presumption in favour of the claim that autocracy is morally superior to democracy all things considered? Three countervailing concerns are pertinent. One is "Quis custodiet custodies?" Concentrating political power in the hands of an elite can produce horrible consequences if the elite becomes corrupt or incompetent. In choosing forms of governance, we should give special weight to preventing moral catastrophes. (A system of Madisonian checks and balances might mitigate this problem.) A second consideration is that political science has not devised a feasible reliable procedure for distinguishing competent from less competent agents and installing only the former as rulers. A third consideration, prominent in democratic theorists such as J. S. Mill, is that aside from a possible tendency to produce better legislation and policies and better implementation of these laws and policies, democracy tends to produce other indirect morally valuable results such as social solidarity and the moral and intellectual development of the democratic citizens. A fourth consideration is that if people are somewhat disposed to use whatever power they have to advance their interests, it is better (though not good), other things being equal, that laws and policies cater to the interests of majorities than to the interests of smaller groups.

6. David Estlund, "Making Truth Safe for Democracy," in *The Idea of Democracy*, eds. David Copp, Jean Hampton, and John E. Roemer (Cambridge: Cambridge University Press, 1993), 88. It should be noted that Estlund himself is trying to defeat the claim that authoritarianism in the form of rule by moral experts is morally required. I am treating his argument as though he were making a positive argument for the right to a democratic say.

7. John Stuart Mill, "Considerations on Representative Government in John Stuart Mill," in *Collected Works*, vol. 19, ed. J. M. Robson (Toronto: University of Toronto Press, 1977), 474.

8. Waldron, *Law and Disagreement*, 253.

9. However, Waldron overreaches in stating that the point of political procedures is to settle the truth about what rights we have. A vote can fix the content of legal rights in some political jurisdiction, but this does not settle the issues (1) whether it is morally right that these legal rights are instituted and enforced and (2) whether these legal rights coincide with the moral rights that people have in this setting.

10. G. E. M. Anscombe, "War and Murder," in *Ethics, Religion and Politics: Collected Papers*, vol. 3 (Minneapolis: University of Minnesota Press, 1981), 52.

11. Waldron, *Law and Disagreement*, 250–1.

12. See Christiano, "Knowledge and Power in the Justification of Democracy." Christiano deploys a narrow publicity requirement in his argument.

CHAPTER 29

1. Walter Bagehot, *Physics and Politics* (Kitchener: Batoche Books, 2001), 89.

2. John Dewey, *The Public and Its Problems* (New York: H. Holt and Company, 1927).

3. John Dewey, "Creative Democracy: The Task Before Us," in *The Later Works of John Dewey, 1925–1953*, vol. 14, ed. J. A. Boydston (Carbondale: Southern Illinois University Press, 1981), 228.

4. Dewey, *The Later Works of John Dewey, 1925–1953*, vol. 14, 227–28.

5. See Elizabeth Anderson, "The Democratic University: The Role of Justice in the Production of Knowledge," *Social Philosophy and Policy* 12, no. 2 (1995): 186–219, and "Racial Integration as a Compelling Interest," *Constitutional Commentary* 21, no. 1 (2004): 101–27.

6. John Rawls, "Kantian Constructivism in Moral Theory," *Journal of Philosophy* 77 (1980): 543.

7. John Dewey and James Tufts, *Ethics* in *The Later Works of John Dewey, 1925–1953*, vol. 7, ed. J. A. Boydston (Carbondale: Southern Illinois University Press, 1981), 216.

8. John Stuart Mill, "Subjection of Women," in *Three Essays* (Oxford: Oxford University Press, 1975), 192.

9. John Stuart Mill, *Considerations on Representative Government* (New York: Harper & Brothers, 1862), 173.

10. John Stuart Mill, *Utilitarianism* (Indianapolis: Bobbs-Merrill, 1957), 40.

11. Dewey, *The Public and Its Problems*, 283.

12. Dewey, *The Public and Its Problems*.

13. Mill, *Utilitarianism*, 12.

14. John Dewey, *Human Nature and Conduct*, in *The Middle Works of John Dewey, 1899–1924*, vol. 14, ed. J. A. Boydston (Carbondale: Southern Illinois University Press, 1976), 193–99.

15. John Dewey, "Valuation and Experimental Knowledge," in *The Middle Works of John Dewey, 1899–1924*, vol. 13, ed. J. A. Boydston (Carbondale: Southern Illinois University Press, 1976).

CHAPTER 30

1. Perhaps an example may clarify this procedure further: let us take the cases of Great Britain, the United States of America, and Israel as three models of liberal-democratic societies whose political and legal order is based upon some form of recognition of the norm of moral respect for persons. Certainly all three societies enjoy a system of parliamentary democracy in which, through legislatively or constitutionally determined periodic elections, public officials are brought to and removed from office. In all three societies individuals enjoy certain rights and liberties that are upheld by the political system and protected by the courts. However, these societies have radically divergent and at times incompatible views of what constitutes the legitimate exercise of the right of free speech. Whereas in the United States considerations of public propriety, fair trial, or national security would hardly serve as routine grounds on the basis of which to curtail First Amendment rights, in Great Britain and Israel they are commonly invoked. In Great Britain the media's access to court hearings and trials is restricted, while in Israel even the publication of certain scholarly articles can be subjected to the prohibition of the military censor if they are deemed to contain "security sensitive information."

The relevance of this example to the theoretical principle of discursive validation is the following: just as differences in the extent and application of the fundamental right of free speech would not lead us to deny that Great Britain and Israel are democratic societies just as the United States is, so too a number of more specific interpretations of the norms of universal moral respect and egalitarian reciprocity are compatible with democratic political dialogue. What results from a deliberative theory of democracy based upon the discourse model is not a catalog of unabridgeable basic rights and liberties but two most general moral norms that are compatible, within certain well defined limits, with a variety of legal and political arrangements.

2. See Kenneth Baynes, *The Normative Grounds of Political Criticism: Kant, Rawls, Habermas* (Albany: SUNY Press, 1992), 1ff.

3. Iris Marion Young, "Impartiality and the Civic Public," in *Feminism as Critique*, eds. Seyla Benhabib and Drucilla Cornell (London: Polity Press, 1987), 73.

4. Iris Marion Young, *Justice and the Politics of Difference* (Princeton, NJ: Princeton University Press, 1990).

CHAPTER 31

1. See Joshua Cohen, "Pluralism and Proceduralism," *Chicago-Kent Law Review* 69, no. 3 (1994). Of theorists who reject using independent standards to judge demo-

cratic outcomes, few offer any clear account of the basis of democratic legitimacy. Thomas Christiano is more clear in defending a version of Fair Proceduralism in "Social Choice and Democracy," in *The Idea of Democracy*, eds. David Copp, Jean Hampton, and John E. Roemer (Cambridge: Cambridge University Press, 1993), 183–86. He develops the view in detail in *The Rule of the Many* (Boulder, CO: Westview Press, 1996). Stuart Hampshire also endorses Fair Proceduralism quite explicitly in his review of Rawls's *Political Liberalism*. See "Liberalism: The New Twist," *New York Review of Books* (August 12, 1993): 43–47, esp. 46.

2. Bernard Manin provides a clear statement of Fair Deliberative Proceduralism: "Because it comes at the close of a deliberative process in which every one was able to take part . . . the result carries legitimacy." See "On Legitimacy and Deliberation," *Political Theory* 15, no. 3 (1987): 359.

3. See, for example, Seyla Benhabib, "Toward a Deliberative Model of Democratic Legitimacy," in *Democracy and Difference*, ed. Seyla Benhabib (Princeton, NJ: Princeton University Press, 1996), 67–94: "It is not the sheer numbers which support the rationality of the conclusion [under majority rule], but the presumption that if a large number of people see certain matters a certain way as a result of following certain kinds of rational procedures of deliberation and decision-making, then such a conclusion has a presumptive claim to being rational until shown to be otherwise" (72).

4. Joshua Cohen, "The Economic Basis of Deliberative Democracy," *Social Philosophy and Policy* 6, no. 2 (1989): 32.

5. Joshua Cohen, "Deliberation and Democratic Legitimacy," in *The Good Polity*, eds. Alan Hamlin and Philip Pettit (Oxford: Blackwell, 1989), 26.

6. Cohen, "Deliberation and Democratic Legitimacy," 29.

7. That they all involve procedure-independent standards of something like justice or the common good does not determine whether or not they involve procedure-in-dependent standards of legitimacy. Epistemic Proceduralism, for example, does not. Cohen's view apparently does.

8. While this probabilistic case is more intuitively compelling, I believe the same results are obtained even if it is accepted that all 1,000 cards are correct. The more general question then is whether epistemic authority (probabilistic or not) supports moral judgment.

9. This is the epistemic conception of democracy defended in Carlos Santiago Nino, *The Ethics of Human Rights* (Cambridge: Cambridge University Press, 1991), 245–55. For example, he claims "the democratic origin of a legal rule provides us with a reason to believe that there is good reason to accept its content and to act accordingly" (255). This is deference to the expertise of the procedure with a vengeance.

10. Availability is understood, of course, to be constrained by which considerations can be accepted by all reasonable citizens.

11. There is some controversy whether there is a duty to do what you believe right. But it is perfectly obvious that in normal cases it is blameworthy not to try to do what is morally required, and you cannot try except by doing what you believe is morally required. Therefore, it is blameworthy not to do, and so morally required to do, what you believe is morally required. This does not deny that there could be especially

perverse people whose moral beliefs are so distorted that we cannot count it in their favor that they are true to them.

12. This requirement is probably too high in the case of personal agents. You get moral credit for trying to do the right thing unless your judgment is much worse than random, perhaps because there is, in the personal case, a phenomenology of seeming right that is not present in the collective case, and that provides on its own some reasons for action.

13. This is puzzling to some, though it is not an uncommon view among political philosophers. Socrates had this view in Plato's *Crito*, and Rawls defends it in *Theory of Justice*, as have many others.

CHAPTER 32

1. Rita C. Manning, "Air Pollution: Group and Individual Obligations," *Environmental Ethics* 6, no. 3 (1984): 217.

CHAPTER 33

1. Jason Brennan, *The Ethics of Voting* (Princeton, NJ: Princeton University Press, 2011).

2. I will assume that it is plausible to expect the average citizen to be able to make an effort to acquire and process a minimal amount of (nonexpert) information that would make her choice at the ballot box better than random. I do not pretend to ignore the daunting problems that affect societies where uneducated and politically disinterested citizens are faced with the duty to vote, but detailed attention to this problem is impossible in an article this short. I would like to say, however, that the normative case for the duty to vote is not affected by the existence of incompetent voters. Moral duties can be consistently justified despite the empirical existence of some individuals that are ill equipped to discharge them satisfactorily. Finally, the arguments in this article may also be interpreted as calling those disinterested in politics, but cognitively able, to change their minds about their role in political society.

3. Being a good Samaritan does not require that we bring the person being assisted to an ideal state of health, nor that we bring the society being helped to an ideal (perfect) state of justice. It just requires that we minimize/avert harm or injustice, respectively. Because of this, it follows that we have a moral duty to vote as good Samaritans even if the electoral result we support will be decent but not ideal (because there is no ideal alternative to choose from or because the ideal alternative is nonelectable). From this, it also follows that my arguments for Samaritanism in elections are consistent with viewing lesser evil voting as moral and perhaps required.

4. Jason Brennan, *The Ethics of Voting* (Princeton, NJ: Princeton University Press, 2011).

5. Ibid.

6. J. S. Mill, *On Liberty and Other Essays* (Oxford: Oxford University Press, 2008), 115.

7. Derek Parfit, *Reasons and Persons* (Oxford: Oxford University Press, 2008), 70.

8. J. S. Mill, *Considerations on Representative Government*, in *On Liberty and other Essays*, ed. John Gray (Oxford: Oxford University Press, 2008), 335.

9. Hannah Arendt, *On Violence* (New York: HMH Publishing Company, 1970), 232.

CHAPTER 35

1. Pew Research Center, "Partisanship and Political Animosity in 2016," June 22, 2016. URL: http://www.people-press.org/2016/06/22/partisanship-and-political-animosity-in-2016/: 3.

2. Pew Research Center, "Partisanship and Political Animosity in 2016," June 22, 2016. URL: http://www.people-press.org/2016/06/22/partisanship-and-political-animosity-in-2016/: 8.

3. See Robert B. Talisse, *Overdoing Democracy: Why We Must Put Politics in Its Place* (New York: Oxford University Press, 2019).

4. What I'm calling belief polarization is generally called *group polarization*; see Cass R. Sunstein, "The Law of Group Polarization," *The Journal of Political Philosophy* 10, no. 2 (2002): 175–95. I depart from this term because it invites confusion in the present context; *both* political and belief polarization have to do with groups, albeit each in a distinctive way.

5. Helmut Lamm and David Myers, "Group-Induced Polarization of Attitudes and Behavior," *Advances in Experimental Social Psychology* 11 (1978): 146, write, "Seldom in the history of social psychology has a nonobvious phenomenon been so firmly grounded in data from across a variety of cultures and dependent measures." See the Appendix in Cass R. Sunstein, *Going to Extremes: How Like Minds Unite and Divide* (New York: Oxford University Press, 2009) for summaries of the experimental findings.

6. Cass R. Sunstein, *Going to Extremes: How Like Minds Unite and Divide* (New York: Oxford University Press, 2009), 18–19.

7. S. Moscovici and M. Zavalloni, "The Group as a Polarizer of Attitudes," *Journal of Personality and Social Psychology* 12, no. 2 (1969): 125–35.

8. D. G. Myers and G. D. Bishop, "Discussion Effects on Racial Attitudes," *Science* 169 (1970): 778–79.

9. D. G. Myers, "Discussion-Induced Attitude Polarization," *Human Relations* 28, no. 8 (1975): 699–714.

10. Reid Hastie, David Schkade, and Cass R. Sunstein, "What Happened on Deliberation Day?" *California Law Review* 95 (2007): 915–40.

11. David Schkade, Cass R. Sunstein, and Daniel Kahneman, "Deliberating about Dollars: The Severity Shift," *Columbia Law Review* 100, no. 4 (2000): 1139–75.

12. Norris R. Johnson, James G. Stemler, and Deborah Hunter, "Crowd Behavior as 'Risky Shift': A Laboratory Experiment," *Sociometry* 40, no. 2 (1977): 183–87.

13. Eugene Burnstein and Amiram Vinokur, "Persuasive Argumentation and Social Comparison as Determinants of Attitude Polarization," *Journal of Experimental Social Psychology* 13, no. 4 (1977): 315–32.

14. Cass R. Sunstein, *#Republic: Divided Democracy in the Age of Social Media* (Princeton, NJ: Princeton University Press, 2017), 72.

15. D. G. Myers, J. B. Bruggink, R. C. Kersting, and B. A. Schlosser, "Does Learning Others' Opinions Change One's Opinion?" *Personality and Social Psychology Bulletin* 6 (1980): 253–60; Robert Zajonc, "Attitudinal Effects of Mere Exposure," *Journal of Personality and Social Psychology Monograph Supplement* 9 (1968): 1–27.

16. Cass R. Sunstein, *Going to Extremes: How Like Minds Unite and Divide* (New York: Oxford University Press, 2009): 40–42.

17. Lyn M. Van Swol, "Extreme Members and Group Polarization," *Social Influence* 4, no. 3 (2009): 194.

18. Helmut Lamm and David Myers, "Group-Induced Polarization of Attitudes and Behavior," *Advances in Experimental Social Psychology* 11 (1978): 185.

19. D. Abrams, M. Wetherell, S. Cochrane, M. A. Hogg, and J. C. Turner, "Knowing What to Think by Knowing Who You Are: Self-Categorization and the Nature of Norm Formation, Conformity and Group Polarization," *British Journal of Social Psychology* 29 (1990): 97–119.

20. Eun-Ju Lee, "Deindividuation Effects on Group Polarization in Computer-Mediated Communication: The Role of Group Identification, Public-Self-Awareness, and Perceived Argument Quality," *Journal of Communication* 57, no. 2 (2007): 385–403.

21. Robert S. Baron, Sieg I. Hoppe, Chaun Feng Kao, Bethany Brunsman, Barbara Linneweh, and Diana Rogers, "Social Corroboration and Opinion Extremity," *Journal of Experimental Social Psychology* 32, no. 6 (1996): 537–60.

22. Cass R. Sunstein, *Going to Extremes: How Like Minds Unite and Divide* (New York: Oxford University Press, 2009), 29.

23. Hence Robert S. Baron, Sieg I. Hoppe, Chaun Feng Kao, Bethany Brunsman, Barbara Linneweh, and Diana Rogers, "Social Corroboration and Opinion Extremity," *Journal of Experimental Social Psychology* 32, no. 6 (1996): 559, write, "simple attendance at certain events . . . laughter and applause at a joke . . . the wearing of political buttons or other symbolic garb or stigmata . . . may be all that is necessary to create such corroboration" (and thus belief polarization).

24. Cass R. Sunstein, *Going to Extremes: How Like Minds Unite and Divide* (New York: Oxford University Press, 2009), 24; Eli Pariser, *The Filter Bubble: What the Internet Is Hiding From You* (New York: Penguin, 2011); Siva Vaidhyanathan, *Anti-Social Media: How Facebook Disconnects Us and Undermines Democracy* (New York: Oxford University Press, 2018).

25. Jacob Westfall, Leaf Van Boven, John R. Chambers, and Charles M. Judd, "Perceiving Political Polarization in the United States: Party Identity Strength and

Attitude Extremity Exacerbate the Perceived Partisan Divide," *Perspectives on Psychological Science* 10, no. 2 (2015): 145–58.

26. Of course, there are limits to what citizens are required to see as within the bounds of properly *democratic* politics. Surely there are certain political commitments that are *out of bounds* in a democracy, the holding or which disqualifies a person for democratic citizenship. Persons holding such views pose problems that the account here is not meant to address.

Index

About the Editors

Steven M. Cahn is Professor Emeritus of Philosophy at The City University of New York Graduate Center. He is the author or editor of more than sixty books, including *Navigating Academic Life: How the System Works* (2021), *A Philosopher's Journey: Essays from Six Decades* (2020), *Philosophical Adventures* (2020), *The Road Traveled and Other Essays* (2019), *Inside Academia: Professors, Politics, and Policies* (2019), and *Teaching Philosophy: A Guide* (2018).

Andrew T. Forcehimes is Associate Professor of philosophy at Nanyang Technological University in Singapore. He is coauthor of *Thinking Through Utilitarianism* (2019), and coeditor, with Steven M. Cahn, of *Exploring Moral Problems* (2018), *Foundations of Moral Philosophy* (2017), and *Principles of Moral Philosophy* (2016).

Robert B. Talisse is W. Alton Jones Professor of Philosophy and Professor of Political Science at Vanderbilt University. He is the author of over 100 scholarly articles and eleven books, including *Overdoing Democracy* (2019), *Engaging Political Philosophy* (2016), *Pluralism and Liberal Politics* (2012), and *Democracy and Moral Conflict* (2009).